Resisting
Hostile Takeovers

Resisting Hostile Takeovers

THE CASE OF GILLETTE

Rita Ricardo-Campbell

Westport, Connecticut
London

Library of Congress Cataloging-in-Publication Data

Ricardo-Campbell, Rita.
    Resisting hostile takeovers : the case of Gillette / Rita Ricardo-Campbell.
        p.   cm.
    Includes bibliographical references and index.
    ISBN 0–275–95830–2 (alk. paper)
    1. Gillette Company.   2. Razor industry—United States.
3. Consolidation and merger of corporations—United States.
I. Title.
HD9999.R34G557   1997
338.7'6885—dc21   97–12811

British Library Cataloguing in Publication Data is available.

First published in 1997

Praeger Publishers, 88 Post Road West, Westport, CT 06881
An imprint of Greenwood Publishing Group, Inc.

Printed in the United States of America

The paper used in this book complies with the
Permanent Paper Standard issued by the National
Information Standards Organization (Z39.48–1984).

10 9 8 7 6 5 4 3 2 1

Copyright Acknowledgment

Every reasonable effort has been made to trace the owners of copyright
materials in this book, but in some instances this has proven impossible.
The author and publisher will be glad to receive information leading to
more complete acknowledgments in subsequent printings of the book,
and in the meantime extend their apologies for any omissions.

To my husband, in appreciation of his tolerance
for my frequent out-of-town trips on Gillette business,
and to Colman M. Mockler, Jr. without whose recognition
of my talents this book would not have been written.

Contents

Acknowledgments

Retired directors of corporations do not usually write books such as this for publication. However, I am not a typical retired director of a Fortune 500 company. As a woman, an academic with a Ph.D. in economics, I believe that The Gillette Company story is too good not to tell.

I could not have written this book without the help of many persons. The draft was read for accuracy in its entirety by Milton Glass, Gillette's treasurer, who became vice president for finance and investor relations at Gillette until his retirement at the end of 1991. I am especially grateful to him for providing a copy of the formal chronology of The Gillette Company, covering its history from 1895 through 1988. The corporation was chartered as The American Safety Razor Company in 1901. No other member of Gillette's management staff has read this manuscript. As a courtesy, copies of the draft manuscript were sent to a few members of the Gillette Board.

In addition to Milton Glass, my colleagues at the Hoover Institution at Stanford University responded with detailed comments. I thank Edward P. Lazear for his detailed and helpful comments on the first three chapters, and Kenneth Judd for his comments on Chapter 4. Additionally, the first three chapters were improved by the editing of Lynn Chu. Additionally, I thank Murray Weidenbaum, chairman of the Center for the Study of American Business, Washington University in St. Louis, who read the manuscript and encouraged me to publish the book, and Abraham Sofaer of the Hoover Institution, for his comments on Chapter 9.

During 1995 I presented the essence of the attempted takeover efforts by Ronald Perelman before a Law and Economics faculty seminar, hosted by Professor Mitch Polinsky of Stanford University Law School. Other people at these occasional seminars spoke on similar topics, and because of the high level of discussion I found attendance at them most helpful.

Without the aid of my secretary, Ada Afanasieff, whose superb computer skills enabled her to act as my research assistant, this book would probably never have been finished.

I also wish to acknowledge the influence of Colman M. Mockler, Jr., who was chairman and CEO of The Gillette Company during the twelve years for which I was on the Company's Board, and to thank Alfred M. Zeien, current chairman and CEO of The Gillette Company, for permission to use various Company printed reports. My long-time friend, Mary Lee Mack Ingbar, provided intellectual and emotional support.

During the period of writing the book I remained a senior fellow of the Hoover Institution. In September 1995 I became senior fellow emerita and was allowed to retain my office with a grant for expenses to, among other things, finish this book. For this I thank Director John Raisian.

And last, but not least, I thank my husband Glenn Campbell, director emeritus of the Hoover Institution, who encouraged the writing of this book and with whom I discussed general matters of corporate finance (as, for example, the advantages and pitfalls of debt capital in comparison to equity capital).

None of the persons or organizations mentioned here is responsible for any omissions or interpretations that I have made.

Abbreviations

CalPERS	California Public Employees' Retirement System
CIPAF	Compagnie Internationale de Participations
ERISA	Employment Retirement Income Security Act of 1977
FASB	Financial Accounting Standard Board
FDA	Food and Drug Administration (U.S.)
FTC	Federal Trade Commission
GEICO	Government Employees Insurance Company
GNP	gross national product
GTO	Gollust, Tierney and Oliver (Coniston Partners)
IRRC	Investor Responsibility Research Center
KKR	Kohlberg Kravis Roberts & Company
LBO	leveraged buyout
MIT	Massachusetts Institute of Technology
OPEC	Organization of Petroleum Exporting Countries
OTC	over-the-counter drugs
PRC	People's Republic of China
PRO	Perelman/Revlon/Orange Group
S & Ls	savings and loan associations
SEC	Securities and Exchange Commission
TIAA	Teacher's Insurance Annuity Association
TPR	transferable put rights
VRC	Valuation Research Corporation

Resisting
Hostile Takeovers

1

Introduction

The Gillette Company was 94 years old in 1996. It took the name "Gillette Safety Razor Company" a year after its inception. The patent on its remarkable innovation, the Gillette safety razor, was granted in 1904. Gillette was a target of hostile takeovers from November 1986 until August 1989, when investor Warren Buffett purchased $600 million worth of its newly issued preferred stock (11 percent of the company). One of the questions I will attempt to answer in this book is: Why was The Gillette Company an unrelenting takeover target during this period?

Many theories have been developed by economists and others to explain why a specific company becomes a target of takeovers. The most common explanation is that the company is poorly managed, and a would-be acquirer believes he or she could do better. But as stated in a *Forbes* magazine cover article, published the day before the unexpected and untimely death on January 25, 1991, of Gillette CEO Colman Mockler, Jr., "Gillette was not a flabby company that needed its belt tightened. It was a tightly run outfit. [Colman M.] Mockler took over in 1975 . . . sold or closed 21 businesses. . . . Productivity has improved at a compound rate of 6% a year during Mockler's tenure."[1] In an analysis of 115 unsuccessful tender offers, a 1963–1987 study of several hundred firms (including Gillette) supports the claim that "target firms can create the same value independently" as a would-be acquirer. In restructuring, regardless of whether the target or an acquirer does it, value is created.[2] This appears to be the case for Gillette.

A Brookings Institution study published in 1990 attempted to find out why, among the many companies targeted by hostile takeovers during the years 1984–1986, twelve remained independent. Gillette was one of those twelve. The authors concluded that "Gillette did not make significant selloffs after defeating the bid, and its employment cuts, while large, could not have justified a large fraction of the proposed premium. As a result, we cannot clearly infer what Revlon was up to"[3] in attempting to take over Gillette. This academic study depended entirely on the sources in the public domain, newspaper articles, proxy statements, annual reports and 10-Ks. This book attempts to resolve these somewhat differing academic points of view. Although my study depends largely on the same printed items, as a director emerita, I have, additionally, my memory of events as they occurred and the minutes of board meetings to guide my analysis.

A board member of a Fortune 500 corporation has, to my knowledge, never before attempted to analyze for the public in book form the day-to-day events, together with an objective economic analysis, of such a significant episode of American business history as a failed takeover attempt. Some commentators regard takeovers as merely venal attempts to disrupt established business enterprises for narrow short-term gain, primarily for the acquirer. Others regard takeover attempts as driven by a conviction (whether warranted or not) that the would-be acquirer can make the firm more profitable for shareholders by restructuring it in accordance with a different plan than that of its present management.

I believe that the (Michael) *Jensen cash-flow theory* explains why Gillette was targeted for takeover. Jensen believes that free cash flow, that is, in excess of that needed to fund projects that are known to have positive net values after the cost of the capital, should be paid out to shareholders. This is discussed in detail in Chapter 7. In seeking ways to hedge against an anticipated continuing decline in the sales of the higher-profit razor blades, as compared to the rising sales of the lower-profit disposable razors, the Board sought to diversify. The large cash flow from the sales of blades made possible investments in new lines of business. Complementarity was sought. Not all the new ventures by Gillette were successful investments, but some were markedly successful. Gillette's large cash flow also made possible the simultaneous development of a remarkable, high-tech, high-quality new razor and blade, the Sensor. Gillette gambled $200 million for research, engineering and retooling, plus over $100 million in advertising costs for this new razor and blade. The Sensor was launched in the United States, Canada, Europe and Japan in January 1990. Advertisements accompanying the Super Bowl, professional football's championship game, blared the name of "Sensor" across television screens nationwide. It was expensive, but the saturation advertising and promotion campaign helped to push market shares for the new brand to levels not met previously by any Gillette shaving system during its introductory period. The encroachment by disposables was reversed.

Gillette is far more than a one-product company. Gillette owns Braun, a manufacturer of award-winning, high-design and high-quality electric razors, coffeemakers and other household appliances. Gillette also owns Paper Mate and Waterman pens, Jafra cosmetics, Oral-B toothbrushes and many brand-name toiletries. However, Gillette's profit margin on razors is the highest among its many products. A male who is clean-shaven spends about three minutes a day shaving, which adds up in 50 years of adult life to well over 90 eight-hour days spent in shaving. Manufacturing and selling razor blades is a terrific business.

Why was the late 1980s in the United States a period of increasing numbers of hostile takeovers of an increasing number of larger and larger firms? How did The Gillette Company defeat takeover attempts three times from Ronald Perelman and Revlon Group, Inc., starting in November 1986, and also defeat Coniston Partners' takeover attempt and win the proxy contest in April 1988? Answers to these and similar questions are the core of this book.

Razors and blades are the expertise of Gillette, and they generate high profits. Gillette management was pushed (some would say kicked) into speeding up their restructuring (selling off low-margin lines) and accelerating the development and launch of its new shaving system. Plans to diversify further in order to make up for the cannibalization of blades by the disposable razor were halted; and a strategy of speeding up development of the revolutionary Sensor, which might stop and even reverse the success of disposables, was adopted.

Four attempts to achieve a legal takeover failed, but the economic effect of the initial and later attempts may have approximated what might have occurred under a successful takeover. The development of the Sensor shaving system was accelerated, and several million dollars in its development, advertising and launch costs were gambled. Whether the would-be acquirers would have followed this same path is unknown. Perelman/Revlon stressed the synergistic fit of Gillette toiletries with their international cosmetic lines, but Gillette's profits from toiletries have always been low. It is hard to believe that Perelman would have sold the core business of blades and razors and stressed Gillette's toiletries. Coniston Partners announced in the spring of 1988 during the proxy battle that they would sell off parts of the Company. But they never, to my knowledge, identified which parts they would sell. It is also hard to believe that either would-be acquirer would have gambled hundreds of millions of dollars on developing and launching the Sensor.

Other books written about the financial deals of the 1980s describe and analyze successful mergers, acquisitions and takeovers. Only recently have there been a few analyses of some of the eventual failures in takeovers, often stemming from the acquirer paying too much and incurring too much debt. This book attempts to analyze why the attempted hostile takeovers of The Gillette Company failed, starting in late 1986 and continuing into 1988, and evaluate whether this was a bad or good outcome for Gillette shareholders.

I was asked to become a member of the Board of Directors of The Gillette Company in 1978. I did not anticipate that the sole reason for Chairman of the Board Colman Mockler to ask me to lunch in California (where I worked, nearly 3,000 miles from Gillette's headquarters in Boston) was to ask whether I would be willing to serve on the Board of The Gillette Company.

After a short talk in my office in the Herbert Hoover Memorial Building on the Stanford University campus, we walked to the faculty club for lunch. Upon our return, I asked Mr. Mockler whether he wished to meet my husband, Glenn Campbell, whose office, as the director of the Hoover Institution, was in the Hoover Tower, not far from mine. "Not really," he answered. I agreed to inform him of my decision within a few days, and he departed.

Mockler and my husband eventually met later that year in London at a dinner hosted by Gillette. This was the only Gillette board meeting in the twelve years during which I served as a director to which spouses were invited. It was also the only board meeting during that time period that was held outside of Boston or the Andover, Massachusetts, plant. My husband and Mockler never saw each other again after that one encounter in 1978.

As an elected alumna member of the Simmons College, Boston, board of directors, I earlier had met Mockler, who was also chairman of the Simmons College board. I have been told that when he was asked why he proposed me for the Gillette Board, Mockler answered, "Whenever Rita spoke at Simmons College board meetings, she had something to say, and this was not true for the other women on that college board."

I read the Company's latest annual report and its more complete financial 10-K filing to the Securities and Exchange Commission (SEC). I also consulted with my husband and a colleague, Dan Throop Smith, who was a member of corporate boards and had been a professor of economics at the Harvard Business School, as well as Under Secretary of the Treasury in the Eisenhower administration. Dan, a good friend, gave me a book, *The Corporate Director*,[4] that helped me to get my bearings in the Fortune 500 company world. However, it was written as if no woman would ever be a director of a large company. With my acceptance, I was thrust into big-business affairs.

As an academic with a Ph.D. in economics from Harvard University and since 1974 a director of Watkins-Johnson, an electronics defense company, I could reasonably assume that I was qualified—but so were thousands of others. Additionally, I had considerable public service experience as chairman of a compact of thirteen western states, the Western Interstate Commission for Higher Education (WICHE); as a member of several national commissions, including the Quadrennial Advisory Council on Social Security and the National Advisory Food and Drug Committee; and also as a member of two presidential committees: the Health Services Industry Committee, which guided federal price controls during 1971–1974 in the health sector, and the President's Advisory Council on the Status of Women during most of the 1970s. I had written numerous books and articles and given speeches on such topics as national health policy and Social Security and women's roles in society. Given the political climate of the late 1970s, it did not hurt that I was a woman. Mockler and the Board had decided it was time to have their first woman on the Board of Directors of Gillette. Gillette was following the trends of the 1970s forward: more outside directors on corporate boards, more women, more minorities.

Before I went to my first directors' meeting, I read an article, "The Boardroom Is Becoming a Different Scene,''[5] which stressed the recent growth in the number of outside directors and the pressure on corporate boards to subordinate profits for shareholders to *higher goals*. Public policy areas of pollution, unionization, apartheid in South Africa, women and minorities were designated areas for advocacy positions for a new generation of board members. I believe now, as then, that each such issue has to be considered by a company board at the individual company level and within the context of answering the overriding question of what action will maximize the company's long-run profits. That boards have expanded their outside representation by appointing from beyond the traditional business community, appointing more academics, Hispanics, blacks and women, does not mean that these individuals are necessarily advocates of any particular group; but, rather, they give advice on how to achieve profit maximization, drawing on their own particular knowledge and perspectives. This widens the board's acumen. That a board member is a woman does not qualify her to speak for women in general. Women, like men, are not a homogeneous group.

I dwell on the subject of women as directors of Fortune 500 companies because it continues to be a relatively rare occurrence and because most women have no concept of how it comes about. Although today 80 percent of the Fortune 500 boards have one woman director, she is likely to be the only woman on that board. At Gillette, as at many other companies in 1978, it was the chairman of the board, primarily, who nominated directors, with the concurrence of other directors. Unless a woman is known by other corporate directors, she does not stand a chance of becoming a director herself. Women do not belong to all-male clubs, and unless women write books or articles, give speeches or in some other way appear in the public eye, individual women remain largely unknown outside their own personal, social circle and do not meet businessmen. Large companies prefer a director, whether a man or a woman, with considerable experience. Thus the person asked is likely to be in his or her fifties.

The flood of information that hits a new director of a Fortune 500 company with manufacturing facilities in over 20 countries and marketing in over 200 countries, for probably over a thousand products, is enormous. So enormous that it took, at least in my case, two years to grasp how the data fit together, never mind the intricacies of corporate decision-making. The bottom line, whether the company is making a profit or not, is the easiest part of the information to absorb. It is not the mere accounting data but the larger questions: Why the company makes bigger profits this year than last year; why geographic expansion should dominate; whether a new acquisition is advisable. These questions, which form the texture of a business, are within a director's role. The inside director has the company's database in mind when making decisions. The outside director may bring a new insight, a wider frame of knowledge and broader thinking in which to set a management problem. Initially the outside director may not know enough about the company to make a good decision.

That is why most new directors keep quiet for a long period of time, before offering opinions that later mature into informed judgments.

In this book I will attempt to describe how a corporate board of a multinational company actually handles such events as a hostile takeover. As an academic economist, I held many of the misconceptions of academics. For example, I thought that the academic definition of *greenmail* was essentially a fixed guideline that could be followed. Greenmail is generally defined as the repurchase of shares of stock at above the market price from a hostile acquirer, who in return agrees to go away. Academic economists are generally against paying greenmail. George Stigler, a Nobel prizewinning economist who for lengthy periods occupied an office next to mine at the Hoover Institution, made this quite clear to me. However, market prices can fluctuate, and at the time of Ronald Perelman's November 1986 attempt to acquire The Gillette Company they did so markedly because of Ivan Boesky's almost simultaneous sell-off of his bloc of Gillette shares. The Gillette price fluctuated so much that a market price was difficult to establish. The academic definition of greenmail, therefore, was not precisely on target, and the directors believed that the repurchase of the stock at a reasonable price was justifiable. Chapter 2 of this book details those rather exciting events of November 1986. The issue of greenmail is discussed in Chapter 8 along with the proxy contest because it became the main issue in that battle.

In order that the general reader may better understand the Gillette story and have his or her own benchmarks to judge the Board's actions, Chapter 3 relates a brief history of The Gillette Company, and Chapter 4 discusses the significance of some of the common terms and actions in the takeover climate: poison pills, junk bonds, stock price and even industrial espionage.

There were two additional attempts by Ronald Perelman and his Revlon Company to buy The Gillette Company: one in mid-June 1987 and the other in August of the same year. With a proxy fight in April 1988, the Company remained vulnerable into the summer of 1988.

What made Gillette a continuing target for nearly two years was, I believe, its large cash flow from its razor blades, which have dominant market shares in many countries of the world. Some argue that The Gillette Company illustrates the theory held by the Chicago school of economists who argue that if a company does not return to its shareholders its excess free cash, but rather invests it in nonrelated businesses, then it will become a target and will be judged as poorly managed. Gillette, however, was not poorly managed in the decade before the November 1986 tender. However, it paid out as dividends only about 50 percent of its excess cash flow and used the remainder partly in acquiring new plant and equipment and partly in purchasing new firms. Colman Mockler in 1975 became the CEO, and he cut costs and sold or closed over 20 businesses. It is true that the Gillette Company invested some of its free-cash flow in what it may be argued were several unrelated businesses. But other purchases (for example, the manufacture of Oral-B toothbrushes) were related, here both on the production side, where toothbrushes use hard plastic, and on the marketing side, where there was and still is great synergy. Toothbrushes are marketed in drugstores and food stores in the United States and abroad much as razor blades are. The decision to buy the Waterman Pen Company of France in 1987, thus adding higher-priced pens to the Paper Mate lines, made Gillette the largest writing instruments company in the world. Gillette, continuing to build this core business, later bought Parker Pen. Studies of other multinational companies show that they also have used free-cash flow to invest in peripheral business; these other companies, as well as Gillette, gained some winners and some losers. On balance Gillette was in the process of ridding itself of more losers than it was adding, and in the 1990s it is reaping the gains from this activity and its geographic expansion.

A fourth takeover attempt, this one by Coniston Partners, a proponent of strategic-block investment, was defeated in a proxy battle in April 1988 by a 52 percent to 48 percent vote. That proxy contest and the subsequent legal settlement show that company boards do learn. My more business-oriented colleagues believed that a settlement with Coniston was absolutely necessary in view of the closeness of the vote. Although in politics 52 percent is a clear winner, the businessmen believed that Coniston should get some payoff, but there could be no tinge of a greenmail payment. A complicated *transfer put rights* transaction evolved that met this criterion. It cost the Company $720 million from future free-cash flow. But all shareholders of record benefited on a one-to-seven ownership-of-shares basis. Then arriving on the scene was Warren Buffett who, by his $600 million purchase of 11 percent of Gillette stock, in conjunction with the Massachusetts 1987 antitakeover law, protects Gillette today from any further hostile takeover attempts.

Companies act in ways that are different from what academic economists might expect. Academic economists believe that companies rigidly follow the rule to maximize profits without any leeway for *go along to get along*. The latter rule can often be rationalized by using a maximization of long-run profits defense. It is difficult to reconcile pressures from different stakeholders in the company. Employees who have worked for a company for 30 years or more usually believe they have a right to some consideration during such battles. Today, labor forces are more mobile than those in earlier generations. Fewer individuals stay at one company for a long period of time. As the economy moves from manufacturing to telecommunications and the computer-based information age, workers are more quick to change jobs in response to the changes in the economy. They also use computers to find where new jobs are. Companies that are quick to fire very long-time employees may end up with less well trained, poorer-quality labor.

Additionally, the book discusses, but only peripherally, the role of women in business. I was the first woman member of the Gillette Board, and in 1977 fewer than 2 percent of the company's over 100 top executives were women. Today that percentage is somewhat higher, about 5 percent. However, with two-thirds of Gillette's profits coming from razor blades, items that men use far more than women in any society, it is not difficult to understand why it is male-oriented, although a consumer-products company. This orientation persists despite the exceptional gains made by the Sensor and Sensor Excel razors for women in the mid-1990s.

Gillette's story sheds light on important issues, such as whether the federal government should try to increase its regulation of corporate governance, takeovers and procedural rules. The book also depicts how an individual company under existing state laws, especially Delaware's, can protect itself and succeed. In 1990 Gillette's cash flow neared $500 million, and its stock price closed on January 25, 1991, at twice the tender offer of 1986; by December 31, 1991, after three splits, the stock price was close to triple the tender price. This performance would seem to justify the Board's decision to resist a change in management.

If the Gillette experience can be generalized, it serves to illustrate, among other things, that directors are not present during the negotiations with the principals of the opposing party. Such negotiations are conducted by lawyers and investment bankers representing the principals of either side; generally speaking, because these *hired hands* get a percentage of the deal, they drive up the size of the deal. However, they do want to settle and earn money. It is true that if the principals negotiate directly, what might be considered *premature disclosure* would be legally required. To avoid such disclosure and comply with the law, companies use lawyers and investment bankers as go-betweens. Those responsible for whatever decision is reached are thus denied the opportunity to read body language and be actively engaged, which dilutes some of the functions of directors. Being a woman may be what makes me see this as somewhat of a loss. Women are generally perceived to be, on average, more *intuitive* than men—a belief that probably stems from their being, on average, more often than men in day-to-day interaction with children. However, there are men who are similarly intuitive, and they too may see this practice as a loss.

Hopefully, this book will help future corporate boards to evaluate and act wisely in situations of other hostile takeover attempts.

NOTES

1. Subrata N. Chakravarty, "We Had to Change the Playing Field," *Forbes*, February 4, 1991, p. 83. (Issues of *Forbes* usually appear a week before the printed date.)

2. Sayan Chatterjee, "Sources of Value in Takeovers: Synergy or Restructuring—Implications for Target and Bidder Firms," *Strategic Management Journal* vol. 13 (1992), p. 267.

3. Sanjai Bhagat, Andrei Shleifer and Robert W. Vishny, "Hostile Takeovers in the 1980s: The Return to Corporate Specialization," in Martin Neil Baily and Clifford Winston (eds.), *Brookings Papers on Economic Activity: Microeconomics* (Washington, D.C.: Brookings Institution, 1990), p. 44.

4. J. M. Juran and J. Keith Louden, *The Corporate Director* (New York: American Management Association, 1966).

5. Lee Smith, ''The Boardroom Is Becoming a Different Scene,'' *Fortune*, May 8, 1978, pp. 150–170.

2

November 1986: In Play

THE TENDER, PERELMAN I

A cash tender offer in *doomsday* advertisements in major newspapers on Friday, November 14, 1986, put The Gillette Company *in play* until late summer 1988. The tender for Gillette shares at $65 each by the *Orange Acquisition Corporation*, newly formed for the purpose of acquiring Gillette, was a surprise. A telephone call the night before and a letter (also dated November 14) to CEO and Chairman of the Board Colman Mockler, Jr., was followed by telephone calls made by top Gillette management to the directors. It can be argued that theoretically a company with greater future profits than the market price of its shares recognizes is always in play. This assumes that the information about its prospects is fully known. In a sense, the company is in play and is heavily traded every day. Even so, such a company is not in play in a legal sense until an offer is made. The offer makes clear to the public that the company is undervalued.

The cash tender offer made directly to shareholders without prior consultation with Gillette's management was viewed as a hostile-takeover battle cry. It was likened by one director to a situation where a stranger says, "I like your house and will pay you so many dollars—amount not negotiable—for it," and this offer places your house on the market and you must sell. Revlon/Perelman, by their $65-a-share tender, had put Gillette on the market.

The Orange Acquisition Corporation was made up of the Revlon Group, Inc., and the MacAndrews & Forbes Group, Inc.; the major controlling person behind them was Ronald O. Perelman. No one in a small group of directors, informally talking just before the November 20 board meeting, knew at that time precisely who MacAndrews & Forbes were.

The total cost of the initiated tender would be over $5 billion, which made this, in dollar terms, a "megadeal." The Orange Acquisition Corporation et al. (Perelman/Revlon) estimated in their Securities and Exchange Commission (SEC) filing that their cost of the 9.2 million shares already purchased was $514.9 million. The money came from the working capital of the Revlon Group and a bank loan agreement to MacAndrews & Forbes. The amount of the filing fee was 1/50 of 1 percent, or $802,438.96, a fee that goes to the SEC. Only $1 billion of the needed $5 billion would be equity capital from the Revlon Group and MacAndrews Group.[1] The remaining billions needed were to be raised by Drexel Burnham Lambert Inc. The filing indicated that expenses included initially $1.5 million to Drexel Burnham Lambert; upon consolidation of the deal, they would receive an additional $22.5 million. Investment bankers are well paid, but very rarely receive a fixed, negotiated, preset sum; rather, their fees range upward from half of 1 percent of a deal. For a $5 billion transaction, that is $250 million for advising and arranging for the needed capital. This method of determining their fee acts as an incentive to inflate the amount negotiated, that is held in check because they want to close the deal. The old saying, "A bird in the hand is worth two in the bush," still commands respect. A dollar in hand today is worth more than one after the several years it may take to negotiate a deal.

Although the *Boston Globe* of November 6, 1986, had carried a story highlighting rumors stemming from the heavy trading of Gillette stock at "10 times the normal volume" on the previous day, that story was not mailed or faxed to the directors. Indeed, none of the *Boston Globe* stories throughout the takeover battles was mailed or faxed to directors by the corporate secretary or public relations officer except in response to an individual's specific request. The impact of a news story stressing heavy trading and listing the names of likely suitors would have been greater on the out-of-town directors than was the very low-key employee bulletin dated November 5, 1986, that the directors did receive. The latter began, "The unusually high volume of trading in Gillette common stock over the past few days has generated a variety of reports in the media of takeover rumors. The Company is adhering to its long-standing policy, as it has in the past, of not commenting on rumors of takeover activity. The reason for this policy is that it affords the company maximum flexibility and legal protection."[2] This single-page item set the tone for the period of the three takeover attempts by Ronald Perelman and that by Coniston Partners, the latter ending in a proxy fight April 1988 and being legally settled August 1 of that year by a private agreement between the two parties. A Gillette memorandum dated November 12, 1986, requested all insiders to notify the Company's legal staff if they wished to buy or sell company stock.

On November 14, 1986, a "Perelman, Orange, Revlon" advertisement in the *Wall Street Journal*, the *New York Times* and other papers offered $65 a share, all cash, starting December 12 and expiring January 13, 1987. The advertisement also declared a 13.9 percent or 9.2 million share ownership of the 66 million shares of Gillette common stock, then outstanding. Although the tender seemed solid, the Perelman/Revlon and Orange Group reserved until January 13 to pull out for lack of financing. The estimated limit on their immediately available cash of less than $1 billion would mean a need for close to $4 billion in loans to cover the purchase of nearly 56 million shares at $65 each and related fees and expenses.

The Second Circuit Court of Connecticut, on April 11, 1986, had sustained the legality of starting a tender offer with no financing in place. In *Wainaco Inc. v Glaeph* (civil number B-86–146), the court held that it is sufficient for the intended acquirer to have a letter from an investment banker stating that it is "highly confident" that the financing can be obtained. This legal interpretation and the promotion of junk bonds enabled most of the large takeovers with junk-bond financing during the late 1980s. Small firms could take over companies several times their size because small firms could borrow the money and eventually pay it back by selling off parts of the takeover target, once acquired.

Warren Buffett, who is generally recognized as the second richest man in the United States and has successfully invested in all grades of stocks and bonds, wrote in a letter to shareholders of his Berkshire and Hathaway, Inc., about junk bonds as follows:

A kind of bastardized fallen angel burst onto the investment scene in the 1980s—"junk bonds" that were far below investment-grade when issued. As the decade progressed, new offerings of manufactured junk became ever junkier and ultimately the predictable outcome occurred: Junk bonds lived up to their name. In 1990—even before the recession dealt its blows—the financial sky became dark with the bodies of failing corporations.

The disciples of debt assured us that this collapse wouldn't happen: Huge debt, we were told, would cause operating managers to focus their efforts as never before. . . . At the height of the debt mania, capital structures were concocted that guaranteed failure: In some cases, so much debt was issued that even highly favorable business results could not produce the funds to service it.

Warren Buffett also emphasized, as did the dean of financial analysts, Ben Graham, the need for a "Margin of Safety."

Drexel Burnham Lambert Inc. was the investment banking firm for Perelman/Revlon. The concomitant Boesky insider-trading scandal, which involved the same investment firm, made it necessary for Drexel Burnham to repeat its first, "highly confident" letter that it could raise the needed $4 billion. The Boesky scandal had made Drexel Burnham so suspect that a second "highly confident" letter was sent to directors and announced in the *Wall Street Journal* of November 20 (p. 4).

Throughout the November 1986 period, Perelman stressed that he considered that a merger of Revlon and Gillette would have a synergistic, revenue-enhancing effect. Revlon's vice chairman Howard Gittis was quoted in the *Wall Street Journal* as calling Gillette "a great fit for us. They're selling to the same customers as us, and we've both got the same distribution channels.''[3] From the point of view of Revlon, this was true, but Revlon had a much smaller range of products. Where was there synergy with razor blades and small household appliances? Revlon was a cosmetics firm.

Gillette directors and management did not view the proposal as one that would benefit Gillette. Only a small part of Gillette's 1986 dollar sales, 30 percent, came from toiletries and cosmetics, Revlon's primary product area, and an even smaller portion of Gillette's profits, 14 percent. Gillette was and still is classified by *Fortune* magazine as a steel-products manufacturing company because the majority of its profits come from steel razor blades. Gillette, even with several sizable toiletries brand names—deodorants such as Right Guard and Dry Idea, White Rain shampoo and others—as well as ownership of Jafra cosmetics, a door-to-door selling company, was not generally viewed as a cosmetics firm.

In 1986, 80 percent of Gillette's operating profits came from the manufacture and sale worldwide of blades and razors. By 1989 this percentage had decreased to a historically more usual 65 percent; toiletries and cosmetics profits had shrunk to 11 percent of Gillette's total profits; while Braun products, headquartered in Germany but owned by Gillette, with its small household appliances and electric razors, accounted for 16 percent. The leading European electric razor was Braun's, but because of antitrust restrictions Gillette could not market it in the United States until 1985. Gillette did and does have a strong international marketing network ideally suited for retailing cosmetics, as well as Gillette blades, Paper Mate pens and Oral-B toothbrushes, through food- and drugstore chains. Gillette had bought a few foreign cosmetic companies, such as La Toja in Spain, and was negotiating for Unisas Princeton Cosmetica in Chile in November 1986.

Gillette directors and management were well aware of the company's strong balance sheet at the time of the tender. On October 24, 1986, *Value Line* had rated Gillette as A+.

THE BOARD

To respond to the tender, a special meeting of the Board was called for Monday, November 17, at 12 noon. Most of the outside directors, all of whom were in attendance, were on telephone hookup. At that time, the Board numbered eleven persons. At the meeting in Boston were Boston-area residents Raymond (Ray) Foster, chairman of the board and chief executive officer of Stone and Webster, Inc., a civil engineering firm; Lawrence (Larry) Fouraker, a fellow of Harvard University's Kennedy School of Government and ex-dean of the Harvard Business School; Colman Mockler, Jr., chairman and chief executive officer of Gillette; Joe Turley, then president and chief operating officer of the Company; and Al Zeien, who was vice chairman of the board. Each of the management directors had long service with the company. Colman had joined the Company nearly thirty years ago, only three years after graduating from the

Harvard Business School in 1954. Initially assistant to the comptroller, he became treasurer in 1965 and rose rapidly to CEO and then chairman and president of the company in 1976. Joe and Al both had joined Gillette just over 25 years ago. Among the outside directors, Charles Meyer and Larry Fouraker had been board members for nearly 25 years and 12 years, respectively.

The six directors connected by the conference call included Stephen Griffin, who had joined the Company over 40 years ago in 1941 and risen to president and chief operating officer in 1976. Gillette has a retirement age of 65, and Griffin joined the board when he became 65. An exceedingly well-read man in the area of history, Griffin added years of management experience to the Board's deliberations. In the minds of most, however, because of his 45 years with the Company, he represented management and not the general public.

Herbert H. Jacobi (Herb), who at the time was general manager of U.K.'s Midland Bank and chairman of the managing partners of West Germany's largest private bank, Trinkaus and Burkhardt, was in Duesseldorf, where he lived and where it was 6 P.M. Herb, like Ray Foster, had joined the Gillette Board in 1981.

Charles A. Meyer in Chicago had been senior vice president of public affairs of Sears Roebuck and Company after serving as Assistant Secretary of State for Inter-American Affairs. He was the senior outside board member, having served for almost 25 years.

Richard (Dick) Pivirotto at that time headed his own management consulting firm. When elected to the Board in 1980, Dick, a former retail executive, was chairman of the Associated Dry Goods Corporation, a retail department store chain that then included Lord and Taylor, a retail specialty store selling primarily women's and children's clothing.

Joseph Sisco in 1986 also ran his own management consulting firm, Sisco Associates, in Washington, D.C. In 1979, when he became a board member, Joe was chancellor of American University in Washington, D.C. He had worked for the State Department for 25 years, 1951 to 1976, and rose to Under Secretary of State for Political Affairs. Joe, an astute negotiator and observer, continues to consult, lecture and work as a television analyst specializing in the Middle East.

An economist and academic, whose home base is the Hoover Institution at Stanford University in California, I had joined the board in 1978. From the time I went on the board until I left in 1990, the management did not try to influence directors by providing excessive perks. Board members did not have limousines meet them at the airport but, rather, took taxis to their hotel. Lunches initially consisted primarily of sandwiches, fruit and cookies, and no alcohol was served in the boardroom or other Company localities. The time allowed for general conversation was sometimes well under a half hour. There were no scheduled evening-before dinners, except prior to the December meeting. A few special luncheons were held at the Harvard Club on Commonwealth Avenue, which was within walking distance from the Prudential Center, where the Board met.

These occasions were usually in honor of retiring Board members. By the time of the takeover attempts, there was one upgrade: Board-day lunches had become hot-buffet affairs, but the time allowed for eating before business was discussed was still about a half hour.

Needless to say, we had no ready access to private jets, although Gillette did own several. After all, the geographical spread of the company was worldwide, and a hardworking top management was expected to visit plants in well over 20 countries. When Gillette opened its plant in Shenyang, China, Colman Mockler attended the ceremony; and he frequently visited Gillette facilities whether in Europe, the United States, South America or Africa. An option to buy a new Gulfstream jet obtained prior to the November 1986 takeover attempt was sold early in the restructuring. For directors, commercial first-class travel was the rule. Gillette was not run in the extravagant mode of RJR Nabisco, as depicted in the now-famous book, *Barbarians at the Gate: The Fall of RJR Nabisco*.[4]

Not all Gillette directors were strong-minded, but then none was, I believe, ''bought,'' as is claimed of RJR Nabisco's directors in that book. Unlike RJR's case, no contributions were made to any organization, to the best of my knowledge, at the request of a director. I do not believe that any of the Gillette directors owed anything to the CEO: rather, they were selected primarily for their abilities and knowledge, which Mockler believed would enhance discussions and decisions by the Board. Gillette's Board did not meet in a headquarters building that ''fairly screamed of opulence, waste and nouveau-riche excess.''[5] Rather, Gillette met in rented headquarters on the 39th and 40th floors of the Prudential Tower Building in the Copley Square area of Boston. The boardroom did have wood-paneled walls and a magnificent, highly polished, oval table. The top-management offices were well furnished. Its shareholder meetings were, during this period, held in a large, tented space, especially covered, at the Andover plant, about a 40-minute drive from Boston. From the time I joined the board through 1991, board directors were paid a retainer and fees for attending a board meeting and each committee meeting at levels consistent with other companies of similar size.

Gillette was not, to my knowledge, a large giver of money within the United States. The company did give to the Boston Symphony and the Boston Fine Arts Museum and also gave money in the so-called compassion area within those Third World countries where Gillette had employees for medical clinics, medical education, legal assistance, sports for children and schools.[6]

The style of Colman Mockler was hardworking and frugal. Mockler enjoyed driving himself in his open red, Chevrolet convertible. Unlike RJR Nabisco's head, the care and feeding of directors was to him of no special concern. Directors came to meetings on their own. The only time I rode in a company plane was in the early 1980s, when one engine fell off a twin-engine plane that I had jointly hired from New York to Boston because all commercial flights to Boston were canceled because of computer failure at Logan Airport. My private plane had first dropped off its two other passengers in Providence, Rhode Island. One of these passengers was Lyn Nofziger, whom I knew. After takeoff from Providence, the engine fell, and we returned to Providence. When I telephoned Gillette in Boston, where the meeting was already in progress, they said that they would send a Gillette plane from Fall River, Massachusetts, to pick me up. It was a new, four-seater Cessna that took me to Fall River, as Logan was still closed. A car and driver and also a sandwich were waiting for me at Fall River, and we began the short drive to Prudential Center in Boston, where the Board was meeting. But even before I ate my sandwich, the car had a flat tire. I arrived finally just as the Board meeting broke up, rather early, just before 2:30 P.M.

The head of Gillette, unlike Ross Johnson, who had headed RJR Nabisco, did not really participate in sports. Mockler followed baseball. Although he owned a half-interest in a summer place in Chatham, on the ocean at the beginning of Cape Cod, and in January usually went for about a week to Bermuda, he was reported not to swim. Mockler was a reserved, basically shy, man who did not like to give speeches and repressed within himself any emotional response to such things as hostile takeovers. This probably contributed to his early and unexpected death at age 61 from a heart attack, at his desk, on January 25, 1991. Colman Mockler did not take vacations of any length or eat what most would consider to be a sensible diet. He loved meat, potatoes and ice cream and was a heavy smoker of cigarettes. During the takeover period, newspaper reporters often referred to him as calm, and on the surface he always was calm and exceedingly courteous.

In 1988 a columnist for the *Boston Globe* found what he believed to be a common link among the directors: "[Colman] Mockler attends twice-monthly meetings of the powerful Harvard Corporation, which oversees all university affairs. It is perhaps no accident that six of the company's 10 American directors hold degrees from the World's Greatest University."[7] Such a high proportion from one university, however, was true for boards of several other Fortune 500 companies.

These ten men and I made up the Gillette Board in November 1986. Two Board members, Fouraker and Pivirotto, were each, in 1986, on seven additional boards, which I believe is too heavy a time commitment for a person who wishes conscientiously to perform the duties of a director. Among us there were represented over 30 additional directorships of private companies, including the boards of the eventually leveraged-buyout company, R. H. Macy Company, Inc. Some Gillette board members were also on the boards of several megacompanies: Citicorp, Citibank, Dow Jones and Company, Chemical Bank, Westinghouse Electric and Tenneco. Additionally, some served on boards of well-known Boston companies, including First National Bank of Boston, John Hancock Mutual Life Insurance Company, New England Mutual Life Insurance Company, Shawmut Bank, W. R. Grace and Company, Polaroid and Raytheon. I served on the board of a West Coast defense electronics firm, Watkins-Johnson Company.

NOVEMBER 17 MEETING

In addition to Gillette's directors and management, the board meeting of November 17, 1986, included representatives of Skadden, Arps, Slate, Meagher and Flom, the law firm well known for corporate legal advice during takeovers, as well as Patrick McCarten and others of the Cleveland law firm Jones, Day, Reavis and Pogue. Joe Flom, the astute, legendary takeover lawyer of Skadden, Arps, was in attendance by telephone at that meeting.

Although the doomsday tender offer was the impetus for the November 17 meeting, it was little discussed. First, it was made very clear that the legal duties of directors in any takeover situation are to maximize the shareholder value and to act in the best interest of shareholders. I do not recall a real discussion at that time on how to define *best interest*; one assumes maximum shareholder value, but over what time period? It is almost always assumed that the current market price of a stock represents all the available information about future events that will affect a corporation and thus its stock price. But investors, even if equally informed, can place different valuations on a share of stock because of different expectations, and thus one person will sell a share at a price that someone else is willing to pay. Trading reflects differences in perception of value. Additionally, the marginal price for one share of stock is usually well below the average price per share if all the shares or a very large percentage of outstanding shares have to be purchased to complete a tender. There can be a conflict between the short-run and the long-run interests of the same individual and among shareholders. Tax positions vary over a lifetime, and individuals and institutions selling stock may value immediate gain differently. This topic is discussed further under voting in the proxy contest.

A time-consuming task for the Board was amending the various benefit plans: retirement, bonus, severance pay, and so on, to protect the benefits of about forty upper-management employees in the case of an "unapproved" change in control. The original wording of the benefit plans had used "approved change," as if an unapproved change were unimaginable. The lawyers informed the directors that an assessment of the company's value by recognized outside experts was needed. Gillette's expiring contract with its then investment advisor, Morgan Stanley, had bogged down on fees. Messrs. Mockler, Turley and Zeien, the three management directors, were instructed to negotiate to retain Morgan Stanley. Although the time squeeze imposed by the tender offer gave Morgan Stanley an undue advantage, the complexity of a business with hundreds of products selling in over one hundred countries seemed too great for a new investment firm to grasp within the time available. A crisis attitude evolved.

The Jones, Day representative summarized legal actions taken by Perelman/ Revlon in seeking a ruling that Gillette's poison pill was illegal. Gillette's lawyers had already filed a countersuit charging that Perelman/Revlon's tender offer might be illegal. Such legal battles became common, raising the fees of the investment and legal advisors, who develop an increasing stake in the course of takeover battles.

There was an early emphasis by the Gillette Board, steered by upper management, on protecting management's benefit packages, especially their severance benefits. From the Board's viewpoint, such action helped ensure that upper management would stay throughout the course of what might ensue. Otherwise, some of the top management, believing a hostile change in the control of the company would terminate their employment, might well very early seek a new job. A federal law limits such severance payments to 2.999% of average annual salary. Gillette did not exceed that limit; and, as the formulae worked out, the provisions yielded up to one year or less of salary in most cases. The Board did not, nor did boards in general at that time, use any pretension of continuing consultancies to disguise higher severance pay.

The Board decided that not until Thursday, November 20, the day of the regularly scheduled board meeting, would it consider all options of action in response to the tender offer. Morgan Stanley advised the Board that their "preliminary indication" was that $65 per share was "inadequate." On advice of in-house counsel, the following press release was issued on November 17, 1986:

Gillette Files Suit against Perelman-Revlon Group

The Gillette Company Board of Directors, at a meeting today, authorized the filing of an amended claim in Federal District Court in Boston seeking to enjoin Ronald O. Perelman, Orange Acquisition Corp., and a number of Perelman affiliated corporations from continued violation of the Massachusetts Take-Over Act. The suit also seeks a judgment that The Gillette Shareholders Rights Plan is valid. Gillette, in addition, seeks to enjoin further purchases of its stock by the Perelman/Orange Group on the grounds that the purchases are in violation of the Federal securities law. Gillette also has requested a hearing on the preliminary injunction in Boston Federal District Court. The Board continued its review of the tender offer by the Revlon Group and voted resolutions to protect the rights of all employees under the Company's long-standing benefit plans.[8]

Thus the stage was set.

PRE-PERELMAN DEFENSES

The Gillette Board had adopted a poison-pill plan on December 30, 1985; and at the following shareholders' meeting, April 7, 1986, the shareholders approved the issuance of five million preferred shares so that the plan could be made operable. The poison pill provided that if a person or group became owner of 20 percent or more of the common stock or made a tender offer for 30 percent or more of the stock, then "Rights" on each share of common stock would be exercisable to buy any newly issued preferred stock at half price.

Although these rights would not interfere with a merger approved by the Board, "the issuance of preferred stock pursuant to the Rights or otherwise could impede the completion of an unsolicited acquisition proposal''[9] unless the would-be acquirer could get the Board's support. The would-be acquirer would have to buy more shares, each at a higher price, thus substantially raising the cost of a tender. Negotiation time for the Board would be gained if a takeover attempt occurred. Shareholders and potential acquirers knew that a poison pill existed. The November 14 tender offer was made contingent on the rights provision being made invalid, legally by juidicial or Board action. A cash tender for all the shares compresses the time for negotiation.

A classified board with one-third of its directors elected each year for three-year terms had also been adopted by Gillette shareholders in April 1986. At that time, the Board had no knowledge of any ongoing effort to gain control of the corporation or to organize a proxy contest. In a general climate of takeovers, the Board wished to assure management's continuity and stability. With four seats up for election each year, it would take two years for anyone to gain control. As the 1986 proxy stated, "Classification will strengthen the negotiating position of the board in representing the interests of all stockholders and considering the related interests of employees, customers and suppliers and will allow the board to seek out and select the best possible course of action."

The years 1985 and 1986 had a high level of general hostile-takeover activity, in part because it was cheaper to buy an established company at the relatively low market prices of shares than to buy a new building and machinery. Half of the Fortune 500 companies enacted an antitakeover provision of some nature without a specific takeover threat before November 1986. That other companies had adopted these measures became an argument for a new company to adopt them. The February 1985 *Economic Report of the President* devoted a whole chapter to "The Market for Corporate Control," which became an argument for boards of major companies at least to consider adopting some of the protective measures that the report described. The term hostile takeover had become a part of the businessperson's vocabulary.

VAN GORKOM, TRANS UNION INFLUENCE

The Supreme Court of Delaware had held on January 29, 1985, that the nine directors of the Delaware-incorporated Trans Union Corporation, with $1.1 billion in sales, were liable for agreeing to sell that company without careful review of its value. Each director was held personally liable for the difference between the selling price per share and what the court perceived to be the higher, intrinsic or *real* market value of the company. The directors were held to be "knowledgeable," but there were no charges or proof of bad faith, self-dealing or fraud. The board had approved a $55 per share price, $17 over the $38 market price, but this was deemed to be too low.[10] However, it was not so much the price but the process used to set the price that the court faulted. In a single two-hour meeting the board had discussed the price and made its decision, and the agreement had been signed that same evening during a formal party for the opening of the Chicago Lyric Opera. The court did not believe that enough time had been taken for discussion and thus for protection of the shareholders' interest.

In essence, the Trans Union chairman, Jerome Van Gorkom, appeared to have negotiated the price ahead of the board meeting without getting an outside opinion on the fair value of the company, and the board had concurred with him. The chairman had retained outside counsel to advise only one day before the decision was made. The essence of the Delaware Supreme Court ruling was that the directors were grossly negligent in selling the company after only two hours of deliberation for a price that, although $17 above the market price of $38, had not been substantiated as representative of the value of the company by an outside, fair-price valuation. But current market price does not always represent a single, long-run or intrinsic value of a company. Because reasonable people may differ in assumptions determining a future value, discounted to current price, the process of deciding a selling price of a company, the required amount of deliberation over a measurable period of time, becomes very important. It was the lack of documentation for the Trans Union board's decision and its failure to follow the legal process of lengthy deliberation that led to the downfall of the Trans Union board and were perceived to be the basis of the court's decision for a $23.5 million judgment against the directors. The directors' claims that their collective experience enabled them to determine that the $55 offer was adequate was shot down. ''None of them was an investment banker or financial analyst.''[11] The *business judgment rule* did not protect them, although they claimed to act in good faith, because they did not document their decision-making and were too hasty.

It is a fear of such high personal liability, stemming from the Van Gorkom case ruling, that makes corporate directors faced with a hostile takeover attempt willing to sit through repetitive legal interpretations of *duty of care* and the *business judgment rule*. The necessity to be informed, to seek outside advice, and to recognize that there are no shortcuts dominates the directors who wish to escape heavy personal liability. Legal process, as defined by Gillette counsel, meant presentation of an issue at a board meeting by both management and outside experts, written information supplied and then votes at a later meeting. Thus, at least two meetings were necessary before the Gillette Board would vote on any substantive issue involving the hostile activity issue. The process took a long time, but the risk of personal legal liability for directors who did not follow these rules was perceived to be very high. When the tender began, the individual directors had little knowledge about the would-be acquirer, takeover law and the economic and other literature on the subject of takeovers. Events moved faster than our ability to acquire meaningful knowledge, but the deliberate slowing of the process prevented hasty decisions.

It became obvious that the Board would have to make a written record of being informed and that, within the time limits, there would then have to be lengthy consideration of all the options to assure that we would maximize shareholder value for the owners of the Corporation. Legal advisers instructed us that directors should be entitled to the benefit of the business judgment rule if they acted in *good faith*, on an *informed basis* and in what they believed to be the *best interests of the company*. Those phrases were part of the legal and investment advisers' vocabulary and, indeed, became the directors' vocabulary throughout this period. To maximize shareholder value, or MSV, and phrasing, such as *directors' duties of loyalty and care*, became standard by repetition throughout these discussions.

Despite the large number of investment and legal advisers hired, no outside public relations experts, to my knowledge at that time, were consulted or hired. However, the *Wall Street Journal Index* for 1986 reports for November 20 that ''Kekst is representing Gillette's interest.'' Dependence on legal counsel was high, and a practice of *no comment* and channeling of public responses by directors and top management, initially through one company public-relations person, was mandated. However, because of the complexity of the financial issues involved, the then treasurer, Milton Glass, shortly became an additional and important spokesman for the company.

PRICE OF $65 PER SHARE

Was the tender price of $65 adequate? This was the question that the Board had to decide. The high and low prices (reflecting the shareholder-approved April 1986 stock split of 2 for 1) of Gillette common shares for each quarter of 1986 were substantially above those during 1985, which prices were above those of 1984. During the first quarter of 1984, the Gillette share price was 25⅝ and by the fourth quarter, 29¼. During 1985, there was a steady rise in the high from 29⅞ in the first quarter to 36 at the end of the fourth quarter of 1985. Earnings per share were $5.18 in 1985, and the dividend payout ratio was 50 percent. In 1986 the high price ranged from the first quarter at 44⅛ up to 58¼ on the day of the tender. The stock was split two-for-one during the first half of 1986, and these prices reflect that split, the first since 1961. The trend in price of Gillette shares was clearly upward over these past four years, reflecting ever-increasing profits and higher expectations.

Gillette's profits from operations in 1985 were 15 percent of its $2.4 billion sales; its after-tax profits were 6.7 percent of sales. The closing price on the last trading day prior to the formal beginning of the tender offer was 57¾. The tender and speculation pushed the price to a peak of 68⅞. From this height, it fell on the day of the tender's withdrawal, Monday, November 24, to 45⅞ and then rose slowly to 50⅛ on the last day of 1986.

Generally speaking, tender offers are 30 to 50 percent higher than the existing stock price, but what was Gillette's existing stock price? According to the SEC filing,[12] Perelman/Revlon started buying Gillette shares Friday, October 31, 1986, when the initial price was $42.75. It closed at 44¾. Not until the 5th of November did Perelman/Revlon make a single purchase that exceeded 100,000 shares, although in the course of one day they made multiple purchases of large numbers of stock. For example, on November 4, when the price started at $48, they bought 37 lots, ending with a thousand shares at $54. This was the first day during which a big jump in the stock price occurred. Whatever price is selected to be the unaffected price on that day, the choice would be difficult to defend.

The total number of shares purchased by Perelman/Revlon on November 13 was well over three million; the total purchased, October 31–November 13, was 9,226,300. All of the shares were purchased on the New York Stock Exchange except for the last trade, which was made on the Midwest Stock Exchange for 2,750,000 shares on November 13.

How the market price was defined in terms of time, the closing price before the tender or an average over how many days before the tender offer, became important to the Board's decision on how they should respond to the offer. The average price during the ten days prior to the tender was $56.60. Although the average reflected some of the heavy buying by the would-be acquirers, it was nearly a dollar less than the price on the day just prior to the tender offer. The Board needed to determine the long-term intrinsic value of the Company, in line with the Trans Union case decision. We did not believe that we could merely add a percentage to an agreed-on base in mechanical fashion, even if we could agree on the base, as a prior ten-day average. If 50 percent were added to the prior ten-day average, it would have yielded almost $85.

The Board opted for obtaining time-consuming estimates of the intrinsic worth of each portion of the Company, based on the projected total sales and profits of each product. There was a five-year plan. Some estimates of the impact on total sales and profits of Gillette's potential but not yet assured new, face-hugging razor, which would become the Sensor, had to be made. Other questions included, What would happen to Braun's sales of its electric shaver when in mid-1985 the Federal Trade Commission (FTC) had lifted the ban on its marketing in the United States? It would take some time for manufacture to "gear up" and for advertising to take hold. It was not until 1986 that Braun's key product—its specific, unique rechargeable shavers—had been introduced throughout the United States. How fast would the Oral-B toothbrush sales increase once Gillette's international marketing was fully implemented? For such questions, the directors' judgments become more important than any assumed rigid percentages derived from past trends.

In general, takeover premiums range from 30 to 50 or more percentage points over the perceived market price. It is not plausible that acquirers would estimate a higher present value of the Company's future value for no reason. The sources of their anticipated gains, however, may be a puzzle, and sometimes significant gains are not experienced. For example, one astute observer of many takeovers notes that "It is hard to explain gains of the size consistently observed across a broad variety of transactions. Even harder to explain is the failure of accounting studies to find evidence that takeovers significantly improve the target's performance."[13]

The various common explanations for a takeover premium seem to be complementary. Improvement in management and creating synergies from dovetailing the manufacture of several competitive lines or from using common selling channels are some of the anticipated, profit-yielding efficiencies expected. Money can be saved by sharing common overhead functions, as of finance and personnel, and advertising can be cleverly shared. The restructuring subsequent to a takeover, especially of large companies,[14] usually results in layoffs. Duplication of personnel is eliminated. This has been especially true in banking mergers in the mid-1990s. Synergy is created by dovetailing the strengths and weaknesses of the buyer and the target company. Conglomerate firms such as Gillette divest their losers (for example, those product lines that sell poorly) more rapidly. These actions create dollar gains. After-tax profits change, in part because interest payments on debt capital are expensed before the company pays corporate income tax, while dividends on equity capital cannot be expensed. Thus, depending on interest rates, recapitalization with a substitution of loan capital for equity capital can create gains if only because the amount of corporate income tax paid is lessened.

Another set of reasons for gains evolve from an *empire-building* theme. A larger firm is considered to be more prestigious than a smaller one, and it may be easier to buy size than to acquire size by expansion. Control over a large, successful company yields ego satisfaction as well as a potential large economic gain. Justification of a takeover price above the market price is sometimes based on a perception that a share of stock, when part of a block that controls a corporation, is worth more than the market price of a single share to those who wish to control. Such an expansion of empire, in order to gain prestige, I believe was a factor involved in Ronald Perelman's attempts to take over Gillette. By ownership and management of Gillette, he would gain prestige, visibility and the social and business acceptability that he apparently had not gained in taking over Pantry Pride and the cosmetic firm Revlon.

Gillette's top management had spent their careers rising through the ranks at Gillette, and they would have looked askance at any entrepreneur-type raider and especially one such as Perelman, whose colleagues have said that he was "pushy, demanding, impatient, a screamer seeking some sort of recognition and wanting to get someplace fast, but polite, too,"[15] and sometimes referred to as "the plague." There was an antipathy toward anyone who has also been described as "the antithesis of the buttoned-down corporate chieftain," a description that fitted several of Gillette's top executives.[16] In 1986 the top five officers of Gillette had an average of 23 years of service under the company's retirement plan. They were professional managers who did not want outsiders to take over "their" company—not one that they owned, but one from which they earned their incomes and gained prestige. There was an initial reaction by management of "No," even though as of February 28, 1986, all directors and officers, as a group, owned approximately only "1.4% of total shares outstanding."[17] Perelman wanted himself to run Gillette and enjoy its cash flow and have the prestige being the head of Gillette might bestow.

Perelman's reputation was such that the management of any profitable, independent company with over 80 years' history would probably reject his unwelcome attempt to take over the firm. His actions promised that he would be tenacious. It took until July 1995 for him to win the 1983 legal battle over, whether he paid a fair price for Technicolor, Inc., despite the directors having been held negligent.

Perelman had business training and experience. Ronald Owen Perelman earned an MBA from the highly ranked Wharton School of the University of Pennsylvania and worked for his father's Philadelphia metal-fabricating business. Helped by family money, he bought an interest in Cohen-Hatfield, a jewelry retailer, and then MacAndrews and Forbes, a licorice extract and chocolate supplier. In 1984, with $90 million raised by Drexel Burnham Lambert, Perelman took MacAndrews and Forbes Holdings, Inc., private to act as an investment vehicle for other acquisitions. Among those acquisitions were Technicolor, Inc., and, in 1985, Revlon. In an article that I did not see until I was writing this book, Perelman was described in *Advertising Age* as follows: " 'It's mogulmania. It's a case of power at its rawest. He makes Carl Icahn look like a polished stone,' said one cosmetics industry executive, noting that some of Revlon's vendors have recently complained about a certain arrogance at Revlon as a result of Mr. Perelman's aggressiveness. One Revlon executive didn't like the way a department store was treating the company and said, 'You'd better watch it or we'll buy you.' "[18]

That this description was not far off the mark can be illustrated by events of six years later. In July 1995, Ronald Perelman was being questioned in a deposition and answered as the following exchange indicates:

Q. Do you derive any income from Revlon?

A. I am not sure.

Q. Consolidated Cigar, what is your position with them?

A. I am not sure.

Q. Do you derive any income?

A. I don't know. . . .

Q. Is there someone in existence that would know the answers to any of these questions?

A. Yes.

Q. Who would that person be?

A. I don't know.[19]

Skadden, Arps had successfully defended MacAndrews & Forbes when they charged that Revlon had in 1985 put itself up for sale because, through its management leveraged buyout (LBO), Revlon had transferred control of the company to management. It was successfully argued that because the LBO had resulted in not preserving the corporate entity, Revlon had, in effect, put Revlon up for sale and therefore should seek the highest price for the company. Because MacAndrews & Forbes had offered the highest price, Revlon's board had to accept it.

That decision in the Revlon case by the Delaware Chancery Court, upheld by the Delaware Supreme Court (506 A.2d 173; Del S. Ct. 1986), made clear that recapitalization by Gillette's management, as through a private LBO with Gillette's existing management running the company, would be a tricky defense against the hostile would-be acquirer, Perelman/Revlon. However, Gillette's lead lawyer, also of Skadden, Arps, Joe Flom, to my recollection, never directly advised against a management LBO. Rather that option was very early shot down as one in which Gillette's management was not interested because of the huge debt that they would incur. To escape cleanly a charge that a change in control takes place when a management LBO occurs, the stockholders must first approve a major recapitalization by management. A Gillette management LBO was never discussed within this context.

SOME ANALYSIS

Perelman/Revlon was aware of the huge potential increase in Gillette's cash flow from the Company's worldwide geographical expansion of manufacturing and sales of shaving systems and Oral-B toothbrushes through Gillette's existing worldwide marketing and distribution systems. Braun, which Gillette had bought in 1967, was also a well-known entity to Perelman, but one that Perelman/Revlon would probably have tried to spin off despite the successful stripping away of its losing product lines in previous years and its huge potential sales of electric razors, clocks and coffee makers in the United States. Its classic design and high-performance products have a status image that attracts higher-income buyers worldwide. With the lifting of the U.S. antitrust ban on marketing of Braun electric shavers within the United States and the possible extension of the aura of Dieter Ram's designs into new products, Braun was poised to take off. Perelman/Revlon probably saw Gillette's superb marketing and distribution system principally in terms of what it could do for the sales of cosmetics. Insiders saw it primarily for how it could increase sales of blades and razors.

It is Gillette's longtime practice, as it is in many other companies, to start development of a new product, an improvement on the old product, as soon as the latter is marketed. The Atra razor, with its pivoting head, took five years to develop and was first marketed in 1977. The Trac II, with its twin-blade cartridge, had first been marketed in 1971, six years earlier. During the 1980s, Gillette added a lubricating strip to its blades, as in Atra Plus and in Good News Plus, where the "Plus" stands for the lubricating strip. This simple, incremental innovation did boost sales. But profits in the core business of razors and blades, although substantial, were not rising because the disposables were cutting into the more profitable, traditional metal razor and blade market.

Although Gillette dominates the U.S. shaving market and most of the world markets, the shaving industry is highly competitive in production and marketing. Gillette's competitors in 1985 included Warner-Lambert with its Schick products, Société Bic with its well-known disposables, Wilkinson Sword (bought in 1990 by Gillette through a group of companies) and American Safety Razor Company, which manufactures several private-label brands. To compete successfully, management believed that a new revolutionary shaving system was needed. By 1986 a prototype of what became the Sensor, a unique razor with twin blades mounted on tiny springs, had been developed; but how to mass-produce it in a cost-effective manner proved to be elusive. "Gillette had hoped to introduce the new system in 1984 or 1985, but it couldn't figure out how to mass produce the cartridges. . . . A test line in 1986 indicated its technology was feasible. Gillette spent the next two years—and $150 million—to build manufacturing equipment for mass production."[20] This level of activity could not have existed without knowledge of the new razor and blade among many workers. However, this development was not, to my knowledge, publicized until early 1988. An April 2, 1988, letter from Gillette's chairman to Gillette's stockholders stated,

Gillette expects to introduce in late 1989 or early 1990 a superior new shaving system that it believes will have a material positive impact on the earnings from the Company's largest and most profitable business segment—blades and razors. Gillette's international manufacturing and distribution network, enhanced by the recent reorganization, will enable the Company to roll out the new system worldwide on an accelerated basis compared with past major system launches. Gillette believes that this capability will increase profit margins once the new shaving system is in full production.

On February 25, 1990, a *New York Times* story stated that in respect to the 1988 proxy fight, "Colman M. Mockler Jr., Gillette's taciturn chairman, had to scramble to keep Gillette independent, partly by convincing doubters that a then-secret 'super blade' could make a lot of money for shareholders."[21]

Whether Perelman or others who became hostile acquirers knew about the progress in developing the new razor and blade in November 1986, I do not know. To analysts and other watchers of the shaving industry, that a new product was being developed could not have been a surprise. (See Chapter 4 under the heading "Stock Price" for an in-depth discussion of why it was probable, in my opinion, that others knew of the potential of Gillette's new blade.) Although the mass production of a new razor giving a closer and more comfortable shave seemed feasible by November 1986, it was not known whether it could be mass-produced at a price low enough to reverse the incursion of the cheaper, less profitable disposables. By then, disposables had over 50 percent of the wet-shaving market.

Analysts and others must have been aware that the company had replaced $157 million in debt capital with equity capital prior to the tender offer, as reported in the 1987 10-K released to the Securities and Exchange Commission (SEC). The Company had called and converted into common stock its convertible debentures worth $151 million, and in July 1986 it had issued 7.5 percent notes to foreign investors in Europe for approximately $58 million. Clearly, the Company had signaled to those who watched the financial markets that it needed cash. That cash was used for continuing research and development on the yet-to-be-named Sensor. Although in the 1987 10-K such financial information was carefully tagged ''prior to the repurchase activity,'' it was probably overwhelmed in readers' minds by the reported $750 million that Gillette had borrowed to finance its repurchase of stocks and restructuring costs after the tender.

The Company took a risk in borrowing $150 million to complete the development for the mass production of the Sensor. It was also a gamble whether the new manual, permanent razor would reverse the incursion of the cheaper, less profitable disposables. Gillette made comparatively little on these throwaways. Each Sensor razor would require periodic purchase of new thin, stainless-steel high-quality blades with twin cutting edges, an item that Gillette could make in huge quantities and with profit margins of over 30 percent; this was where real money could be made. The hope was to return the market of razors to the high-quality, permanent-metal product that Alfred Zeien (who in 1991 became chairman of Gillette) and others envisioned.

Although Perelman thought that the Company was worth more than it was trading at, the Gillette Board did not want to sell the Company for the price he was offering. To the typical institutional investor, a small gain in price may look good, but not to the many long-term individual investors in Gillette who, if they sold shares bought many years ago at far lower prices, would then be subject to sizable taxes on their profits. A small percentage gain, even 30 percent, to some did not always look to be worthwhile. This distinction between institutional and individual holders of Gillette shares is discussed in more detail in connection with the proxy contest in April 1988.

After the tender, the market pressure from more buyers, relative to sellers entering the market, forced an immediate increase in the stock price. (A more theoretical discussion of the economic theory of takeovers, including the claim that the demand for common stock is *infinitely elastic* in competitive markets with perfect information, appears in Chapter 4.) Arbitrageurs and other new buyers seeking quick profits were attracted because they anticipated further price increases up to at least the offered $65 a share. The percentage of stock held by institutions increased, and that held by individuals fell.

Assessing the intrinsic value of Gillette meant estimating the liquidation value of the different parts of Gillette. In a takeover financed mostly by borrowed money, it was very likely that parts of the business would be sold to pay off debt. ''Larry the liquidator'' in the 1990 off-Broadway play *Other People's Money* was aptly named.

It was common to finance takeovers in the 1980s by selling off parts of a whole, and Gillette had many parts: Braun with its coffeemakers and coffee grinders, clocks, mixers and other small household appliances; the newly acquired Oral-B toothbrushes; Paper Mate pens; Liquid Paper, an eraser fluid; and the loosely connected mix of well-known brands of toiletries, ranging from Right Guard and Dry Idea deodorants to White Rain shampoo and Mink hair spray and to Jafra's direct-selling cosmetics and recently acquired La Toja and other European brand cosmetics. The total value of selling off the parts of Gillette not involved in the core business of razors and blades probably would yield a greater total value than selling the business as a single unit.

Losses incurred by parts of Gillette's diversified operations were discussed during the early 1980s by the Board, but few of its separate operations had been sold before the restructuring in 1987. Exceptions were Braun's high-quality Hasselblad camera and its hi-fi business, sold in 1983. Additionally, worry over safety and potential consumer lawsuits stemming from Gillette's Cricket disposable-lighter business, which also was losing money, had resulted in its sale to Swedish Match AB late in 1984. Cricket had originally come from the S.T. Dupont Company, which along with Jafra, a direct sales cosmetics company, dominated the diversified group. Gillette had partially acquired S.T. Dupont, with 48 percent in 1971 and reaching 80 percent in 1973. S.T. Dupont's luxury lines of high-priced lacquer-design pens and lighters and leather wallets, lost money in the United States, and not until 1985 did it earn enough abroad to offset this. It was not sold until 1987.

But it was the toiletries and cosmetics division that Perelman/Revlon alluded to when talking of Gillette synergy with Revlon, and not blades and razors. In 1986 Gillette's toiletries and cosmetics sales were almost equal to blades and razor sales, but the profits earned were only about one-fourth of those earned by blades and razors. Two-thirds of Gillette's profits come from razors and blades. They were and are the major source of cash flow to the Company.

Many concepts, assumptions and projections entered into the Board's perception of the long-run, intrinsic value of the Company. An additional overwhelming fact, however, was that Perelman/Revlon/Orange Group (PRO) had only $1 billion in cash and would need to borrow nearly $4 billion. The question was: Would the financing be available at interest rates acceptable to Perelman?

The difficulty in determining the intrinsic value of a company, especially one with valuable trade names, such as Gillette with its many world-famous brands, can be shown from the much written-about $26.4 billion takeover of RJR Nabisco in 1989. The initial bid for that stock, in what evolved into a bidding war, was $75 per share, "higher than the stock had ever traded—around $71,"[22] and the takeover price paid by Kohlberg Kravis Roberts (KKR) reached $109. For most informed people, that price was too high. George Shultz, who knew Ross Johnson, has remarked to me that Johnson, president and chief executive officer of RJR, had early on remarked to him that $80 would have been right. Even well-informed insiders do not necessarily know the intrinsic value of a company.

In January 1990 the price of RJR reset bonds fell to 56 cents on the dollar, and KKR, which had backed their reset, was faced with a financial dilemma. They would have to force up the price of reset bonds or be forced in a reset to pay huge interest rates, 25 or 30 percent. Eventually, a compromise position was reached. George Roberts of KKR refinanced the bonds with a special equity issue. On July 16, 1990, "Some two-thirds of the reset bonds would be retired; the remaining ones would carry new interest rates of 17% and 17⅜%—higher than KKR wanted, but bearable nonetheless."[23]

The Ivan F. Boesky insider-trading scandal had exploded on November 14, 1986, the same day as the tender was made for Gillette. Front-page newspaper articles detailed how Boesky had been charged with trading on inside information and fined $100 million. As a *Wall Street Journal* article stated, there was "concern that the growing insider-trading scandal ultimately could hurt financing for mergers and acquisitions." Boesky, in order to meet the fines, began to sell his holdings. Among the stocks Boesky liquidated were large holdings of Gillette shares, which as a result "dropped almost $11 a share in the past three days [November 17 to November 19] to $57.75."[24] Drexel Burnham Lambert was the common investment banker for Revlon and Boesky. Even though a second confidence letter to Gillette arrived to affirm that Drexel and Revlon anticipated no trouble in raising the needed $4 billion to complete the deal, several of Gillette's directors doubted whether Drexel would be able to fulfill that commitment. A few even wondered whether Drexel was implicated in illegal junk-bond activity and whether parking of Gillette stock occurred during the accumulation of the 13.9 percent holding prior to the SEC filing.

High-risk but high-yield junk-bond securities had financed many hostile takeovers by large companies in the 1980s. Now they were tainted, at least for the time being, by the Boesky scandal. As an aftermath of the recession continuing into 1982, the market prices of most stocks had become cheap relative to the replacement value of a company's assets. Gillette had little corporate debt, many written-off plants, and trade names that were undervalued in an accounting sense. With its large cash flow, it was a takeover target.

BOARD MEETING, NOVEMBER 20, 1986

The November 20, 1986, board meeting followed the company's usual pattern of committee meetings in the morning, followed by the main board meeting, that was scheduled for 11:00 A.M., somewhat earlier than usual. (The usual Gillette board procedures were for the committees to meet in the morning of the third Thursday of the month; if necessary, the joint finance and executive committee continued to meet during luncheon. The full board meeting usually began at 1:30 P.M. In October 1986 the Board had decreased from ten to nine the number of scheduled meetings each year. Months that the Board had no scheduled meetings were January, May and August.) The personnel committee met at 9:00 A.M., and the joint executive-finance committee started shortly after

10:00 A.M. Because the latter meeting was a joint meeting of two committees, neither the chairman of the executive committee, Charles Meyer, or the chairman of the finance committee, myself, chaired this meeting, but rather, as was customary, Colman Mockler as chairman of the board conducted the meeting with a calm, business-as-usual approach. The agenda was set by the chairman, and no one suggested that the order of business be changed. Apparently, all the directors wanted the usual company business settled before an in-depth discussion of the takeover threat. In less than an hour and a half, the committee recommended to the Board spending millions of dollars to bolster investment in retail eyewear (one of the miscellaneous areas under "other"), to increase production of Good News razors and to purchase a small cosmetics company, Unisas Princeton in Chile. The main issue on each director's mind, the tender offer, was not addressed.

Even when the main board meeting was called, attention was first given to the same business matters that the executive-finance committee had discussed; in addition, management reports were received on the new blade plant in India and the completion of the Waterman Pen acquisition, which later proved to be a substantially good investment. Amendments to the savings and retirement and other benefit plans to meet the new 1986 tax law provisions, discussed by the personnel committee earlier, were also approved.

Not until a quick lunch with all the usual business items out of the way did the Board consider the immediate problems presented by the Perelman/Revlon/Orange tender offer. Present again were representatives from the law offices of Jones, Day and Skadden, Arps. Because no one in upper management was impressed with the original Morgan Stanley person assigned, Gillette in renegotiating for Morgan Stanley's services had obtained Eric Gleacher, who already had a reputation as an investment banker who could give good advice in merger matters.

Again, the directors were advised as to their duties of loyalty and care, that is, to protect the interests of the Corporation and its stockholders. Although, as I recall, there was mention of short-term valuation versus longer-term valuation of the Company, the interrelation between short- and long-run values was not directly addressed. The Board's horizon had been shortened to the legal requirement of up to 20 days for their response to the tender. The market's actions were anticipated to condense greatly this period of time. Each individual director's assessment of the company's value depended on his or her estimate of future company earnings. It became quite clear during that discussion that a potential conflict between short-term and long-term values would become a major facet of the decision that would evolve. Good short-term decisions can turn out to be good decisions in the long run. The rejection of the $65 per share price was such a decision. The Board did not accept the old axiom, "A bird in the hand is worth two in the bush."

Morgan Stanley was expected to make a valuation of the company to help the directors judge whether or not the offer fell within the range of the intrinsic value of the Company. We were told that this is standard practice in such situations. It was Andrew Liu of Morgan Stanley who did the valuation and reviewed all the financial variables from the income and balance sheet statements and set out his assumptions. Like many such exercises, the valuation reflected a fairly static situation without extreme assumptions as to the possible outer limits of Gillette's future sales and profits. No specific mention, as I recall, was made of a potential new razor.

Advisors pointed out that the Perelman/Revlon offer had many conditions. Since each director had his own copy of the advertisement, which had the conditions in bold print, this was no surprise to the directors. Although some of the conditions were of a technical nature, the last one was basic: "the purchaser obtaining sufficient financing to enable it to purchase all outstanding shares of common stock on a fully diluted basis and to pay related fees and expenses." The directors were skeptical. Would Perelman/Revlon/Orange get financing despite the Boesky scandal, via loans, for nearly another $4 billion?

The detailed evaluation of data presented to the Board by Andrew Liu supported Morgan Stanley's very early call of $65 as being too low, although it was about 44 percent above $45 and 18 percent above $55, the range of the market price before the tender. The long-run price was viewed as much higher. After being briefed on the Van Gorkom case, where directors had been ruled liable for accepting a too-low bid, Gillette's directors were eager to avoid that scenario.

Valuation of a company with as many products and wide geographical dispersion as Gillette is complex. The realistic, immediate valuation of a company depends primarily on the value of its physical assets; trademarks, of which Gillette had many; general goodwill; comparisons to competitive companies; and projections of future earnings, which depend on future sales and costs. The physical valuation of assets was affected by Gillette being an old company with most of the physical assets on its books already depreciated. Additionally, complicating the valuation were the ever-changing foreign-exchange rates. Gillette owned plants and facilities throughout the world: in the United Kingdom, Berlin, Mexico, Argentina, Africa, Australia, Brazil, Canada, Ireland, Spain, India, and so on. The Gillette trade name we believed to have high value; Braun, which had been bought in 1967, was just being allowed to market its electric razor in the United States under Braun's trademark and had yet to gain its envisioned sales momentum in the United States. Because Braun's electric razor had over a 60 percent market share in Germany and a similarly high share in Japan, the Board believed that its U.S. market would be substantial and profitable.

The directors had a gut feeling, supported by the Morgan Stanley analysis, that a $65 Gillette share price was far too low, even though the market price per share had recently been lower. The directors, as well as the general investing public, knew that the Company was doing well. On October 24, 1986, *Value Line* rated the Company's financial strength at A+ and stated, "All things considered, a 14% profit gain seems achievable in 1986."

In 1985 earnings per share had been $5.18, and the 1986 projections were somewhat higher. The net (less cash equivalents) debt-to-equity ratio was 46 percent, and before the takeover attempts it had been anticipated to decline. Return on stockholders' equity had been improving annually, and sales and net profits were projected to rise by 14 percent and 17 percent, respectively.

The year 1985 was the 80th consecutive year that Gillette had paid dividends. Gillette, as is true of most companies that pay dividends, had a policy of increasing the amount only if it were believed that the higher level of dividend payment could be maintained indefinitely. Most directors, I believe, perceive that lowering a dividend rate is admission that a company is in financial trouble. Gillette, during the period when I was on the board, kept its dividend payout ratio between 40 and 50 percent of profits, and in 1985 it was at 50 percent. The surging profits of the Company had been recognized by dividend increases and by a two-for-one stock split approved by the shareholders in April 1986. The last previous stock split had been 25 years earlier, in 1961. The stock had been trading during 1985 between $55 and $70 per share and had closed on December 31 at $69.50. Thus, the Board had been accustomed to hearing Gillette's stock prices quoted, before the split, above the $65 tender. It is possible that this fact helped to make the perception of a $65 tender seem low. Prior to the split in early 1986, 31 million shares were outstanding, and 4 million had been reserved for convertible debentures and stock options. The two-for-one split resulted in increasing the authorized number from 75 million to 150 million shares.

The Board decided on November 20, 1986, that they should seek the highest price possible for the company and directed management to seek a *white knight* or other buyer. A white knight was viewed as a new, more friendly buyer who would pay more and would rescue the Company from an unfriendly acquirer, who would probably break up the company and fire many long-term employees. It was the Board's belief that the first order of business was to protect the Company from an immediate threat to its immediate business plans and that this would best maximize the shareholders' long-run value. The Board decided to leave the poison pill in place and noted that the "Rights" were not yet separated from the common stock.

Discussed during the November 20 meeting (and later by the media and in testimony during 1988) as potential white knights were various well-known companies, which included Unilever, Ralston Purina, and Hanson Trust P.L.C. Probably the best summary in the public record of what occurred in seeking white knights is in the "Findings of Fact and Conclusions of Law in the Civil Action No. 88-0862-WF in the U.S. District Court, Massachusetts, *The Gillette Company v RB Partners et al.*, June 30, 1988, Federal Court House," a case involving the Coniston Partners proxy contest in April 1988.

Judge Wolf in the ruling recalled that "Mr. Zeien said that Gillette had contacted potential buyers. Some of those buyers, he said, had reviewed confidential information, but none, he said, were seriously interested in acquiring the company. . . . [Those] discussions occurred . . . primarily during one week in November 1986.''[25] A few pages later, Judge Wolf summarized,

With regard to the confidentiality agreements, as I noted earlier, in November 1986, Revlon attempted a hostile takeover or tender offer for Gillette. For one week Gillette, among other things, urgently looked for possible buyers for the whole company. They were looking for the so-called 'white knights.' Nine companies contacted by Mr. Gleacher expressed sufficient interest in getting confidential information to consider a possible transaction. All of them signed what are in the industry standard agreements restricting their use of confidential information for two years. . . . Several companies who signed such agreements made friendly offers for part of the company. Nobody ever offered to buy all of the [Gillette] company.[26]

During the Coniston hearings after the proxy fight in April 1988, the names of all companies that Gillette had sought out in its search for potential white knights in November 1986 were disclosed. Five companies were invited to review Gillette's books in late 1986: Metromedia Company, PepsiCo, Ralston Purina, Anheuser-Busch, and Colgate Palmolive. Additionally, five investment firms also had access to the books: Kohlberg Kravis Roberts (KKR), Forstmann Little, Citicorp Industrial Credit, Salomon Bros. and Kidder Peabody. As was common in such circumstances, the ten firms agreed not to disclose for two years without Gillette's written consent information about Gillette's confidential data and not to bid for the company without Gillette's written consent.

None of these companies wished to purchase all of Gillette. However, both KKR and Forstmann Little were reported to want to purchase new Gillette convertible preferred stock or to loan money to the company via a subordinated convertible debt,[27] and Ralston-Purina, according to Eric Gleacher's testimony, wanted a ''cross minority ownership.'' Among the variables involved in white knight negotiations are the percentage of equity a company will sell and the price and the length of a standstill agreement before further purchase of stock. With these and other variables involved, agreement can be difficult to reach.

A primary reason for not finding a white knight was that many of the potential white knights were involved in other buyout negotiations at this time. For example, Unilever, N.V., was negotiating to acquire Cheseborough-Pond's, Inc., which agreed to be acquired on December 2. Additionally, a December 4 *New York Times* news article mentions that ''traders were hearing speculation that Proctor and Gamble or Hanson Trust P.L.C. might also be interested in Gillette.''[28] But, Hanson had agreed to purchase Kaiser Cement Corporation on November 28. Henkel KGAA in Duesseldorf had agreed to acquire Occidental Petroleum Corporation's Diamond Shamrock Chemicals Company on December 10.[29] Takeover activity by large firms peaked in the United States in 1986, and finding a large firm that was able and willing to buy all of Gillette proved to be a nonachievable goal.

MEETING, NOVEMBER 23/24, 1986

The November 20 meeting broke up about 5:30 P.M., and I returned to California and Herb Jacobi to Germany. Over one million shares traded on Friday, November 21. The normal daily trade at that time was well under 200,000 shares. Worry about a possible sweep of the market or a Coniston purchase of 51 percent of the shares on the Monday resulted in a hurriedly called directors' meeting in Boston on Sunday evening, November 23. Rumors about stock market activity in Gillette stock were everywhere. Was Perelman achieving purchase of 51 percent of shares? No one knew, but with such a large number of institutional holders, the Board was worried. The meeting adjourned at 1:15 A.M. Monday morning and reconvened at 8:30 A.M. on the same morning.

That Sunday evening the directors talked informally over a catered roast-beef dinner set out on the board table. The last to arrive at the meeting was Herb from Germany. He and I had both missed our scheduled six-hour, nonstop, Thursday evening flights to return home, and our flight time had therefore increased far beyond usual. As the two directors then living the farthest from Boston, we flew a lot of miles in that period.

As far as the Board was concerned, on that Sunday night it had to decide whether Perelman/Revlon could obtain a $4 billion loan from Drexel Burnham Lambert, despite the ongoing Boesky insider-trading case that had recently broken. Two confidence letters from Perelman's investment bankers assured us that the $4 billion was available. Should we risk the potential sweep of the street on the Monday? Nearly 14 percent of the outstanding shares were in Perelman's hands. We believed that the past week's stock market action, in which the price of the stock was rising rapidly, meant that the Board and management had no time to discuss with Unilever or others their potential holding of substantial shares of Gillette stock as a neutralizing action. The Board's belief was that if the loans were announced, then close to the 17 percent of shares needed for control would quickly trade hands.

The November 23/24 meeting had greater tension and excitement than had the preceding meeting. It was clear that, although the poison pill seemed to give us time to negotiate, the market actions might not allow sufficient time to negotiate an alternate deal. On November 14 over 7 million shares had traded; and for the week ending November 21, over 12 million. There were about 62 million shares outstanding.

The meeting of November 23/24 was a fascinating experience with its fast-moving exchange of ideas, heightened at times by revealed emotion. The same investment bankers and legal advisors already mentioned were present. Many options were debated: A leveraged buyout with Kohlberg Kravis Roberts (KKR) financing to possibly negotiations for Ralston Purina to buy about one-fifth of control. (Ralston Purina had bought Union Carbide's battery business, Duracell, on June 30, 1986, for $1.42 billion and was possibly hard pressed for acquisition money.) Bargaining without ever dealing face-to-face with the principals was artificial and difficult. It was my understanding that if the CEOs got together, then SEC rules would require disclosure of all the discussions and negotiations. Our investment banker, Eric Gleacher, could, however, sound out Perelman's investment banker on specific points and then only the final outcome need be disclosed and not all the twists and turns prior to the final agreement. The president of Natomas, a target of a hostile tender, has described this artificial process as follows:

Investment bankers are able to sound each other out without speaking directly for the principals. One banker could say, "I am willing to recommend this," and the other banker could counter with, "If you did, then I might recommend that." So long as the investment bankers were talking and the principals themselves were not, no immediate disclosure would be required. If those conversations succeeded in leading to an agreement between the principals, then only that agreement—and not the interim moves—would have to be disclosed.

In one sense, it seemed like a very expensive approach, at the rates both sides were paying their lawyers and bankers—but it worked.[30]

Perelman was intimating that he wanted to be bought out of all of his 13.9 percent of shares, nearly $600 million. He also wanted, as part of the deal, Oral-B, the toothbrush company that Gillette had bought for $188.5 million in 1984. Perelman stated that he would pay substantially more for Oral-B than Gillette had paid. Additionally, a face-saving third demand was that Gillette dismiss the legal suit that the company had filed against him and Revlon Group, charging illegal leaks of intention evidenced by unusual movements in the stock price prior to the tender.

Very early, a leveraged buyout by management was dismissed, largely because it would have required management to get large quantities of capital via the junk-bond route and that management did not want to do. Gillette directors and officers, as a group, owned only about 1.5 percent of shares outstanding, as reported by the March 1987 proxy statement. A high percentage of the seven outside directors might be called professional directors, and three had been or were academics. A high level of personal wealth was not, to my knowledge, an attribute at that time of any Gillette director. It may have been that the top management were wealthier than the directors. It has been documented that hostile tenders are more likely to occur than friendly acquisitions in a situation when a very small percentage of stock is owned by management and directors. Gillette fitted this pattern. Management did not have the ready availability of one billion dollars in cash that Perelman/Revlon had. Almost all of the total of any management bid that topped the $65 per share would have to be borrowed. Management did not want a company with the huge debt that an LBO would require. And the lawyers with knowledge of Perelman's success in obtaining Revlon by depicting its LBO as a change in management remained silent. As the economics ruled out this option, why, the lawyers probably reasoned, muddy waters with legal objections?

The Board had instructed their investment bankers and management to seek out white knights. But if the potential of a sweep of the street threat had any reliability, time was short. Unilever had been approached, but they replied that they could not meet to consider buying Gillette until the following Tuesday. At that time we did not know that they were already negotiating with Chesebor-ough-Pond. All negotiations were through our investment adviser Eric Gleacher and the lawyers, primarily of Skadden, Arps. Gillette had hired the legendary Joseph Flom, who gave advice over the phone on Sunday evening, November 23, while listening to, rather than attending, as he had planned, a special Boston Symphony concert to benefit the Boston Museum of Fine Arts. Negotiating through agents was not a common experience. I, and probably others, missed the nonverbal communication of body language, the changing tones of voice, and the like that might have given clues to Perelman's main goals.

Throughout these negotiations and the later Coniston attempt, many directors were thinking that the larger the dollar amount involved, the more the investment bankers and lawyers involved will earn, which must slant their advice. Because these advisers are usually paid a percentage of the deal, the larger the settlement amount, the more each would get.

No buyer for all of Gillette had surfaced. Gillette's future was, in the eyes of the directors, under the current management's plans "bright," a term first used, I believe, by the company's treasurer, Milton Glass. It was a term picked up by news writers throughout the country to describe the directors' view of the company in the days ahead.

At the same time, Gillette's legal advisors reported that Perelman was inti-mating that he wanted to be bought out of all his 13.9 percent of shares. Ne-gotiations began. The Gillette Board adamantly refused to sell Oral-B, which creates a good cash flow and has a valuable trade name. The Board initially refused to dismiss Gillette's suit against Perelman/Revlon for illegal leaks of their intentions. The Board believed a dismissal would in effect be stating that Gillette had no basis for its charges. This position was later traded off during negotiations.

Perelman also insisted that Gillette was not to use, as in press releases, the term *greenmail*, regardless of what price might be negotiated for his 13.9 percent of shares. This was a term of opprobrium to Perelman and also to some members of the Gillette board. It was argued that "special repurchase of stock" was just as acceptable a description of the eventually agreed on action. With a Ph.D. in economics, I believed that a buyout of Perelman/Revlon's stock at a price not available to other shareholders on Monday, November 24, regardless of the level or the size of the differential above the market price, would be greenmail. (See the Chapter 8 section on antigreenmail provision for a further discussion of greenmail.) But "repurchase of stock" prior to the market trading was techni-cally acceptable in the sense that it was paid in exchange for Perelman to go away. It was argued that other shareholders had also had an opportunity to sell their shares at a price higher than the actual repurchase price, over several days earlier. As throughout this discussion, the question of defining market price hinged on over what period of time was the price extant.

Joseph Mullaney, Gillette's senior vice president for legal affairs, advised the Board that the payment of a premium up to 3 percent over Friday's (November 21) market price was reasonable and generally acceptable and that such a small amount above the market price does not automatically imply the stigma that the term *greenmail* does. This opinion offered by in-house counsel was stated to be in accord with a recent Delaware Supreme Court decision, but I do not recall that the case was specified. Because Perelman would not own any Gillette stock after the repurchase, his threat to take over the Company would disappear. Because the repurchase of stock was not meant to perpetuate the directors and management in office but was rather a response to a perceived threat to the Company's long-run plans and the stockholders long-run interests, the lawyers advised that the action was defensible under the business-judgment rule. This doctrine has been defined in layman's language as follows: ''As long as members of a board of directors acted in good faith, were not negligent, and did nothing to enrich themselves at the shareholders' expense, then their decisions concerning all aspects of the company's affairs would be given the benefit of the doubt and not [be] interfered with by the courts.''[31]

When writing this book, I found through a computer search under *greenmail* a reference to the Delaware Supreme Court decision in *Polk v Good and Texaco* (March 10, 1986), which involved the Bass Group's acquisition of nearly 10 percent of Texaco stock. The directors of Texaco countered by repurchasing at a premium of approximately 3 percent over market price the holdings of the Bass Group. The Delaware Supreme court upheld the Chancery Court decision that the payment was ''reasonable'' in relation to the potential long-term threat and the immediate disruptive effect which the purchase and holding of Texaco's stock by the Bass Group would have created.[32] The Bass Group agreed on a 10-year standstill, and Texaco paid them $650 million for 12.6 million shares. The term *greenmail* was not used in the settlement.

The Delaware Supreme Court in reaffirming the 1985 state Chancery Court's decision in that case stated that ''the presence of the 10 outside directors on the Texaco board, coupled with the advice rendered by the investment banker and legal counsel, constitute a *prima facie* showing of good faith and reasonable investigation''[33] and that the directors were protected by the business judgment rule. This seems to me to be the legal decision to which Gillette's counselor Joe Mullaney referred.

The Gillette Board met the Delaware courts' criteria. There was a dominance of outside directors. In November 1986, 8 of the 11 Gillette directors were outside directors, or 73 percent. The Gillette Board also sought advice from an outside investment banker and outside legal counsel. Thus Gillette, incorporated in Delaware, would seem to meet this precedent if the repurchase price was 3 percent or less of the market price. Because the market price was fluctuating widely, what was the market price was difficult to determine. It is necessary in volatile markets to define the market price over a specific period of time. The Gillette Board defined the market price as the average of the closing prices for ten days preceding the tender, or $56.60. Three percent of that amount is $1.70. But the buyback price of $59.50 was $1.20 above a premium of 3 percent over the market price, as defined by the Gillette Board, although 10 cents less than $3.

It is my recollection that there was confusion during the discussion whether 3 percent or 3 dollars was at issue. The directors never saw the ruling in the *Polk v Good and Texaco* case, unless they sought it out afterward, nor as I recall was that case ever specifically cited to the Board. The payment to the Bass Group by Texaco was about 3 percent above the market price, but they defined their market price as that on the single preceding trading day. Gillette's closing share price on the preceding trading day was $57¾, and 3 percent of this is $1.73, which totals $59.48, which rounds off to $59.50, the amount that Gillette paid. Thus, the repurchase price reflected the Delaware Supreme Court ruling, and greenmail was not paid.

The closing Gillette share price on the day after the initial tender was announced, Friday, November 14, was $67.75. The Board authorized payment of considerably less, at $59.50 per share.

The total amount paid for the 9.2 million shares was $558 million, plus $9 million of Revlon's expenses. The latter amount was not initially acceptable to all directors, but their position was lost during the negotiation by the lawyers. Although this repurchase action was not called greenmail by Gillette and arguably it was not in view of *Polk v Good*, many economists and journalists thought otherwise. "Gillette pays, Revlon scrams; greenmail is in," headlined the *USA Today* story beginning, "Gillette Co. deflected a takeover attempt Monday in a sign that Wall Street's inside trading may be prompting some takeover artists to settle for 'greenmail' instead of control."[34]

Some journalists intimated that the junk-bond financing just had not been available. This could have been true. But Gillette's Board did not choose, despite the ongoing Boesky insider-trading scandal, to risk that Perelman/Revlon might get the $4 billion loan on acceptable terms. Two "confidence letters" from Perelman's investment bankers had assured the Board that the $4 billion was available. Nearly 14 percent of the outstanding shares were in Perelman's hands. The Board believed that the past week's stock market action meant that it had no time to discuss with Unilever or others their potential holding of substantial shares of Gillette stock as a neutralizing action. The Board's belief was that if the availability of an investment bank loan were announced, then close to the needed 37 percent of shares would become available. The Board was, in an economist's jargon, *risk-averse*.

Perelman made $34 million, a relatively low rate of return of nearly 6 percent on his original investment over a short period of time. His or PRO's average price paid for the 9,226,000 shares acquired was close to $56; and $34 million, or 5.7 percent on his nearly $600 million investment (share price and costs) of under one month, was his profit. A ten-year standstill agreement was written into the stock-repurchase agreement, under which Perelman/Revlon agreed not to purchase Gillette stock for a period of ten years and Drexel Burnham Lambert agreed not to finance any acquisition of Gillette stock for three years. A ''price protection'' clause over a period of one year was included to benefit PRO if Gillette were sold in that period at a higher price. PRO would then get the differential between the higher sales price and the $59.50. The Board also authorized repurchase of up to seven million Gillette shares in the market, an action that could be used to stabilize the share price, if necessary. By May 1987 only 600,000 shares had been bought back under this authority.[35] That Gillette was willing to buy in shares was initially presented as a way to calm those possibly disgruntled shareholders who would have preferred to have gotten $59.50 for each of their shares immediately rather than wait for a possibly much higher price a year or so hence. The owners of Gillette shares were a diverse, shifting group about whom generalizations were difficult. Some long-term holders did not want to sell and pay high capital-gain taxes, while other short-term holders wanted a quick turnover with gains. The fluctuation among shareholders during a takeover fight is too little examined.

The meeting broke at 1:15 A.M., when the lawyers on each side were deadlocked over wording: Gillette was not to use the term *greenmail*, and in return Gillette's dismissal of its legal suit against PRO was not to be described in words that would imply criticism of Gillette.

The meeting reconvened at 8:30 A.M. Monday morning. The directors reviewed the already described items and then took action; the takeover threat was over before the stock market opened.

The Board at a special November 26 meeting redeemed the preferred stock purchase rights, or poison pill, only to issue a slightly revised new poison pill. Gillette stock price plunged 10¾ points to 45⅞.

Without a poison pill, the outcome might have differed, but I doubt it. Although the tender can be an action against which the pill has little force, that is, if a sweep of the market occurs, it may still buy time for a board. The breaking of the Ivan Boesky scandal on the same day as the tender had a greater effect, because it placed in doubt the financing of the tender. If Perelman had had more cash earlier, he might have bought more than 13.9 percent of the stock. *CPC International*, a food corporation with $5 billion in sales, had bailed Perelman out in early November 1986 ''at peak prices and Transworld gave him a valuable option to buy its Hilton International unit.''[36] Perelman was a risk-taker, and the Gillette board and CEO were risk-averse.

Some directors believed that the debt created to buy back Perelman's stock was an advantage for Gillette because the new, heavy debt would make the Company less attractive to potential buyers. It was argued by others that the heavy interest payments on the debt, which would subtract from the cash flow, would make the Company also less attractive to existing shareholders. Arguments about the pros and cons of equity and debt financing were not new at the board meetings. Trained at Harvard Business School, Colman Mockler did not believe that corporations should go into long-term debt. A few directors thought that Gillette with its sizable cash flow was a sitting duck for a takeover. The Board readily went along with the defenses of the poison pill and the staggered board and accepted management's opposition to long-run debt. The hostile-takeover attempt finally resolved the argument, as the repurchase forced a large amount of debt.

It may have been the lesser cash flow of 1985 that attracted hostile takeovers. Informational asymmetry between insiders and outsiders over the potential long-run effects of actions in 1984 and 1985 probably existed, and some must have questioned why such a strong company had a falling cash flow. The surface reaction to this among some may have been that I as a decision-maker could do better. With credit available via junk bonds, why not buy the company?

I first talked with Colman Mockler about finance in the mid-1970s, when I was serving on the Simmons College Corporation board, which he chaired, and then it was in connection with the U.S. social security system. He had just read my book *Social Security: Promise and Reality* and, I believe, for the first time had realized that the social security system then had a long-run financial imbalance. The future benefits then promised were going to require a more rapidly increasing labor force to tax than demographics were predicting. Mockler believed that social security and corporations alike should not go into long-term debt. Social security had future tax revenues, but corporations had only anticipated profits. Promises to pay out in the future, whether benefits or interest on corporate bonds, needed secure assets. This was conservative financial thinking.

NOTES

1. Tender Offer Statement filed with the Securities and Exchange Commission on November 14, 1986, by Orange Acquisition Corporation, Orange Partners I, et al., regarding The Gillette Company, Section 10, p. 16 (hereafter referred to as "Filing").

2. The Gillette Company, General Bulletin, No. 138-86, November 5, 1986, memo signed by Joseph F. Turley.

3. Michael W. Miller and William M. Bulkeley, "Revlon Begins $4.12 Billion Bid for Gillette Co.," *Wall Street Journal*, November 14, 1986, p. 3.

4. Bryan Burrough and John Helyar, *Barbarians at the Gate: The Fall of RJR Nabisco* (New York: Harper and Row, 1990), pp. 59–60, 94–96.

5. Ibid., p. 96.

6. William T. Poole, ed., *Patterns of Corporate Philanthropy: Funding False Compassion*, with a summary essay by Marvin Olasky and with a preface by Rady A. Johnson (Washington, D.C.: Capital Research Center, 1991), p. 15, table 3.

7. Alex Beam, "T.G.I.W.: Gillette: Who Are They?" *Boston Globe*, July 13, 1988, p. 67.

8. "Gillette Files Suit against Perelman–Revlon Group," *Gillette Company News*, November 17, 1986.

9. The Gillette Company, Proxy Statement, March 11, 1986, p. 5.

10. Arthur Fleischer, Jr., Geoffrey C. Hazard, Jr. and Miriam Z. Klipper, *Board Games: The Changing Shape of Corporate Power* (Boston: Little, Brown and Company, 1988), p. 31.

11. Ibid., p. 32.

12. Filing, pp. II-1 through II-4.

13. Bernard S. Black, "Bidder Overpayment in Takeovers," *Stanford Law Review* vol. 41 (February 1989), p. 598.

14. Frank R. Lichtenberg with Donald Siegel, *Corporate Takeovers and Productivity* (Cambridge, Mass.: MIT Press, 1992), pp. 41, 45.

15. Fleischer, Hazard and Klipper, *Board Games*, p. 136.

16. Amy Dunkin, Laurie Baum and Lois Therrien, "Dealmakers: This Takeover Artist Wants to Be a Makeover Artist, Too," *Business Week*, December 1, 1986, p. 110.

17. The Gillette Company, Proxy Statement, March 11, 1986, p. 9.

18. Pat Sloan, "Perelman Eager to Snare Gillette: Bitter Takeover Fight Expected," *Advertising Age*, November 17, 1986, p. 108.

19. Margaret A. Jacobs, "Settlement Closes Trial Pitting Perelman against Fired Executive," *Wall Street Journal*, July 19, 1995, p. B10.

20. Lawrence Ingrassia, "Face-Off: A Recovering Gillette Hopes for Vindication in a High-Tech Razor," *Wall Street Journal*, September 29, 1989, p. A6.

21. Anthony Ramirez, "A Radical New Style for Stodgy Old Gillette," *New York Times*, February 25, 1990, p. F5.

22. Burrough and Helyar, *Barbarians at the Gate*, p. 165.

23. George Anders, "Marketplace: KKR in Peril: The Fight to Save RJR," *Wall Street Journal*, April 6, 1992, p. B8.

24. Randall Smith and Ann Monroe, "New Insecurity: Insider-Trading Jitters Deal Another Setback to Junk-Bond Market," *Wall Street Journal*, November 20, 1986, p. 1.

25. Judge Mark L. Wolf, Findings of Fact and Conclusions of Law, Civil Action No. 88-0862-WF, United States District Court, District of Massachusetts, *The Gillette Company, Plaintiff, v RB Partners et al., Defendant*, June 30, 1988" (hereafter referred to as "Findings"), p. 54.

26. Ibid., p. 57.

27. Joseph Pereira, "Trial Discloses Identity of 10 Firms Gillette Co. Contacted as White Knights," *Wall Street Journal*, June 27, 1988, p. 8.

28. John Crudele, "Buyout Rumors Spur Gillette's Stock," *New York Times*, December 4, 1986, p. 35.

29. Margaret McAllister (ed.), *The Merger Yearbook '87: Yearbook on Corporate Acquisitions, Leveraged Buyouts, Joint Ventures and Corporate Policy*, 9th ed. (Boston: Cambridge Corporation, 1987), p. 207.

30. Dorman L. Commons, *Tender Offer: The Sneak Attack in Corporate Takeovers* (Berkeley: University of California Press, 1985), p. 98.

31. Roy C. Smith, *The Money Wars: The Rise and Fall of the Great Buyout Boom of the 1980s* (New York: Truman Talley Books/Dutton, 1990), pp. 148–149.

32. Martin Lipton, Theodore N. Mirvis and Andrew W. Brownstein, "Takeover Defenses and Directors' Liabilities," typescript [1986], pp. 32–33.

33. *Polk v Good*, Del. Supr., 507 A.2d 537 [11] (1986). *William J. Polk, Jr., et al. v*

Howard Good et al., Plaintiffs, and Texaco, Inc. et al., Defendants, Supreme Court of Delaware, submitted: Oct. 1, 1985; decided: March 10, 1986; p. 537.

34. William Giese, "Gillette Pays, Revlon Scrams; Greenmail Is In," *USA Today,* November 25, 1986, p. 1B.

35. Joseph Mullaney, "Gillette after the Tender Offer," in House Committee on Banking, Finance and Urban Affairs, *Oversight Hearing on Mergers and Acquisitions,* May 12, 1987, Serial No. 100–20 (Washington, D.C.: U.S. Government Printing Office, 1987), p. 181.

36. Linda Sandler, "Heard on the Street: 'Pale Green Greenmail' Is Spreading as Firms Buy Out Raiders as Part of Broader Purchases," *Wall Street Journal,* November 25, 1986, p. 59.

3

The Gillette Company: Brief History

EARLY YEARS: KING C. GILLETTE

The Gillette Company was started with the deliberate attempt by its founder, King Camp Gillette, to invent a product that would be purchased over and over by individuals. Gillette was a son of an inventor, each of his three brothers was also an inventor, and each held a number of U.S. patents.[1] Author of *The Human Drift*, first published in 1894, Gillette was an independent thinker who supported simultaneously free enterprise and a utopian, unique form of socialism. Gillette envisioned ''a gigantic, joint-stock company that would take over the world's production and distribution of all goods and services and be governed by the people—each stockholder having one vote.''[2] Gillette later termed this a *World Corporation* under his United People's Party. Gillette was a dreamer and also an entrepreneur.

Not until Gillette was forty years old did he think of the idea of a razor for men's shaving with a removable blade, both sides of which could bear a sharp edge. After several attempts to find a partner, he met William Nickerson, a Massachusetts Institute of Technology (MIT) graduate and a successful machinist and inventor, who was persuaded to develop machinery for the low-cost production of a quality blade. Nickerson and Gillette founded a company that in 1903 sold 51 razor sets and 168 blades. In 1904 Gillette received a U.S. patent and had raised sufficient money to increase production, and by 1906 he could pay a cash dividend to stockholders. By 1911 his major South Boston plant employed 1,500 persons. Very early, Nickerson developed automatic sharpening machines and automatic steel-hardening equipment, improving greatly the quality and output of the blades.

The Company, which started as a small, one-product firm, producing safety razors, has grown into a multinational conglomerate that produces—in addition to manual razors and blades—electric razors, small household appliances, pens, toothbrushes, and toiletries and has manufacturing facilities in 28 countries on every continent of the world. About 70 percent of Gillette's sales and profits and 75 percent of its thirty-one thousand employees are overseas. This is a truly global company that, with joint ventures in many countries, uses the foreign financial markets to float Eurobond issues, whose stock trades on several foreign stock exchanges, and that markets identical products worldwide.

The Gillette Company was originally chartered in the state of Maine as the American Safety Razor Company on September 28, 1901, and began production of razors and blades two years later. Its annual sales in 1904 were 91,000 razors and 124,000 blades. Production, especially of the blades, very early soared. By 1917, when Gillette was incorporated in Delaware, one million razors and 115 million blades were sold annually. Manual shaving in one's home became a masculine ritual.

The first overseas sales office was opened in 1905 in London, England, and in that year the Company adopted a trademark which featured King Camp Gillette's portrait and signature. By 1910 Gillette was well established in France and Germany, as well as in the United Kingdom and the United States.

King Gillette had designed a low-unit-cost, replaceable product that most men use daily and that would wear out, in a kind of strategic obsolescence that would support demand. The product consisted of blades to be inserted in a handle, and in order to shave in comfort one would have to purchase new blades over and over again. Until then, a razor and a blade were one unit and thus relatively expensive. A man had to strop and hone his razor frequently if he were to shave in some comfort. The word *hack* rather than *shave* better connotes the discomfort of removing facial hair prior to the development and spread of the safety razor with its blade that could be removed and sharpened. As Gillette wrote,

It is manifestly true that no one—previous to the Gillette invention—had conceived the idea of producing a blade in which the purpose in view was to produce a blade that would be so cheap to manufacture that its cost to the consumer would permit of its being discarded when dull, thus avoiding the annoyance and difficulties of stropping and honing. Furthermore, it was true up to the time that the Gillette razor went on the market that there were hundreds of thousands of men who did not shave themselves, for the reason that they could not keep a razor in condition—they had not the knack or mechanical skill to strop and hone a razor, and there being no razor on the market that was of such low cost as to permit of the blade being discarded when dull and a new one substituted, they were obliged to be content to go to the barber, which involved large expense, annoyance and loss of time.[3]

Gillette reduced the art of shaving to such a cheap and simple process that hardly anyone today gives the procedure a second thought.

Early geographic expansion of the company was rapid. A Gillette plant was started in Paris in 1905; blades were sold in Montreal and in St. Petersburg in 1906. During the next twenty years Gillette incorporated in Belgium, Denmark and Italy and established branch offices in Copenhagen, Madrid, Milan, Istanbul, Calcutta, Sidney, Brussels, Geneva, Buenos Aires, Singapore, Shanghai, Tokyo and other cities. Razor blades were marketed worldwide. Manufacturing plants were incorporated in England, Brazil and Germany, and the Canadian and South Boston plants were expanded. Very early, worldwide expansion of Gillette was the axiom that the Company followed.

William Nickerson's fully automated blade-sharpening machine reduced manufacturing costs substantially and at the same time improved the quality of the blades. With the U.S. entry into World War I in 1917, the government placed an order for 3.5 million razors and 36 million blades, enough to supply the entire U.S. armed forces. This acted like a giant marketing program that spread the word about the advantages of self-shaving with a Gillette razor and blade. For several years after the invention of the Gillette safety razor and blades, many men in the United States still went to the barber for shaves. After World War I Gillette had a vast pool of new customers, who bought new blades to fit into the razors that had been given them in the army. The French soldiers had been similarly supplied since 1914. By 1923 nearly 23 percent of Gillette sales were overseas. Thus, although World War I initially destroyed European production, after the war Gillette was on a roll within the United States and also rapidly expanding abroad.

Gillette's basic patent protection expired in 1921. Henry Gaisman of the AutoStrop Safety Razor Company developed a new razor that Gillette blades would not fit and also the Probak blade, which would fit both AutoStrop's razor and Gillette's. Gillette continued to be profitable; and in 1926 with 2 million shares outstanding, dividends of $4.50 were declared.[4] The shaving market was a gold mine.

Competition, the Depression and financial scandal, however, forced Gillette stock to plunge from $125 a share in early 1929 to a low of $18. Gillette shipments to its overseas subsidiaries had erroneously been recorded as sales, while the full warehouses abroad indicated that the actual sales badly lagged behind the shipments. Competition abroad from low-cost German razors and the U.S. AutoStrop Company intensified. Then Gillette had to acknowledge that top management had overstated profits and that unearned large bonuses had been paid to executives. Talk of merger with AutoStrop evolved as their blade, designed for restropping or sharpening, continued to have high sales. AutoStrop, with its already patented Probak blade, forced an outside review of Gillette's books prior to its merger with Gillette, which resulted in the discovery of the overstatement of Gillette's profits. Gillette announced, as a counterattack to its financial errors, its new Gillette Blue Blade with heavy advertising and linked the announcement with its confessed mistake. A typical advertisement carried the headline, "A Frank Confession," with a smaller inserted box headed "The Gillette Blue Super-Blade."

The Company's recovery was slowed by the need to correct overstatements of actual sales abroad in previous years. Gillette wrote off large inventories in warehouses full of obsolete blades. Profits had been overstated by about $12 million over a five-year period,[5] and a minority group of stockholders sued the directors in late October 1930. The ensuing trial was settled with a $400,000 payment. The dividend payment was deferred. Management was tarnished, and King Gillette was replaced.

A new president was chosen. The top management who were also on the board were forced to resign, and five new directors were elected. The merger of AutoStrop Safety Razor Company and Gillette was completed, but the merged company was expected to have "only about 55 percent of the industry,"[6] a figure less than what Gillette alone had sold in some previous years. Years of price-cutting competition and variable discounts to dealers followed under Henry Gaisman, who had been president of AutoStrop.

A milestone was reached in the history of Gillette when King C. Gillette died in 1932 at age 77. But recovery from the Great Depression was slow. Within the United States, competitors with cheaper but arguably poorer-quality blades were cutting Gillette's market share. Gillette's advertisements stressed a strong connection between being clean-shaven and being successful. Prices were cut, quality improved, but profits fell.

In 1938, under a new president, Joseph P. Spang, Jr., Gillette stopped price cutting, emphasized quality and increased its advertising. Over the next several years, Gillette not only expanded geographically but also introduced several new products. A brushless shaving cream was distributed nationally in 1937, and an electric shaver was introduced shortly after, only to be withdrawn in 1940. Braun did not manufacture its electric razor until 1950.

WORLD WAR II AND EXPANSION

Not until 1939, with the beginning of World War II overseas, did the real gross national product (GNP) of the United States exceed that of 1929. U.S. entry into the war in December 1941 assured that the Great Depression was over, and the real (in 1982 dollars) GNP of the United States soared to one trillion dollars in 1942. World War II again disrupted European production of blades, but it also greatly increased the future demand for Gillette's razors and blades, as it introduced many young men to the habit of frequent self-shaving. War, once again, acted as a huge promotion and marketing program. The federal government limited the distribution of new razors and blades to only the armed forces. Not until 1944 did the War Production Board rescind its prohibition on sales of razors and blades to civilians. Several years of having to make each individual blade last for many additional shaves convinced the U.S. public that the higher-priced but higher-quality Gillette blades were truly superior to the cheaper penny blades. And military duty had established among hundreds of thousands of men the habit of a daily shave.

During the 1940s, Gillette for the first time handled products designed for women. Home permanent-wave kits, with curlers, a waving lotion, and neutralizer were being cleverly marketed under the "Toni Twins" concept—"Which twin has the Toni?" Over a million kits a month were being sold by the mid-1940s. The Toni permanent-wave kit could successfully be used by oneself at home. Toni parties among high-school girls and older women with each person doing another person's hair were common. Cost-saving over beauty salon visits, the home permanent-wave kits had many repeat customers among women.

Some giant cosmetic companies, as well as Gillette, had become interested in purchasing the Toni Company. Gillette bought it in January 1948 for an initial payment of $12.6 million, from two brothers, Neison and Irving Harris. It was the latter who had had the brilliant marketing idea of using identical twins[7] for comparative advertising. The services of these successful entrepreneurs were retained as managers, and their salaries were tied to a percentage of profits. It was the advertising slogan and the promotion that milked it—as by sending sets of identical twins around Europe and the United States, who asked audiences to judge which twin had the Toni—that made this home permanent so successful. Other companies had sold home permanents since the early 1930s, but it was Toni that captured the market with its expensive but innovative advertising and promotion. Eventually, sales of home permanents were stabilized, as opposition by beauty parlors grew as they lost customers and a cultural change that favored straight-hair styles occurred. In 1979, shortly after I had joined the board, an attempt was made to stimulate the home permanent's stable sales by introducing Toni Lightwaves, which creates a more relaxed curl than the original Toni, and in 1989 Epic Wave was introduced. But the one-time fad of home permanents was not revived.

Gillette continued to add successful new modifications to its very profitable razor/blade line. For example, in 1946 the Company introduced the Blue Blade dispenser, which eliminated the need to wrap and then unwrap the blade. During the 1970s, Trac II and the Atra blade, each an incrementally improved product over the old, were introduced. The Gillette Safety Razor Company also continued to expand geographically, for example, opening a new factory in Annecy, France, in 1953; it was closed in 1990. Gillette companies in Puerto Rico, Columbia, Brazil, Finland and Spain were incorporated, as well as Gillette Austria, Chile, Portugal and Japan, all before 1970. New manufacturing facilities were established in Australia, West Germany and Argentina. Jointly with native financial ownership, manufacturing plants were established in Malaysia, Iran, Indonesia and Jamaica.

DIVERSIFICATION

The Gillette Company in the mid-1950s had bought Paper Mate, a manufacturer of ballpoint pens, for $15 million; and in 1967 it purchased a controlling interest in Braun A.G. of West Germany, a manufacturer of many kinds of appliances from the electric razor, hair dryers and coffeemakers to high-fidelity speakers and cameras. Both companies were to become major parts of Gillette, Paper Mate with close to a half billion and Braun with over one billion dollars of sales in 1990.

By 1973 Gillette was a multinational, diversified, consumer-products company, whose sales reached $1 billion, with just over $156 million in profits from operations and net income per share of $3.06. Although only 31 percent of its revenue was from sales of blades and razors, they earned 66 percent of pretax profits.

Braun AG sold in 1978 its products in over a hundred markets and had five manufacturing facilities outside its home base near Frankfurt, Germany. Because of the small production runs of some of its very high-quality products, such as Braun's high-fidelity equipment, the unit costs of production were too high for competitive pricing. Similar well-designed products by Japanese companies at lower prices squeezed Braun out of these markets. The distributorships of the Hasselblad camera and hi-fi businesses were sold in 1983, as had been, somewhat earlier, Braun's moderately expensive but handsome black and steel table lighters, which for many years had sat on Gillette's boardroom table during meetings. The lighters were an early casualty of the decline in smoking and also of the greater popularity of both low-price disposable lighters and the very elegant, cloisonné high-price lighters, such as S.T. Dupont's, which Gillette also then owned. The latter appealed especially to customers in the Middle East and Asia.

The initially somewhat bloated Braun Company, headquartered in Frankfurt, was revitalized when Paul G. Stern became head of its technical operations in January 1976 and then chairman and CEO in late 1979. Stern had a Ph.D. in physics, had worked many years at IBM and was a no-nonsense administrator. The title of his 1990 book states his personal goal—*Straight to the Top*. Some idea of the excessive perquisites for executives at Braun when he arrived is given by Stern's comment that the executive parking area for company cars then "looked like a Mercedes-Benz car dealership,"[8] while the CEO and chairman of the parent Gillette board, Colman Mockler, drove his own classic red convertible Chevrolet in Boston. Stern not only reduced many of the executive perks, but he also increased plant productivity so that "three times as many shavers per day with half the number of employees"[9] were being produced when he left. Braun was making some profits when Stern arrived; but by the time he left, it was doing substantially better.

The public's perception of Braun products was and is that they combine high quality with distinctive design and advanced technology. They are premium products. Braun's chief designer from the time I joined the board of Gillette in 1978 has been Dieter Rams, who is listed as a member of Braun's headquarters staff in Gillette's 1991 annual report. The superb industrial design of Braun products has been widely imitated and has won many industrial design awards. I recall receiving for Braun in the early fall of 1980 an award for the best industrial design of all Europe over the past 25 years. What amazed me then was that even the Braun cafeteria was designed and furnished in the squared-off, round cornered, black and steel-gray and off-white trademark Braun-look. Having recently designed the interiors of the Herbert Hoover Memorial Building at Stanford University, I found it astonishing that a designer could impress his own trademark on a building to such a degree, as well as on small individual products.

In 1988 the 39th Braun product (the Braun solar-operated pocket calculator) was added to the collection of the industrial design section of the Museum of Modern Art in New York. During that year, seventeen Braun products were honored with design awards from various institutions.

Braun's electric razor was then in 1993 Europe's leading shaver. The purchase of Braun assured Gillette access to Braun's major product markets. Gillette hoped to market Braun's electric cord and rechargeable shavers within the United States. However, this goal was not realized until mid-1985, when the U.S. federal ban under antitrust law on Gillette's marketing the Braun electric razor within the United States no longer applied. The barring of Gillette from selling Braun electric razors within the United States during that period delayed the realization of Braun's achievable profit returns for several years. In 1980, 9 percent of Gillette's profit from operations was created by Braun; in 1985, 13 percent; and in 1991, 16 percent, with that percentage representing more than double the amount in dollars in 1985.

Gillette continually followed a policy of product diversification in addition to geographic expansion. During the early 1970s, before Colman Mockler became chairman and president in 1976, Gillette bought several small companies whose products had little if any relationship to razors and blades. Among the especially far afield companies were La Giulia, a small Italian chewing-gum and candy manufacturer, and several small household-plant and potting-soil companies. Gillette also bought in 1971 the Welcome Wagon business, an offbeat form of marketing. It was sold in 1978 as part of the company's effort to deemphasize and eliminate "product and business areas [with] limited growth or profit potential."[10] Additionally, Buxton, Inc., of Agawam, Massachusetts, a manufacturer of personal leather goods, was bought in 1972 and sold five years later. Also in 1974, Gillette bought an 80 percent interest in an Australian sunglasses firm, Sunoroid Party Limited, and in the same year sold North American Fashions, Inc., which had been acquired in 1970.

In 1971 Gillette had acquired a 48 percent interest in S.T. Dupont Company, a French manufacturer of luxury goods, such as cloisonné pens and lighters. This company, founded by Simon Tissot Dupont, had developed a superior, unique Chinese lacquer finish. Chinese lacquer is a finishing technique that resists water, heat and acids but provides a deep brilliancy of color. From 1973 to 1980, the sales and profits of the luxury products of S.T. Dupont tripled even though the company's premier product, the Dupont lighter, had a high rejection rate when subject to quality-control checks. The initial 20 percent reject rate declined to 2.5 percent. The handsome Dupont lighter became very popular among Middle East and Asian customers, as also did Dupont's deep-blue Chinese lacquer pen. By 1980 Dupont had six international marketing subsidiaries: one covering Belgium, the Netherlands and Luxembourg; another in Switzerland and Austria; and one each in Germany, Italy, Japan and the United States. Additionally, there were a Hong Kong sales office and commission agents in the Middle East. Despite the seemingly thriving business during 1980, S.T. Dupont did not continue to grow, and its profit margins declined from 15 percent of sales during the depression of the early 1980s. During the early 1980s, buyers were sought, and the company was eventually sold in 1987 to Dickson Concepts Limited, a Hong Kong–based company that marketed luxury goods primarily in the Far East.

Gillette acquired Jafra in 1973; this cosmetics company, known for its skin-care products subsidiary that sold primarily door-to-door, evolved into an international business with its manufacturing plants in Southern California and abroad. Jafra hires thousands of beauty consultants, who sell directly in the customer's home, either individually or at a beauty class or party arranged for the purpose of sales. As a professional woman, I thought that direct selling in the home went against the global demographic trend of many more women working outside the home. Jafra, however, under Gillette, has more than survived, with over 150,000 consultants in 1990 worldwide (many are part-time workers) in thirteen countries, including Germany, Mexico and the United States. Although fewer women do not work outside the home, many women with families prefer to work with the number of hours and timing under their own control. Jafra permits this and does not require the capital that most self-employment does. Jafra may attract more women with greater zeal and competence than do similar jobs with similar earnings and fixed hours.

Jafra is one of the few direct-selling companies that has been constantly profitable, which, I believe, is primarily because of its continuing geographic expansion. Avon, which has expanded into Asia, has a similar experience. When Jafra was acquired, its net sales were almost $4 million, and by 1980 they were over $33 million. In 1984 Jafra businesses were opened in the Philippines and Australia. Its sales in Europe, Mexico and South America continue to be strong even though the percentage of women working outside the home in those areas has grown, as it has in the United States. By 1984 there were 26 Jafra operations abroad. Jafra was reorganized in 1987 and increased its consultant sales force to a total of 186,000 women in 1991, when it led the skin-care and color-cosmetics markets in Mexico.

Diversification in the earlier years into nonrelated lines was not very successful. For example, in 1970 Gillette purchased a wig manufacturer, North American Hair Goods of New York, which by the time I joined the board in 1978 had disappeared. Ever since, Gillette has tried to weed out its unrelated, low-margin product lines. Some sales, like that of the small Italian chewing-gum factory, La Giulia, in 1981, took longer than others. Another example is the Hydroponic Chemical Company, a manufacturer of plant-care products, which was sold earlier. These products had no synergy with Gillette's core businesses.

During the early 1970s, Edward Gelsthorpe, a man known as a marketing whiz, was brought in from the outside to become president. Gelsthorpe's "reputation was for quick-fire launching of new products in the hope that some would succeed,"[11] and under him the acquisitions continued at a quick pace. Apparently, his theory was that good managers can successfully manage widely different product lines. Management is a transferable skill. Discomfort between the more conservative, traditional Gillette players and the new expansionists evolved. Gelsthorpe, elected as president and chief operating officer in 1973, resigned after fourteen months to take a job at United Brands. He was replaced by Colman M. Mockler, Jr., as president. Mockler, with a Harvard College and a Harvard Business School graduate, had come up through the financial area of the Company. Mockler became chairman of the board in 1976, when Vincent C. Ziegler retired. At that point, Stephen J. Griffin became president, a position he held until his retirement in 1987. Griffin had begun to work for Gillette in 1941, served in the U.S. military, and after his return was repeatedly promoted over the years. The two men, Mockler and Griffin, were the top team for nearly twenty years.

In 1976 and into the early 1980s the direction of the company began to change. The emphasis was shifted to divestment rather than acquisition. For example, the Braun Company's hi-fi business was sold in 1983, along with its distributorship of the famous Hasselblad camera. Although the products were of superb quality, profits, in face of Japanese competition, did not occur. The surgical supply business in the United kingdom was also sold in this period. It is hard to justify just how these products had fitted in with Gillette's manufacturing and marketing strengths.

Recent studies on the percentage of divestitures by other large companies indicate that 33 percent and possibly as many as 50 percent of large companies also sold their earlier acquisitions during the 1980s. "Grimm's *Mergerstat Review* reports that divestitures make up at least 35% of mergers and acquisitions transactions in the 1980s. In a more systematic study, Ravenscraft and Scherer (1987) estimate that 33% of acquisitions in the 1960s and 1970s were later divested, while Porter (1987) finds that over 50% of the acquisitions made by 33 conglomerate acquirers in 'new' or unrelated industries were later divested."[12] Kaplan and Weisbach found that 44 percent of acquisitions in their sample between 1971 and 1982 were divested by 1989.

Although some believe that the data show that firms that diversify lost in this process, others point out that buying a firm and then reselling it is no proof of loss. For example, it could be argued that Gillette found synergies with partial-equity investment and invested in the late 1970s oil and gas exploration in order to assure, despite potential Middle East disruption, the petrochemical feedstocks from which the Company's hard plastics are made. Gillette divested these after the Desert Storm war because the emergency threatening Gillette's major raw material was over. It could be argued that these were originally synergistic acquisitions; but once the markets changed and the price of a barrel of oil had so drastically dropped and losses increased, it made sense to divest. Gillette, as already pointed out, almost invariably during the 1980s made partial-equity investments. In 1971 Gillette had acquired a 48 percent interest in S.T. Dupont, increased it to 80 percent in 1973 and sold it in August 1987 at a small profit.

As Kaplan and Weisbach point out, "Many divestitures are not failures from an *ex post* perspective. For example, of the divestitures with a reported gain or loss of sale, 42% report a gain on sale; 44% report a loss; and 14% report that the gain or loss is immaterial. Based on accounting results as well as comments by reporters and managers, we classify only 34% of the divested acquisitions as unsuccessful; that is, the reason for the divestiture appears to be performance-related."[13] Gillette's experience is close to these norms. Moreover, Gillette's high-tech manufacturing capability was not needed to manufacture the unrelated products, such as chewing gum or sewing kits to make ski vests, that were divested.

Innovation to support the existing core products continued. The Atra pivoting-head twin-blade razor and cartridge and the disposable razors, Good News, Swivel and Daisy, were introduced before 1981. In 1984 Good News was upgraded to feature a moving cartridge head that automatically adjusts to facial contours—the Good News Pivot Disposable. Blades and razors approached 70 percent of total profits.

Paper Mate entered the stick-pen market with Write Brothers pens, and Paper Mate had 21 percent of market-share dollars in 1980. The early success of Eraser Mate with its new erasable ink technology was pivotal. Demographics support production and sale of writing instruments as well as razor blades and toothbrushes. The world's population is continually increasing, and there is worldwide demand for these easily transported products. Sales in Latin America and the Asia-Pacific region have soared. Rising educational levels and, in Latin America, high birth rates accompanied by initially low but rising per capita income, foster purchases of personal grooming aids such as blades and toothbrushes and of new pens.

COLMAN MOCKLER, BOARD CHAIRMAN

One of the first tasks as board chairman in 1976 that Mockler had to confront head-on was that charges of "political contributions or illegal or other questionable payments" had been made by Company officials. A special report of the audit committee, composed of four outside directors, found that no such payments were made "in the United States or in any foreign country" but that "over the four year period [1972–1975], certain illegal or questionable payments were made in foreign countries by foreign units of the Company totaling $400,000, all or part of which may have been paid to government officials."[14]

Probably because of this early experience, Mockler ran the company during the twelve years that I was on the board to avoid any perception of even the slightest impropriety. During these years, I was a member of the audit committee, which monitored very closely the potential for any illegal actions under the Foreign Corrupt Practices Act. Mockler almost always attended the twice-yearly audit committee meetings.

In 1976 Gillette had a thirteen-person board, four of whom did not stand for election in 1978, the year in which I was elected as the only new member. The Board was thus reduced to nine members in 1978, including one past Gillette top executive and five outside directors. The latter included the former chairman of Raytheon's board, Charles Francis Adams; a Texan oil and gas producer, Edwin L. Cox; the dean of the Harvard Business School, Lawrence Fouraker; and Senior Vice President for Public Affairs, Sears Roebuck and Company, Charles A. Meyer.

While on the Gillette board, I worked at Stanford University in California, where there were continuing demonstrations against big corporations maintaining plants in South Africa. Gillette had started operations in Springs, near Johannesburg, in 1930, to mix and bottle toiletries and to package blades for local distribution. Blade operations were started in 1953 and the manufacturing of toiletries in 1960. Generally speaking, over the years the South African plant accounted for about 1 percent of Gillette's worldwide profits and employed about 300 persons, the majority of whom were blacks. At Stanford University and the University of California some believed that large U.S. companies should punish the apartheid government of South Africa by removing their plants. Gillette management and Board, however, both opposed apartheid and believed that The Gillette Company was helping, not harming, blacks by employing them. South Africa provides a market for Gillette's products. Gillette, as many other large companies, grades jobs, and each grade carries a salary range. There are no separate or special ranges for blacks. Gillette provides equal pay for equal work for the same period of time.

Gillette was an early signatory, in May 1977, of the Reverend Leon Sullivan's guidelines. The statement of these principles includes nonsegregation of the races, equal employment practices, equal pay for equal work for the same period of time, training programs to prepare non-Caucasians for management and supervisory positions, and "Improving the Quality of Employees' Lives Outside the Work Environment in Such Areas as Housing, Transportation, Schooling, Recreation, and Health Facilities."[15]

Gillette was classified in the top level of companies "making good progress" toward these goals. Gillette's housing program in South Africa is multiracial. Typically, Gillette became involved not only in financing projects but also in dealing with the bureaucracy that South African blacks encountered in daily living. Gillette funded four additional classrooms in Kwa Thema, where most of its black employees live, and has generally provided ongoing assistance in the form of books and video equipment and facilities. The Company also funded training seminars for local black businessmen and started a legal-aid clinic. Annually at the shareholders' meetings while I was on the Board there were stockholder proposals to require that the Company either leave South Africa or, minimally, not expand investment in South Africa until apartheid was removed. Typical were proposals submitted by the ministers and missionaries benefit board of the American Baptist and United Methodist churches and others such as Sisters of Charity of the Incarnate Word and Daughters of the Holy Spirit. All of these and others who sponsored motions owned a number of shares, and their representatives spoke at the annual meetings.

The Board's response to requests that it move its plant from South Africa can be summarized simply. South Africa is a worthwhile market for the Company's products; the Company makes a small profit from this operation and believes that its continual employment of blacks helps them. The shareholders, on average, voted 90 percent against removal of Gillette's operations from South Africa. Although Gillette continued to stay there, it did not expand but rather retrenched.

On December 4, 1986, I met Mangosutchu Buthelezi, president of Inkatha, at Stanford University, where he spoke. He, as the Zulu chief, was of course against apartheid and labeled it "the vicious apartheid home land policy," but he, as did the Gillette board and management, also believed that it was desirable for large U.S. corporations to remain in South Africa. Unemployment would be caused by their withdrawal, an action that the large pension funds of the state governments of California and New York supported. Pressure on Stanford University and state employers to divest themselves of stock in any company that had plants in South Africa, such as Gillette, somewhat depressed the stock price of those companies. In 1993, when the ban on purchase of stock by the large state-government pension funds was lifted, price of Gillette stock rose somewhat.

Concerns over the South African situation did not hinder Gillette's continued progress. As analysts reiterate, blades and razors consistently have been the major source of Gillette profits. Although one-third of Gillette's total sales are from blades and razors, two-thirds of Gillette's operating profits are from blades and razors. In 1977 the toiletry division, with such strong product lines as Right Guard and Soft & Dri deodorants, White Rain hairspray, and Foamy shave cream, still contributed only about 13 percent to profits, although toiletries accounted for 25 percent of net sales. During the recession years 1990–1991, the writing-instruments division of Paper Mate and Waterman's contribution to profits declined, while razors and blades increased their share and Braun also continued its upward climb. Toiletries in 1990 accounted for 22 percent of sales but only 14 percent of profits.

In his 25 years as chairman, Colman Mockler was able to change slightly the statistical relationships of sales and profits among the major product lines, as the company sales quadrupled to over $4 billion in 1990. In 1976 "blades and razors accounted for 29% of Gillette sales and 73% of profit,"[16] while in 1990 blades and razor sales were 36 percent of the sales and earned 60 percent of the total profits. Gillette's greatest expertise is in the manufacture of razors and blades. A *Wall Street Journal* article reported Mockler's goals in 1977 as follows: keep good products strong, develop one or two new areas to gain a foothold in world markets and weed out those product lines with only marginal profit. These goals were followed all during Mockler's period of control. For example, Braun eliminated during 1974–1977 about 200 products; new product lines, among them Oral-B toothbrushes, were developed that increased both sales and profits. Product diversification strategies, geographic expansion and specific cost-cutting policies continued throughout the years of Mockler's leadership. .

During the late 1970s diversification was used to widen knowledge of selling techniques beyond traditional, in-store sales. Companies were bought that used different selling techniques, such as ''party-plan sales,'' to help the Jafra cosmetics selling program. These included Athena Crafts bought in 1976 and direct mail-order Frostline in 1978.

By 1978 disposables were eating into Gillette's then traditional profit lines: inexpensive pens, razor blades and pocket lighters. The Company's greatest competitor in all three areas was a French company, Société Bic S.A., which owned 63 percent of the stock of the Bic Corporation in the United States. The parent company's stock was first listed in 1972 in the Paris Stock Exchange's Official List, but with three of its four directors a Bich, and the fourth, E. Buffard, listed as founder and director, Bic acts much like a private company. Under French law, it is not necessary for a privately held company to disclose manufacturing processes. In the United States, the French company Société Bic has only some 2,300 employees, but the parent French company, a conglomerate, employs over 8,000 employees worldwide. Its net sales are about one billion U.S. dollars. *Barron's* reported that by 1978 Bic had ''the greatest share of the retail over-the-counter ballpoint business. . . . Gillette has the largest share in the soft-tip business. Bic and Gillette, of course, are facing off on each other in lighters. And together, they have over 80 percent of the market in disposable razors.''[17] Others commented that ''Bic and Gillette have a real hate relationship. . . . It is much more than your normal market competitiveness.''[18]

By 1980 Gillette made and sold a wide variety of products, including cigarette lighters and both the disposable Cricket and the luxury model, S.T. Dupont's jewelry-like Chinese lacquer lighter. The main competitor to the Cricket was the Bic lighter, whose manufacturer was able to produce small-item plastics more cheaply than Gillette. Additionally, the oval design of the Bic lighter was generally preferred to the more angular Cricket. Gillette directors, as well as management, felt pressured by the increasing publicity given to accidents with disposable lighters: if there were not an increasing occurrence of such accidents, there was an increasing fear of potentially large product liability suits. Gillette sold Cricket to Swedish Match A.B. in 1984, just after I had met Bruno Bich, who had become CEO of Bic Corporation, headquartered in the United States in 1983, at the America's Cup races in Newport, Rhode Island. After all, the

1994 *Moody's International* lists "sailboards for wind surfing" as one of the products manufactured by Bic (p. 2874). Gillette had sold Cricket well before the *New York Times* front-page story of April 10, 1989, that described in gruesome detail the effect of an exploding lighter (not Bic's) on several victims. Whereas the French company did not realize the effect of such accidents on the sales of all companies manufacturing butane lighters, Gillette had done so much earlier and divested. Later Bic revealed that they had paid out in 1977 over a million dollars in a death caused by a discontinued Bic model and "faced 42 other exploding-lighter lawsuits."[19]

Gillette's strength lay in the refillable razors and their blades, the source of two-thirds of the Company profits, which were being threatened by the rapid growth of plastic disposables worldwide. By 1984 disposables had gained 40 percent of unit sales and 30 percent of dollar sales. Bic could produce disposables—blades, ballpoint pens and their more favored oval-shape lighters—more cheaply than Gillette could their directly competing products. The company was being outsold.

A new product, the Widget, a handy scraper and cutter into which single-edge stainless blades could be safely fitted, was introduced in 1982. Colman Mockler enjoyed using the then unpatented word *widget*, commonly used according to Webster for "an unnamed article considered for purposes of hypothetical example." I myself enjoyed twitting my theoretical economist friends who would assume the existence of a company manufacturing an unknown product, *widget*, to explain some microeconomic theory.

Gillette invested in other acquisitions during the 1970s and 1980s, and many made very good sense. After Paper Mate pen had been bought, in the mid-1950s, Liquid Paper, a correction fluid, was added in late 1979. This company was founded by Bette Nesmith (now Graham), who, as secretary to the chairman of a Dallas bank, discovered that her new electric typewriter did not erase her errors as cleanly as did her manual typewriter. Ms. Nesmith invented a paint-out fluid, Mistake Out, and began supplying it to other secretaries in the same large building in which she worked. Within a decade it became the Liquid Paper Corporation. After being turned down by the IBM Corporation, to which she tried to sell the product, she increased her efforts and expanded her own manufacturing. The Liquid Paper Corporation was a success and had plants in four countries and sales in nearly three dozen countries. When Gillette bought it, it had a net income of $3.5 million.[20]

Argentina's Sylvapen was added in 1986, and Waterman pen in 1987. Sylvapen added coloring sets as well as a South American base for manufacture of ballpoints. Waterman, in France, both traded on its established name, that of a different family from the Waterman pen family of the United States, and promoted an upgraded image that has been exploited by advertisements in upscale periodicals. For example, in 1989 a full-page advertisement in *Forbes* stated, "My 1949 Chateau Lafite, they say, is too valuable to drink. My Studebaker Classic should never be driven. Don't even think about eating off the English china. All I can say is, thank goodness for my Waterman. Finally, a priceless possession I can actually use.''

GEOGRAPHICAL EXPANSION: A GLOBAL COMPANY

The Gillette Company, although headquartered in Boston, became very early an international company with establishment of its London, England, office in 1905. Factories in France, Germany and Canada soon followed. Soon after World War I, which had acted as a marketing program, Gillette-owned factories were in Italy, Belgium, Switzerland, Spain and Denmark.

Prior to World War II, Holland, Sweden, South Africa and Brazil were added to the countries with Gillette plants, and even during that war a new manufacturing plant was opened in Argentina. After the war, Australia, Colombia and Hong Kong became part of the Company's worldwide operations.

Overseas expansion meant a need for skilled money managers who could deal with fluctuating exchange rates and varying degrees of inflation. Gillette has met this challenge with astute managers, including in 1991 Gaston R. Levy, executive vice president of the International Group, who made money for Gillette Argentina during several years of hyperinflation, and Milton Glass, vice president for finance and for investor relations, who with others astutely steered the Company's borrowing abroad and financial maneuvering during the hostile-takeover period.

Overall geographical expansion grew rapidly, increasing Gillette's international business from 32 percent in 1965 to over 50 percent in 1978 and by 1993 to over 70 percent. Gillette brands for many years have ranked first or second in Latin American, European and Asian markets.

Marketing of Gillette's razors and blades was pushed worldwide. During the 1980s Gillette moved strongly into Asian markets. By 1982 Gillette owned companies in several Asia-Pacific countries: Australia, Japan, New Zealand and the Philippines. These companies varied in size from just over 200 employees in Australia to 33 in New Zealand. Additionally, there were smaller marketing operations in Hong Kong, Singapore and Taiwan. In 1982 a joint venture was started to produce blades and plastic razors in Shenyang City in Northeast China. Some Asians may not shave every day, but there are over one billion persons living in China. In 1983 a mini-plant to manufacture twin-edge disposables was set up in Morocco, and a sizable joint venture for razor and blade manufacture was began in India. Gillette started a new manufacturing plant in Thailand to replace Gillette's existing practice of importing from other countries razors and blades, pens, and so on and then selling them in that country.

Gillette's methods of geographical expansion were two-pronged. Joint-manufacturing ventures, usually with rented plants equipped with already-depreciated machinery shipped from elsewhere, followed the earlier exploratory approach of selling products in a country to see if it had a market large enough to support manufacturing within the country. These methods allowed a small investment in new areas and a gradual upgrading of the Gillette products selling throughout Gillette's geographic spread. Whereas Americans and Europeans might insist on an Atra and today on Sensor blades, the Asians, Indians and Chinese in remote rural areas prized the older Gillette blades because they were so much better than the alternatives available to them. Under this continual upgrading process linked to geographic expansion, it was unusual for Gillette to discard any manufacturing machinery.

By 1982 Atra cartridges, on a pivoting head, outsold in the United States the twin-blade Trac II system, which had been the U.S. market leader for nine years. Lubra-smooth, a blade with a lubricating strip, was in 1985 another new version of blades. Trac II was still the twin-blade leader abroad. Atra blades, the new top of the line, cost a little less to make than Trac II and were priced a little higher, thus increasing profits.

Research to upgrade razors and blades was always started even before a new version was marketed. "Gillette has never launched a new shaving product without having in development the succeeding product and this is the case with the Sensor shaving system as well."[21]

By 1983 Gillette had secured five patents for a new razor with a pivoting head and individually mounted, moving blades that were designed to adjust to facial contours. This was the forerunner of the Sensor. The prototype outperformed both Atra, which was moving towards 20 percent of market share, and Trac II, which had peaked in market share at near 30 percent in the 1970s and was gradually falling to below 15 percent. The prototype was judged to be better in closeness of shave, comfort and appearance. However, it required Gillette to develop laser welding to produce this high-volume, high-speed and yet high-precision equipment. By 1987 Gillette had been able to produce this prototype, "making almost 100 welds per second with a production reject rate of only 10 blades per million. The last major technical obstacle to mass production"[22] of Gillette's yet-to-be-named Sensor had been overcome. It was with confidence, therefore, that the 1988 Annual Report contained the statement that "The Company has announced that, within the next year, it will introduce an innovative shaving system whose superior performance represents a significant advance in consumer satisfaction."[23] Gillette's top expertise was demonstrated to be high-tech manufacture at low cost.

Gillette continued its expenditures to expand by acquisitions and in June 1984 acquired a real winner with the Oral-B Laboratories, Inc., the dental-care business of Cooper Laboratories, Inc., Palo Alto, California, for $188.5 million in cash. The Company borrowed $100 million in order to make the purchase, and Oral-B turned out to be an excellent investment. There was synergy in both the production—hard plastics—and the marketing of toothbrushes. Toothbrushes can be sold at checkout counters of food and drug stores alongside razor blades, and worldwide there was an unsatisfied demand for improved dental hygiene. The Oral-B toothbrush had an international market waiting for it. Gillette was in an excellent position to increase the market shares of Oral-B abroad. The

Oral-B brand held a 25 percent share of the U.S. toothbrush market when purchased. In 1991 its sales of $308 million were more than double its first full-year sales under Gillette, at $135 million. In 1991 the anticipated worldwide geographical expansion of Oral-B was in full swing; Oral-B entered four new European countries, Chile and Indonesia. Additionally, Liquid Paper and Waterman pen, whose sales quadrupled in the four years of ownership to $108 million in 1991, were very successful acquisitions.

ACQUISITION PHILOSOPHY

In evaluating whether or not to buy a proposed acquisition the Board would always consider management's estimate of its expected return on investment, or ROI. Although there was often a great deal of discussion about the marketability of a product, rarely was the predicted ROI or the assumptions that lay behind it questioned. When the board members did question in depth a suggested acquisition, a vote was not usually taken; rather, a quiet consensus not to pursue was reached. The Board probably made a few errors in rejecting some proposals, primarily by not offering a high enough price (Duracell batteries in 1987), but it probably erred more in agreeing to purchase others. This subject is discussed in more detail in Chapter 5.

As I recall, at one of my first board meetings the acquisition of a Denver company, Frostline, was proposed and agreed to. As a new board member, my surprise about the intent to purchase a mail-order sewing-kit company was only weakly expressed. But investment in a company whose kit to make a down vest, which my youngest daughter had once ordered and completed, was really a surprise to me, who had viewed Fortune 500 companies as somewhat apart from everyday life, engaging in big financial deals. To Gillette, Frostline was of interest because it used a mail-order catalog in selling, which could become a new method to sell Gillette blades. Frostline did offer firsthand experience in starting up such a business and was, relative to alternative means, available and inexpensive. That experience had value. To my knowledge Gillette has never tried to sell blades through a mail-order catalog.

Gillette sold Frostline in the early 1980s and then bought a 40 percent equity in Misco in 1983. Misco sold computer supplies through a mail-order catalog. The concept was test-marketed in the United Kingdom and West Germany; although this venture was profitable, Misco was sold in the 1987 restructuring to Electrocomponents PLC of London, and my recollection is that Gillette sold it for more dollars than had been paid for it.

Gillette has been extraordinarily successful in marketing razors and blades to both men and women, but it has not been very successful in marketing cosmetics and toiletries where advertising and creating an image play a more important role than manufacturing expertise. A major exception to this is Gillette's Jafra line of cosmetics, marketed by thousands of beauty consultants to customers in their homes. Jafra comprises about 20 percent of Gillette's toiletries and cosmetic sales and had a compound sales growth rate of 16 percent, 1987–1991, with the larger share coming from rapid growth in international markets, where Gillette's international marketing pays off.

Although the sales of toiletries and cosmetics peaked in 1989 at $1 billion, the profits at $71 million, a 7 percent margin on sales, were relatively low. Profit margins on razor blades were always well over 30 percent and on Braun products, 12 percent. Oral-B, by 1991, also had profit margins of about 12 percent.

In 1989 Gillette decided to strip off most of the women's cosmetic lines and to group shaving cream, deodorants and other men's toiletry products, linking them with the same marketing slogan used for the Sensor, "The Best a Man Can Get."

Although it seemed feasible during the late 1980s to attempt to dominate the international cosmetics market for women, the competition of L'Oreal and Revlon was increasing. Cosmetic products themselves are not that distinguishable; rather, advertising and packaging play the defining role in consumer purchasing. Gillette's top expertise is using advanced technology to manufacture at low cost high-quality products, which is not an expertise easily transferable to the production of cosmetics.

During the 1980s, support of the existing major product lines of Gillette by capital expenditures was substantial. The purchase of Sylvapen Argentina for $4.5 million in 1986 and Waterman in 1987 promised a high return on investment because of the excellent fit between their products and Paper Mate products. Large expenditures were also made for cost reduction through increasing the capacity to manufacture Braun's products, Jafra cosmetics in the United Kingdom and United States, Atra blades in the United Kingdom and Fil-flow Contour pen cartridges in Berlin.

The 1982 recession and the weakening foreign-exchange rate resulted in an overall sales decline, but operating profits remained stable. Gillette's directors willingly considered management's proposals to diversify further and purchase noncontrolling percentages of several companies through its newly formed North American Venture Council. Gillette was in the venture business. However, as a resident of Silicon Valley, I argued against venturing even small amounts of capital into the complex software industry. Gillette had little expertise in this area, and there was no marketing synergy with traditional Gillette products. I could not sway my fellow board members. To Datasoft, Inc., went $2 million, plus future loans and options for 20 percent equity; and to Digital Learning Systems, New Jersey, went $1 million, plus future loans and options for 20 percent equity. These were relatively cautious expenditures, but in an industry that management did not really understand. Gillette does have a company-wide information and accounting management system that enables it to compile consolidated financial and other data rapidly; but Gillette did not have experience with creating computer software or in handling the independent, creative personalities who do that type of work. Eventually these small equities were sold off.

In the eighteen-month period of March 1983 to September 1984, the Gillette North American Venture Council acquired the mail-order computer-supplies company Misco; 81 percent of Elizabeth Grady skin-care salons; 40 percent of two retail eyewear companies; 20 percent equity in Digital Learning Systems and 40 percent of Data Soft, two computer software companies; 20 percent of a hearing-aids company; and 5 percent of Repligen, which was doing research on hair, in addition to its other better-known biotechnology research.[24]

During the early 1980s, the Gillette Board had lengthy debates on how best to hedge against the rising costs of the company's most important raw material, oil, for which there was no clear substitute. Hard plastics are manufactured from petroleum feedstocks, and the company's core products—the handles of disposable razors, Paper Mate pens and Braun appliances—are made from hard plastics. This was the period of the rapid price rise in oil resulting from the Iranian revolution (1978–1979) and the operations of the Middle East cartel, the Organization of Petroleum Exporting Countries (OPEC), which also included Venezuela and Ecuador but not Mexico, whose activity had begun in 1960 but did not significantly affect market prices until 1973. OPEC was intended to limit competition and induce the price of petroleum to rise. The surge in Mexico's oil production in response to the higher world-market price during the late 1970s and early 1980s was insufficient to contain the price of oil, shortages developed and lines to buy gasoline to operate personal cars were not uncommon. The Company, in order to assure the continuing availability of hard plastics at reasonable prices, decided to buy into oil and gas ventures in the United States. Gillette was fortunate to have a successful independent oil and gas producer on the board, Edwin Cox, who greatly added to the debate, but who resigned in April 1980 because of other business pressures.

The Board and management were worried. The rise in world oil prices in 1974–1980 had been spectacular. No one could predict when the oil cartel might break up and when Middle East Islamic wars might push the prices even higher than the cartel could. The directors argued over whether any cartel ever existed over a long period. With Cox's expertise and the help of Gillette's Don Kissel, the decision was eventually made in November 1980 to join with Kidder Peabody Exploration and M.P. Capsimalis and Associates in finding standby sources to gain cost protection. Joint ventures and minimal equity positions were secured in March 1981. With Kidder Peabody Exploration and Lomak Petroleum, Inc., Gillette sought little "bleeders" in the already-mined areas of Texas and Oklahoma. More costly oil became feasible to produce as the world price at the barrel head rose. Gillette's risk was kept small by joining partnerships in oil exploration in Oklahoma and Texas. Gillette was, of course, not the only company caught in this price squeeze. Gillette risked company-created cash, and mostly the Company got dry holes. These had been expected. Although I had argued that no cartel in history has ever lasted and that the price of oil would eventually fall, I could not say in what year this would occur. My fellow directors argued that the company could not risk continuing rapid rise in the price of its most needed raw material. We unanimously approved substantial Gillette investment beginning in 1981 in the risky oil and gas business. Gillette added to its partners Colton East, Inc., which eventually became a wholly owned subsidiary. A $10 million letter of intent signifying a joint venture with Huffco Petroleum, Inc., was also agreed to in 1982. The higher world price would have made reopening of the fields profitable for a brief period, with a very rare chance, but a chance, of striking it rich.

During the 1981–1983 period, Gillette spent almost $70 million in oil and gas exploration projects. These investments were funded from operations and also tax credits; intangible drilling costs were taken in the year that they occurred, rather than extended over a series of years of product life. The Iranian revolution ended, the Middle East cartel broke up and the price of oil fell; in the restructuring that occurred following Perelman, Gillette sold its gas and oil investments.

Organization: Geographical or by Product

Problems of organization in such a wide-flung company with diversified products were early apparent. In 1966 Gillette operated under five principal divisions: The Gillette Safety Razor Company, The Toni Company, The Paper Mate Company, the Eastern Hemisphere Division and the Western Hemisphere Division. Razor blades, the dominant product, were marketed worldwide and also produced in different countries. With the addition of Braun, product diversification increased to include household appliances as well as the electric razor.

Gillette struggled with how best to organize the company with its several hundred product lines and wide geographical dispersion in manufacturing and distribution. Should product line or geographic area dominate? This struggle was reflected in the Company's advertising strategies. The name *Gillette* and its symbolic insignia, of a circle, with three small parallel lines at right angles to the inside of a circle was rarely used in marketing, except in marketing razor blades; and even there the symbol was rarely recognized as a Gillette trademark. The circle corporate logo was not adopted until 1970, by which time Gillette no longer used the familiar portrait and signature of King Gillette on its razor-blade packages. This corporate logo, designed by Fritz Eichler of Braun, was apparently intended to look like an impressionistic "G."[25] This may be the only Braun design that seems to have failed in its mission. But then it was not designed by Braun's top designer, Dieter Rams, who gave the logo a clearer and more dashing, oblique look in 1992.

As explained in the Company's 1992 annual report, Gillette's new Omnimark is "repositioned . . . to suggest the letter G. The three bars represent the three factors that account for our global achievements and who we are: Our *world-class brands*, . . . Our *world-class products*, . . . Our *world-class people*."[26]

The problem of organizational structure was to plague Gillette into the 1980s, when it was broken into two major geographical divisions, each with a senior executive vice president and with no overall president under the chairman. This organization was created in a period of defense against a takeover. The company continually has faced a management puzzle: how to weigh the importance of geographical areas and product lines in managerial decisionmaking. Today razors and blades are marketed worldwide under the same logo and advertising slogan, "The Best a Man Can Get," which has been translated into many languages. The manufacturing facilities have been located in accordance with common-sense logic that favors internationally those cities with special tax incentives: for example, Berlin, when Germany was divided, and hot, steamy Manaus, in Brazil.

Toiletries and Cosmetics

In 1983 the division of toiletries and grooming aids was renamed "toiletries and cosmetics," reflecting greater emphasis on women's products. The division had included deodorants, antiperspirants, hairspray, shaving cream, shampoo, hair conditioners, home permanents and skin-care products such as Aapri skin cleanser. Brand names such as Right Guard, Adorn, Foamy, Silkience and Dry Idea represented toiletries, not cosmetics. None, except possibly White Rain hairspray, contributed at a level of profits that the early Toni home permanents had. It may have been Gillette's move toward acquiring more cosmetic-type products that helped initially to attract the attention of Ronald Perelman, even though the profits from cosmetics and toiletries were never substantial. Gillette's flurry of purchases of various foreign cosmetics companies was an attempt to create an effective mass concentration that would increase the profits from sales of their cosmetics and toiletries worldwide.

In 1986 Gillette bought La Toja Cosmetics S.A., a Spanish maker of bath products, and also Lustrasilk Corporation of America, a leading manufacturer of ethnic hair products for blacks. During 1987 Gillette purchased UNISA, a leading Chilean manufacturer of cosmetics and skin-care products that made the lipsticks and other color lines of Princeton cosmetics. As late as 1988, Antica Erboristeria, an Italian herbal-based line of toiletries, was bought. It was not until 1990 that Gillette management finally gave up the idea of expanding its area of cosmetics for women. With the success of the Sensor under its slogan, "The Best a Man Can Get," Gillette declared itself interested primarily in toiletries primarily for men, with its new male Gillette series emphasizing Clear Gel products in 1992. Gillette's successes have been those products where manufacturing expertise, even to the extent of manufacturing its own production equipment, has been important.

Razors and Blades

In the mid-1980s, Gillette's directors still had no idea whether the revolutionary concept behind the spring-mounted Sensor razor and blade could result in manufacture at a low-enough unit cost to be competitive. Management and the directors continued to worry that the company would be continually losing its profitable blade market to the cheaper and much lower-profit disposable razor. As disposables steadily increased their market share, some of Gillette's management argued that the Sensor system should be marketed as a disposable. Because Bic had a lower cost of manufacturing for its molded one-piece plastic razor and blade, Gillette's pricing of any new disposable would have to be low enough to compete. From Gillette's point of view, disposables, including Gillette's own Good News and Daisy, aimed at the men's and women's markets, respectively, were eating into the market for steel blades designed to fit into metal razor handles. This was Gillette's core business. Gillette could not be competitive and still charge enough to make profits from disposables. Gillette's 1988 Annual Report announced that it would introduce an innovative shaving system that was a significant advance. "Shaving system" is Gillette's phraseology for a nondisposable razor and blade. The argument between those supporting the development of disposables and those who believed in the traditional razor and blade that promise a higher quality shave was over. The latter group had won. The Sensor had brought about the needed turnaround. Before 1989 was over, Gillette's two major razor factories, South Boston and Berlin, were running seven-day weeks and three shifts a day. By the end of 1994, Gillette had worldwide a 67 percent share of the dollar market for razor and blades.

Diversified Acquisitions

It was because of the continuing growth in sales of disposables worldwide that Gillette management advocated during the early 1980s a widely diversified acquisitions program that included buying several minority equity positions in promising new small companies. Management was viewed as a technique that, if successful with one business, could be successful with other businesses. Some of the ventures were not clear fits with Gillette's operations. It is easier to say in hindsight that there were some errors. Some in management believed that acquiring an interest in beauty-parlor chains would increase the sales of Gillette's cosmetic and skin-care and hair-care products. Sandra Lawrence, in charge of new business at the time of purchase of equity positions in beauty salons, was convinced that beauty parlors would be a coming source of profits to Gillette. As the only woman on the Board and therefore presumably the only director with direct experience with beauty parlors, I argued against the proposals to buy an equity position in the Elizabeth Grady Face First International Corporation in the Boston area and also an 81 percent interest in Beauty Resources, Inc., with "Noelle" spas located in Bethesda, Maryland, and Atlanta, Georgia. I argued that when a beauty parlor does sell products, it sells only designer-level lines, and most beauty parlors do not compete directly with drugstore marketing. Gillette's products were not, except for the Paul Mitchell hair-care lines, even close to designer-level products. A major problem was that

beauty parlors sell primarily services, while Gillette's strength is in the manufacturing of products. Gillette sold both beauty operations in the 1988 restructuring.

Sandra Lawrence was the only woman who made a presentation to the Board
during my twelve years on it. She and I had a long discussion about possibly
introducing to the eastern part of the United States the California concept of a
merged beauty salon and spa, which would provide in one place hair and skin
care, exercise programs and therapeutic massage and in addition offer advice on
skin care and nutrition. The Yellow Pages of many California telephone books
illustrate this expanded range of services in California in comparison to the more
traditional beauty salon in the East. This concept was never adopted by Gillette,
and wisely so. It would also have been wise, I believe, not to have invested at
all in this generally very small-unit, very service-oriented business.

Gillette also in the 1980s invested several million dollars in the retail eyeglass
area, a business that management and the Board believed should, with our aging
population, expand, barring a recession. It was then customary for individuals
to obtain eyeglasses by first getting a prescription from an optometrist or oph-
thalmologist and then waiting several days for an optician to produce the eyeglasses. This was a time-consuming procedure for the individual consumer.
Retail optical chains were being established, with even a few express superstores
that could provide both an eye examination and eyeglasses in one or two hours,
thus meeting many consumers' desire for both speed and choice. In some large
stores such as Sears Roebuck and Company, eyecare retail outlets were established, where one could leave a prescription, shop for other items and return
the same afternoon or evening for one's new eyeglasses. This struck me, a
working mother always short of time, as an excellent idea. When management
proposed a limited equity investment of 40 percent of the shares of Spectron,
Inc., and Eye Optics, the directors enthusiastically supported this action. These
investments were sold in the 1987 restructuring, Spectron to Mitani Corporation
of Japan and Eye Optics in 1988 to the Pearle Vision Center, which shortly
became part of the large British conglomerate Grand Metropolitan. Grand Metropolitan also owned Burger King, Heublein and other food and beverage lines.
This was the world of conglomerates. If Gillette could have retained these operations, it might eventually have made substantial profits. The amount of capital
invested in the companies was relatively low, and the idea seemed good. There
was some transferability of skills and materials between their production and
Gillette's production, between Gillette's sales force and marketing and their sales
force and marketing.

The Sensor

However, these and other areas of new business for Gillette probably would
never earn the 30 percent margin of profits that the nondisposable razors and
blades did. It, therefore, made more sense to use free cash to improve shaving

systems and to continue to expand sales of these worldwide. Gillette had always improved its blades after every successful launch, and this pattern of continuing innovation was expected to persist. With high-quality advanced technology, geographic expansion and heavy advertising, the razor and blade business grew rapidly and profitably. The manufacture of an improved prototype, however, was far easier than the mass production, at a competitively low unit cost, of a new complex blade system envisioned as using tiny springs to impart a more face-hugging quality to a shave. A twin-blade razor, with each blade individually mounted on responsive springs that automatically adjust the blades to different facial contours, is a far different concept than the original single, nonflexible, thin, tempered-steel sharp blade attached to a razor handle by two screws.[27]

The initial retail price of Gillette's first silver razor (silver does not rust) and 20 blades was $5. This was a high price in 1905, even though each blade was to provide 20 to 30 shaves (and according to some advertisements, 10 to 40). The revolutionary Sensor, initially marketed in 1990 with five blades at $3.75 (price not corrected for inflation), is manufactured by computer-driven, laser-welding machinery. Directors and the management made an expensive gamble that a low unit cost of mass production was attainable and they won. By April 1992, the Sensor, with its advertising tag, "The Best a Man Can Get," captured 43 percent of the nondisposable-razor market annually with its one billion blades.[28] Gillette's 10-K for 1988 (p. 2) states that the Company's "major competitors worldwide are Warner-Lambert Company (with its Schick product line)."

ADVERTISING

Extensive advertising has always supported Gillette's products, all of which are consumer products. King Gillette, as early as 1912, wrote in a memo to his fellow directors, "The whole success of this business depends on advertising."[29] And indeed, advertising, at times sparked by military images, has been very important in expanding both the domestic and the international markets of Gillette. The following jingle accompanied by a drawing of a sailor and a young woman dancing to music from a record player, was typical of wartime advertisements during World War I.

> You look your best—your face feels swell—
> You get more shaves per blade as well
> With Thin Gillettes, four for a dime—
> They breeze through beards in record time!
> Thin Gillette Blades: 4 for 10¢, 8 for 19¢, 12 for 27¢.[30]

Both World War I and World War II acted as massive marketing programs for Gillette. Later sports and radio and then television transmitted Gillette promotions worldwide. Slogans such as "Look Sharp, Feel Sharp, Be Sharp. Use

Gillette Blue Blades'' have since 1939 been broadcast worldwide through Gillette's World Series of baseball. The early ''Gillette Cavalcade of Sports'' series, sponsorship of championship heavyweight boxing and the international game of soccer have served as advertising bonanzas for Gillette's razors and blades.

Gillette has long recognized the importance of sponsoring male team sports for advertising in its world markets. The television rights to advertise on baseball's World Series games and for other all-star baseball games were acquired in 1950. In 1970 the Company was asked to conduct the balloting for the selection of the major-league baseball players for the annual All-Star Game. Gillette advertises and promotes razors, blades, and male toiletries through its sponsorship of baseball, of cricket in the United Kingdom, and of soccer, football and basketball worldwide. With their major regional and international events, male sports have been pivotal in advertising and promotion. The 1986 World Cup soccer finals in Mexico involved 24 national teams, and the television and radio audience numbered in the millions. With the advent of television the name of Gillette is displayed worldwide, whether for soccer, football or tennis, in huge letters along the sidelines, just in front of the fans. As television viewers follow the ball, often they also see ''GILLETTE'' as well as the play on the field. In the tradition of highlighting male team sports, the Sensor was launched in the United States and Canada and in most of Europe at football's 1990 Superbowl. In 1980 nearly 15 percent of Gillette's revenues were spent on advertising and promotion. With the worldwide launch of the new Sensor razor and blade in January 1990 at the Super Bowl, that percentage rose to 15.6; in 1991 it rose to 16.1, or a total of $754 million—an amount greater than Gillette's total sales in 1970. The television visuals that launched the new Sensor were identical in Japan, Europe and the United States, with voice-over narrations in different languages. Television has greatly widened and intensified the impact of advertising dollars; by using the same or similar advertising themes worldwide, dollars that might otherwise be spent on the creation of new advertising themes are saved. Although the competition has the same opportunity, Gillette may have spent more and been the more successful advertiser.

A GLOBAL COMPANY

Gillette, a multinational well before World War I, early evolved into a global company that in the 1990s sells in 200 countries and territories and manufactures in about 30. The complexity of running a large international company can be envisioned just by listing the legal jurisdictions in which its subsidiaries are incorporated and thus the many governments and diverse laws with which the company must deal.

A global company differs from an international company in that it considers the whole world when deciding company policy, such as where to locate a new plant, at what level to set prices in different countries or in what languages to advertise. Gillette operates within the world as a large domestic company operates within a single country. Gillette seeks the least-cost manufacturing site indicated by taxation laws and labor costs. Joint ventures in many countries secure an initial toehold in their markets. Gillette stock and bonds are sold on several exchanges throughout the world. Some international companies have many sales offices and even manufacturing subsidiaries abroad, but their U.S. headquarters may favor construction of new plants within the headquarters country, and few of their high-level management are foreign-born. Among Gillette's top executives are many foreign-born, and many U.S. employees are living in foreign countries. In 1993, five hundred U.S. nationals lived and worked abroad for Gillette. Among Gillette's twelve directors in 1993 were three who lived abroad, one each in Germany, Mexico and the United Kingdom. Although Gillette's policy is to hire into upper-level positions the natives of the countries where a plant is positioned, its training of managers includes, as does IBM's, carefully assessed geographical transfers of executives from one country to another. Among Gillette's 40 top executives in 1992, 50 percent have worked in at least three countries. Transferability of managers across national boundaries makes it possible to create uniform business policies, but it also, apparently some claim, discouraged blacks from moving into the company's executive ranks. To my knowledge this claim has not been fully explained.

"It takes at least 25 years to build an international management corps that possesses the skills, experience and abilities to take a global organization from one level of success to the next."[31] Fewer than 15 percent of Gillette's overseas staff were born in the United States; at least 85 percent come from a country in which Gillette operates. Typically, Gillette identifies individuals to hire for overseas employment while they are studying in the United States for an MBA. This solves the problem of finding capable young people who also speak English. Another problem is to find people who can become international, that is, at home in more than one country, and also have a global understanding of the business. An example of this type of person is Dieu Eng Seng, who in 1993 was the area vice president of Oral-B, Asia Pacific and has worked for Gillette in his native Singapore and in Australia, China, Hong Kong, Malaysia and the United States. Gillette's 1995 Annual Report describes in interesting detail how more than 150 men and women are being trained through several successive eighteen-month assignments in different countries, how they and their families cope and how they move up in the Company.

Gillette continued to build on its five major profitable centers: small Braun appliances, writing instruments, old-line toiletries such as deodorants and shampoo, toothbrushes, and its crown jewel—razor blades and razors. During the April 16, 1992, stockholder meeting, chairman of the board Al Zeien stated, "Internal projections of our current core businesses are quite attractive and, since a new leg must measure up to this standard and thereby add to our rate of earnings growth, it is easy to see how difficult this task is. Any new opportunity would have to be on familiar ground product-wise and be able to utilize our powerful international structure. Oral-B, acquired in 1984, has met this test,'' and also Duracell in 1996, that ''is an excellent strategic fit for our tightly focused, technologically driven consumer products business. Duracell and Gillette share numerous characteristics, including global brand franchises, common distribution channels, exceptional merchandising opportunities and geographic expansion potential.''[32]

The corporate culture of Gillette has at times been described as stodgy and dull. Persons who view Gillette in this fashion are usually unaware of its wide range of products and continuing geographical expansion. There is nothing dull to me about a company that can report, ''During 1991, Gillette entered five new markets in Eastern Europe and substantially expanded operations in Egypt, India, Pakistan and Turkey.''[33]

Viewed from Silicon Valley, Gillette may appear to some to be stodgy and dull compared to the high-tech, innovative companies that populate that area of California. In Silicon Valley a common company culture is always to be at the cutting edge—first to discover ''something new'' and then to consider the costs of producing it. Many such companies are started but do not become successful producers because their founders do not find reducing the costs of production as exciting as inventing a new product, and therefore the company may not spend the needed time on streamlining its cost of production. In newer fields the yield from innovation may be greater and the attainment of innovation easier than in an older industry.

The painstaking approach of trying out different technologies to minimize manufacturing costs to reach a declining cost curve as the output grows may never be fully addressed by some companies. It is in thus perfecting their manufacturing techniques that the older and even sometimes bureaucratic companies may excel. Gillette developed its prototype Sensor blade with heavy cash investment in engineering prior to the November 1986 takeover attempt by Perelman. The cost-cutting manufacturing techniques for mass production and innovative marketing were yet to be developed. Developing them was seen as exciting to Gillette's management as creating a new product is to possibly many more innovative entrepreneurs. During the first two years of making the Sensor, Gillette reduced its unit costs by 30 percent. Keeping up with advances in technology worldwide, Gillette applies different new techniques to its own manufacturing. Japanese companies have perfected the incremental change in manufacture, and so has Gillette.

Companies with primarily innovative cultures are likely to pay their midlevel employees in part under profit-sharing plans. An entrepreneurial employee will risk a lower base wage for a potentially higher total. On the other hand, more bureaucratic companies are unlikely to have profit-sharing that goes very far down their executive ladders, even though the very top management will usually have bonuses linked to profits. The bulk of their employees are less likely to accept risk, and risk-taking is not really encouraged among even middle-management employees.

In retrospect, when all the various investments by Gillette of the early 1980s are added up, the argument against the company's diversification program is weakened because of the actual sizable gains from the company's successes: acquisition of Oral-B toothbrushes and Waterman pens. To gain, one must risk. There are very few instances where a company's size remains constant. It either grows or shrinks, and Gillette in recent years has grown, primarily through geographical expansion.

The Gillette Company is, as are over three-fourths of the Fortune 500 firms, a diversified, multiple-line business firm or, as some people think of it, a conglomerate. In negotiating mergers to add new products, managers do not think that this activity runs counter to the long-term interests of shareholders, but at times they overestimate their ability to add value to a business by increasing its size.

Among Gillette's fellow firms of the Fortune 500, diversification increased from 1985 to 1992, although for a sample of 6,505 firms of all sizes, it decreased from 1985 to 1989. Gillette was in step with the times. "It is widely acknowledged there were high numbers of unrelated acquisitions in the late 1960s and early 1970s. . . . We also know that a substantial number of business units acquired in the late 1960s and early 1970s were later divested . . . and that acquisitions were more likely to be followed by divestitures when targets were not in businesses highly related to those of the acquirer."[34]

"The pure pleasures of Empire-building"[35] may be a supplementary reason for managers to support excessive expansion, but in my view this was less compelling than the alluring potential increase in market power that would yield benefits at the expense of the firm's competitors.

During the 1980s I was involved in a business roundtable that included executives of several large well-known Japanese firms. Their emphasis was that a firm should always continue to expand its markets and profits will follow. Their emphasis was on long-term profits and incremental change to existing product lines. In actuality, this was Gillette's approach as it improved its existing line of razors and blades with the development of the Sensor. Gillette has been closer to this Japanese model, which emphasizes market size and incremental improvement, than to a U.S. model that places emphasis first on short-run profits and only second on market size. Gillette's emphasis on incrementally improving its existing product lines in contrast to dramatic innovation is also more Japanese than American. There was at Gillette the belief that growth was a good thing and that company growth would pay off in higher profits.

During the early 1980s most Gillette directors thought that the Company was a sitting duck for a takeover, and thus the Board readily went along with adoption of the poison pill and a staggered board, both in place because of a potential, not an actual, threat. The Board and management did not want a bigger long-run debt, but they did want to find potential synergistic products to replace eventually, in part, what seemed to be a stable or even declining razor and blade market that disposables threatened to dominate. The cash flow accommodated small equity investments. The only alternative, if the Company were to grow, was to speed up innovation and marketing of new razor and blade products, with the Sensor.

The excess of Gillette's sources of cash over its uses of cash, its cash flow, was after taxes $113 million in 1983. In 1984 Gillette bought Oral-B, and in 1985 the Company had higher capital investment as it increased its production capacity to manufacture blades and also spent money on developing the Sensor. This resulted in negative cash flow in each of these years. The repurchase of stock in 1986 explains that year's negative cash flow, and by 1987 Gillette once again had a positive cash flow in the amount of $207 million.

Gillette's new Sensor razor and blade system was unveiled in Europe and the United States on October 3, 1989. Gillette had tested the Sensor starting in October 1988, holding a continuing dialogue with about a hundred thousand consumers, who rated it in comparison with Gillette's Atra Plus and with Bic's and Wilkinson's shaving systems. In the rankings, Atra Plus was the closest competitor, and in all categories, such as from comfort to maneuverability and after-shave appearance, the Sensor ranked 26 percent better than the Atra Plus and 35 percent better than its nearest non-Gillette competitor. The simultaneous launch on October 3 was in the United States, Canada and seventeen European countries. Colman Mockler was quoted as saying, "If the public reacts to these Sensor blades as they reacted to the Super Blue Blades in the late 1950's and the Trac II in the early 1970's, then we're going to sell as many as we can make."[36] He was right.

Rapid geographic expansion of Gillette went far beyond the United States and Canada, into Japan, Latin America, Australia, Africa, and indeed the rest of the world.[37]

The Company continued its profitable growth into the 1990s. Operating cash flow continued, and some was used to pay off the long-term debt created by the close to $600 million payment to Perelman in 1986 and the stock repurchase in 1988. In 1988 the debt peaked at $1.675 million and remained at over a billion dollars until 1991, when it was reduced to $742 million, and in 1992 to $554 million. The cash flow continued to be substantial, and money continued to be spent on research and development, advertising and marketing and geographic expansion.

The compounded annual return to shareholders on Gillette stock for the five years after Perelman was 35 percent, as compared to 15 percent for the Dow Jones Industrial average and 16 percent for Standard & Poor's 500.

Gillette was poised to take off when Colman Mockler died unexpectedly in January of 1991. As a *Forbes* cover story entitled "Triumph for Gillette's Colman Mockler: Technology as a Marketing Tool" ironically stated,

Gillette management's real triumph was not in warding off raiders—other companies have done that—but in reasserting the principles that had made this old multinational company great in the first place and which were in danger of being lost. . . . While from the outside Gillette in the mid-1980s looked like a company that had settled into middle age and offered a tempting breakup target, it was in fact very much on the move. . . . Even while warding off the predators, Gillette management was working full time to bring the Sensor to market.[38]

As Mockler's successor, the Board elected as CEO and chairman a soft-spoken engineer, Alfred Zeien, who had an MBA from Harvard University. Zeien had worked since 1968 at Gillette, primarily on the technical side, and had been chairman of the management board of Braun AG. Al Zeien did not attend Harvard as an undergraduate, as had Mockler, but graduated from the little-known but very well respected Webb Institute. Under Zeien, the Company is expected to grow with new products and geographic expansion and continue to be very profitable.

APPENDIX: CHRONOLOGY OF THE GILLETTE COMPANY[39]

1901   The corporation is chartered as the American Safety Razor Company on September 28 and begins operations in an office located over a fish store at 424 Atlantic Avenue, Boston.

1902   The name of the corporation is changed to the Gillette Safety Razor Company.

1903   Production begins and, by year end, Gillette sells 51 razors and 168 blades.

1904   A U.S. patent on the Gillette Safety Razor is granted on November 15, and annual sales rise to 90,884 razors and 123,648 blades.

1905   An overseas sales office is opened in London, England, and the first overseas manufacturing operation is established in Paris.

A trademark featuring King C. Gillette's portrait and signature is adopted.

1906   The first dividend is paid on Company stock.

Gillette opens a plant in Montreal, Canada.

1908   A Gillette sales company is established in Hamburg, Germany.

1911   Blade sales for the year reach a record 35.6 million.

1914   William Nickerson, MIT graduate and machinist, who worked with King C. Gillette on the original Safety Razor, invents fully automatic blade-sharpening machinery.

A sales company is established in France.

1917   Gillette razor sales total one million, and blade sales total more than 115 million.

During World War I, Gillette European factories close, and production in other Gillette facilities increases substantially.

The Company is reorganized as a Delaware corporation.

1918   The U.S. government issues every soldier and sailor his own shaving equipment, and the Company ships 3.5 million razors and over 36 million blades to the armed forces.

1919   Branch offices or companies are established in Copenhagen, Madrid, Milan, Istanbul, Calcutta, Sydney, Brussels, Geneva, Buenos Aires, Singapore, Shanghai and Tokyo.

      Gillette Belgium, Gillette Denmark and Gillette Italy are incorporated.

1924   Gillette Holland is incorporated.

1926   Two new factory additions are completed in South Boston, bringing capacity to 150,000 razors and three million blades daily. Plant and warehouse floor space increases to cover sixteen acres.

1927   Company earnings since incorporation reach nearly $100 million. Approximately half is returned to stockholders, and the remainder is reinvested.

1929   Gillette Sweden is incorporated.

1930   The Gillette Safety Razor Company and the AutoStrop Safety Razor Company merge.

      Gillette South Africa is incorporated.

1931   Gillette France is incorporated, and manufacturing operations begin in Rio de Janeiro, Brazil.

1932   Gillette Blue Blade is introduced, and Gillette Austria is incorporated.

1936   Gillette chemists develop Brushless shaving cream.

1938   The Gillette Thin Blade is added to the product line.

      Gillette Norway is incorporated.

1939   Gillette embarks upon the "Cavalcade of Sports" broadcasts and sponsors the first radio broadcast of the World Series.

1942   The War Production Board limits production of razors to quantities authorized for sale to the armed forces and for export.

      Construction of a new plant is completed in Buenos Aires, Argentina.

1943   Gillette Argentina is incorporated.

1944   All manufacturing facilities for the production of razors are devoted to military requirements.

      Company begins sponsorship of televised weekly boxing bouts from New York City.

1946   Production facilities increase. The Boston and London plants produce manufacturing equipment for their use as well as for plants in Argentina, Brazil, France and Switzerland.

      Gillette Switzerland is formed.

1948   The Toni Company is acquired on January 2, with an initial payment of $12.6 million.

Six sets of twins tour England, Belgium, Scotland, Ireland and Holland to introduce Toni and launch the "Which Twin has the Toni?" ad campaign in Europe.

1949   A new plant in Mexico City is completed and begins operation.

1950   Television rights for the World Series and All-Star baseball games for the next six years are acquired for $6 million.

The stock is split two-for-one.

1952   The name of the Company is changed to The Gillette Company—the razor, blade and shaving cream business being operated as the Gillette Safety Razor Company, a division of The Gillette Company.

1953   Gillette France opens a new factory in Annecy, transferring operations from Paris, and manufacturing operations begin at Johannesburg, South Africa.

1954   Gillette Venezuela is incorporated.

1955   The Paper Mate Company, a manufacturer of ballpoint pens, is acquired for $15 million.

1956   Gillette New Zealand is incorporated.

1957   A new factory is completed in Sydney, Australia, for the manufacture of Gillette and Toni products.

Paper Mate operations are consolidated in a new plant in Santa Monica, California.

Facilities are expanded in Boston, Chicago and England.

1959   Toni produces its 450 millionth home permanent kit.

Operations of the company's research laboratories move into new facilities in South Boston; Washington, D.C.; Chicago; and Reading, England.

Gillette Puerto Rico and Gillette Colombia are incorporated.

1962   Gillette Surgical at Reading, England, begins manufacturing disposable hypodermic needles.

1963   The Gillette Safety Razor Company completes a new $8 million South Boston factory addition, creating the world's largest facility designed exclusively for razor blade manufacture.

Gillette Hong Kong is incorporated.

1965   Gillette Brazil, Gillette Finland and Gillette Spain are incorporated.

1966   Gillette Austria, Gillette Chile and Gillette Portugal are incorporated.

1967   The Gillette Company acquires a controlling interest in Braun AG of West Germany.

Corporate headquarters of The Gillette Company move from the South Boston facility to the Prudential Tower Building, Boston.

1968   Braun North America, a division of The Gillette Company, is formed to market Braun AG household appliances and photographic products in the United States and Canada.

1969   The Company begins construction on more than 1.7 million square feet of manufacturing, office and warehouse space around the world.

1970   Gillette combines its Research and Development Laboratories in Reading, England.

1971   The Company buys a 48% interest in the S.T. Dupont Company, a French manufacturer of luxury writing instruments and disposable lighters.

The Trac II twin-blade shaving system is introduced by the Safety Razor Division.

1972   Buxton, Incorporated, of Agawam, Massachusetts, a manufacturer of high-quality personal leather goods, is acquired.

1973   Net sales exceed $1 billion for the first time.

Jafra Cosmetics, Inc., a small California-based skin-care company, is acquired. Jafra consultants conduct classes and demonstrations in the homes of consumers.

The Company acquires the Hydroponic Chemical Company of Copley, Ohio, a manufacturer of plant-care products for the home.

By year end, GII, the international version of Trac II, is available in 50 countries.

1974   Colman M. Mockler, Jr., is elected president and chief operating officer in July. He succeeds Edward Gelsthorpe, who resigns to join United Brands.

The Company sells North American Fashions, Inc., which was acquired in 1970.

The Plant Care Division is established to further the home plant-care business.

1975   The United States District Court in Boston approves a consent decree settling an antitrust suit brought by the United States Department of Justice against Gillette as a result of the 1967 acquisition of Braun AG.

In April, Colman Mockler, Jr., is elected chief executive officer.

The Company acquires LaGuilia, a small Italian chewing-gum and confectionery manufacturer.

1976   Gillette establishes a new company, Cambridge Shaver Imports, Inc., to market Braun-made electric shavers in the United States under the Eltron trademark.

The Braun Control, a new pocket electronic calculator, is introduced in Germany.

Jafra Cosmetics begins operation in Brazil, its first overseas market.

1977   Atra automatically adjusting twin-blade razor and cartridge becomes the best-selling razor in the United States.

Fluorocarbon propellants in all domestic Gillette aerosol products are replaced by hydrocarbon propellants.

Buxton, Incorporated, is sold to Beatrice Foods Company of Chicago.

1978   Jafra Cosmetics International begins operations in Austria, Germany, Holland, Italy and the United Kingdom.

A major facility for the manufacture of blades and razors, writing instruments and disposable lighters opens in Manaus, Brazil.

The Welcome Wagon business in Memphis, Tennessee, is sold to a group of former Welcome Wagon employees.

1979   Braun enters the dental hygiene appliance field in Europe with the introduction of electric toothbrushes and water jets.

Gillette buys the Liquid Paper Corporation, a Dallas-based manufacturer of type-writer correction fluid and typewriter ribbons.

The Company sells Cambridge Shaver Imports, Inc.; The Hyponex Company, Inc.; the Autopoint mechanical pencil business; and the domestic transfer games business.

1980   The Gillette Company's 1980 net sales exceed $2 billion.

The Swivel disposable razor featuring a pivoting head is introduced.

The Company signs a contract for promotional rights and stadium billboard space for the 1982 World Cup Soccer games in Spain.

1981   The new lighter-weight Daisy disposable razor with a shorter handle is introduced in the United States.

Jafra continues its international expansion with operations beginning in Argentina, Belgium, Guatemala, Panama and Switzerland. Jafra now has eighteen international operations.

S.T. Dupont, the Paper Mate Division and Braun AG in West Germany each introduce new products.

Over the last five years, more than a dozen business and product areas have been sold or discontinued.

1982   Atra cartridges become the top-selling cartridge in the United States markets, outselling the Trac II brand, which had been the market leader for nine years.

The Widget handy scraper and cutter is introduced.

Toiletries and cosmetics continue to expand, with Soft & Dri Solid antiperspirant added to Right Guard and White Rain shampoo and Silkience hairspray added to hair care.

Jafra operations open in Chile, Peru and Spain, bringing the number of international Jafra businesses to 21.

Gillette becomes the world's largest marketer of a broad range of writing instruments, with unit volume of pens and refills climbing to a total of e billion units.

Braun broadens its most important product category, shavers, with the entry of three new lower-priced cord shavers for men.

The Board of Directors approves an agreement with the Shenyang Daily Use Metal Industrial Company to establish a joint venture for the production of coated and uncoated blades and plastic razors in Shenyang City in northeast China.

A joint venture is formed for the production of double-edge razor blades in Giza, near Cairo, Egypt.

1983   Backed by $28.2 million in media and promotional support, the Right Guard line of deodorants and antiperspirants is restaged with improved product formulations, bold graphics and new packaging.

Jafra expands operations to Malaysia, Singapore and Venezuela, increasing the number of overseas markets to 24.

Permission is received from the governments of India and Thailand for the establishment of two new plants. The blade-manufacturing joint venture in India will be called Indian Shaving Products Limited. The Gillette-owned facility in Thailand will manufacture double-edge blades and assemble stick pens.

The company acquires a 40 percent equity position in Misco, Inc., a privately held New Jersey company that sells computer supplies and accessories via catalog.

Divestiture of the Braun photo and hi-fi businesses is completed.

1984   The Company purchases Oral-B Laboratories, Inc., the leading marketer of toothbrushes in the United States, from Cooper Laboratories, Inc., for $188.5 million.

Swedish Match AB buys the worldwide Cricket disposable lighter business.

The Company sells its surgical supplies business located in the United Kingdom in November.

1985   A new company, Braun Inc., is established to market the full range of Braun products in the United States.

S.T. Dupont opens its first U.S. boutique in New York City.

1986   In November, Revlon Group, Inc., launches a $4.12 billion hostile-takeover attempt at Gillette.

Gillette buys Sylvapen, Argentina's leading manufacturer of writing instruments.

Gillette buys La Toja Cosmeticos, S.A., a Spanish manufacturer and marketer of toiletries products.

Indian Shaving Products, Ltd., a joint-venture blade-manufacturing facility in Bhiwadi, India, is inaugurated.

Jafra Japan and Jafra Colombia are established.

Gillette contributes $107,000 in Mexico relief aid to help rebuild vital public facilities damaged by earthquakes.

For events after 1986, the reader is referred to this book and the annual reports of the Company.

NOTES

1. Albert S. Leonard, *The Gillette Company 1901–1976* (Boston: The Gillette Company, 1977).

2. King C. Gillette, *The Human Drift* [1894] (Delmar, N.Y.: Scholars' Facsimiles and Reprints, 1976), pp. ix–x.

3. Quoted in Russell B. Adams, Jr., *King C. Gillette: The Man and His Wonderful Shaving Device* (Boston: Little, Brown and Company, 1978), pp. 49–50.

4. Gillette, *The Human Drift*, p. 138.

5. Ibid., p. 159.

6. "Gillette Review: Hat in Hand," *Fortune* vol. 4, no. 4 (October 1931), p. 48.

7. Ibid., p. 206.

8. Paul G. Stern and Tom Shachtman, *Straight to the Top: Beyond Loyalty, Gamesmanship, Mentors, and Other Corporate Myths* (New York: Warner Books, 1990), p. 212.

9. Ibid., p. 218.

10. The Gillette Company, *Annual Meeting of Stockholders April 20, 1978, and First Quarter Report 1978*, p. 2.

11. Adams, *King C. Gillette*, p. 281.

12. Steven N. Kaplan and Michael S. Weisbach, "The Success of Acquisitions: Evidence from Divestitures," *Journal of Finance* (March 1992), p. 107.

13. Ibid., p. 108.

14. *Notice of Annual Meeting of Stockholders and Proxy Statement*, The Gillette Company, March 22, 1977, pp. 16, 17.

15. "Gillette South Africa," The Gillette Company, internal document, typed, undated, p. 2.

16. Neil Ulman, "Gillette Chairman Takes a Long View in Program to Brighten Profit Picture," *Wall Street Journal*, June 28, 1977, p. 14.

17. Louis M. Rusitzky, "View from New England," *Barron's*, April 2, 1979, p. 4.

18. Nathaniel C. Nash, "How Bic Lost the Edge to Gillette," *New York Times*, April 11, 1982, p. F7.

19. Wendy Cooper, "The Case of the Exploding Cigarette Lighters," *Institutional Investor* (December 1987), p. 210.

20. Eric Morgenthaler, "At Council on Ideas, It Is Helpful to Be a Daydream Believer," *Wall Street Journal*, July 29, 1994, p. A5.

21. Al Zeien, "Stockholder Participation," in *Annual Meeting of Stockholders, April 16, 1992, and First Quarter Report 1992* (Boston: 1992 The Gillette Company), p. 9.

22. Benjamin Esty (doctoral candidate) in collaboration with Professor Pankaj Ghemawat, "Gillette's Launch of Sensor," Harvard Business School Case Study No. 9-792-028, September 15, 1992, p. 7.

23. *Annual Report 1988* (Boston: The Gillette Company, 1989), p. 4.

24. Dean Witter Research, Table 5, Gillette North American Venture Council, October 31, 1984.

25. Adams, *King C. Gillette*, p. 265.

26. The Gillette Company, *1992 Annual Report*, inside cover.

27. Adams, *King C. Gillette*, p. 56.

28. Lawrence Ingrassia, "Technology: The Cutting Edge," *Wall Street Journal*, April 6, 1992, p. R6.

29. Adams, *King C. Gillette*, p. 85.

30. Leonard, *Gillette Company 1901–1976*, quoting a special issue of *Gillette News* commemorating the 75th anniversary of the Company's founding, p. 15.

31. Jennifer J. Laabs, "Gillette: Building a Global Management Team," *Personnel Journal* (August 1993), p. 75, quoting Al Zeien.

32. Alfred M. Zeien and Michael C. Hawley, "Letter to Stockholders," March 3, 1997, *1996 Annual Report* (Boston: The Gillette Company, 1997), p. 3.

33. *Annual Meeting of Stockholders April 16, 1992*, The Gillette Company, p. 3, quoting Al Zeien.

34. Cynthia A. Montgomery, "Corporate Diversification," *Journal of Economic Perspectives* vol. 8, no. 3 (Summer 1994), p. 170.

35. Ibid., p. 166.

36. Anthony Ramirez, "A Radical New Style for Stodgy Old Gillette," *New York Times*, February 25, 1990, p. F-5.

37. "Chronological History of Gillette, as Delineated by the Company," Shearson Lehman Hutton report on Gillette, Table 10, October 19, 1989, pp. 17–19.

38. Subrata N. Chakravarty, "We Had to Change the Playing Field," *Forbes*, February 4, 1991, p. 83.

39. Abbreviated from a 47-page "Chronology" of The Gillette Company through 1986, issued by The Gillette Company's Corporate Public Relations Office.

4

The Takeover Climate: Poison Pills, Junk Bonds, Stock Price, Industrial Espionage(?), Insider Knowledge

The decade of the 1980s was a period of mergers, as corporations and takeover specialists sparred for control over large companies and their income streams. Companies with a large excess cash flow and multiple divisions—and Gillette was in this category—attracted other firms to take them over. After acquisition, the acquirer would sell the less profitable divisions and then enjoy the cash flow from the highly profitable remaining segments. Prior to any specific move by any particular company or takeover specialist, Gillette had adopted various protective devices that would give directors and management time to consider fully any offer and, if they did not believe the offer was a good one, time to fight off attempts to gain control. Gillette was not unusual in adopting such measures prior to any announced intent to buy the company. Colorful characters and colorful articles in the business press, and terms such as *white knights, white squires* and *poison pill* only partially masked the intensity of some corporate battles. A general climate of takeovers prevailed.

The development of the high-risk but high-return bond market by Drexel Burnham Lambert, under Michael Milken, made cash available for companies and individuals such as Ronald Perelman to buy—at relatively high prices with other people's money—the common stock of many companies. The economic climate for takeovers was fostered during the first half of the 1980s by this ready availability of cash, the expectation that the economic boom would continue, the differential treatment of dividends and interest under the corporate income-tax law and the relatively weaker Reagan antitrust policy. The increasing use of personal computers and fax machines enabled more rapid transfer of information and money to facilitate big deals. The movement of takeovers accelerated in 1986 with the more than $6 billion deals of Kohlberg Kravis Roberts & Co. (KKR) in acquiring Beatrice in a leveraged buyout (LBO) and of General Electric in purchasing RCA. The impending change in the corporate income-tax law, which would raise the federal rate from 20 percent to 28 percent on capital gains effective in 1987, probably speeded up the number of takeovers at the end of 1986. Gillette was caught in the same takeover fever that swallowed up several large companies: Bendix, Getty Oil, General Foods and Republic Steel.

Gillette's management and directors were well aware from the general business literature (the *Wall Street Journal, Fortune, Business Week, Forbes* and so forth) that Gillette was a likely target, even though it was becoming clear that not all takeovers were the financial successes that an acquirer usually, at least initially, claimed.

Some directors possessed firsthand experience from other companies on whose boards they were members. For example, Larry Fouraker was a member of R.H. Macy's board before its leveraged buyout in the mid-1980s. Richard Pivirotto had been chairman of the board of directors of the Associated Dry Goods Corporation from 1976 to February 1981 and continued to serve as its director. These stores, including Lord and Taylor, became involved in the takeover frenzy. Additionally, Joe Sisco's wife, Jean Sisco, was a director of the Carter, Hawley and Hale stores until 1986 when they were taken over. The Federated Department Stores and Allied Stores were bought in 1988 with excessive debt by Robert Campeau. Herbert Jacobi in 1985 was a general manager of the British Midland Bank, whose Crocker National Bank in San Francisco was bought in 1986 by Wells Fargo. Herb, for a short period of time, had to visit San Francisco regularly in order to smooth this transition. Talk about takeovers was common among the directors just prior to a formal board meeting of Gillette.

My files contain a newspaper clip dated as early as 1980 in which Gillette was mentioned as a candidate for a takeover bid from Seagram Company, which had received $2.3 billion from its sale of U.S. oil and gas properties to Sun Company.[1] Clearly, although no specific bidder for Gillette surfaced until November 1986, the Board, at least at the end of 1985, acted as if eventually a bid would occur. For example, in November 1985 the Board was briefed, as it had infrequently been in the past, about the general takeover climate: the percentage of Gillette stock owned by institutions, recent Delaware Chancery Court decisions (the state in which Gillette was and is incorporated), company guidelines for directors to handle media and also detailed information about staggered boards and poison pills. Gillette adopted in 1986 a staggered twelve-person board; four directors were elected annually, each for three years. With that change, it would take a minimum of two years to change control of the board solely by shareholder voting. In late December 1985 Gillette's Board adopted a poison pill during a special telephone meeting, even though no specific bidder had surfaced. Management was nervous, and the Board acted.

POISON PILL

The aptly named *poison pill* is designed to make the price of a hostile takeover prohibitively expensive. If a set amount of the target company's stock is bought, commonly 20 percent, by a hostile acquirer, the sale triggers an issuance of rights to all shareholders other than the would-be acquirer to buy at half price, or even less, the target company's stock. This dilutes the value of its stock holdings for the acquirer. The increase in shares may make it prohibitively expensive to complete purchase of the target company. It also forces negotiation between the acquirer and the target's board of directors.

In the case of Gillette, as in many other companies, its December 30, 1985, poison pill gave all its shareholders but the acquirer the right to buy additional shares of stock at half price, when 20 percent or more of outstanding stock had been acquired by a hostile-takeover purchaser. The resulting increase in stock shares outstanding would make Gillette, as a target company, prohibitively expensive. Gillette's December 30 letter to shareholders stressed that its poison pill was ''to assure that all stockholders receive fair treatment and maximum value in the event of any proposed takeover of the Company. The distribution protects against unfair two-tier tender offers and other coercive tactics to gain control of the Company on inequitable terms. It also guards against improper self-dealing transactions which could arise if a takeover occurs.'' The aim was to give directors time to negotiate a price higher than an initial, unilaterally determined price. This line of argument appealed to the boards of many other companies. By 1988, between four hundred and five hundred companies had poison pills, a concept that was first introduced in 1982.

Evidence of the effect of a poison pill on a company's valuations, as shown by stock-market prices, varies, depending on the period of time used in the calculation. Should the period be measured from the time after a pill is adopted until a tender occurs or over a shorter period beginning when a pill is first used to forestall a takeover? The immediate post-adoption effect usually is a drop in stock price, but the long-run effect on a company's valuation can be favorable. The effect of a poison pill on the final outcome of a specific hostile tender is not predictable. Should that effect cover a period of time long enough to include company restructuring, which will affect earnings and stock price? The longer the period, the more confounding variables enter the calculation.

Often cited in opposition to enactment of poison pills is Michael Ryngaert, who analyzed a sample of 380 companies that adopted poison-pill defenses, 1982–1986. Ryngaert's mild conclusion was that ''on average, poison pill defenses have seemingly had only a modest effect on firm valuation.''[2] Ryngaert assumed that poison pills were adopted to protect managers. However, he states that:

The results for 293 nontargets analyzed in Table 3, do not support the managerial en-
trenchment hypothesis. I do not find any excess returns that are statistically significantly
different from zero.

. . . this result may indicate that pill defenses are not very important unless the firm
already has a substantial expectation of a control premium built into its price. Conversely,
the pill adoption may signify that the firm is a takeover candidate and this new information may lessen the impact of the pill, itself.[3]

Gillette fitted the latter speculation, I believe. Gillette also fit the description
of the typical firm described in the economic literature as one that adopts a
poison pill: low ownership by management and directors (in the case of Gillette,
less than 1.5 percent) and having a staggered board in force.

Although Ryngaert's article involves a tremendous amount of research work,
much of it done while he worked at the Securities and Exchange Commission
(SEC), it does not answer the question of what happens when a board of directors lets a poison pill actually take effect—rather than redeeming it, as Gillette
did, for the nominal sum of 1 cent a share, thus in effect nullifying it. To my
knowledge, until at least the end of 1988 and probably much later a poison pill
has not been allowed to become effective. The literature has a reference to a
preferred stock plan of two relatively unknown companies, Bell & Howell and
Enstar, where a special form of the pill was allowed to proceed.[4] However, a
Wall Street Journal tax note of October 26, 1988, states in a brief, page-one
reference to income tax and poison-pill rights that "the issue of what happens
if a right is exercised (*none ever has been*)" makes clear that to the paper's
knowledge a poison pill had not been put into effect by late 1988.[5]

Legal battles over whether poison pills protect shareholders or merely deter
potential hostile takeovers and help entrenched management were common in
the 1980s. The percentage ownership of all voting common stock outstanding
by institutions, as compared to individual owners, increased during the 1980s,
when assets of public and corporate pension funds grew rapidly. Institutional
investors seeking to increase their short-run or immediate gains may try to dis-
mantle takeover defenses when they are board-enacted, without shareholder approval. With the marked increase in institutional ownership of stocks,
shareholder sentiment against poison pills has increased. In 1991 a survey by
the Investor Responsibility Research Center (IRRC) of Washington, D.C., found
that 57 percent of their institutional respondents, including managers of large
pension funds and investment, college and foundation managers generally op-
pose company-proposed poison-pill plans. However, as in the case of Gillette,
these plans are usually not specifically voted on by the shareholders; but where
they have been voted on by shareholders, to "IRRC's knowledge, all of these
proposals have passed."[6]

Defenders of poison pills state that the Delaware Supreme Court upheld their
viability in *Moran v Household International Corporation*, 1984. Further, New
York's Georgeson and Company's proxy lawyers in their March 31, 1988, study

state that among 48 target companies, the 27 companies (January 1, 1986–
October 19, 1987) with poison pills had final offers averaging 78.5 percent
higher than their stock price before a takeover attempt, while the 21 companies
without a poison pill had offers showing only a 56.7 percent gain.[7] But this
Georgeson report was criticized because it analyzed only those companies with
poison pills that were actually takeover targets. Georgeson did a second study
that analyzed a random sample of all companies with poison pills, whether
publicly known takeover targets or not and matched to nonpill controls of com-
parable-size companies operating in the same industry and in the same time
period, and compared their changes in shareholder value. They found no negative statistical effects from poison pills. ''The study shows that poison pills do
not prevent takeovers nor do they diminish the value of a company's stock . . .
stocks of companies with poison pills outperformed companies without poison
pills'' and thus had benefited their shareholders at the end of 21 months, September 1987.[8] The finding that the stock of companies with a pill appreciated
more, 54.8 percent as compared to 45.2 percent for those without,[9] may reflect
the effect of variables other than the poison pill over the time period of the
study, which was longer than Ryngaert's study, which had covered only six
months. Among the ten companies where a deal occurred, there was a 44 percent
differential in favor of companies with poison pills. And even among the 90
without a deal, there was a 5.8 percent average differential that favored the
poison-pill company. This is not complete statistical proof that poison pills, on
average, helped companies during the turbulent period of the late 1980s, primarily because there was probably self-selection by undervalued companies to
adopt a pill. Although this factor has not been corrected for, the data are sug-
gestive.

Critics also argue that such studies do not take into account that shareholders
may lose because a poison pill may deter some takeovers from ever being initiated. Deterrence is a major goal of a poison pill. However, there are by their
nature no data on deterred takeovers. Whether the deterred takeovers would in
sum have been beneficial is therefore unknown.

The often-quoted Securities and Exchange Commission (SEC) study that
found that stock prices fell 1 percent, on average, within 48 hours of adoption
of a poison pill also does not prove that a poison pill, per se, is detrimental to
the shareholder.[10] The pill's impact has to be measured over a longer period of
time and in actual takeover situations. Adoption of a poison pill, I believe, does
increase the possibility of defeating takeover attempts, because it lengthens the
time for response. A poison pill centers decisions onto the directors. Only the
directors can repeal the rights as issued or can vote to redeem them at a nominal
cost. Adding these matters to the necessary decisions of whether to sell the
company and at what price does create delay. The board has more time to seek
other buyers in order to negotiate a higher price. However, since a cash tender
was made for Gillette, a benefit of more time was minimal. A ''sweep of the
street,'' the purchase of a majority of shares, is always possible with a cash

tender, and while a target company delays its decisions the company could be sold.

Professor Michael Jensen and others have argued against poison pills and other deterrents to takeovers such as staggered boards on the general ground that they weaken pressure on management to become more efficient in managing a company's resources. Where several antitakeover defenses have been adopted, as in the case of Gillette, it is very hard to isolate the effect of any specific defense. Moreover, the expressed intention of a hostile acquirer to take over may itself spur a company to reassess, reduce excess and restructure to focus on winning strategies. These are also the aims that hostile takeovers strive to accomplish.

As Gillette learned, a poison pill may not prevent a cash tender but it will exert pressure on the would-be acquirer, giving the target company some time to negotiate. Its benefits are not dependent on the exercise of the pill but rather on the exercise of the threat of it. Martin Lipton, who is usually credited with originating the poison pill, stated in 1988 that it '' 'was not designed to, and does not, alleviate' the pressure on target companies brought about by today's most common takeover threat: the cash tender offer made directly to shareholders for all of a company's stock.''[11] With this I concur. Shareholders sell stock without consulting the board.

JUNK BONDS

The creation of a sizeable market for junk bonds available to finance takeovers made it possible for Ronald Perelman to envision taking over Gillette, a company that was in 1986 two to three times the size of the would-be acquirer's Revlon. *Junk bonds* are bonds issued by corporations judged by the two chief credit-rating agencies, Moody's and Standard & Poor's, to have a high probability of not repaying their loans. A bond is a loan. Bonds can be arrayed by degree of risk from the safety of those issued by an asset-rich, Fortune 500 company to those of heavily indebted firms with little or even close to nonexistent assets whose high-return bonds are viewed by some people as wild gambles. Junk bonds have been defined by Michael Milken as "a debt instrument that trades more on the underlying credit risk of the company or the industry than on movements in interest rates. They have legal characteristics of debt, but if things go bad you're generally the first creditor to take on the rights of an equity owner.''[12] Junk bonds make capital readily available to people who want to buy other people's businesses but who do not have enough money of their own to do so. Would-be acquirers are willing to pay a high price for the availability of money; the price is the interest rate on the funds they borrow. The money is loaned because the high yield possible offsets the high risk of nonpayment.

Some persons dealing in junk bonds view them not as investments but as lotteries. But not all junk bonds are even close to being wild gambles throughout their lives. Successful turnarounds do occur. In early 1991 Warren Buffett invested $440 million in high-yield bonds of RJR Nabisco and in two weeks had already gained $175 million,[13] or a 40 percent return. Under the astute management of Louis Gerstner from American Express, RJR Nabisco was in 1991 being turned around, although it still had a double-B investment rating. The book that tells the tale of the past management's excesses, *Barbarians at the Gate*, might well have been entitled "Barbarians *within* the Gate."

Warren Buffett states his pros and cons in making a judgment call on whether to buy junk bonds in his 1990 letter to Berkshire Hathaway's shareholders.

In the case of RJR Nabisco, we feel the Company's credit is considerably better than was generally perceived for a while and that the yield we receive, as well as the potential for capital gain, more than compensates for the risk we incur (though that is far from nil). RJR has made asset sales at favorable prices, has added major amounts of equity, and in general is being run well.

However, as we survey the field, most low-grade bonds still look unattractive. The handiwork of the Wall Street of the 1980s is even worse than we had thought: Many important businesses have been mortally wounded. We will, though, keep looking for opportunities as the junk market continues to unravel.[14]

Buffett had not changed his 1985 opinion: "Before it's all over, junk bonds will live up to their name."[15]

The growth in junk bonds went hand-in-hand with the deregulation of the savings and loan banks (S & Ls) that were caught in the squeeze between thin, low-interest-rate returns from the fixed-income home mortgages they held and the competitive higher interest rates that they had to pay out on savings or lose those deposits to competitors. Some S & Ls invested in the high-interest-yielding junk bonds that would, if all went well, provide them with far more money than would the lower interest rates on their more customary holdings of home mortgages. Money to buy junk bonds was readily available.

In 1977 Drexel made its first new issue of junk bonds, and increasingly Drexel provided through sales of junk bonds the standby credit frequently used to finance a hostile takeover. In 1985 Drexel Burnham Lambert junk bonds financed, among others, Carl Icahn's purchase of TWA, James Goldsmith's purchase of Crown Zellerbach and T. Boone Pickens' purchase of Unocal. In 1986 the continuing development of the junk-bond financial markets by Drexel made it possible for Ronald Perelman (initially as MacAndrews & Forbes), KKR and others to borrow large amounts of cash, which they could then use to purchase large blocks of shares of large companies. These firms paid back a substantial part of their new heavy debt from gains realized when they sold parts of the new acquisition, sometimes to the experienced managers of the same parts of the business they had bought. Perelman, KKR and others would then concentrate on the core business left after the sell-offs and develop its cash flow. For example, in 1985 Perelman bought Revlon for $2.3 billion and sold off its health-care, noncosmetic business for $2.06 billion.[16] Perelman then tried to build up Revlon's remaining core cosmetic lines with heavy advertising and new acquisitions.

However, as Chapter 2 relates, Perelman did not succeed in acquiring Gillette's cosmetics and toiletries lines, whose sales in 1986 were 30 percent of total Gillette sales of $2.8 billion and yielded only 16 percent of Gillette's profits.[17] It is not known whether Perelman, in order to fashion a fit with Revlon, would have expanded Gillette's cosmetics lines at the expense of the research and development for razors and blades or would have sold off Braun. Would Perelman have sought with the same zeal as Gillette management did the technological secret of how to mass-produce at low unit cost its new concept of a razor and blade? By 1991 Gillette's sales of toiletries and cosmetics were only 20 percent of its total of $4.7 billion sales and generated an even lesser share of profits, only 13 percent of the total of $862 million. Except for Jafra, which had spread to 24 countries, cosmetics, with their lower profit margins, were not envisaged by the board or management as a growing part of Gillette. Perelman, however, saw the product lines of Gillette's cosmetics and Oral-B toothbrushes worldwide as dovetailing with sales of Revlon's cosmetics. Without Gillette's international marketing advantage, Perelman in early 1991 found it necessary to sell Revlon's Max Factor cosmetic line and its German beauty-aids subsidiary, Betrix, to Procter & Gamble for $1.14 billion. The proceeds were reported to be needed to pay off some of his $800 million bridge loans, due by 1992, which had been floated to pay for the Revlon purchase in 1985.[18]

Junk bonds can be viewed as a form of equity with very high risk and potentially very high equity returns. However, because they are called bonds, the interest paid for the loan of the capital is deductible as a business expense before paying the U.S. corporate income tax. The dividends paid for use of equity capital cannot be expensed and are also taxed as income to the recipient. This makes the takeover market financed by junk bonds more viable in the United States than in most other countries, where accounting rules differ and taxation of dividends may not exist. When an American company acquires another American company, the value of the latter's *good will* buried in its trade names must be amortized against income and not against shareholders' equity, as is required in some countries. The latter procedure lowers the after-tax selling price of an American company to some foreign buyers below the after-tax price available to an American buyer.

The easy availability of credit via junk bonds helped to create excessive zeal for takeovers and a climate in some circles that favored debt over equity financing. Rarely discussed in the financial pages of newspapers was that nonpayment of interest on bonds could force a company into receivership and bankruptcy, while reducing or not paying dividends on common stock, while regrettable, does not provoke such dire consequences.

Warren Buffett of Berkshire Hathaway, considered by *Forbes* to be the richest man in the United States in 1993, spoke at a November 1985 Columbia Law

School symposium on hostile takeovers. His comments on the behavior of CEOs in spending other people's money are very interesting and jibe with my experience. In commenting about gifts to charitable causes he describes an individual who raises money for a charity as follows. "In the last five years he's raised about 8 million dollars. He's raised it from 60 corporations . . . in the process of raising this 8 million dollars from 60 corporations from people who nod and say that's a marvelous idea, its prosocial, etc., not one CEO has reached in his pocket and pulled out 10 bucks of his own to give to this marvelous charity. They've given 8 million dollars collectively of other people's money. And so far he's yet to get his first 10-dollar bill."[19] Buffett comments further that you will find similar behavior by CEOs when they are purchasing corporate aircraft and comments, "I think they probably maybe even eat a little differently when they're eating on the company . . . the equation of the CEO is frequently very different from the shareholders' equation. . . . my equation might be a little different if I could rationalize some way to buy that with somebody else's money. If I get the ego satisfaction and the check is written on someone else's bank account—say, the shareholders'—the equation can change."[20] With some company directors thinking along these lines, it is obvious that many would be bothered by junk-bond financing.

Junk-bond issues peaked in 1986 at $40.8 billion. As James Van Horne, a Stanford University professor of finance, was quoted as saying, "By 1986, 'virtually any dumb deal could get done.' "[21] It is this perception rather than that academic research found positive efficiency gains in many LBOs and takeovers that dominated corporate board thinking in November 1986.

STOCK PRICE

A hostile takeover attempt, whether successful or not, forces directors of corporations to concentrate on the shareholders' dominant interests as owners. But the perception of that interest may be unclear as between the short run and long run. New institutional holders of stock may want an immediate price rise, but many long-term individual holders have invested for the long run. Their preference is for a steady long-run price rise stemming from later large gains in profits. Of course, they additionally welcome any immediate increase in the stock price.

There is not usually a precise trade-off ratio of short-run against long-run gains. Insiders should be better able than outsiders to project long-run gains. Many new shareholders are attracted by the potential of immediate sizable profits from a company in play. In a takeover situation shareholders who hold are usually predicting that the stock price will rise even higher than the initial tender price. Some new holders act as arbitrageurs, buying stock at prices below the tender with hope of a quick gain as the tender is completed. Most of these arbitrageurs are institutional holders, whose cries are usually the loudest when a tender fails.

Among the individuals who hold stock as a permanent, long-run investment are those who bought earlier and at a lower price and who do not want to pay the large capital-gains taxes that would be imposed if they did sell. One such person at the April 21, 1988, Gillette shareholder's meeting in Andover, Massachusetts, stated not only that Gillette stock had been a better investment than a pension fund, and in fact he considered it his pension assurance, but also that selling would force him to pay a large capital-gains tax, which he did not want to pay.

Financial economists believe that selling and buying stock is always dependent on a rational decision made after comparing the average or mean returns for a given risk. Individuals who do not wish to take a high risk probably buy into mutual funds, where an "expert" makes decisions for them. Although this may be generally true, not all individual investors are alike. Some never invest in mutual funds, as they believe that they have better judgment on individual companies and can provide their own diversification. The computer age has widened the knowledge of many individual investors, and there are some who view buying and selling stocks as a game to win, not as a substitute for a pension.

The ownership of a company's stock usually shifts rapidly once a takeover is announced as arbitrageurs and institutions buy in. This intensifies a possible conflict between short-run and long-term gains. The potential of the latter may be clearer to insiders such as directors, which may inspire them to adopt defensive measures such as staggered boards and poison pills. Some company directors are irked because companies are buying other companies not with their own money but with, as the 1990 off-Broadway play title so aptly states, *Other People's Money*. Some directors merely shrug, because debt financing has become so commonplace.

A surge in the price of stock is common in most takeover situations. More units are demanded at a given price as arbitrageurs enter hoping to make a quick gain from buying and then reselling at a higher price. The demand curve for the stock shifts up and to the right.

The Chicago school of economists believes that tender offers are a good thing because they result in ownership shifts and increased pressure to perform on management, who then reallocate corporate resources for their highest returns, which maximizes the gross national product from existing resources. The takeover premium in stock price is believed to reflect potential gains in efficiency from acquirer innovation and also a gain from more information.

Others believe that some people will pay a higher price for the enhanced prestige that comes from owning a larger company. This might be called a *hubris* concept. It is ego-boosting to be known as the chairman of The Gillette Company. Sidak and Woodward claim that "if the hubris hypothesis were correct," as I believe in part it was for Ron Perelman in the case of Gillette, "then some takeover premiums would be, after nontrivial transactions costs [that is, when payments to investment and legal advisors have been deducted], merely wealth transfers from the bidder's shareholders to the target's shareholders."[22]

The belief that hostile takeovers are beneficial to society because they dislodge incompetent managers has been supported by Michael Jensen, a Harvard Business School professor, who defined *free cash flow* as follows: "cash flow in excess of that required to fund all of a firm's projects that have positive net present values when discounted at the relevant cost of capital."[23]

Many persons, including Jensen, want such excess free cash flow paid out to shareholders in dividends. Although dividends are the major form of distribution of equity returns, they fell from 80 percent of cash distributions overall in 1977 to 40 percent in 1987. Cash distribution to shareholders via acquisitions and share repurchases increased.[24] As Chapter 3 documents, Gillette followed a similar pattern.

Gillette used some of its sizeable free cash flow to purchase many small companies, well aware that this use of cash for acquisitions would not be subject to the scrutiny of the capital markets that occurs when a new firm goes public. Chapter 3 documents some of the purchases made by Gillette. It is interesting to me, as a past director, that potential acquisitions were never presented to the Board as possible hostile takeovers. For example, the purchase of Waterman Pen in France was presented as "accommodating" the woman who inherited the company, Francine Gomez, because she was, management claimed, "more interested in French politics than she was in making money." A *New York Times* magazine article described her as a "strong-willed chief executive and board chairman who took over her family's floundering company and led it to a 65 percent share of the French market in nondisposable pens. Always outspoken and occasionally imperious, Mme. Gomez is accustomed to having her own way"[25] and ran Waterman as "a fashion boutique." Mrs. Gomez resigned in December 1988 in reported disagreement with Gillette management on how best to market the Waterman pen.[26]

The purchase of Oral-B toothbrushes was presented as a response to a cash shortage of the owner company, Cooper Laboratories. As far as I can recollect, in these and other cases, such as Liquid Paper, Frostline and other Gillette acquisitions, whether the target was willing or not willing to sell was not discussed. It was just assumed that they were all willing to sell, and, of course, one can argue that "Everyone has his price." However, in the case of Gillette as a target, a price at which Gillette was willing to sell was never offered.

I believe that Michael Jensen was correct in thinking that managers have incentives to expand a firm beyond the size that may maximize shareholder wealth. The larger a company, the higher the pay for management, and an expanding company does have more jobs into which to promote middle managers than if it were shrinking. I did not then nor do I now, attribute this concept to Jensen; rather, I attribute it to the intellectual exchange within an international business roundtable to which I belonged that included several executives of well-known large Japanese firms. Their emphasis on long-term profits and incremental change to gain profits made a contrasting counterpoint to the American businessmen I knew, not all necessarily at Gillette, who tend to emphasize short-run profits, often from money transactions, rather than gains derived from production and selling. To my mind, Gillette seemed closer to the Japanese model than to the U.S. short-run model. At times, Gillette investments may have stemmed more from a desire to increase the size of the Company than immediately to increase profits. There was at Gillette a belief among some top management that growth was a good thing, and that company growth would eventually pay off in higher profits.

Gillette did not use all of its cash flow to purchase small companies; it also spent sizable amounts on plant and equipment, research and development and payment of dividends that were maintained at just under 30 percent of cash from operations during this time period. For the period 1983–1988 there was a slight, continuous dollar rise in dividends from $71 million in 1983 to $86 million in 1986 and to $95 million in 1988, but as a percentage of all uses, dividends fell from 47 percent in 1983 to 20.3 percent in 1988. The largest use of cash in that period was not for acquisitions, except in 1984 when Oral-B was bought, but for spending on plant and equipment; acquisitions of oil and gas investments were close behind. The latter were driven by fear of higher prices of this resource vital to the manufacture of hard plastics.

Based at the Hoover Institution, where several Chicago-trained economists also work, I was well aware of the arguments that favor hostile takeovers. During the late 1980s I found myself not infrequently discussing with Nobel Prize–winner George Stigler, whose office at the Hoover Institution was then close to mine, whether it is acceptable to an economist for a company to approve greenmail payment for any reason. Although initially George Stigler, whom I greatly respect, did not budge from his resolve against a company paying greenmail, eventually the fairly steady price rise of Gillette stock after November 1986, and possibly my arguments, resulted in his agreeing that special circumstances could support a company repurchase of its shares from a preselected seller at a higher-than-market price. Stigler bought 100 shares of Gillette stock so that he would watch the company more closely and possibly also make money. It greatly saddened me when George Stigler unexpectedly died in December of 1991 and I lost my friend and best critic.

The Chicago school believes that in competitive, efficient markets with perfect information, which never in actuality exists, that the market price of a stock reflects its long-run, intrinsic value. They also assume that both the supply and the demand for a common stock are *perfectly price-elastic* and that heavy buying per se does not necessarily raise a prevailing market stock price. Rather, a price rise signals new information, and the additional information triggers the rise in price.

Whether or not the early price rise after a takeover announcement stems from anticipated increased efficiency and higher profits or from the additional information about the company made available or from a perceived inevitability of a price gain from speculator involvement during any takeover attempt, whether completed or not, the stock price does rise. An acquirer that makes a tender offer must offer a price at least somewhat higher than market. The question is how much higher and what determines the excess. If the tender is too low, a large percentage of owners may continue to hold and wait for a higher price. As ownership shifts to institutions and away from individuals, the pace of trading usually quickens.

When arbitrageurs sensing price gains and profits enter the market, they increase demand, and the number of shares traded soar. Arbitrageurs usually represent investment institutions but may also be individuals trading for themselves. The increasing percentage of shares held by institutions, such as mutual and pension funds, may mean that there is a quicker buy-and-sell reaction time to new information. Their business is to obtain knowledge, and they do so through electronic means. Increasingly, individual owners also use personal computers and electronic communications. However, individual investors do not have the time, except in rare instances, to learn the multiple activities of a firm. It can be asked whether even all corporate directors have the time for acquiring detailed knowledge of a large multinational, especially when its products are high-tech. It is true that managements answer directors' questions, but managements rarely offer detrimental detailed information until it is specifically asked for. The director must know the correct questions to elicit the information wanted.

Every investor always seeks the highest possible after-tax return from a given amount of investment dollars. For some investors, the required payment of capital-gains taxes can be a dominant factor, which makes them not act as quickly to sell in a price rise. All holders do not wish to sell and be liable for taxes at a takeover's timing. Some older individuals buy common stock that pays dividends and wish to hold the stock virtually as a form of pension. They may be less informed than institutional investors about alternative investments.

For all investors to be willing to pay the same price for an anticipated return on all stocks with a given degree of risk would require investors frequently to shift stocks held, to have no company loyalty and to hold identical individual tax positions and assessments of each stock's long-run valuation. But the quality of information held by shareholders varies. Two stocks currently each yielding 6 percent may not be perceived as perfect substitutes for each other. Investors perceive differences among companies: Expectations of future gains may differ, judgment about products differ, assessment of geographical dispersion of sales among countries and perceived management style differ and so do perceptions of alternative investments in small or large ways. Perception of risk and individuals' degrees of risk-aversion also reflect different personality traits among individuals.

At times, it is claimed by would-be acquirers that a target company's stock price is too low. Indeed, both Ron Perelman and later Coniston Partners stated this about Gillette's stock at different times in the press. Consider also the 1985 remark of that highly successful investor Warren Buffett: ''Over a good many . . . of the past 10 years, the very best managed companies I know of have very frequently sold in the market at substantial discounts from what they were worth that day on a negotiated basis."[27] In his 1990 Berkshire Hathaway Report, Buffett refers to three different prices of a Company's stock. "In 1989 intrinsic value grew less than did book value, which was up 44%, while the market price rose 85%; in 1990 book value and intrinsic value increased by a small amount, while the market price fell 23%."[28] Market value changes constantly, and buyers believe that they buy at a low market price compared to the long-run intrinsic value of the stock and that, therefore, the price will rise over time. For example, Warren Buffett stated that he accumulates on the open market a large number of shares—for example, 9.8 percent of Wells Fargo & Co. common[29]—when the market price appears undervalued to him.

There are economists who believe that stock prices are often wrong, that they do not always reflect the intrinsic value of a company. The theories of economist Mordecai Kurz (of Stanford University) have been described in a recent article as follows:

Kurz shows that most of the time equity prices do not correctly reflect all the information about companies. For Kurz, new data aren't unambiguous facts fed into a mechanical market. They are more like concrete clues in an ongoing mystery. As more information appears, the meaning of the clue can change, and investors can adjust their outlook accordingly. Kurz replaces the idea of rational expectations [Chicago School] with that of rational beliefs. This boils down to the idea that investors price stocks not strictly on the basis of new information but also on how well they understand that information. And that depends on how well they comprehend the economic structure of a world that Kurz emphasizes is changing all the time.[30]

To me, this describes the situation for many stocks, but especially the Gillette stock during the period when the Sensor was being developed. It is also interesting to me, as one who has not kept up with the highly theoretical work (mostly mathematical equations) of Kurz, that he uses the same argument that I have used. Some individuals do beat the market, and Warren Buffett is one of his major examples. In Terence P. Paré's 1995 article in *Fortune*, "Yes, you can beat the market," it is shown over time that Buffett/Munger have substantially beat the market by gains of 31 percent, compared to the S&P 500 gain of 14 percent, from 1983 through 1994. Paré also selects two other persons who have substantially beaten the market over this time period: Walter Schloss, who runs a limited partnership, and Bill Ruane, head of Sequoia Fund.

For a would-be acquirer to say that the market price of a target stock is too low implies that she or he has information not available to others that makes the acquirer believe that the stock is underpriced. In November 1986 the directors of Gillette and, as far as I know, the Company's top management did not know how to mass-produce, at a low enough unit cost to make it competitive, the spring-mounted razor blade representing the new concept that became the Sensor. The precise date when the specific process became feasible I do not know. Top management does not wish to pin down the precise date. It is probable that the knowledge that Gillette knew how to mass-produce the Sensor at a competitively low unit price was known to many outsiders by March 1988. "The company began working on the process to produce it as early as 1984, making a heavy upfront investment in engineering, prototyping and pilot lines."[31] The company's 1988 Annual Report was confident. In October 1989 the successful low-cost production of the Sensor was formally announced, but this date seems far too late for the first knowledge that it would be successful. The advertisement campaign had been launched in December 1988 with "a $75 million ad campaign which depicts shaving as an emotional rite of passage for men. This entire campaign with the tagline of 'Gillette, the best a man can get' " was a precursor of the Sensor launch and was referred to in a May 26, 1989, analyst sheet with the comment that "the expected margin [of] improvement should be particularly significant . . . as an inordinate amount of advertising expenditures for the product is being done in advance."[32] With a hundred thousand consumers rating the Sensor in 1988, how secret could its successful development have been in late 1986?

INDUSTRIAL ESPIONAGE(?)

At Gillette's shave-testing lab in South Boston, employees came to work unshaven each day and tested the Sensor "throughout its development cycle, going back eight or nine years."[33] This places in the early 1980s widespread knowledge of the Sensor's development among employees. Later, in the same interview with Derwyn Phillips, in 1986, executive vice president in charge of Gillette North America, agreed with an interlocutor's question that "product development cycles are generally too lengthy in U.S. corporations."[34] (Phillips, along with John Symons, who late in 1987 became president of the North Atlantic shaving group, retired, each at age 60, in 1990.)

I am not aware of printed references to the precise date of the attainment of the necessary low unit cost of manufacturing for the Sensor prior to its announcement date, but industrial spies, would-be takeover experts and many others could easily have learned of it earlier. For at least one outsider who did and paid for extensive research on the Company, that is, Ronald Perelman, to have known early seems not unlikely. After the repurchase of shares in November 1986, no new acquirers surfaced until the Coniston Partners in the spring of 1988. If no new buyer thought it profitable to take over Gillette for almost two years, then detailed private information may have been very closely held at the end of 1986. If Ronald Perelman did not have this information, why did he persist, despite a signed ten-year standstill agreement, in trying twice more, in June 1987 and August 1987, to buy Gillette? Was it solely for reasons of perceived synergy among existing products, the large cash flow and an attempt to purchase respectability? We may never know the answer. But the sharp, overall stock-market fall in October 1987 did end Perelman's attempts.

Surrounded as I was at Stanford University's Hoover Institution primarily by

Chicago-school economists, it was not until somewhat later that I became aware of an economic literature that disputed Jensen's theories that economic takeovers are almost invariably desirable because they allocate resources to better ends. Ravenscraft and Scherer,[35] using data dating from 1974 to 1977 (apparently available only for this short period), estimated that takeovers created an average loss, not a gain, to manufacturing output of about $3 billion. Further, professors Lawrence Summers and Andrei Shleifer[36] wrote that it was the employees, bond-holders and others with stakes in a company who lost when a takeover occurred. Takeovers may affect unfavorably older employees who under the usual implicit labor contract had been underpaid in their younger years. Older workers, especially, whose wages may over their lifetime exceed their marginal product, that is, what they contribute to the firm, might be laid off in a hostile takeover and then never make up for the lower-than-marginal-product wages paid them in their youth. Golden parachutes protect the higher-paid employees in most takeovers, even with the SEC's limit of three times the annual salary. Jensen argues that efficiency in a company improves when there is a threat that someone will buy it. It may be unknown whether the buyer would invest capital or retained earnings as the target company would have invested prior to a takeover. Certainly in the case of Gillette, the question can be raised whether Perelman would have invested in the development of the Sensor to the degree that Gillette management did.

Supporting my unproven theory that there probably was limited early outside knowledge of the development of the Sensor are other cases of industrial espionage. Gillette itself is no stranger to industrial espionage. Very early its patent was under attack as others, for example, the Gem Cutlery Company, also began marketing a double-edged blade. Charges of stealing patent rights were made very early, as by Julius Bueno de Mesquita of Gem Cutlery, an older relative of a colleague of mine.

Kenneth A. Clow, who developed Gillette's worldwide security operations, said in 1988 that Gillette has engaged as many as fifty different investigators in one year:

One particularly memorable scam against Gillette surfaced in the spring of 1981. Gillette started receiving complaints from small businesses that they had been promised prizes if they ordered Paper Mate pens. While the ordered pens were delivered, and paid for c.o.d., no prizes were included. And to add insult to injury, the pens didn't work. . . .

Gillette launched an investigation in the summer of 1981, hiring outside investigators who eventually infiltrated the companies [who bought poorly made imitations of Paper Mate pens]. . . .

By October, the U.S. Postal Service, the Internal Revenue Service, the Federal Bureau of Investigation and local police, using Gillette's information, arrested more than 300 people at three locations in one morning to shut down the scam. . . .

Fighting counterfeiters is a constant battle at Gillette, especially counterfeiters of Gillette razor blades. "You stop one and there's another," Mr. Clow laments.[37]

At one time in Colombia,

the Colombian market was flooded with U.S.-manufactured Write Bros. Paper Mate pens being sold at prices below those for the Colombian-made product.

Gillette's investigation uncovered the reason: Drug dealers were laundering their money by buying the Write Bros. Paper Mate pens from office supply houses in the United States and sending them to Panama as payment in kind for Colombian marijuana.

"We found out who was doing it, gave the information to the Colombian authorities and they shut it down," Mr. Clow said.

By that time, normal sales fell from $65 million to $70 million to an annual volume of $20 million in sales and $200,000 in profits [down from $6 million]. But when the drug dealers were stopped, sales immediately shot back up to the normal volume, as did profits.[38]

Obviously, Gillette's products are fair game for industrial espionage. The article from which these quotes are taken was published at the time of the Coniston proxy fight.

It was reported that in the early 1980s "some Gillette employees in England [tried] to sell a Gillette process to Wilkinson Sword Group. Not interested in industrial espionage, Wilkinson Sword notified Gillette and their joint efforts sent the people to jail."[39]

Reverse engineering, of course, makes it easier to imitate already marketed products. It is much more difficult to obtain knowledge about yet-to-be marketed products. Competitors and takeover professionals may hire industrial spies, but the company's own employees, whether disgruntled or overenthusiastic, may also carelessly reveal valuable industrial secrets.

Often reported during my twelve years on the board were sizeable sales of imitations of Gillette products; for example, of fake cloisonné Dupont pens being sold in Hong Kong and elsewhere around the world. And I encountered, rather predictably, imitation Braun products in Hong Kong. I had gone to the Far East during the late 1980s without an electric hair curler but had taken with me a Braun cartridge-style curling brush, which had been seized by the customs office of the People's Republic of China because they viewed it as dangerous. The cartridge contained butane gas and was actually very safe. I replaced it with an imitation Braun curler in Hong Kong, where imitations, but not the real thing, were readily available in the open-air market.

Other imitations of Braun products were highly publicized. In 1983 the Plagiarius design award of the Busse Design Institute of West Germany was awarded to the Russian Mikromaschine for its copy of the Braun Sixtant hand shaver; and in 1984 the Plagiarius was awarded to the Chiau Huei Enterprises Company, a Taiwanese company, for its product, "Prince Dental a blatant copy of the Braun electric toothbrush."[40] The Plagiarius Award, a dubious accolade, was initiated by Rido Busse, who founded Busse Design Ulm Company and today the Plagiarius award is officially recognized by the German government.[41]

Obviously, it is not far-fetched to believe that knowledge of how to manufacture Gillette products could be in the public domain even if this leakage is not known to the company.

Various articles[42] have discussed how Gillette, as one among several U.S. corporations, has continually collected intelligence on its competitors. Employees of government agencies such as the FBI and CIA have patiently combed library files to trace instances of industrial espionage that placed valuable information into unfriendly hands. They screen the readily available news clips services and the *Wall Street Transcript*, which discusses, by industry, company presentations to financial analysts and brokerage houses. Other printed sources range from the help-wanted advertisements in daily newspapers to highly sophisticated industry analyses by commercial firms and the U.S. government. Companies sometimes reveal their own plans. "For example, a while back [a] Gillette [employee] told a large Canadian account the date on which it planned to begin selling its Good News disposable razor in the U.S. The date was six months before Bic Corp. was scheduled to introduce its own disposable razor in America. The Canadian distributor promptly called Bic and told it about the impending product launch. Bic put on a crash program and was able to start selling its razor shortly after Gillette did."[43]

It seems to me that it would be impossible for a large company to spend about $200 million on a specific project and not have leaks and gossip, some clues dropped about what they were doing. The high number of people employed in the research and development of the Sensor makes it very probable that there was some careless discussion, whether in bars, during lunch, at trade shows or in some other settings.

Different people process fragmented information differently. Maybe Perelman saw the outside potential of the Sensor while others with just as much knowledge didn't. When in December 1992 and April 1994 I informally queried the current chairman of the board, Al Zeien, about the possibility of early knowledge obtained by either Perelman or Coniston, he understandably did not comment. I wish to stress that at no time have I discussed this hypothesis with management at Gillette.

As a director of a defense electronics company, Watkins-Johnson Company, since 1974, I was accustomed during the Cold War period to receiving regularly its *Security Newsletter* and a quarterly, *Employee Security Connection*. These stressed the importance of employee vigilance, detailed foreign-travel reporting requirements and other matters critical for a company that had to obtain federal security clearance for its top-level employees. From time to time these letters would report industrial spying cases. Also, living in Silicon Valley, I was well aware of Hitachi's attempt to buy IBM's secrets in 1982. Although this type of activity may be more common in the defense electronics and computer industries, consumer industries have also been involved in industrial spying. Among older documented cases is that of a Procter & Gamble employee offering a marketing plan for Crest toothpaste to Colgate-Palmolive Company in 1965 and a later attempt to sell the recipes of the Oakland-based Mother's Cake and Cookie Company to its rival firm Pepperidge Farm in 1981.[44]

INSIDER KNOWLEDGE

At a point of time, the market price of a share of common stock of any company may be perceived as undervalued or overvalued. Many people do not believe that this can be so if information is equally available to all parties. Stock dealing by insiders is prohibited during periods when confidential knowledge would give them a special advantage in stock trading. Disclosure of stock trades by insiders are required by the SEC shortly after they occur. The Securities and Exchange Commission (SEC) regulations Sections 16 a and b require monthly reporting to the SEC of the buying and selling of shares of stock by directors, officers and other insiders of a corporation, and Rule 14e-3 prohibits trading by insiders once a tender has begun. Insiders may not trade on any specific knowledge about the company that is not public knowledge. To avoid any perception of trading on nonpublic information Gillette always carefully advised when it was advisable for directors not to trade its stock.

But *insider trading*, or trading on inside information, has not always been clearly defined. As late as December 1994, it has been argued that insider trading is still not legally defined in precise terms.[45] Economist Henry Manne, the U.S. authority on this issue, continues to argue against laws that make insider trading illegal, on the grounds that they never can be very effective, as they are impossible to implement against a shareowner holding shares because of insider good news or deciding not to buy because of bad news. In these instances, no securities are trading and thus there is no transgression. Enforcement is difficult even against actual buying and selling of stock based on insider information. Professor Manne maintains that it is "a victimless crime, certainly so far as the trading partners of insiders are concerned. Yet in 1988 Congress increased criminal penalties and the civil liability of anyone trading 'contemporaneously' with an insider who had undisclosed information."[46] It can be argued that shareholders who are not trading with and who have not traded with an insider can be harmed by such trades. Large shifts among shareholders of takeover stocks before a potential buyer is announced raise public skepticism about who gains from having information not available to others.

Simply put, insider trading, I believe, occurs when a person has specific information that will affect the stock price and then acts in the securities markets, while other people do not have that information. This was the case, for example, when Nathan Rothschild made the family fortune when he obtained news of Wellington's victory at Waterloo a day ahead of the London financial markets and bought British government consols before their subsequent sharp price rise. In today's world of fax and cable television transmission, it is very unlikely that such an informational advantage about meaningful world events could be obtained early.

On the other hand, the top management and directors of a company could have inside information about specific events, such as the status of the development of new technology processes that could give them an informational advantage in selling and buying stock.

It has been argued that any individual with a good analytical mind who takes the time can come to know virtually as much as the insiders. A person who follows a company and brings a background from the social and physical sciences to have good judgments of how external developments can affect a company may be in a position to make sound forecasts. . . . So, developing knowledge expertise and making good forecasts about a company does not necessarily involve inside information.[47]

Could this reasoning be applied to Ron Perelman and to those who worked for him in developing knowledge about The Gillette Company?

Newspapers report on a regular basis trading by insiders. Critics dispute that a general insider knowledge yields an advantage in stock trading and point to how few individual insiders sell at a low or buy at a near-high as evidence. "A look at six of the largest insider sales reported to the Securities and Exchange Commission by top executives so far this year show that, in most cases, the executives would have been better off waiting to trim their holdings. In three cases, the executives lost out on hundreds of thousands of dollars of potential profits by selling shares too early.[48]

Insiders may sell for cash to meet their personal needs, and they may have to sell regardless of whether it is financially a good time to sell from the corporate point of view. They need money. Also different people make different assessments of identical data. Additionally, many insiders have received, as part of their earnings and as an incentive to do their job well, bargain-priced stock options that the Company issued when the stock price was much lower than the current market price. Reported large amounts of buying by insiders often reflect that they have exercised their options. A 1992 University of Michigan study of 8,000 insider trades made during 1975 through 1989 was reported to find that such trades "substantially outperformed the market."[49]

However, some insider trading does take place using selective specific information to make profits. Thus the SEC Rule 14e-3 makes it illegal for inside directors to trade when they have unique specific knowledge, as may occur during a struggle for corporate control or, more commonly, when an increase in dividends has been voted. Gillette's Board, as other company boards, was always very careful to announce a dividend increase on the news wire immediately after the Board voted, because the Company wished to avoid any possibility of a charge of insider trading. Information is a very valuable good, but how to define trading by insiders is difficult. At least one textbook points out, "Gray areas abound. A corporate raider has inside information about his own intentions as to his next target. Is he prohibited from trading before he has announced those intentions, when he knows the announcement will drive up target stock price?"[50]

Sensitive reading of widely available company annual reports and the SEC-required 10-Ks yields close to insider knowledge to perceptive outsiders. The ability to fit individual company data into economic and industry trends and to project earnings on more than a specific company's past performance helps create the "genius" investor such as, for example, a Peter Lynch, who for many years outperformed the market with Fidelity Magellan. Should the market reward persons who are more perceptive in analyzing whatever information is out there about a given company and its economic environment?

NOTES

1. Leonard Anderson, "Seagram to Go Slowly on Any Purchase Using $2.3 Billion from Properties Sale," *Wall Street Journal*, September 16, 1980, p. 2.

2. Michael Ryngaert, "The Effect of Poison Pill Securities on Shareholder Wealth," *Journal of Financial Economics* vol. 20 (1988), p. 377.

3. Ibid., pp. 392–393.

4. Paul H. Malatesta and Ralph A. Walkling, "Poison Pill Securities: Stockholder Wealth, Profitability, and Ownership Structure," *Journal of Financial Economics* vol. 20 (January/March 1988), p. 351.

5. "Tax Report: A Special Summary and Forecast of Federal and State Tax Developments," *Wall Street Journal*, October 26, 1988, p. 1.

6. Ann Yerger and Elizabeth Lightfoot, "Voting by Institutional Investors on Corporate Governance Issues," Investor Responsibility Research Center, Corporate Governance Service (IRRC), Washington, D.C., December 1991, p. 33.

7. Elliott D. Lee, "Heard on the Street: 'Poison Pills' Benefit Shareholders by Forcing Raiders to Pay More for Targets, Study Says," *Wall Street Journal*, March 31, 1988, p. 53; and *Poison Pill Impact Study I*, Georgeson and Company Inc., March 31, 1988, preface.

8. Richard A. Wines, Poison Pill Impact Study II, Georgeson and Company Inc., October 31, 1988, [p. 1] unpaged.

9. Ibid. [p. 12] unpaged.

10. Michael Ryngaert, "The Effects of Poison Pills on the Wealth of Shareholders," Securities and Exchange Commission Staff Paper, September 5, 1985, pp. 36–37.

11. Tim Metz, "Heard on the Street: Promoter of the Poison Pill Prescribes Stronger Remedy," *Wall Street Journal*, December 1, 1988, p. C1.

12. Michael Milken, as told to James W. Michaels and Phyllis Berman, "My Story—Michael Milken," *Forbes*, March 16, 1992, p. 83.

13. Jennifer Reese, "News/Trends: Buffett Buys Junk," *Fortune*, April 22, 1991, p. 14.

14. *Berkshire Hathaway Inc. Annual Report*, 1990, p. 18.

15. John C. Coffee, Jr., Louis Lowenstein, and Susan Rose-Ackerman (eds.), *Knights, Raiders, and Targets: The Impact of the Hostile Takeover* (New York: Oxford University Press, 1988), p. 17.

16. Andrei Shleifer and Robert W. Vishny, "The Takeover Wave of the 1980s," *Science* vol. 249, no. 4970 (August 17, 1990), pp. 746–747.

17. *Annual Report 1990* (Boston: The Gillette Company, 1991), pp. 29–30.

18. "People" section, *U.S. News and World Report*, April 22, 1991, p. 13.

19. Coffee, Lowenstein and Rose-Ackerman (eds.), *Knights, Raiders, and Targets*, p. 14.

20. Ibid., p. 15.

21. Jonathan Peterson, "Junk Bonds: a Financial Revolution That Failed," *Los Angeles Times*, November 22, 1990, p. A34.

22. J. Gregory Sidak and Susan E. Woodward, "Takeover Premiums, Appraisal Rights and the Price Elasticity of a Firm's Publicly Traded Stock," *Georgia Law Review* vol. 25 (1991), p. 799.

23. Michael Jensen, "Agency Costs of Free Cash Flow," cited in Sidak and Woodward, "Takeover Premiums," p. 797.

24. Laurie Simon Bagwell and John B. Shoven, "Cash Distribution to Shareholders," *Journal of Economic Perspectives* vol. 3, no. 3 (Summer 1989), p. 132.

25. Paul Chutkow, "Her Nibs," *New York Times*, Business World section, December 4, 1988, p. 28.

26. Deborah Wise, "Waterman Rift: A Tearful Farewell," *New York Times*, December 16, 1988, p. D1.

27. Warren E. Buffett, Michael D. Dingman, Harry J. Gray and Louis Lowenstein (Moderator), "Hostile Takeovers and Junk Bond Financing: A Panel Discussion," in Coffee, Lowenstein and Rose-Ackerman (eds.), *Knights, Raiders, and Targets*, p. 13.

28. *Berkshire Hathaway Inc. Annual Report, 1990*, p. 5.

29. G. Christian Hill, "Buffett Is Said to Hold 9.8% of Wells Fargo," *Wall Street Journal*, October 25, 1990, p. A2.

30. Terence P. Paré, "Yes, You Can Beat the Market," *Fortune*, April 3, 1995, p. 74.

31. William H. Miller, "Gillette's Secret to Sharpness," *Industry Week*, January 3, 1994, p. 28.

32. Mary B. English, "The Gillette Company," report, Furman Selz Mager Dietz & Birney Inc., New York, May 26, 1989, p. 1.

33. "Product Development: Where Planning and Marketing Meet—An Interview with Derwyn F. Phillips," *Journal of Business Strategy* vol. 11, no. 5 (September/October 1990), p. 14.

34. Ibid., p. 16.

35. David J. Ravenscraft and F. M. Scherer, *Mergers, Sell-Offs and Economic Efficiency* (Washington, D.C.: Brookings Institution, 1987).

36. Alan J. Auerbach (ed.), *Corporate Takeovers: Causes and Consequences* (Chicago: University of Chicago Press, 1988).

37. Kathryn J. McIntyre, "Fighting Crime: Name Recognition Makes Gillette Target for Fraud, Theft," *Business Insurance*, April 18, 1988, p. 53.

38. Ibid.

39. Auerbach, *Corporate Takeovers*.

40. *The Gillette Company News* vol. 12, no. 2 (October 1985), p. 2.

41. Dominic Stone, "Rational Thinking," *Design* (March 1992), pp. 35–37.

42. Steven Flax, "How to Snoop on Your Competitors," *Fortune*, May 14, 1984, p. 29.

43. Ibid., p. 31.

44. Norman R. Bottom, Jr., and Robert R. J. Gallati, *Industrial Espionage: Intelligence Techniques and Countermeasures* (Boston: Butterworth Publishers, 1984), pp. 17–19.

45. Stan Crock, "Insider Trading: There Oughta Be a Law," *Business Week*, December 12, 1994, p. 82.

46. "Insider Trading," *The New Palgrave Dictionary of Money and Finance*, vol. 2, F–M (London: Macmillan Press Limited, 1992), p. 417.

47. J. Fred Weston, Kwang S. Chung and Susan E. Hoag, *Mergers, Restructuring, and Corporate Control* (Englewood Cliffs, N.J.: Prentice-Hall, 1990), p. 558.

48. Alexandra Peers, "Inside Track: Insiders Are Not Always Best Judges of Future Course of a Company's Stock," *Wall Street Journal*, April 3, 1991, p. C19.

49. Alexandra Peers, "Inside Track: Are Big Insider Purchases 'Buy Signals'?" *Wall Street Journal*, October 21, 1992, p. C1.

50. Weston, Chung and Hoag, *Mergers, Restructuring, and Corporate Control*, p. 574.

5

The Restructuring of Gillette

In 1977 a news story on Gillette began, "Colman M. Mockler, Jr., chairman and chief executive officer of Gillette Co., is a man with a plan who takes the long view." Mockler detailed his "three-prong program" as follows: to "keep its product lines strong . . . weed out marginal product lines" and enter "one or two new areas to gain a foothold in world markets."[1] These guiding precepts were followed during the twelve years that I served on the company's board. They were emphasized again and again by Mockler in Gillette's restructuring plan after the rejection of the Perelman tender offer.

"Maximize Shareholder Value," or MSV, became the motto of the directors, who were given green baseball caps on which MSV was inscribed in white letters during the annual dinner before December's board meeting in 1986. During dinner an apparently original jingle entitled "Maximize Shareholder Value" was read. In part, it follows:

> What do you do,
> When they tender for you?
> You maximize shareholder value!
> Does anyone here
> Have something to fear?
> Only, that shareholder value!
>
> So what's to be done,
> When you're under the gun,
> And the tender has run,
> And the raider has won,
> The management's gone,
> The employees forlorn.

All you can say,
At the end of the day,
We maximized shareholder value!

But what if, instead,
Gillette isn't dead,
The Directors believe
From what they perceive
There's no need to sell,
To Perelman—Drexel,
To maximize shareholder value!

. . .

Some changes we'll make
For shareholders' sake,
The cash flow will roar,
The earnings will soar,
To maximize shareholder value!

And when it's all done
Shareholders have won,
With a new infrastructure
And a will to restructure,
The Directors can say,
At the end of the day,
We maximized shareholder value!

The jingle, acknowledged to be the work of Counsel Joseph Mullaney, served a major purpose: It supplied a uniform, ready phrase with which directors could answer queries about the Company's goals and why they had voted to repurchase stock—to maximize shareholder value. The jingle was also predictive: the earnings did soar.

Although it turned out apparently to be impossible to serve me a summons at my home because I was working, the Delaware Chancery Court succeeded in having me served at my office on January 5, 1987, with a class and derivative complaint by plaintiff Max Grill. That plaintiff claimed that the directors "breached their fiduciary duties" (p. 8) and, among other things, requested that the enactment of Gillette's poison pill be enjoined and the directors be required "to negotiate in good faith with Revlon and any other persons" (p. 10).

Gillette had no meeting scheduled in January, and a directors' meeting was not held until the scheduled meeting on the third Thursday, February 19. I went to Washington, D.C., on a planned business trip on January 12 and returned home on Thursday, January 15.

On February 12, 1987, a man who later identified himself as Warren Black entered unannounced into my office and served me with a Santa Clara County, California, Superior Court summons in a class action case filed by plaintiff

"Sandra Miller, on behalf of herself and all other persons similarly situated." These were shareholders of Gillette. Unknown to me, attempts had been made since early January 1987 to serve me at home. I had taken a brief vacation starting January 29. The server was not very assiduous, and it had taken him until February 12 to serve me personally in my office. The January 5 summons had been accepted in the mailroom. The case was against not only myself but all the directors of the Gillette corporation, and I was not too concerned. The directors had already been told to mail to the general counsel's office any such documents that might come our way, and I was assured that the Jones, Day firm would represent me and that I would not even have to make an appearance. I did receive a letter from Gillette's counsel, Joe Mullaney, making clear that the suit was filed in the Santa Clara County Court because that was where I lived and not because of Gillette's ownership of an Oral-B plant in that county. Eventually the Miller case was settled, as were all other similar suits across the country with which it was combined. The complaint was "for breach of fiduciary duty; intentional interference with prospective economic advantage; conspiracy." In reading the summons, I was glad that I had been informed to hand such suits over to the company's lawyers. Thus directors are shielded from a legal suit's reminders of the huge potential personal liability costs if "the business judgment rule" defense and directors' liability insurance fail to protect them and their assets.

There is a difference between personal/physical risk and financial risk. One of my truly risk-taking friends, Ellen Lapham, tried as part of a team to climb Mount Everest in October 1986. Although the team reached 24,000 feet, they failed to climb the 29,000-foot peak because they withdrew from exposure to the 100-mile-per-hour winds and the bitter, unseasonable cold. Risks that involve life are more urgent than investment risk. Business risktakers can also withdraw, and many shareholders in a company do so by selling their stock. The directors of Gillette, once their decision to repurchase stock had been made, remained steadfast. Their risks differed from shareholders' risks but at no time approached that of my mountain-climbing friend.

The Santa Clara suit protested the Board's adoption of the poison pill because, in its opinion, it created "irreparable harm to shareholders" (p. 11). The suit also protested the buy-back of stock from the Perelman Group on November 24, 1986, as a "waste of corporate assets" (p. 14) and, probably most important in the minds of the persons for whom the suit was filed, "removed an opportunity of Gillette's shareholders to sell their common stock of Gillette at $65 per share" (p. 15). This suit clearly raised the major shareholder argument against payment of greenmail: "I've lost the chance to make an immediate gain." *Greenmail* is referred to in Chapter 2 and discussed in depth in Chapter 8. There, as here, I maintain that to define greenmail as payment at a premium over market price for stock is not a precise enough definition in actual situations. When there is a volatile daily market price prior to a tender, defining the time period over which the market price applies becomes very important. The Gillette

Board chose the average of the daily market Gillette share price over the ten days prior to the repurchase announcement.

GILLETTE ACTIONS, LATE 1986 INTO EARLY 1987

A Gillette Board meeting was held on November 26, at which the Board withdrew the 1985 poison pill by redeeming the preferred-stock purchase rights at 1 cent apiece. The Board then adopted a new, very similar poison pill, with an exercise price of $160 for each new right. These rights were to expire on December 9, 1996. Obviously, the directors believed, whether correctly on not, that the poison pill gave them time to negotiate. Additionally, the Board tripled the company's maximum short-term borrowing limits, thus enabling it to obtain the cash needed for the stock repurchase. During the Board's December 1986 meeting, capital expenditures were also authorized for manufacturing new dies and molds and other equipment to produce Gillette razors and blades. Additionally, manufacture of Braun's new Lady Shaver and a new steam iron were approved and, most important for Gillette's future geographical expansion, equity holdings in India were increased to about 40 percent, with the long-run goal of continually maximizing that percentage equity.

Gillette continued to restructure to strengthen its existing technical expertise, marketing and distribution strengths. In December 1986 Gillette announced that about 8 percent of the Company's worldwide workforce, about 2,400 people, would be laid off, primarily through retirements and attrition. This was expected to cost about $205 million, primarily in early-retirement benefits to employees. Misco, Inc., a mail-order computer-supply company bought in 1984, was sold to a London firm, Electro Components PLC, for a profit in March 1987.

The concept of the Sensor had been fully developed by 1986, but production at a low-enough unit cost to sell at a competitive price had not yet evolved. Work on that continued. Management and the Board finalized the purchase of Waterman, S.A., a publicly owned French manufacturer of premium pens, in early 1987. Acquisition of this company had been first discussed in October 1986. Waterman pens, like Oral-B toothbrushes, were a synergistic fit with Gillette, providing Gillette with high-quality pens in the middle to upper price range. By adding these to the lower-priced Paper Mate pens, Gillette solidified its world leadership in the manufacture of writing instruments. The Board continued to conduct the normal course of business into the first part of 1987. Management responded to media criticism by working many additional hours, both to conduct normal business and to fight off rumors stemming from newspaper articles. The financial press portrayed the Company as a continuing potential target for takeover.

The directors did not believe that all takeover threats had completely dissolved with the repurchase of stock and the signed 10-year-standstill agreement with Perelman. Their apprehension was reaffirmed by a headline in the February 6, 1987, *Wall Street Journal*: "Gillette Stake of Substantial Size Is Held by Investor Irwin Jacobs, Sources Say'' (p. 5). There was speculation about whether Gillette might again be forced into a greenmail situation, this time by Jacobs, who had in the past invested in other companies' stocks and successfully brought about greenmail payments to himself. Once a board of directors has been viewed as being willing to pay above-the-market price for a stock buy-back, it may be seen as always being willing to repeat this action. This interpretation was made clear to many directors in their normal social interactions with others. Using that line of reasoning, the directors viewed Jacobs more as a greenmailer than as an investor, and this was reinforced because in the past he had resolved his large holdings of other companies in this fashion.

Despite its uneasiness, the Board continued to operate in its usual fashion. On advice of management and after a somewhat long debate, the directors authorized in February of 1987 the purchase of an Italian toiletries firm, Antica Erboristeria, for $27 million. Management's argument for the purchase was mainly that a company needs a significant segment, a *critical mass*, of a market in order to make money and that this purchase would help Gillette gain that significant base in toiletries. La Toja Cosmetics of Spain had been bought in 1986, and Princeton Cosmetics of UNISA in Chile had been purchased in 1987. Additionally, there were anticipated tax gains for Gillette from the purchase.

The Board was also pressed at this time to do something for the disgruntled shareholders—those who felt they should have received a repurchase offer for their stock at the same price paid to Perelman. Gillette stock had traded over a million shares at $61, on February 5, 1987, somewhat less than Perelman's November 1986 tender offer of $65, but higher than the repurchase price. On February 19, 1987, the Board announced a two-for-one stock split with a 12 percent dividend increase. Gillette's general dividend policy was to distribute about 50 percent of earnings and to sustain the level of the dividend rate indefinitely into the future. Gillette had announced earlier its intention, in conjunction with the settlement with Perelman, to buy up to seven million Gillette shares on the open market, a move that was intended to support the market share price. However, as of March 24, 1987, the Company had purchased only 638,000 shares, well under the seven million authorization.

Gillette as a major international firm had several financial options available to reduce its interest payments on its greatly increased debt and also to reduce its tax burden in early 1987 when the new U.S. 1986 tax law went into effect. In January of 1987, U.S. companies were allowed to allocate to foreign-source income nearly 55 percent of their interest expense, almost double the 28 percent limit allowed until that year. To benefit from this Gillette borrowed Euro-French Francs, Euro Sterling, and in a somewhat complicated transaction, shifted parts of its U.S. long-term debt and interest payments to Braun in Germany. The Company also substantially benefited because foreign governments allowed more favorable interest expense deductions. To get immediate cash, Gillette also sold Oral-B assets to its own subsidiary, Gillette Canada, gaining $1 million immediately in reduced interest expense and $2.5 million in year two.

These financial maneuvers were brought to the Board by Milton Glass, who had been the treasurer and was elected to vice president for finance in April of 1987, when Lloyd Swaim became treasurer. Throughout the period that I was on the board, I found that the financial expertise of these men was, on the whole, superb. Prior to the tender, Milton Glass was named by the *Institutional Investor* as "the top CFO," or chief financial officer, in the cosmetics industry. The highlighted quotation read: "solid, hardworking guy, a ramrod as a CFO. Helped acquire close to $1 billion in financial-services entities in last three years, while spinning off close to $100 million in businesses. Intelligent, conscientious, creative and imaginative."[2]

RESTRUCTURING

During the first part of my twelve years on the Board of Gillette, 1978–1990, the Company had pursued a deliberate strategy of diversification. During the early 1980s management believed that disposable razors would replace eventually most of the nondisposable metal razor and blade business such as Trac II and Atra. Disposable razors are relatively low-cost, low-price, single items made of plastic. Gillette could make little profit on them because of the low unit price set by its major competitor, Bic. "By the late 1980s disposables had a share of nearly 50% in dollars and some 60% in units. While it held a narrow lead over Bic in units and a wide lead in dollars in disposables (Gillette's are priced higher), its profit margins were being squeezed."[3] Although a serious loss in the worldwide razor and blade market in retrospect seems unlikely during the 1980s, management and the CEO were worried because the low-cost unit production of Sensor was not assured.

To protect against a possible worldwide declining market share of the very profitable durable metal razor and blade, Colman Mockler and many others in top management desired to make new acquisitions with an eye to expanding the number of product lines and also to improving Gillette's expertise in marketing techniques. Mockler believed that a knowledge of direct-mail selling through catalogs would be useful as the market share of disposables increased. Small companies with mail-order catalogs, Frostline and Misco, were bought for the firsthand experience.

Gillette's general corporate strategy on diversification was to buy a consumer business where the product has repeat sales. Gillette was willing to pay a premium for a quality product with a relatively low unit price. Pens, for example, are often lost, resulting in repeat sales, thus Paper Mate. Toothbrushes wear out, customers often buy more than one at a time, and they were not well-marketed worldwide, thus Oral-B. Worldwide demand for batteries has been soaring, and batteries wear out, and thus a long look at Duracell in 1987, which was sold in late 1988 to KKR for $1.8 billion, an amount above what Gillette had been considering to offer. By May 1991, when Duracell's stock was offered to the public, its value was triple what KKR had paid. The Board discussion on Duracell in 1987 centered around how long their then nickel-cadmium batteries could resist being overtaken by the newer, longer-lasting batteries that could power computers and mobile phones over longer periods of time—several weeks, as compared to a few days. The expanding market for batteries and the prevalence of repeat customers were appealing to Gillette with its superb marketing expertise.

Events indicate that the Gillette Board may have been too conservative in their assessment of Duracell. Gillette's Board and other company boards worried about potential competition from new, longer-life batteries and did not foresee that Duracell would be the lead company in developing the new technology in the manufacture and marketing of rechargeable nickel-metal hydride batteries used in personal computers, and also of alkaline batteries. In 1994 the rechargeables were selling for $250 each. In September 1996 Gillette bought the revamped Duracell Company for $7 billion, after Duracell initiated some standardization industry wide of the sizes of rechargeable batteries for computers and camcorders. Since 1987 Duracell has grown faster than Gillette, but with Gillette's market strength behind it Duracell probably could have grown even faster. Duracell has continued major research investments in new alkaline technology and high-power rechargeable batteries. Future trends in technology and who among the competitors would win were difficult factors to gauge in 1987. Duracell was a good buy in 1987 and also in 1996. In both periods continuing innovation—in Scotland, PRC and Japan—makes it a highly competitive industry.

Gillette wanted to manufacture products that Gillette's expertise in marketing internationally, as well as in the United States, would act on to increase their value. The Oral-B toothbrush fits all the criteria: repeat business, low unit price, easy placement beside razor blades on store shelves and high potential for international sales.

The idea that mail-order marketing of disposable blades would be feasible continued to drive acquisitions, and in 1984 Gillette bought into Misco, Inc., a mail-order company that sold computer supplies through a catalog. Intrigued by this initial successful foray into a specialized portion of the computer industry, the Company then invested in minority ownership positions in several small computer-software companies. Although the cost of these investments was low relative to Gillette's cash flow, software companies had no product or marketing synergy with Gillette. Further, this line of business and its culture were new to Gillette. Although Gillette has a worldwide computer management information system, its computer expertise did not extend to the creation of software. As the only member of the Board who lived in California's Silicon Valley, I was surprised that the management of a traditional manufacturing company would believe that they could compete in the unique culture of creating software. My disagreement was of no avail at board meetings, and 20 percent equity of Datasoft and Digital Learning systems were acquired. In the restructuring after November 1986 these small equities were readily sold.

Also sold in the restructuring were the retail eyeglass business and the beauty spas, Elizabeth Grady Face First International, acquired in 1984, and Noelle, each, again, a relatively small investment. Although beauty spas may seem to be superficially synergistic in that they could sell Gillette toiletries, it was not a real fit. Gillette toiletries are not at the high-price end, the premium area of cosmetic products that most beauty salons push. The Paul Mitchell line of hair products with which Gillette had partner agreements was a very small exception.

Gillette also invested in oil and gas exploration and development, as detailed in Chapter 3, because the extraordinary increases in the price of oil during the late 1970s and into the 1980s appeared to be continuing indefinitely. The Gillette Board had lengthy debates on how to hedge against the rising costs of the company's most important raw material, petroleum needed for manufacture of hard plastics. Then the Gulf War ended, and Gillette's losses from the gas and oil businesses in 1986 rose to $41 million as the price of oil declined. In 1987 gains of $3 million were made. The Company used the *successful efforts* method of accounting that permits costs of unproved properties to be capitalized.

Gillette rarely lost sight of the fact that roughly two-thirds of its profits come from the shaving business. During the period of takeover attempts and into 1988, Gillette continued to seek low unit manufacturing costs for its new concept of a razor and blade, eventually the Sensor. Trac II had been launched in 1971, and the Atra in 1977. In 1986 the Sensor was comparatively overdue. Success in gaining a unit cost of its manufacture low enough to price competitively took until March 1988. Blade prices were set to earn higher margins on the newer blades, higher margins than from the sale of the razor handle. Gillette blades fitted only the Gillette handle, as was true for razors and blades manufactured by other companies. Interchange among brands is made impossible. Gillette, with a market dollar share of over 60 percent, had every economic incentive to be the first to market a greatly improved blade.

During 1987, Gillette sold S.T. Dupont to Dickson Concepts, Ltd., of Hong Kong for $52 million. This was the result of Gillette seeking a buyer well before the first takeover attempt. Dickson Concepts (International) Ltd., a luxury-goods company, appears to have made a success in marketing Dupont's status products, which Gillette had in the past marketed primarily to Middle East buyers. Since purchasing S.T. Dupont, Dickson has also purchased a top-status department store in London, Harvey Nichols, and the well-known European brands of Charles Jourdan and Guy Laroche. Mr. Poon, the chairman, founder and 51 percent owner of Dickson, took substantial risks in buying S.T. Dupont and marketing to the Far Eastern market the high-status, Western-style goods already favored by the Middle East market.[4] Mr. Poon's concept seems similar to what Gillette earlier envisioned for S.T. Dupont, a division that at the time of sale was not financially successful. It may be that in the long run Gillette would have succeeded at profitably marketing high-status, luxury goods, but their very low earnings margin made them inadvisable at Gillette as an alternative to investment in the high-margin razor blade manufacturing business. The equity investment in Eyeworld was sold to Mitani Corporation of Japan, and later the equities held in the two computer-software companies were sold. Gillette's research and medical evaluation laboratories were also sold, as was the company's one Gulfstream airplane and a hangar facility in Bedford, Massachusetts.

It was hard to gain cash from streamlining routine expenses, because Gillette had not been extravagant in spending on perks for directors or luxuries for employees. Gillette did not have, as compared with, say, RJR Nabisco, a large fleet of airplanes; and company policy did not reimburse first-class air fares, except for very top management and directors. I recall that I, along with my fellow director, Herb Jacobi, personally argued for reimbursement of first-class air fare for the treasurer, Milton Glass. It was fortunate that the frequent-flyer programs permitted him and other heavily traveled top-level employees to upgrade most of their overseas flights. I personally feel that it is "penny wise and pound foolish" not to reimburse employees who travel on average two times a month on international flights for at least business-class fare.

Gillette was not lavish in spending on buildings, and the company could not squeeze out millions of dollars by scaling down this type of excess. Gillette's headquarters were several rented floors in the Prudential Tower, in Boston, and the factories were no-nonsense industrial buildings. The only sign of lavishness that I saw—but I did not see many Gillette manufacturing plants—was a large outdoor swimming pool in Isleworth, England, and this could be justified as a forerunner of the wellness programs promoted by U.S. corporations in the 1980s. Certainly, I never saw or heard about anything even remotely comparable to the recent description of RJR Nabisco's Taj Mahal airplane hangar and its adjoining

building of tinted glass, surrounded by $250,000 in landscaping, complete with a Japanese garden. Inside a visitor walked into a stunning three-story atrium. The floors were Italian marble, the walls and doors lined in inlaid mahogany. More than $600,000 in new furniture was spread throughout, topped off by $100,000 in objets d'art, including an antique Chinese ceremonial robe spread in a glass case and a magnificent Chinese platter and urn . . . a walk-in wine cooler; a "visiting pilots' room," with television and stereo; and a "flight-planning room," packed with state-of-the-art computers to track executives' whereabouts and their future transportation wishes. All this was necessary to keep track of RJR Nabisco's thirty-six corporate pilots and ten planes, widely known as the RJR Air Force.[5]

I do not accept as desirable the excessiveness of RJR Nabisco's provision of private planes, cars and apartments for directors. Gillette was very moderate in its provision for upper management and directors. However, as air travel became more arduous with the upswing in the number of persons traveling during the 1980s, Gillette could have provided more business and first-class fares to upper management. There are some also who argue that the directors' reliance on taxicabs to get to and from the Logan airport for meetings was not a time cost that most other large corporations apparently would impose. Before the takeover attempts were far along, limousines were regularly ordered for after-meeting rides to Boston's Logan airport, which had in 1986 and for several years later a bottleneck approach created by narrowing many lanes down to only two lanes each way in the tunnel under the harbor. Missing scheduled flights did annoy directors already under stress from the many extra meetings imposed by takeover attempts. A new tunnel has been built since this period.

ANONYMOUS LETTER

An anonymous letter was mailed to each director before the February 1987 board meeting. I received a copy as I left to take the plane for the Boston board meeting February 19, 1987. Selected quotations from the three-page single-space letter follow:

We are a group of Gillette middle managers who have lost confidence in our company's senior management. We believe their incompetence resulted in our being vulnerable to the Revlon raid, and we do not think they are capable of successfully restructuring the company. We strongly urge you to replace this management with more capable people. If you do not, the Gillette Company is unlikely to remain independent.

We have outlined below our assessment of the shortcomings of the key senior managers and our recommended course of action. Be assured that we are not crackpots, but responsible managers who are anxious to preserve this fine company and see it prosper.

The unsigned letter disparaged with often inaccurate generalities and very few specifics. The letter criticized Colman Mockler, Joe Turley, Derwyn Phillips and Rod Mills. Phillips for involving "himself in all company issues" and Mills because he is "a bureaucrat who responds only to his managers' proposals."

The letter asks:

What should be done about this management crisis at Gillette? Only you can do something. These people are incapable of changing their management behavior. They are wedded to the past and cannot successfully restructure and redirect the company. The current restructuring is indicative of this as it is merely a cost reduction program. New management with new ideas is necessary to ever rebuild the company.

The anonymous letter called for retirement of Mockler, Turley, Phillips and Mills and then endorsed Tony Levy, Lorne Waxlax, Bob Ray, Al Zeien and John Symons.

Such a letter, apparently mailed to each outside director, was bound to be discussed by board members prior to the formal meeting. One director said that because it was anonymous it should be ignored, while another said that he could not privately talk it over with Mockler because he never had talked with him privately about anything. I and a few other board members agreed to talk individually to Mockler about the letter. In the Board's opinion, the anonymous letter erred in its assessment of CEO Mockler, who had used his 30-year company experience and skills to reposition the Company and increase its profits substantially. There was no support for the idea or even discussion that Mockler should resign, but there was weak support for the early retirement of Joe Turley and Rod Mills, which eventually occurred. It is less difficult for a board to induce and, if need be, force the early retirement of individual members of top management than just firing them. Gillette's upper management were typically long-term employees.

In the 1987 reorganization, Derwyn Phillips and Al Zeien became vice chairmen of the Board, and no new president was named. Tony Levy, John Symons and Lorne Waxlax were each named executive vice presidents, while Bob Ray resigned for personal reasons.

The letter modified the fragile, subtle relationship among outside directors and between the CEO and directors. As a recent book, *Pawns or Potentates*, states: "There are also norms about how to deal with fellow directors, one of which is not to assert leadership over them. All are peers on the board, and being openly assertive is bad form. . . . Also *de riguer* is not contacting fellow directors outside of meetings."[6] But it can be argued that corporations under economic and leadership stress have a need for leadership among the directors and also a need to encourage communication among directors apart from the board meetings. Observation of other companies' struggles in takeover situations through newspaper accounts is intriguing. It may be that IBM's late 1992 and very early 1993 crisis might have been averted if there had been strong, early leadership among its outside directors. Newspaper accounts of the succession battle in late January 1993 over who would head IBM indicated a lack of the type of discussion that might have occurred in informal meetings among informed outside directors. Apparently IBM badly lagged in understanding the rapid changes in information processing and did not believe that the market for mainframe computers would drastically decline as the demand for personal computers and networking rose. Its stock price slid by one-half before action was taken.

Among IBM board leaders in forcing out their CEO and two top managers were, according to newspaper accounts, outside directors, retired Johnson & Johnson chairman James Burke and Capital Cities/ABC chairman Thomas Murphy. At least one story implied that Drew Lewis, a director and chairman of Union Pacific Corporation and also a past U.S. Secretary of Transportation under President Reagan, became an informal leader.[7] The struggle was over not only whether the CEO and his lieutenants would retain their jobs but also how much to cut the then $4.84 per share annual dividend payout rate in face of a nearly $5 billion loss in 1992. The January 26 meeting cut it by slightly more than one-half to $2.16. Could earlier leadership among the directors have stemmed the excessive bleeding of profits? From newspaper articles alone, I believe it could have. An insider's knowledge may change my opinion.

From my experience, I do not know if any informal restraints on individual relationships among fellow directors are, as Lorsch claims, generally followed by directors. As the only woman on an otherwise all-male board, I initially assumed that members of all-male luncheon clubs would discuss such matters when involved, even if only very briefly. Because I did not have social interaction with other directors at all-male clubs, either in San Francisco or Palo Alto or in the Boston-based clubs that many other directors had, I did not know. It is interesting that all-male luncheon clubs exist in each locale, and at least the Californian ones claim that no business is conducted at lunches on their premises. They are private social clubs. As I wrote in 1985, "All-male luncheon clubs are self-advertised as social in nature, but only the naive would believe that no business arrangements result from the informal contacts from which women are excluded. Self-employed lawyers and real estate sales persons are only two common occupations which benefit from such social contacts."[8]

On the few occasions that I and a fellow director met at a non-Gillette function, we did discuss Gillette if no outsiders were present. Rarely, I and another director would have dinner or a prearranged drink in order to talk about Gillette in an informal manner. I believe that the presence of outsiders should limit insiders talking about a specific company's business but also that informal, general discussions among informed directors of several companies can be very helpful.

The anonymous letter and the takeover attempts made the Board less cohesive, but despite this, Board support for the CEO did not weaken. The main effect of the anonymous letter to Gillette directors was to speed up the Company's needed and already planned reorganization.

By December 31, 1988, $169.7 million had been charged to the restructuring provision for costs related to employee reductions, the closing of several operations in domestic and international markets and the net impact of the sale of some assets.

The Company closed Jafra Canada and eleven other small Jafra businesses abroad. Gillette was stripped down to its core operations: razors and blades, writing instruments, Braun products, the new Oral-B toothbrush and high-profile toiletries lines (such as Right Guard and Foamy), and door-to-door selling of Jafra Cosmetics. The Company's cash flow increased despite its need to pay off sizeable interest payments on the loans incurred for the buy-back of stock from Perelman. From its very beginning, Gillette had expanded geographically, and worldwide sales continued to grow throughout the Mockler period. Gillette's response to the threat of a takeover was to speed up existing trends, not to change direction but to cut costs and streamline operations. Gillette was forced to use any excess cash to pay off its new debt, rather than buying small equity positions in sometimes unrelated companies. It was the unrelated diversification that had weakened, not strengthened, the Company. Gillette was not alone in this misdirection of resources; moreover, as a recent paper on corporate governance reports, "The evidence strongly suggests that unrelated acquisitions degrade corporate performance" of many companies.[9] But the related acquisitions enhanced the financial position of Gillette. It is a primary board function to accept or turn down the acquisitions proposed by management. During the early 1980s investment bankers hoping to make money on a deal shopped many companies to other companies such as Gillette that had the cash flow to buy. Management turned down those that they perceived to be losers. It was the Board's function to help select winners from the remaining few that management presented after culling the field.

Why did Oral-B, primarily a toothbrush-manufacturing concern, and Waterman pens, also bought during the 1980s, produce such outstanding profits? Oral-B used hard plastics as do many of Gillette's manufacturing processes, pens and disposable razors, and also it was easy to see the potential close synergy with marketing of razor blades, by selling in drug stores and food markets. Oral-B toothbrushes initially were primarily marketed in the United States via endorsements of dentists. Gillette planned to build on this base. In other countries, brushing teeth after each meal or even at bedtime was not an established habit as in the United States. Dentists' endorsements could be a good entry. Gillette's market research showed that there was a big market abroad for selling toothbrushes, and Gillette had an international distribution system for selling small items that would occupy little shelf space in multiproduct drugstores, as in France, that could ideally be used to sell toothbrushes, often side-by-side with the Gillette razors.

Waterman pens was clearly a fit because Gillette already manufactured pens. Primarily, Waterman extended Gillette's higher price lines in easier and probably less expensive fashion than developing the same in-house. Pens, like toothbrushes, could also be sold alongside razor blades.

Was Gillette unique in the percentage of companies that it bought and then sold after a short period of time? I do not think so. Michael Porter, in his 1987 *Harvard Business Review* article, documents that among 33 major U.S. companies seeking diversification in 1950–1980, 53.4 percent had divested some of their acquisitions by 1987. These 33 companies had acquired 3,788 companies, joint ventures or start-ups over that period, and of those outside the acquirer's own industry, more than 60 percent were divested.[10] Once the decision to diversify is made, the discriminating selection of which companies to acquire is difficult because it involves so many unknowns.

Sales of Gillette's products rose in 1989 to $3.8 billion, an increase of $1 billion over 1986 sales of $2.8 billion, and profits from operations nearly tripled to $664 million in 1989 from $229 million in 1986. In March 1990 Chairman Mockler could observe in his letter to the stockholders,

Gillette stock continued to outperform the stock market averages during 1989 in terms of total return. The annual return to stockholders on Gillette common stock was 50.6%. This compares with returns of about 32% for the Dow Jones Industrial Average and the Standard & Poor's 500 in 1989. The Company's stock has been an outstanding long-term investment. The value of a $1,000 investment in Gillette stock at the end of 1979 grew to $11,511 by the end of 1989, more than twice the value of a comparable investment in either the DJIA or the S&P 500.[11]

REORGANIZATION

But Colman Mockler, like most people, had a weakness: Not all his choices of his immediate subordinates were discerning. Actions by the Board to retire early Joe Turley and Rod Mills, by April 1988, and the promotion of Tony Levy to executive vice president of Gillette were actions in the spirit of the anonymous letter.

In November 1987 the Board approved a reorganization of the Company into two major operating units: one, under Derwyn Phillips, Gillette North Atlantic, covered Europe as well as the United States and Canada. This was primarily the Safety Razor Division, which had been headed by Derwyn Phillips. He was supported by John Symons of the United Kingdom, who, as head of the Shaving Group headed up the Sensor's strategy. The other major division was Gillette International/Diversified Operations, headed by Al Zeien, acting as an umbrella over Braun, Oral-B toothbrushes and Jafra Cosmetics and also handling all international operations outside of Europe and North America. Zeien was supported by Lorne Waxlax as head of Diversified Operations and Tony Levy as the head of the Gillette International group, handling all international operations outside of Europe and North America. Gaston ("Tony") Levy of Brazil had been very successful in running Latin America operations and this widened his area to include India, Australia and the Far East. This restructuring grouped operations under two distinctly different areas: the more mature, slower-growth markets of North America and Europe and the faster-growing, less-developed areas of the world. Each of the geographical divisions were organized along product lines. Under the complicated reorganization there was no president of the company, but two vice chairmen (Phillips and Zeien) and three executive vice presidents (Levy, Symons and Waxlax).

LEGISLATIVE CLIMATE: FEDERAL

Although a change in the ownership of a corporation, such as would have occurred if the tender for Gillette had been successful, may at first seem to be solely a private, nongovernmental affair, the surge in such corporate ownership transactions during the 1980s sparked public debate.

In February 1985, the U.S. Council of Economic Advisers to the president issued its annual report that contained a chapter entitled "The Market for Corporate Control." It summarized without specific examples the public debate over the tactics used by both sides in contests for control of corporations, as follows:

The outcome of this debate over takeover tactics is significant for the economy as a whole. The set of tactics permissible in contests for corporate control determines both the probability that takeover attempts will be made and the probability that they will eventually succeed. To the extent that government regulations impose costs on bidders, or reduce a bidder's chances for success, fewer takeover attempts will be made. This tends to insulate corporate managements from the competitive pressures of the external market for corporate control. Stockholders, as a group, will also suffer as a result of excessive regulation because it reduces the chance to earn takeover premiums. However, to the extent that takeover practices are abusive, either because they allow bidders to acquire corporations through manipulative means, or because they allow entrenched managements to defeat takeovers that are in stockholders' and the economy's best interests, certain controls may be appropriate. . . .

The central policy question regarding takeovers should be whether the benefits to the economy as a whole resulting from takeovers exceed their costs . . . there is powerful evidence that takeovers as a group are beneficial.[12]

The major argument in favor of takeovers has already been stated: the belief that takeovers reallocate resources to more efficient management and thus increase the national production of goods and services. A takeover almost always forces a company to restructure and, at least initially, lay off employees. Those who believe that their jobs are threatened by a specific takeover are against that takeover. This hostility may become generalized against all takeovers. From corporate management's point of view, a major argument against them is that an impending takeover diverts the time and attention of existing management away from the main purpose of running a business: producing goods and services and selling them to make profits for the loaners of equity capital in return for their risking their capital. As the chairman of Sony, Akio Morita, has been quoted: ''Unfortunately, American industry is now being distracted by a game called mergers and acquisitions. America's brightest managerial talent is engaged in takeover moves and empire building. The best students do not study engineering but become MBA's or lawyers and, eventually, professional money-makers. This is not a productive enterprise.''[13] In my several conversations with Mr. Morita and other Japanese businessmen, this quotation correctly reflects their views and those of many other foreign businessmen. Takeovers are a redistribution from one group, the existing shareholders, management and employees, to a new group of the same designations. The main beneficiaries are the investment bankers and lawyers who usually receive a percentage of the price. Although there are many other general arguments pro and con that could be presented, the essence of the debate has been summarized, but there are questions to be answered. Can a company threatened with a takeover act to restructure and perform more efficiently? The experience of Gillette says it can.

In the case of Gillette, the *threat* of a takeover was sufficient to stimulate some restructuring that resulted in a more efficient allocation of resources. An actual takeover was not necessary. The restructuring probably was somewhat different from that which an outsider's takeover would have forced. Whether the mere threat of a takeover creates benefits less, equal to or greater than an actual change in governance might have spurred is unknown. The lines of business curtailed by Gillette and thus the number of immediate job losses and their specificity probably differed from what would have occurred under Perelman.

To integrate two independent businesses would require a different business strategy than to improve an existing business standing alone. Is a threat sufficient for efficient restructuring? Can a threat exercise enough power to spur desirable change without outsiders exercising their threat? The case of Gillette raises the question of whether societal benefits might be gained by other companies without some of the societal losses that occur in an actual change of corporate governance.

In the short run, who lost and who gained? By December 31, 1986, Gillette's annual earnings had dropped substantially by $142.7 million in 1986, as compared to 1985. Year-end earnings per share were only 25 cents, compared to $2.59 in 1985. Obviously, in the short run Perelman/Revlon had gained several million dollars, and Gillette and its share owners had lost several million. Additional substantial short-term losers were those employees who lost their jobs. One cannot forget, however, that among the big gainers in the short-run were the investment bankers and the merger and acquisition lawyers, who got their percentage of the deal.

The Company, however, immediately began to recoup, and in 1987 profits from operations were up by over $250 million. Getting rid of the lines of business that were losers was beneficial to the Company. During this period the Board could increase dividends per share only in small part because fewer shares were outstanding after the buy-back. Continuing the payment of dividends per share and even raising them was deemed essential by the directors despite the negative first-quarter financial report in the spring of 1987. With the Company's loans graded at far below their earlier, more usual AA ratings, the directors believed that confidence in the Company would fade if dividends were reduced. Therefore, a special company valuation and a legal judgment were obtained to permit the Company, even in a negative position, to pay out dividends in 1987 totaling $85.2 million, almost as high as the 1986 total of $86.4 million.

In December of 1987, the Senate Committee on Banking, Housing and Urban Affairs issued a report on the Tender Offer Disclosure and Fairness Act of 1987 that discussed potential federal reforms designed to regulate what some considered to be abusive takeover tactics. The Senate committee covered existing and potential rules over disclosure of large stock purchases, procedures in tender offers, greenmail, poison pills and the role of regulation by the states. The congressional policy debate was not simply over whether hostile takeovers were good or bad but also about federal control and state rights. Corporations are incorporated by the states and thus owe their existence to the states. It is state laws and state courts that regulate them. But the federal government regulates the stock markets, and the federal Securities and Exchange Commission oversees these markets, in which corporations float their stocks to obtain equity capital.

Congress debated legislation for controlling takeover activities. Despite the October 1987 stock-market crash, mainly a one-day affair, and the fall-off in takeover attempts, in large part due to Delaware's new (February 1988) anti–hostile takeover law, the Senate debate over bill S-1323 lasted intermittently until mid-1988. During this period, pressures by the public and corporations continued. On June 21, 1988, the Senate adopted by a 98-to-1 vote, "to ban so-called golden parachute payments to corporate officers who lose their jobs in the event of a takeover, unless the payments are approved by a majority of stockholders."[14] On the same day, however, the Senate rejected a ban on corporate enactment of poison pills, unless they were also approved by a majority of stockholders. Although S-1323 contained antigreenmail provisions and reform of the way in which shareholder ballots were to be counted, these items were not voted on, and the whole bill, S-1323, died when Congress adjourned.

The long-run aftermath of the merger and acquisition activity of the 1980s includes many new state laws that reflect the belief that corporations have responsibilities to others in addition to their shareholders. In the category of others, I would place employees. State governments are in general more sensitive because of geographic immediacy to business within their state and because of the large numbers of employees who are voters and who may fear that they might lose their jobs.

Even before Congress failed to enact federal legislation, several states passed new regulatory laws governing corporate control. Massachusetts legislation was passed in June 1987. This is discussed in more detail in the next chapter. Perelman's renewed attempt to obtain control of Gillette spurred Delaware's antitakeover legislation, which was adopted on February 2, 1988, but became retroactively effective December 23, 1987. The predating saved Texaco, a company that Carl C. Icahn was believed to have been planning to take over.

In general, state laws support the freedom of corporations to continue to act in what their directors perceive under the "business judgment" doctrine to be the company's best interests. The state of Delaware, in which nearly 60 percent of large firms are incorporated, in February 1988 made it virtually impossible for a would-be acquirer to take over a Delaware-incorporated company, such as Gillette, except by a successful cash tender for 85 percent or more of its stock. Because an hostile takeover through purchase of stock became more difficult, more proxy fights for corporate control could be expected. Gillette's struggle in a proxy fight with Coniston Partners in April 1988 carried out this expectation.

NOTES

1. Neil Ulman, "Gillette Chairman Takes a Long View in Program to Brighten Profit Picture," *Wall Street Journal*, June 28, 1977, p. 14.

2. Beth McGoldrick, Gregory Miller, Beth Selby, Fiammetta Rocco, Ellen James and Fayette Hickox, "Cover Story: America's Best CFOs," *Institutional Investor* vol. 20, no. 9 (September 1986), p. 101.

3. Lawrence Ingrassia, "Keeping Sharp: Gillette Holds Its Edge by Endlessly Searching for a Better Shave," *Wall Street Journal*, December 10, 1992, p. A6.

4. Marcus Brauchli, "Dickson, Hong Kong Luxury Goods Company, Sees Gold in Opening 'Status' Shops in China," *Wall Street Journal*, March 1, 1993, p. A10.

5. Bryan Burrough and John Helyar, *Barbarians at the Gate: The Fall of RJR Nabisco* (New York: Harper and Row, 1990), p. 94.

6. Jay W. Lorsch with Elizabeth MacIver, *Pawns or Potentates: The Reality of America's Corporate Boards* (Boston, Mass.: Harvard Business School Press, 1989), p. 93.

7. Fred R. Bleakley and Peter Pae, "Clark Is Barred from American Express Meeting," *Wall Street Journal*, January 25, 1993, pp. A3–A4.

8. Rita Ricardo-Campbell, *Women and Comparable Worth* (Stanford, Calif.: The Hoover Institution on War, Revolution and Peace, Stanford University, 1985), p. 21.

9. Bernard S. Black, "Institutional Investors and Corporate Governance: The Case for Institutional Voice," *Continental Bank Journal of Applied Corporate Finance* (Fall 1992), p. 26.

10. Michael E. Porter, "From Competitive Advantage to Corporate Strategy," *Harvard Business Review* vol. 65, no. 3 (May/June 1987), p. 45.

11. "Letter to Stockholders," *Annual Report 1989* (Boston: The Gillette Company, 1989), p. 2.

12. *Economic Report of the President*, Annual Report of the Council of Economic Advisers (Washington, D.C.: Government Printing Office, 1985), p. 191.

13. "Tender Offer Disclosure and Fairness Act of 1987," Report of the Committee on Banking, Housing, and Urban Affairs, United States Senate, to accompany S. 1323 (Washington, D.C.: Government Printing Office, 1987), p. 2.

14. *Congressional Quarterly*, Washington, D.C., June 25, 1988, p. 1777.

6

Hot Summer: Unsolicited Bids of 1987

MID-JUNE 1987

During 1987 Gillette demonstrated the sizable free cash flow that the company, once streamlined, could generate. As early as the spring of 1987, Gillette had paid off slightly over $100 million of its long-term debt, split its stock two-for-one and increased its annual dividend rate and payout. The Gillette Company continued to dangle as a tantalizing, missed prize before Perelman's dazzled eyes. The Company was even better than he had thought; and despite the ten-year standstill agreement, he launched a surprise second bid the evening of June 17, 1987, the night before the regularly scheduled June board meeting. Gillette's antagonist would not go away, and he offered to pay many dollars more for the newly split shares.

Both the huge increase in the Company's debt because of the share-repurchase response to the tender in November 1986 and the anonymous letter of February 1987 hastened the restructuring of the Company, and the latter also subtly shifted relationships among the directors. Previously social interaction among directors was limited to lunches during scheduled meetings and a once-a-year December dinner prior to the next day's board meeting. Some of the directors, of which I was one, felt a need to discuss events and the business in more depth than was permitted by the ten agenda-controlled, formal meetings a year. But such informal discussions could take place only among insiders who were fully briefed, and all would be governed by the same legal restrictions on their benefiting from insider knowledge as are directors. Informal discussions rarely occurred.

Some of Gillette's outside directors were also directors of companies that were involved in other takeover attempts. Individual directors, at times, dis-

cussed takeovers in general with outsiders, as I did with some academics, but
company specifics were confidential.

Even as well-informed and intelligent an academic as economist and Nobel
prize winner George Stigler, who during the winter quarter occupied an office
next to mine at the Hoover Institution, could not meet my need for an objective
discussion of Gillette's strategic management decisions. I did not believe that I
could give him enough factual data to make such a discussion meaningful. Although I was a director of another company, it was not involved in a takeover,
and economic and legal concepts were vague without the specifics, about which
I did not feel free to talk. Nor was I as a woman acceptable to the local businessmen's luncheon club, the Palo Alto Club, where such matters at times were
probably discussed by a few members. In retrospect, it is ironic that these dis-
criminatory types of social arrangements deny the very few women directors
the type of intellectual interchange from which they could benefit. Yet some of
that male club's members who are not company directors at the same time
envied the role of a woman on the board of a Fortune 500 company involved
in such an exciting drama as a takeover battle.

To at least a few of the Gillette board members and upper management, the
wisdom of some informal meetings apart from regular board meetings had become obvious. They could be a mutual learning experience.

The treasurer of The Gillette Company, Milton Glass, enjoyed informally
discussing international finance. As chairman of Gillette's finance committee, I
had become very impressed with his knowledge of the money and foreign-
exchange markets in the United States and abroad and often dropped into his
office prior to a board meeting to discuss the financials of Gillette; sometimes
we had breakfast together the day of the board meeting. Milton Glass had spent
all his working life at Gillette, retiring as vice president for finance at the end
of 1991. Milton's father had emigrated from Eastern Europe to the United States.
Milton, as a youngster, worked part-time and graduated from Bentley, a com-
muter business school in Boston. Subsequently, he earned an MBA from North-
eastern University, attending school at night. Milton Glass became Gillette's
financial spokesman during the takeover period and became a vice president of
the Company in February 1987.

I had become chairman of Gillette's finance committee in 1980, and although
I had a Harvard Ph.D. in economics, I had not had a college course specifically
on corporate finance. Milton always informed me about a week ahead of the
meeting what unique matters would be on the agenda—Eurobond financing,
dual-currency convertible bonds, portfolio insurance—giving me a chance, if
necessary, to read and ponder ahead of time about them. For me, it was a
continuing education. For example, in 1984 Gillette was the first company in
the United States to issue dual-currency convertible bonds. I needed to know
more than a brief definition: How did they work? What other companies had
used them? Again, I did not know much about Eurobonds, which were first
issued in 1975 and grew into a world market of a hundred billion dollars. By

1986 over 40 percent of total U.S. corporate borrowing was in Eurodollar bonds. Because Eurobonds are issued outside the jurisdiction of any country, the holders of these bearer bonds can remain anonymous and thus their interest income in practice is often tax-exempt. Eurobonds were a great vehicle for Gillette to finance part of its borrowings as the Company and its foreign subsidiaries could sell them directly; often the bond issue was underwritten by a single bank. The Gillette name was well known abroad, and direct placement of large Eurobond issues made available large amounts of capital at reasonable rates.

During 1985 Gillette had decreased its long-term debt slightly, by $7.2 million, to $436 million. By December 31, 1986, the debt had more than doubled to $915.2 million because of the repurchase of Perelman/Revlon's shares. Although two-thirds of this expense was financed from borrowings under revolving credit agreements and commercial paper, there were also issued ECU notes of $58 million at 7½ percent and, in 1987, of $71.7 million, both due in 1993. During 1986 and 1987 substantially all of the 1984 dual-currency convertible bonds, due in 1994, were called and converted to common stock, resulting in issue of just over 2.1 million new shares. Most of the additional borrowing at the end of 1986, when about $600 million was needed to purchase Perelman's stock, was financed by Deutschmark and by Swiss franc bonds, both at 7 percent and due in 1991. These each represented close to 7 percent of the long-term debt. During 1987 higher-cost French francs, $94 million at 9 percent, and pound sterling at 9⅝ percent enabled reduction of the commercial paper to $150 million and payback of all of the revolving credit loans. The weighted-average interest rate on Gillette's long-term debt was 7.4 percent by December 31, 1987, down from 7.8 percent a year earlier. Gillette had weathered the storm, and its net worth was positive. Net earnings per share were two dollars for 1987 against twelve cents for 1986. Dividends per share in 1987 were 78.5 cents against 68 cents in 1986 and were paid on time throughout this period.

The directors and management were well aware that The Gillette Company continued in play after they repurchased Perelman's shares and a standstill agreement had been signed. Gillette's restructuring, which included selling off small, noncore business units, had pushed the price of the shares higher than the $65 tendered price, and in May 1987 the stock was split two-for-one.

Some media stories on Ronald Owen Perelman, whose personal contradictions and financial success had fascinated many, were openly admiring. His recipe for a successful acquisition was condensed to a simple formula. "Pick a large pool of undervalued assets (it doesn't matter what they are), buy it (or better yet, buy just enough to control it), keep the one or two reliable cash-flow generators, find superb operating managers to handle those cash spigots, reduce the rest of the assets to ready money, and use it to reduce your purchase cost. Leverage liberally to taste."[1] This description of Perelman in action, written after the tender in November 1986 was, I believe, an accurate portrayal of Perelman zeroing in on the assets of Gillette.

Not one director surprised by the tender on November 17, 1986, had remembered at that time and identified the would-be acquirer Ronald Perelman and his MacAndrews & Forbes company as the corporate pyramid builder portrayed in a 1986 *Forbes* story, "Pyramid power."[2] This story had detailed how Perelman built a $4.4 billion empire on the basis of a $1.9 million investment, roughly a 2,300-fold increase. Journalist Allan Sloan writes, "Perelman's secret [is his] superior ability as a business manager and paper shuffler, a sharp eye for tax avoidance and solid support from Drexel Burnham Lambert."[3] Even though this article had probably been read by several directors and upper management personnel when it first appeared, it was not recalled at the time of the tender. It was true that management had little time between receiving the tender offer and the Gillette board meeting, but a computer search would have found this article and several others, which could easily have been circulated among the board members before they considered the tender. At no time do I recall management on their own initiative following such a procedure. There was a lack of internal communication of publicly available information to the Board.

Back in November 1986, the immediate question asked by the Gillette directors was, Who are MacAndrews & Forbes and who is Perelman, that they would be interested in Gillette? That Perelman had pyramided $2 million to over $4 billion was not recalled. The naiveté among some directors showed in their expressed speculation about what an investment company could possibly want with a razor-blade manufacturer. "To make money from the cash flow," was a ready and correct answer. Ronald Perelman had an MBA from the top-rated Wharton School of the University of Pennsylvania and many years of business experience. He could assess the Gillette business from public sources. A story in *Barron's* on August 25, 1986,[4] carried a detailed account of how Gillette was making sizeable profits, ranging from 8 percent on sales of S.T. Dupont's expensive lighters and watches to a 69 percent margin on sales of razors and blades. The story also pointed out that the price of Gillette shares at sixteen times the projected 1986 earnings was relatively below that of shares of other consumer products companies whose prices were up to 20 times projected earnings. Presumably, Ronald Perelman and his top staff read *Barron's* and investment sheets, as well as annual reports and 10-K filings.

On December 1, 1986, *Business Week* carried a detailed account of "Perelman's Route to the Big Leagues."[5] The deals were friendly until his 1985 proxy battle for Pantry Pride, Inc. Perelman used $200 million from selling some of Pantry Pride's assets to buy Revlon, then sold some of Revlon's assets to gain $1.6 billion, and then sold to Salomon Brothers, Inc., his 8 percent stake in CPC International for $41 million. These deals, plus Drexel Burnham Lambert financing, were the source of the somewhat less than one billion dollars of cash needed to make the bid of over $4 billion for Gillette. Obviously, Perelman was an astute financial manager; but in stripping off assets of profitable companies, he could destroy them en route. Gillette's Board wanted no part of being his target.

During the spring of 1987 and into the 2-for-1 stock split and 12 percent dividend increase of May 22, investment houses, as well as the media, built up expectations about the Company's value. Shearson Lehman Brothers' May 4 sheet referred to "spectacular first quarter earnings . . . up 33%"[6] and at $0.96 a share above the street projection of $0.85. But no publicly available information ever hinted that a new razor might be evolving. Perelman still held well over one billion dollars from the $2.5 billion war chest he was reported to hold in March after spending $800 million to take Revlon private in April.

Milton Glass and I had arranged to have dinner on Wednesday evening, June 17, 1987, along with director Herb Jacobi, chairman of the managing partners of Trinkaus and Burkhardt, the largest private bank in then Western Germany. This was a very natural pairing. We were the only two directors at that time who had to come such long distances and would be in Boston the night before the meeting. Thus, we were enjoying an excellent dinner at a French gourmet restaurant, new to me, on Gloucester Street, which was a pleasant walk from the Westin Hotel on Copley Place, where I was staying. We were just beginning our second course when a telephone call came for Milton Glass. The call was from the Company, informing him that Perelman was making a second offer for Gillette shares, this time, after the two-for-one split, at $40.50 per share. There was surprise on both sides, Milton at the offer and the caller at finding that two of Gillette's directors could be easily informed over dinner.

At the board meeting the next day copies of a letter dated June 16 to the Board of Directors carrying the second unsolicited offer from Ronald O. Perelman was distributed. My first recollection is general indignation among the Board members that this time the offer was at $40.50 a share, only 20 percent above the closing price of the previous day at $33⅞ per share, which was, we noted, an amount above the $65 offered for a nonsplit share only seven months previously. By then all the directors were presumably experts on takeovers, and we knew that the premium price in any takeover was customarily at least 30 percent above market. The directors were amazed at Perelman's request to permit him to buy Gillette stock because that request, in the minds of the directors, violated the spirit and intent of the ten-year standstill agreement that Perelman/ Revlon had initiated and Perelman signed. Ronald Perelman had promised to go away. Gillette had agreed to the standstill because it promised ten years of stability needed to carry out the company's future business plans to manufacture at a low unit cost a new generation of razors with the Company's existing technical personnel. A climate of potential takeover swirling around a company does not permit the comfort of the stability necessary to retain key innovative employees.

I, and I suspect other directors, found the June 16 letter itself, even though clothed in the polite language of financial diplomacy, to be insulting. It acknowledged that Perelman/Revlon had signed a standstill agreement not to seek for ten years to buy shares of The Gillette Company, but reiterated that "we are confident that a combination of our two great companies is the best alternative to your shareholders, employees, and the communities in which you conduct your business." The Board did not see a two-way synergy with Revlon. I, the only woman on the board, was annoyed by Perelman's salutation of "Dear Sirs." Further, the Board's hostility was spiked by the inclusion of "your investment banker can feel free to contact our lead lender, Citibank N.A." Gillette's lead investment banker for many years had been Citicorp, with its commercial banking arm being Citibank, a position that placed Citibank in a coveted position among bankers in Europe. Board members and management were understandably angered that Citibank was the lead lender for Drexel Burnham's junk bonds to finance Perelman/Revlon's second takeover attempt of Gillette. The Board authorized that after June 26, when the Board planned to meet again, that a stinging letter be sent to John S. Reed, chairman of Citicorp's board. That letter removed all of Gillette's U.S. and international business from Citicorp, thus breaking a relationship that dated back to 1966 and had included co-managing a 300 million DM borrowing for Gillette during the previous two months. The Gillette Board viewed Citibank's role as Perelman/Revlon's lead lender as a "repudiation of the long-standing relationship between Gillette and Citibank" and did not accept Citibank/Citicorp's argument that a "Chinese Wall" of secrecy isolated Citibank's actions from Citicorp's.

The Gillette Board also questioned the high number of trades in Gillette stock—over 3 million shares on two days, over 2 million on one day and over 1 million on five other days between June 1 and 19—because they gave an appearance that early information about Revlon's proposal might have led to the increased activity in Gillette stock prior to public disclosure on June 18. Under the 1986 standstill agreement, Gillette management was authorized to initiate legal suit if Perelman/Revlon started to buy any Gillette shares without permission.

Perelman had in conjunction with the repurchase also received a one-year *call option*, which would give him the difference between the price ($29.75) that Gillette paid in November 1986 for Gillette's stock held by him and any future price that another buyer of the Company might pay in the ensuing one-year period. The provision expired in November 1987. The Gillette Board denied consent for Perelman to buy stock because he had signed the ten-year standstill and noted that the option gave him an unfair advantage over other companies in bidding. Perelman's second letter, June 18, quickly responded to Gillette's immediate turndown by waiving in advance being paid for the difference between the repurchase price of November 1986 and his offer of $40.50, totaling about $200 million. The Board deemed this June 18 waiver to be a negotiation ploy and worthless because Gillette could tie Revlon up in the courts until the expiration of the option in November 1987.

In the afternoon of June 26, the Gillette Board met and reaffirmed their turndown. Further, the Board again asserted the Company's "bright future and recalled that per-share earnings rose 33 percent during the first quarter of 1987 and that a similar rise was expected for the second quarter. Additionally, although the Board responded as requested by June 26, it stated that in the future it would not respond to any future communications from Perelman/Revlon considered to be in violation of the agreement and would not respond to their imposed deadlines, but rather in the regular course of business.

The Reuters Wire of June 18 reported Perelman's overture in the same fashion as the Gillette Board saw it. Perelman "may be trying to ignite a bidding war for Gillette Company that could draw some big international players and in the process make a lot of money for himself." And, on June 19 it was reported that "Irwin L. Jacobs, the Minneapolis investor, disclosed yesterday that he owned 'a substantial' block of stock in the Gillette Company."[7] There was potential value to Revlon if it could provoke a buyer to buy Gillette before mid-November 1987.

Speculation swirled about the Company. Would Gillette sell a major division to another company? Why did Perelman's request to permit purchase of Gillette's share specify a price of "at least $40.50" a share? Would he offer more, and was anyone else in addition to Jacobs buying shares in the heavy trading during the first part of June?

Because my husband became very ill about this time and on July 14 had a successful mitral valve replacement, I attended the June 26 meeting by telephone. The Board was advised by outside legal counsel that consenting to Perelman/Revlon's request would close off using the standstill-and-call option tactics in the future, when such actions might well benefit Gillette shareholders. Further, acceding to the demands would be placing a for-sale sign on Gillette. The Board with its outside advisors concluded that it was not in the interests of shareholders to sell at this time, nor was it legally required to conduct an auction. The answer was *no*.

During this period the media tried to spur further takeover action, if not by Ronald Perelman, then by others. Commentators agreed that Gillette's refusal did not mean that Ronald Perelman was going away. Immediately after the turndown of the $40.50 per share bid, Irwin Jacobs and other so-called arbitrageurs began speculating in the stock. Fayez Sarofin, a Houston-based investment advisor, was reported as holding about four million or 3.5 percent of Gillette's shares outstanding. Jacobs confirmed that although he owned a substantial stake, it was less than the 5 percent required for disclosure and that he expected the company to act in the best interest of its shareholders. He also pointed out that disgruntled shareholders could file suit, and of course a group did so in the Delaware Chancery Court. Meanwhile, newspaper articles speculated about what Gillette could do. For example, "Several companies have fought hostile takeovers by proposing recapitalizations. But one Gillette source played down the likelihood of such a move, noting that such drastic moves simply aren't Gillette's style."[8] Others mentioned that Gillette could buy back more of its stock, and still others speculated about the possibility of substantial cross-shareholdings.

A shareholders suit was filed in Delaware requesting that Revlon be freed of the standstill agreement in order to allow a *free market auction* for Gillette.

Speculation moved to whether the courts would invalidate a signed contract. The Delaware Chancery Court on June 28, 1987, reviewed the shareholder appeal, and its vice chancellor was reported to state that the plaintiffs would have trouble convincing the court to enter a mandatory preliminary injunction because that would abrogate an existing contract.[9]

The major advisor to Ronald Perelman was Howard Gittis, a top lawyer in Philadelphia and vice chairman of Revlon/MacAndrews. "Mr. Gittis supervises all legal and financial aspects of takeover bids, acquisitions and divestitures. As chief administrative officer, he deals with investment banks as well as internal personnel matters. The 53-year-old Mr. Gittis says his compensation totals 'in excess of a couple of million dollars' a year."[10] Generally speaking, Mr. Gittis was the detail-oriented person behind the acquisitions, while Mr. Perelman did the grand planning of the takeovers. The last two paragraphs of a Wall Street Journal article are revealing:

Though not as flamboyant as his boss, Mr. Gittis enjoys luxury. In Southampton, he lives in a peaked-and-gabled estate with eight bedrooms, 10 baths, a sauna, steam bath, exercise room, tennis courts and a pool. Mr. Perelman summers down the road in equally fashionable East Hampton.

Even in the Hamptons, Mr. Gittis says, he and his boss talk several times a day. But their closeness is best demonstrated, he says, by the layout of the Revlon offices in New York. There are two ways to enter Mr. Perelman's 49th-floor Fifth Avenue office overlooking Central Park. One is down a long hall lined with murals. The other is through Howard Gittis's office. "I have an open door to his office," Mr. Gittis says.[11]

The role of the media in the game plan of takeover strategy can hardly be overlooked. For example, a *New York Times* story on June 4, 1987, headed "Rumors Swirling around Gillette," speculated that among potential acquirers were Sir James Goldsmith, Hanson Trust, Irwin L. Jacobs and, possibly, a one-time conjecture, the Japanese.[12] There were many speculations about who were accumulating stock. Arbitrageurs were buying because they believed that "eventually this company will be acquired," Andrew S. Shore of Shearson Lehman Brothers and others were quoted as saying. The investment houses during May and June released research bulletins and reports by their in-house analysts that supported *buys* based on fundamentals and at times these created rumors. Strong earnings gains were predicted, because of the acceleration of Gillette's learning curve to become more efficient because of takeover pressure. The stock price was projected to rise to between the mid-$40s (Gruntal & Co., Inc., June 3, 1987) and $50 (Tucker Anthony, June 4, 1987) on a takeover basis. Analysts correctly assessed the growing favorable impact of the company's huge geographic expansion and market share gains. Whatever the interpretation, Gillette was clearly still *in play*, and the stock price rose, to close at 40¼ on June 18, 1987.

As the summer wore on, the media attention continued. A June 26th page-two story in the *Wall Street Journal* attributed to "sources" that Perelman/Revlon were considering boosting their buying price to between $41 and $45 a share and reported that "someone else—perhaps a foreign buyer—may be interested in acquiring Gillette."

The *Wall Street Journal* of July 15, the Wednesday before the regularly scheduled board meeting, carried a signed story headed, "Gillette Shares Advance Amid Signs That Big Buyer Is Accumulating Stock."[13] The share price rose to $43.875, and the only buyers named in the story were Bear, Stearns and Co., a New York investment banking firm, and takeover trader Irwin Jacobs. Media speculation also revived again the rumor that the Ralston Purina Co. of St. Louis might become a partner in cross-shareholdings with Gillette.[14] If the media could, it would have ignited a bidding war.

Meanwhile, the state of Massachusetts passed an antitakeover bill that was modeled after Indiana's new takeover law, which had been upheld by the Supreme Court. The Massachusetts legislation asserted its jurisdiction over companies incorporated outside of that state if they also had substantial assets within Massachusetts and/or were headquartered in that state, such as Gillette. Some argued that this legal policy would subject a multistate company, again such as Gillette, to the laws of more than one state. Delaware, where Gillette was incorporated, had not, as of 1987, enacted antitakeover legislation, and thus the Massachusetts legislation was believed not likely to cause a problem in this respect. The legislators who had met with Gillette's CEO Colman Mockler also in June 1987 were reported to have said that "they plan to take action . . . that would strengthen the company's takeover defenses."[15] It is not unusual for corporate executives to seek government's help to attain the corporation's goals. Pressure by the Company's employees to retain their jobs can be exerted through the political process. Gillette had thousands of employees who vote in Massachusetts' elections.

AUGUST 1987

The new 1987 Massachusetts law denies shareholder voting rights in a corporate board election to anyone who buys or offers to buy 20 percent of a company's shares. The law requires that an election be held within 50 days after such action to approve or reject the would-be acquirer. This legislation made it difficult for Perelman or any other would-be buyer to pursue Gillette. Although some believed that the new law would be called unconstitutional, the Indiana law after which the Massachusetts law was patterned was upheld on April 21, 1987, by a 6–3 vote of the Supreme Court as being well within the rights of states to regulate corporations. Despite this in August 1987 Perelman again approached Gillette for permission to buy the Company, his third offer in less than a year. Journalists found the story of Perelman's pursuit of Gillette to be irresistible, and imaginative stories and headlines appeared in the business sections of newspapers.[16]

An analyst who followed The Gillette Company closely was quoted as suc-
cinctly stating, "cash flow, brand names and the worldwide distribution network" appeal to Mr. Perelman. "The blade business is an inherent cash
machine, with 60% market share and in Latin America 80%. We're talking about
a huge appeal."[17]

It was estimated by Gillette's management that a buyer could finance a takeover of Gillette from the Company's ongoing cash flow if the buyer could put
up, up front, $1.3 billion. Important in this scenario was an earlier court ruling
that in order to make a tender offer for a company, it was not necessary for a
potential acquirer to have financing in place. Although legally Perelman's request to purchase shares was not a tender offer, it again placed before the Board
the issue of whether it was the right time to sell the business. No one else, to
the Board's knowledge, was seeking to buy Gillette, and not until the Board
gave permission for Perelman to purchase the shares could he actually make a
tender. Citibank was again Perelman/Revlon's financial backer. The *Wall Street
Journal* reported that Gillette had severed its 22-year banking ties with Citibank
because they had been the lead lender in the June hostile proposal to buy Gillette.[18] But financing for Perelman did not appear to be a problem. The $1.3
billion was available, some in cash and the rest to be supplied by investment
bankers.

The Board had a lengthy discussion with outside legal and investment advisors as to how far the business judgment rule would cover the Board's actions
and the possible taxes that would have to be paid if the company were sold.
The all-important projections of Gillette's future business were analyzed. On a
continuing basis, Gillette had been exceeding analysts' projections of earnings
ever since Perelman's first run. The Board also was fascinated and frustrated by
the fact that because Revlon was a private company, it would not have to report
its earnings. Revlon Group's directors had accepted $20.10 a share from Ronald
Perelman, about $800 million in April of 1987. It was not a secret that Gillette
was still in play, but the only known potential buyer was Perelman, who would
benefit substantially for every dollar over the $29.50 repurchase price of No-
vember 1986 if only another buyer could be enticed to bid successfully prior to
November 24, 1987. Gillette's earnings were up by 40 percent, but new buyers
had not surfaced. As Smith Barney's astute specialist Nancy Hall stated on July
27, the "mystery accumulator is a no-show . . . we believe GS can move back
toward $45. If GS is taken out, we think the price tag is at least $48."[19]

The persistent Ronald Perelman would not go away quietly, and he again
requested by letter of August 17 permission to buy all the Company shares, this
time at $47; $45 in cash and $2 in stock. The *Boston Globe* published an
editorial on Friday, August 21, in support of the Company. "Gillette is an old-
fashioned success in that it makes useful, everyday things. Small wonder it has
paid cash dividends to its shareholders every year since 1906."[20]

Although Gillette did not have a scheduled August meeting, one was called for Monday, August 24; as most observers had expected, the third offer by Perelman was turned down.

Perelman's request again forced discussion of all alternative options. These included a leveraged buyout, seeking another company as a white knight to form some type of partnership or to remain independent based on the Board's high assessment of the potential success of Gillette's future business plans, with the launch of the Sensor. Foremost was to select the path that would maximize shareholder's value. The legacy of the Trans Union decision of January 29, 1985, meant that no company director was free from the threat of a catastrophic personal liability award. It was therefore personally prudent to go once again through all the legally advocated requirements. Otherwise each director's liability insurance would not cover his/her costs.

Going through my mind during these discussions was how precise a reflection of value a share price could be that changed in about nine months from $32.50 in November 1986 to $40.50 offered in June 1987, and $47 in August 1987. On a pre-split basis an increase from $65 to $94 was a 45 percent gain. Perelman might have obtained new information about Gillette to support his continual upping of the price that he was willing to pay. At the same time, because the stock market was soaring, one had to correct for the effect of the general stock market's rising prices on Gillette's share-price increase. In my mind, however, and in most analysts' minds, the market's general rise over nine months did not account for all of the about 45 percent rise in Perelman's assessment of the value of a Gillette share. The Standard & Poor's stock market 500 index rose 34 percent between November 1986 and August 1987.

Even as Perelman kept requesting permission to buy the Company, Gillette was divesting operations peripheral to its core business. Negotiations were in process to sell the computer catalog company, Misco. Also being sold were Gillette's partial equity holdings in two optical retail stores: Eye World, headquartered in Natick, Massachusetts, and Eye + Tech of Houston, Texas. And sold during this period was land and a research building outside of Washington, D.C., in Rockville, Maryland.

Simultaneously, Gillette was expanding geographically its manufacturing facilities to make metal and plastic components of core products abroad, as, for example, in Manaus, Brazil. The business was being carried on, and even the niceties were not overlooked. Management suggested and the Board approved at its September meeting the issuance of 50 shares of Gillette common stock to Mary A. Bray in recognition of her 50 years of employment with the Company. The Board was caught up in a myriad of decisions in international expansion of a large business even as it had to decide on what assets to sell and most important what to do with a would-be acquirer who would not go away.

During the August board meeting, management's success in selling off the more peripheral parts of the business was reported. Sales of S.T. Dupont and Misco were expected to bring in $16 million more than the restructuring plan had envisioned. Although other smaller gains were anticipated from sales of smaller divisions, some small losses were also anticipated. Gillette's management did not have the luxury of concentrating on running the Company.

Before the Board finally made its decision on August 24 once again to refuse Perelman's overtures, it was told that Irwin Jacobs would, depending upon the action of the Board, file a Schedule 13-D and begin a proxy contest. The *Wall Street Journal* reported on August 25 that Irwin Jacobs had been holding a large stake in Gillette and that as a large shareholder he was "becoming increasingly unhappy with Gillette's position." The story speculated on other courses of action open to Jacobs, which included putting pressure on Gillette "to drive it into the arms of a friendly suitor, boosting the price of its stock in the process."[21] The *Journal* article further speculated that Jacobs might call for "a special shareholders meeting to consider Gillette's future—a strategy he employed in seeking to bring about management changes at Walt Disney Productions in 1984."[22] The article cited the several times in the past that Mr. Jacobs had applied pressure to different corporations with similar interesting results. Jacobs sold his various stakes, each for under the 5 percent SEC reporting limit and each for sizeable profits. Once a company has been perceived as paying greenmail, others would like also to be paid greenmail—to get a piece of the pie. Mr. Jacobs appeared to be interested in being paid greenmail.

The directors read with wry amusement an article, "Antic Observations: Fanciful Theories on Perelman's Obsession with Gillette," in the Sunday issue of the *New York Times* of August 23. The article cleverly tweaked Gillette for its stodgy ads, and Ron Perelman because he's greedy. "He yearns to remove the one flaw in greenmail—the fact that it doesn't provide a predictable revenue stream."[23] Although in November 1986 Perelman, as an unknown to the Board, surprised Gillette by his tough business practices, his more recent, carefully crafted, softening public image had become by August 1987 all too familiar.

Three economic factors attracted Perelman to Gillette: steady, sizable cash flow, higher operating profits and Gillette's lead position in drugstores and supermarkets in both the United States and abroad, where Gillette's sales were expanding. The marketing of Oral-B toothbrushes, as well as razors and blades, demonstrated an increasing potential synergy with Perelman's newly added drugstore cosmetic lines: Almay, Max Factor, Charles of the Ritz and Germaine Monteil.

Gillette's refusal in a special August 24 meeting to accept the $47-a-share bid provoked Revlon's Vice Chairman Howard Gittis to state, "We certainly don't intend to abandon the pursuit."[24] Although newspapers are not always correct in their reporting, this phraseology seemed then to be accurate.

It bothered the directors that Perelman was not willing to live up to his earlier agreement not to pursue Gillette or seek to control or influence Gillette. As I recall, the issue of whether Perelman could obtain the money for a takeover was hardly discussed. Probably the other directors, like myself, assumed that with the backing of the Bank of Boston and Citibank, Perelman/Revlon could raise the $1.3 billion needed and finance the rest from cash flow. A *Fortune* magazine article confirmed our estimates of the availability of cash to Perelman. It stated that Perelman's war chest was $1.6 billion.[25] Gillette was well along in its restructuring with divestitures and elimination of jobs and had a slow, continuing increase in sales and profits. The Board, after a relatively brief discussion without outsiders present, authorized at the August 24 meeting issuance of a press release to state that it was in the best interest of the shareholders to refuse the unsolicited request by Perelman/Revlon to be permitted to buy the Company's stock.

Perelman sent another letter to Gillette's Board extending his offer until October 15, but it did not increase the $47 offer, which was about 19 percent above market price. The letter's tone was arrogant in asserting that the Board, still addressed as "Sirs," had not thoroughly reviewed Perelman's request and "accordingly we will extend our request until October 15, 1987, in the hopes that you will be more responsible in your evaluation."

The very stressful period continued. At the September 24 Gillette Board meeting Joe Flom stated that Perelman's request to waive the standstill against purchase of Gillette stock was not a tender offer. This was a legal nicety. There was no legal requirement to sell the Company. Investment advisors reiterated their earlier advice about all the factors that the directors must take into account. But no one among all the financial types present even hinted at the possibility of a sharp overall drop in stock market prices.

Late in September, Perelman/Revlon Group offered to buy from Salomon Inc. a special issue of preferred shares on the same basis that Warren Buffett/Berkshire Hathaway was offering, about $809 million worth. Although a Revlon spokesman was quoted as saying their filing "has no effect on our interest in Gillette,"[26] it would have weakened their cash position. Revlon had been taken private in May 1987, and it was difficult to gauge how much cash they had. In June, Revlon was estimated to have spent $125 million to $150 million in buying major cosmetic brands from Yves St. Laurent International S.A.

"Gillette can hear the footsteps," as a long *Boston Sunday Globe* article that ended with "No one knows who owns Gillette,"[27] put it well. Since the beginning of June through September 25, 113.5 million shares of Gillette had traded. Although this represented almost 100 percent of the 114.6 million shares outstanding, undoubtedly some shares had traded several times. Additionally, future options for 20 million shares had also traded. The company was in play. Some analysts judged that Gillette stock, with the Company's streamlining and higher profits would shortly be worth $50 a share. Although many believed that the market was generally overvalued, this qualification was not raised in connection with Gillette. Rather, analysts were usually quoted as making favorable factual statements, for example, "Gillette has been raising earnings and the stock has been rising in a strong market."[28]

Deal making is a fascinating game. But in a way the directors were on the fringe. It was Eric Gleacher of Morgan Stanley and Joe Flom of Skadden Arps who did the dealing. I, and I believe that this is true for the other directors, never even met Ronald Perelman. We listened to what our negotiators wanted to divulge. We also learned from the newspapers some additional facts. For example, Oppenheimer and Co. was reported as placing Gillette on its "restricted list,"[29] signaling that investment concern might become a player in the persistent takeover speculation surrounding the Boston-based maker of razor and personal-care products. Speculation was that this reflected Oppenheimer and Co.'s purchases of a large stake of Gillette shares for arbitrage gains. Of course, there were so many stories and rumors floating that it was hard to sift the truth from falsehood. In retrospect, it would have been easier if copies of newspaper articles about Gillette from the hometown paper, the *Boston Globe*, and from the *New York Times* and the *Wall Street Journal* had been routinely sent to outside directors. On the other hand, surprises made my daily reading of the *Wall Street Journal* more exciting.

During this period even a *Pacman* defense, Gillette buy Revlon, was discussed. Also floated by Perelman were intermediate positions—one billion dollars for 20 percent of Gillette and two people on the board! Did Perelman want Gillette for social position, as well as cash flow, or did he just want a leg in the door? Should the Board go to the shareholders with the $47 offer?

Some news commentators were writing rather strong stories about how Gillette had become "a sleepy, undermanaged storehouse of untapped value"[30] that was forced into hurried restructuring by the Perelman bid in late 1986. Gillette's restructuring involved elimination of excess, costly inventory storage for too many products. Paper Mate's 400 products were cut to 300. The closing and selling of some operations of Jafra Cosmetics, Inc., and of course the divestitures and the planned selling off of Misco, Elizabeth Grady Beauty Salons and Eye World all helped to reduce excessive inventories. These moves were pushing up the cash flow at Gillette, but not as far as it needed to go.

Gillette and Perelman let the Tuesday, October 15, extension date of Perelman's offer expire. Gillette voted its regular quarterly dividend of 19 cents payable December 4 to shareholders as of November 2. Its October 15 press release reported third-quarter operating profits 27 percent above those of the third quarter a year ago in 1986. No mention of Ronald Perelman was made in that press release.

OCTOBER 19, 1987: BLACK MONDAY

A one-day drop in the Dow Jones Index of close to *100* points on October 14, the Wednesday before Gillette's board meeting, was generally considered "a mere correction in an underlying bull market," and little heed was taken of the warning by the well-respected financial analyst Alfred L. Malabre, Jr., that the fall "may not be reversed so readily."[31] Even though a major newspaper headline warned that it saw the "stock market reeling" from an increasing foreign trade deficit, the market had been considered overvalued for so long that it seemed to be without warning that the precipitous fall on *Black Monday*,

October 19, occurred. Some believed that the wide adoption of computer-based, program trading of stocks intensified the market's fall, and others that the speculative impact was worsened by increased futures trading and so-called portfolio insurance. It also was fairly common to point to Japan's fairly rapid decline in buying U.S. government debt instruments. Regardless of the causes, on October 19, 1987, the Dow Jones Industrial Average plunged by 22.6 percent, or 508 points. Black Monday was only one business day after Gillette's October board meeting. Gillette's share price plunged and its directors sought comfort in that many other companies had the same experience. However, other companies had not turned down a $47-per-share offer in August that had been extended by a letter of September 14 until October 15, 1987, for shares that the market judged on October 19 to be worth only $23.625 a share.

A draft of a proposed letter to Gillette shareholders had been prepared to be sent jointly from Colman Mockler and Joseph Turley and was distributed to the Board, October 15. The three-and-a-quarter page, single-spaced letter explained in general terms how the Board reached its unanimous decision not to sell the Company and touted its success as of September 30, 1987, as evidenced by higher earnings, substantial progress in restructuring and continuing pursuance of its business plans. I, and I believe other directors, called the company on Monday, October 19, not to send this or any similar letter.

Gillette was not the only company that was approached during this period by a would-be acquirer wishing to force its sale to them. For example, there was the widely written-about Newmont Mining Corporation, which had a standstill agreement that restricted Gold Fields, a company that already owned 26 percent of Newmont's stock, to owning no more than one-third of its stock and having a one-third representation on Newmont's board. On September 8, 1987, Ivanhoe made a partial tender offer for Newmont and consolidated Gold Fields in a street sweep to increase its ownership of Newmont to 49.7 percent. Newmont felt itself to be threatened and declared a $33 per share special dividend, permitting Ivanhoe Acquisitions Corporation, controlled by T. Boone Pickens, to make a tender offer for Newmont. The Delaware Supreme Court found, among other things, that the standstill agreement was a reasonable response because it protected public shareholders from an "unbridled majority shareholder" and that Newmont had no legal obligation to sell the company, and further that the directors were not obliged to sell the company.[32] If under these circumstances of a standstill agreement Newmont was not legally required to be for sale, then in the opinion of Gillette's directors, neither was Gillette. The Newmont Mining case decision also reaffirmed the business judgment rule protection and in general gave the Gillette Board and management legal comfort.

Gillette's directors took some legal comfort in the Newmont decision because, like Newmont, Gillette was never for sale and had had only one bidder: Perelman/Revlon. The Board felt justified in its refusal to break a standstill agreement and in its turn-down of a $47 offer (or $94 compared to the pre-split $65 offer of November 1986), even though the stock market subsequently in one day had plunged over 500 points. Although Perelman must have felt relieved on October 19, he and the Gillette directors knew that stock prices fall but they also rise again, and Gillette was a company with a bright economic future. Gillette had been *in play* for almost a year, and there was no sign that the extraordinary amount of media coverage was lessening. Very few had predicted such a rapid fall in stock prices. However, one good thing came out of this large market correction, as new and old bidders for Gillette did not surface for at least a short period of time, affording management some breathing space.

If Gillette had on October 15 accepted a $47-a-share bid from Perelman, he would have been legally committed to purchase the company at that price. The pursuit of Gillette ended only for a short period of time. It had become a company so well-known to potential takeover artists because of its high intrinsic value, international marketing and profits of 30 cents on each dollar of sales of razors that it was too tempting for takeover artists to ignore. This time it would attract the so-called strategic block investors, the Coniston Partners.

At the end of September, Ronald Perelman had put into play Salomon Brothers. John Gutfreund, CEO of Salomon, turned down Perelman and sought the protection of the "Oracle of Omaha," Warren Buffett, a billionaire investor of his Berkshire Hathaway Inc. funds. Warren Buffett paid $700 million for Salomon Inc.'s 9 percent preferred stock, which was convertible, after three years, into a 12 percent stake in Salomon."[33] With $63 million a year in virtually tax-free dividends, this was generally judged a very good deal for Berkshire Hathaway.

About one year later, in the summer of 1988, Warren Buffett similarly protected Gillette and greatly benefited Berkshire Hathaway's shareholders by buying $600 million of special Gillette preferred stock. This action is discussed in detail in a later chapter.

Ronald Perelman publicly disputed that he was a corporate raider, stating, "We just build businesses,"[34] and adding for good measure that incomparable phrase, "I'm dumb, but I am not stupid."[35]

NOTES

1. Anthony Ramirez, "The Year's 50 Most Fascinating Business People: Revlon's Striving Makeover Man," *Fortune*, January 5, 1987, p. 54.

2. Allan Sloan, "Pyramid Power," *Forbes*, January 27, 1986, pp. 30–31.

3. Ibid., p. 31.

4. Gary Weiss, "Razor Sharp: Gillette to Snap Back from a Dull Stretch," *Barron's*, August 25, 1986, pp. 15, 37.

5. Amy Dunkin, Laurie Baum and Lois Therrien, "People/Dealmakers: This Takeover Artist Wants to Be a Makeover Artist, Too," *Business Week*, December 1, 1986, p. 110.

6. Andrew Shore, "The Gillette Company," Shearson Lehman Brothers, May 4, 1987, p. 1.

7. Robert J. Cole, "Jacobs Calls Holdings in Gillette 'Substantial,' " *New York Times*, June 20, 1987, p. 37.

8. Christopher J. Chipello and Laurie P. Cohen, "Gillette's Rejection of Revlon's Proposal Isn't Likely to Deter Chairman Perelman," *Wall Street Journal*, June 22, 1987, p. 7.

9. David Wessel, "Gillette Reaffirms Refusal of Revlon Bid, Argues for Stronger Anti-Takeover Law," *Wall Street Journal*, June 29, 1987, p. 8.

10. Ann Hagedorn, "Gittis Opts for a Low Profile at Revlon," *Wall Street Journal*, June 25, 1987, p. 30.

11. Ibid.

12. Robert J. Cole, "Rumors Swirling around Gillette," *New York Times*, June 4, 1987, p. D2.

13. Bryan Burrough and David Wessel, "Gillette Shares Advance amid Signs That Big Buyer Is Accumulating Stock," *Wall Street Journal*, July 15, 1987, p. 4.

14. Chipello and Cohen, "Gillette's Rejection," p. 7.

15. Wessel, "Gillette Reaffirms Refusal," p. 8.

16. Andrew Feinberg, "Antic Observations: Fanciful Theories on Perelman's Obsession with Gillette," *New York Times*, August 23, 1987, p. F8.

17. Christopher J. Chipello and Ann Hagedorn, "Revlon Proposes to Buy Gillette and Is Rebuffed," *Wall Street Journal*, June 19, 1987, p. 3.

18. Robert Guenther, "Gillette Is Severing Ties with Citibank over Bank's Role in Hostile Revlon Plan," *Wall Street Journal*, August 14, 1987, p. 4.

19. "Bulletin: Cosmetics," Smith Barney Research, July 27, 1987.

20. Editorial, "Gillette's Sharp Identity," *Boston Globe*, August 21, 1987.

21. Richard Gibson and John Andrew, "Jacobs Considers Move in Takeover Fight for Gillette, Confirms McGraw-Hill Stake," *Wall Street Journal*, August 26, 1987, p. 2.

22. Ibid.

23. Feinberg, "Antic Observations," p. F8.

24. David Wessel and Ann Hagedorn, "Gillette Refuses Revlon's Bid of $47 a Share," *Wall Street Journal*, August 25, 1987, p. 4.

25. Thomas Moore and Wilton Woods, "Big Deals: How the 12 Top Raiders Rate," *Fortune*, September 28, 1987, p. 52.

26. Laurie P. Cohen, "Revlon Offers to Buy Interest in Salomon Inc.," *Wall Street Journal*, September 29, 1987, p. 3.

27. Robert Lenzner, "Gillette Can Hear the Footsteps," *Boston Sunday Globe*, September 27, 1987, p. A1.

28. Ibid., p. A5.

29. Bryan Burrough, "Gillette Is Placed on Restricted List of Oppenheimer," *Wall Street Journal*, September 11, 1987, p. 41.

30. Keith H. Hammonds, "Turnarounds: How Ron Perelman Scared Gillette into Shape," *Business Week*, October 12, 1987, p. 40.

31. Alfred L. Malabre, Jr., "Stocks May Face More Than a Correction: Past Linkage with Bond Market Suggests So," *Wall Street Journal*, October 15, 1987, p. 6.

32. Delaware Supreme Court, *Ivanhoe Partners v Newmont Mining Corporation*, no. 341, November 18, 1987

33. "Letter to Shareholders," *1987 Annual Report of Berkshire Hathway Inc.*, p. 19.

34. Steve Swartz, "Home to Roost: Raid on Salomon Inc. Has Turned the Tables on Wall Street Firms," *Wall Street Journal*, October 2, 1987, p. 16.

35. Ibid.

7

A Target

As the decade of the 1980s progressed, the number of hostile takeovers increased, takeovers of increasingly larger firms in the United States. Junk bonds and rising returns to bankers and attorneys who got a percentage of the deal were major driving factors. Junk bonds heightened the availability of credit, and as the deals increased in size the economic incentives were larger for the major players, who were often paid a percentage of the deal. In part the merger boom was helped by the Reagan administration's limited enforcement of antitrust policy and the market's rising real interest rates on government securities, which in turn forced corporations to compete for cash by paying out higher dividends. High real interest rates raised the cost of capital to build a new plant and thus swung decisions by companies towards buying cheaper, existing plants rather than building new ones. "No risk, no gain," ruled, and business increased its appetite for risk. The debt levels of corporations increased dramatically in order to complete the financing of attractive deals. There are some who regard the 1980s as a decade of greed, but others, including myself, view it as an extraordinary period of economic expansion.

The new technology of computers, wireless telecommunications and fax machines made possible the fast interchange of technical and financial information among the widely dispersed parties necessary for planning financial restructuring and the complex deals that made expansion possible. An additional factor was the impending implementation of the 1986 change in the U.S. tax law that would increase the capital gains and decrease the corporate income tax rates and thus placed pressure on takeover dealers to speed up the timing of their transactions.

FREE CASH-FLOW THESIS

Why did The Gillette Company specifically become the target of Ronald Perelman's hostile takeover bids, which started in November 1986 and continued in June and August 1987—to be followed by the Coniston Partners' takeover attempt, which was defeated in a proxy contest April 1988? The simple answer is that Perelman and Coniston were seeking to make money and Gillette had a large, stable cash flow. Economists and others have developed different, more sophisticated theories to help explain why a specific company becomes a target of takeover attempts. But to me, the deciding factor is that Gillette has generated and continues to generate substantial annual, stable cash revenue flow over costs. Michael Jensen's free-cash-flow thesis helps to explain Gillette's great attraction for a takeover attempt. The ultimate answer is that what drives a would-be acquirer is the opportunity to make money.

Michael Jensen, a Harvard Business School professor who also taught at the University of Rochester, has promoted a free-cash-flow theory of takeovers. At a 1985 symposium Jensen presented his concept of acceptable uses of a company's *free cash flow* as follows: "Free cash flow is cash flow in excess of that required to fund all projects that have positive net present values when discounted at the relevant cost of capital. Such free cash flow must be paid out to shareholders if the firm is to be efficient and to maximize value for shareholders."[1]

The last sentence's precept Gillette disregarded. Gillette did not use its free cash flow in the early 1980s solely to pay out dividends to shareholders, shore up the advertising and production of its existing products and geographically expand and fund purchase of only immediately revenue-producing firms at levels above the relevant cost of capital. Gillette spent some of its free cash to acquire companies or part equity in companies that were not all good fits but might, it was thought, eventually provide profitable new markets. The actions were deliberate and made with an intent eventually to replace the anticipated decline in the nondisposable blade market. Selection of acquisitions that would fit was a difficult task. In hindsight, it is clear that the purchase of Oral-B Laboratories and its toothbrush manufacture from Cooper Laboratories Inc. was an excellent move, but equity investment in beauty salons was unwise. Both had some relation to Gillette's existing product lines. Prediction is difficult. Chapter 3 has other illustrations of this point. Many of the Chicago school's economists with whom I informally talked at the Hoover Institution held that at least some of Gillette's purchases were not in the best interest of the shareholders. Critics fault the purchase of small companies whose manufacturing and marketing processes proved not to be synergistic with Gillette's existing products, but these critics have the benefit of hindsight. Gillette was not unique in its failure to assess correctly the future value of acquisitions. As already noted, many large companies buy several entities, keep some and develop them, often for sizeable profit, while selling off their losers. Gillette may have had a high ratio of losers to winners, but it also purchased some real winners. Even as Perelman hovered, Gillette bought Waterman S.A., thus widening and strengthening its position in the writing instruments business. To gain, one must risk.

Buying a company or a partial equity of a company involves all the directors' judgments as well as those of management, and in discussions during a Gillette Board meeting a consensus evolved, although not all involved necessarily would agree with it. For example, Gillette has excellent manufacturing and mass-marketing skills. Beauty salons do not utilize either of these strengths, but I was not successful in convincing the other decision makers to turn down management's proposal to purchase partial equity of Elizabeth Grady and similar salons. To the majority of the Board, beauty salons and Gillette were a synergistic fit. It was argued that beauty salons could sell Gillette's products, most notably Paul Mitchell's shampoo and other toiletries and cosmetic lines. As these products were, I believed, to the consumer a cut above most of Gillette's toiletries, I believed that it was unlikely that the alliance would enhance sales of Gillette's lower-priced toiletry products. Beauty salons sell one-on-one; Gillette sells through mass advertising.

It was rare for a Board consensus to develop against the well-researched and well-presented proposals of management to buy all or part of any company. A proposed action was described by management and then usually supported by the analysis of the investment banker who had initially proposed the company for purchase or investment. Although a final decision by the Board was not always asked for immediately, the sense of the Board to initiate a *due diligence* check of the company was usually sought. I can recall only one clear negative majority reaction of the Board against acquiring a company, and this was in the case of Sani-Fresh, a manufacturer of disposable fluid soap implying qualities of a soothing lotion along with cleansing power that was being used in public restrooms of hotels and airports. Such a company requires product and distribution channels with which Gillette had no experience, and after arguments were made by several directors against the proposal, it was not pursued.

During the 1980s, Gillette continued to pay out nearly 50 percent of company profits as dividends and gambled that it could improve its long-run profit position by investing in research and development of its new, potentially high-margin razor and blade, as well as making purchases of parts of other companies. Gillette, in effect, acted as a venture capitalist when it purchased these minority equity positions. Diversion of its excess cash to purchase existing small companies or to invest experimentally in small percentages of equity of other larger companies meant that the capital markets did not scrutinize this use of Gillette's cash flow as the markets do whenever a new firm goes public. Such a lack of market discipline is also true for many other new ventures that do not start out as initial public offerings or IPOs. New companies may start within an existing corporate framework, some are supported primarily by venture capitalists and some may just be new, very small, nonformalized companies without legal incorporation or partnership, often using primarily the innovator's funds. As a resident of Silicon Valley, I find such entrepreneurial activity to be a not unusual way of economic life.

Managers, including Gillette's, have incentives, such as gains in prestige and new higher-level jobs and salaries, to expand their firms beyond the size that may maximize shareholders' wealth. There are very few instances where a company's size remains constant; it either grows or shrinks. In the case of Gillette, events into the 1990s have shown that the firm could expand well beyond its existing size in the 1980s and with increasing profits. A preferred strategy was to stick to what the Company managers knew best, manufacture of better razors and blades, and with geographic expansion of their markets. In large measure, Gillette did pursue this policy, but additionally Gillette today is the clear world-wide leader in writing instruments as well as in razors and blades.

Gillette until late November 1986 had a very conservative balance sheet. Long-term debt prior to the Perelman takeover attempt was only 18 percent of annual sales, but by the end of 1986 it was 33 percent of sales. Gillette's debt-to-assets ratio doubled from 18 percent to 36 percent from 1985 to 1986, but Gillette's ratio was still at a level well below the average for large nonfinancial corporations. This changed rapidly and dramatically. At the end of 1986, Gillette's long-term debt was twice stockholder equity. By the end of 1987, its debt was reduced to 1.4 times equity. Even after the Perelman buyout of November 1986, the Company's debt was not at a level threatening to Gillette because its large cash flow from its new razor and blade and continuing geographic expansion increased as sales and profits from operations continued to rise.

CONISTON ANNOUNCES GILLETTE HOLDINGS

In February 1988, Gillette directors were requested to sign over power of attorney to Gillette's lawyers because of the Coniston Partners' filing with the S.E.C. that they owned 5.9 percent of Gillette shares and that Coniston intended to wage a proxy fight for the four seats on Gillette's board up for election on April 21, 1988. In a proxy vote shareholders delegate their ownership authority to vote on corporate matters to those whom they choose to be the directors of a corporation. Coniston Partners intended to challenge Gillette's nomination of four directors with their slate of four different nominees. Coniston Partners had paid about $31.50 on average for each Gillette share. Coniston envisioned a sizeable quick profit. If Coniston won the proxy fight and their nominees were elected, Coniston expected Perelman to bid again; and as new directors they would pressure the Board to accept the new bid. Perelman had bid several times before he finally obtained Revlon. It seemed that a sizable quick profit was very probable if Coniston won.

The Board had not met since December 17 when Gillette's quarterly dividend was increased to 21.5 cents from 19 cents per share to shareholders of record February 1, 1988, payable March 4. At the February 18, 1988, board meeting, the Board size was increased to twelve members with the election of Juan M.

Steta, a lawyer and partner of the Santamarina y Steta S.C. law firm in Mexico City.

During that meeting, the legal out-of-court settlement of all cases stemming from the November 1986 takeover attempt was distributed. The settlement was dated February 19, 1988, the day after the board meeting. Although the Company had obtained "dismissal with prejudice and without costs of all claims" stemming from the November 1986 buy-back of Perelman/Revlon's stock, it also agreed to follow stipulated procedures in handling any future takeover proposal and stock repurchases. These included having a committee of only outside directors first review such a proposal. The requirements of initial review by only outside directors and timely public disclosure of details on takeover intents were changes from Gillette's practices already in place. The settlement capped the total of all attorneys' fees, including expenses, at $550,000. A court hearing was ordered to evaluate the settlement on April 13, 1988. The Company and its directors were finally, two and one-fourth years later, off the hook in the November 1986 buy-back. But Coniston Partners had created a new set of problems when they announced ownership of about 6 percent of Gillette stock and their intention to contest the April 1988 election.

CONISTON PARTNERS: STRATEGIC BLOCK INVESTING

In a letter to Gillette stockholders, dated February 24, 1988, Colman Mockler confirmed that "your Company has been drawn into a proxy contest [with] . . . RB Associates of New Jersey, L.P. . . . [who] intend to nominate four representatives for election to the Board of Directors at the upcoming 1988 Annual Meeting of stockholders." The initials "RB" stood for "razor blade" and indeed RB Associates was formed to take over Gillette. The principal owner of RB Associates was Coniston Partners, and they had disclosed with an "affiliated Bahamian limited partnership," on February 10 that they owned about 5.9 percent of Gillette's common stock. Mockler's letter to shareholders of February 24 stressed that Coniston had no "direct experience in managing or running an international consumer products firm." Coniston then announced that they had no intention of running Gillette. Mockler's February 24 letter also stated accurately that from the beginning of 1980 until December 31, 1987, Gillette stock had risen in value by 25 percent a year, more than one-and-one-half times the Dow Jones Industrial Average and that of the Standard & Poor's 500 rise over the same period. The letter made no mention of Coniston's multiple partners and investors, who were not known to the Gillette Board at that time.

When the price of Gillette stock fell to as low as $17 per share after the October 1987 crash (an amount equivalent to $34 on a non-split basis) Gillette directors and management believed that new buyers surely would begin to accumulate the stock. Additionally, Gillette had paid what is termed by many to be greenmail, which alerted Coniston Partners that quick money might be made here. On Friday, October 16, 1987, Coniston bought over a million shares of

Gillette and on the following Black Monday bought almost a million and a half shares. By February, Coniston owned 6.76 million shares, 6 percent of the Company, having bought them, on average, for $31.50 each. But there were 116 million shares of Gillette stock outstanding, two-thirds held by institutions, which was a higher percentage than the average 45 percent of equity of American public companies held in 1986 by various institutional investors.[2] If $65 had been judged too low a year ago, what judgment could be made about just over half that price!

The only major buyer that surfaced after the crash in October 1987 was the Coniston Group, whose primary owners were two bright, well-trained MBAs and a lawyer who had considerable merger experience working for Skadden, Arps. Coniston at that time employed about ten people. Formed in 1982 by Keith Gollust and Paul Tierney, Coniston in 1984 added a merger lawyer, Augustus Oliver. Coniston Partners pursued a strategy, self-labeled as *strategic block investing*, that consists of accumulating enough stock of other companies to force them to act in ways that push up their stock price and thus earn Coniston a high return on their initial investment. Coniston wanted short-run gains, not to run a company. Image-conscious, they understood the importance of a Park Avenue, New York, address and projecting their corporate face as a winner.

The new Massachusetts (1987) and Delaware (1988) antitakeover laws together blocked the way for a company to use a hostile tender route to gain control of Gillette. A hostile acquirer intending to buy control must get approval of a majority of outstanding shares. The Gillette Company with substantial in-state business and headquarters in Boston would be subject to Massachusetts law even though it was incorporated in Delaware. Both the Massachusetts and the Delaware laws forbid a would-be acquirer from joining with the target firm for three years without the board's approval. Ownership cannot exceed 15 percent in that period. Taken together, these laws make very costly a takeover tender in Massachusetts of a Delaware incorporated firm. A better, less costly, route for an acquirer would be a proxy fight and informal pressuring.

Tenders were not in the history or style of Coniston Partners. And even if a company paid greenmail, a new federal tax of 50 percent on greenmail payments stemming from hostile tenders was imposed at the end of 1987. The time seemed ripe for Coniston's preferred instrument, the proxy, as a means to gain large returns on relatively small investments. How this works can be illustrated from Coniston's own past actions. In 1985 Coniston had obtained 5.3 percent of Storer Communications and, after winning a proxy contest, forced that company to be sold in a leveraged buyout. Coniston invested $42 million in Storer stock for 13 months and gained $39 million,[3] an almost 100 percent gain. Of course, other shareholders of Storer also benefited, but not many so dramatically. In 1985 and 1986 Coniston invested $171 million in Viacom and gained $61 million over a brief period of time.

In the case of the Gelco Corporation, in which Coniston also invested, Coniston forced it to recapitalize. Gelco bought in 46 percent of its stock and remained independent. In the case of Allegis, Coniston forced sales of all its units, except the central core, United Airlines. By borrowing about one-third of the over $500 million that they used to buy Allegis stock in 1987, Coniston leveraged their returns as the price of Allegis stock rose. The latter, stripped down to United Airlines, has subsequently been taken over by its employees in a leveraged buyout.

As Gillette could be termed an *old hand* in staving off would-be acquirers, Coniston Partners could be termed an *old hand* in running proxy fights. Coniston Partners had a built-in advantage in waging what became a proxy war with Gillette. They did not need to go outside their own circle to find experts. Augustus (''Gus'') Oliver, with a Yale University undergraduate degree and a summa cum laude from American University law school, was a well-trained, some might say even a brilliant lawyer who worked as a merger specialist at Skadden, Arps, where he had become partner. Keith Gollust, who had majored in mathematics in Princeton and had an MBA from Carnegie Mellon, had interestingly and understandably enough early changed his name from Goldlust. He became an investment banker, as did Paul Tierney, Jr., who had majored in philosophy in Notre Dame and later received an MBA from Harvard University. These three were viewed as intellectually the cream of the crop, trained at the Ivy League schools that gave them all the correct credentials as well as the knowledge to play the market for their own gains. Yet they were identified to the Gillette Board not in these terms but rather as greenmailers and corporate raiders, labels that their recent past actions had earned. The three also ''run a $100-million risk-arbitrage and special situation fund called Sabre Associates and a railroad boxcar leasing business, and [they] own[ed] real estate at a Utah ski resort.''[4] These three men among them coached a boy's soccer team, ran a local PTA, worked ten hours a week on Eugene Lang's ''I Have a Dream'' program, and ''yet they have plenty of time left over to mow the lawn, play with the kids, and take 50-mile bicycle rides, sometimes during business hours.''[5] It was a lifestyle that many could have envied.

An in-depth *Fortune* article in the summer of 1987 states that the three major Coniston Partners, all under 42 years old in 1987, had ''charm, vivid intelligence'' and were ''mild-mannered, soft-spoken, and genial'' and also described them as ''Ivy League buccaneers.'' If the Gillette Board members had met them in a different situation than a proxy contest, it is possible that some of the board members would have liked, or at least not disliked, each of the Coniston Partners.

Because it was a very small group, Coniston could make decisions quickly. They were in the business of taking over companies and were not distracted by day-to-day operational demands, as was Gillette management. By the time they tackled Gillette, Coniston had already built up their media contacts in the major business press: newspapers such as the *Wall Street Journal* and the *New York Times* and periodicals such as *Business Week* and *Fortune*. Since they lived in New York, it is not difficult to imagine that they had good contacts not only at the *New York Times* but also at Boston's major newspaper, the *Boston Globe*. In a proxy battle it is important to make one's case in the public press in a favorable light. Coniston was practiced in this role.

Coniston had "taken stakes in no fewer than 15 corporations since 1982 without ever taking control . . . as in Storer's case, the three win board seats and subsequently 'help' companies recapitalize, spin off assets or liquidate."[6] Their aim was financial gain for Coniston, without regard for the jobs of existing Gillette employees or management. Proponents of takeovers, in general, see them as a preferred way to improve the management of firms and usually underestimate the effect of takeovers on the numbers employed by the target company and the slowing down of the rate of increase in their wages. Workers in firms that are taken over can lose. The resulting downsizing may mean increasing efficiency, but it also means increased unemployment. Some individuals lose their jobs.

Companies in the 1980s became more efficient, often paring off excess middle-management layers after friendly mergers and sometimes hostile takeovers occurred. Gillette had already begun the process of downsizing after the Perelman/Revlon attempt. The Company's annual report for 1987 states, "By December 31, 1987, $79.3 million had been charged to the restructuring provision for costs related to employee reductions, the closing of several operations in domestic and international markets and the net impact of the disposition of certain assets, including the sale of S.T. Dupont and Misco. Management estimates that the balance of the restructuring provision is adequate to complete the restructuring plan."[7] Gillette was well under way to completing its planned reorganization and a reduction by 8 percent of its workforce when Coniston announced its proxy battle.

The prospects of future Gillette Board meetings with an agenda set by four dissident, newly elected Coniston representatives adept in arm-twisting, intent on selling off the Company bit by bit, were not appealing to Gillette directors. The process promised to be arduous and eventually exhausting for those who were opposed to Coniston. The Board and management believed that the bright prospects of an independent Gillette as a long-term business were threatened. Coniston's emphasis on immediate short-term gains was held to be undesirable; for the Company to stay independent was a more appetizing alternative. Gillette's management and board decided to fight. Most directors of almost any Fortune 500 company are accustomed to exercising authority and taking responsibility for their actions. Gillette Board members fitted this description and were willing to engage Coniston, whom they viewed as the enemy.

Coniston's record on hostile takeovers was publicly clear. Moreover, Gillette's chairman believed, as did the CEO of the Wire Company, in the Broadway play, *Other People's Money*, that this was a broader fight than Gillette's. If strategic-block investing became the rule, then any large company whose breakup value might be greater than its current stock market value would be at risk. Only by actually selling parts of a company would it be known how much value could be created. It is tricky to assess the value of a company and also separately the value of its parts. Is the whole worth more than the sum of its parts? It is also difficult to sell individual parts of a company for what one believes each are worth. In a breakup, those parts of a company earning the least return on investment would presumably be unsold. In fact, their price eventually might be so low as to create losses. Whether from the overall economy's point of view the breakup of a given company is good or bad depends on individual situations.

The three major Coniston partners, considerably younger than Gillette's directors, were described by the media as having attractive personalities, and they were also adept at using carefully generated media pressure to force asset sales. Among all the descriptions for Coniston Partners in the media, I like best "Ivy League buccaneers."[8] Individual members of the Coniston Partners repeatedly stated that they did not wish to run a business but to sell it or its parts in order to increase the value of its stock. Coniston Partners had in December 1986 about sixty investors with whom Gollust, Tierney and Oliver shared the risks and the very high returns of their strategy. A high market price per share of stock might have protected companies from such raiders, but the sharp October 1987 fall in stock prices across the board had surfaced good buys. There were bargains available, and Gillette was one.

Who were the Coniston Partners? Gillette wanted to find out. At the March 17, 1988, board meeting, a mock-up of a chart that eventually was headed the "Coniston Group: Who Are They?" was handed out. The mock-up was dated March 14, 1988. The final chart published in newspapers April 19 expanded the March 14 version of 20 to about 31 entities, or names. Many changes were minor, for example, four rectangles that carry a Sabre name as against two on the earlier draft. Other additions may have been more substantial. How important was the addition of *Compagnie Internationale de Participations Bancaires et Financieres S.A.* (CIPAF) "Luxembourg" in the advertisement as a shareholder of two of the other entities I do not know. The April 19 version created by legal counsel also added along the lines connecting the various entities such words as *shareholder* and *general partners* that the earlier draft did not have. Among the refinements of the original chart was the addition of "Witherspoon Associates," an entity that gave a statement in the course of discovery and was defined as "a general partner of the general partner of a 4 percent limited partner in RB Partners."[9] The immediate general effect of the revisions was to add complexity and confusion to the diagram. The board approved what management had produced.

Coniston Partners' remarkable past gains implied to some that they may have been somewhat unscrupulous. Others argued that because they were such bright and well-trained lawyers, it is very unlikely that they ever stepped over the legal boundaries, although they may have skirted close to the edge. To my knowledge, they were never investigated. However, the lead story in the April 6, 1988, *Wall Street Journal* linked Keith Gollust to an investigation of Oakley Sutton, a small investment firm near Princeton University that was raided in December 1987 by fifty federal marshals wearing bulletproof vests. The news story stated that Oakley Sutton accumulated stock ''for corporate raider Coniston Partners'' in connection with their accumulation of Storer stock. Although nothing was ever proved against Coniston, the surfacing of their name with such activities created suspicion of possible indiscretions in their financial moves.[10]

Gillette still had unanswered questions, such as why Coniston did not make all of the public filings required by Bahamian law. The pyramid of parts of Coniston in the full-page Gillette advertisement in the *Wall Street Journal* on April 19, 1988, and in other major papers headed ''The Coniston Group—Who Are They?''[11] suggested questionable foreign entanglements merely by citing the various locations of the Coniston Partners and their banks: Luxembourg, Bahamas, Grand Cayman Island, Panama, Monaco and Nassau. The business press continued to pursue Coniston's offshore link to a bank in the Grand Cayman Island that permits legal passthrough funds for foreign accounts and does not require companies to report sales of stocks.[12] By linking Coniston as a legal customer to banker Marion Gilliam, ''subject of a three-year investigation by the Federal Bureau of Investigations for stock manipulation and wire fraud,'' a 1990 *Forbes* article casts a McCarthy-like stigma and then questions whether securities violations had ever been committed by Coniston. Neither that 1990 article or Gillette's newspaper advertisements in April 1988 allude to the fact that among Coniston's sixty or so investors were the Harvard University Foundation Fund and other very respectable organizations, but these I did not learn about until after the proxy fight of April 1988.

Coniston's March 17 letter to Gillette's stockholders, timed to coincide with the Gillette Board meeting, made Coniston's argument for why they invested over $200 million in Gillette. The price of Gillette stock is ''far less than what we believe could be generated in a sale of the company.'' Gillette by asking you to vote against the antigreenmail proposal is in effect asking you to agree that Gillette may pay greenmail again. Further, Coniston stressed that Gillette refused to negotiate the $47-per-share (Perelman's third) bid of August 1987 and also has a poison pill. All these items taken together made a strong argument to vote for Coniston's slate, especially in the minds of the top institutional holders: California Public Employees' Retirement System (CalPERS), the New York State Employees' Retirement System and the investors, bankers and brokers such as Citicorp Investment Management Inc. and Wells Fargo and investment institutions such as Bear Stearns, Merrill Lynch and Morgan Guaranty that held large depository positions. Among these, more than 71 million shares were involved, about two-thirds owned by professional money managers. As the proxy vote neared, letters and advertisements by Gillette and Coniston directed at shareholders to sway their votes gradually increased in volume. Few were aimed at individual holders and as the actual vote came closer, more were directed at the institutional holders who had been steadily increasing their ownership share.

Most disturbing to Colman Mockler and the Board was the Coniston concept of *strategic block investing*. This translates into purchase of a small percentage of a company's stock and its use as a lever to pressure the company to pursue policies that would increase the short-run price of its stock, even though they usually also would destroy the company's independence and long-term value. Coniston's strategy was in tune with others waging proxy battles in the 1980s. Coniston intended not to manage the Company but rather to sell it or at least to induce someone else to buy it. As the possibility of such tactics being used against Gillette drew closer, management tensed. Gillette's chairman, Colman Mockler, on April 15, 1988, wrote to 175 presidents of other companies, saying that "your company" is also at risk from this tactic. In that letter Mockler stated

So-called "strategic block" investing involves:

* The formation by Wall Street market players of large pools of capital, much of which may be foreign-sourced, based on promises to the investors in the pools of immediate yields that are far in excess of conventional yields.
* The taking of a significant equity stake in a company, not to make a tender offer, but with a view to putting a company "in play," and forcing its immediate sale or break-up by threatening a proxy contest, consent solicitation, or the initiation of a "low ball" or inadequate takeover bid by third parties.

Because market prices of stocks of even well-managed companies can be at times below their intrinsic, longer-term value, companies with breakup values higher than the current market price are at special risk from this tactic.

A major problem for Gillette's Board was to know more, beyond what was published in newspaper and business periodical articles about Gollust, Oliver and Tierney. The Board did not know who additionally were involved in Coniston Partners. For such information, the directors were dependent on Gillette's lawyers and management. Coniston's March 24, 1988, advertisement in the *Wall Street Journal* boasted of their successful track record after winning proxy contests in making gains from strategic block investing that was "sold in a leveraged buyout, *bringing hundreds of millions of dollars of gains for Storer stockholders. . . . In 1986, Coniston investment affiliates invested over $50 million in the Gelco Corporation . . . resulting in $100 million of profit for Gelco stockholders. . . . In 1987, Coniston investment affiliates invested over $500 million in Allegis Corporation . . . resulting in hundreds of millions of dollars of gains for Allegis stockholders."*

But that advertisement did not address who were the "Coniston investment affiliates." Even the Coniston letter of April 4 to Gillette's stockholders that headed its fourth section with "Who is The Coniston Group?" used generalities to answer that question. "Approximately two-thirds of the equity capital managed by Gollust, Tierney and Oliver comes from individuals, corporations, banks, insurance companies and pension funds in the United States with the balance coming from overseas' investors.'' Who the latter were and their ownership shares was not spelled out, and the Gillette Board asked management to find out who they were. Inquiries and computer searches were made by Gillette's in-house lawyers and outside detectives and lawyers were hired. Precisely who was involved with Coniston was hard to learn but a mystery name, Tito Tettamanti, kept surfacing.

TAKEOVER CLIMATE

Meanwhile, the general climate of takeovers and mergers heated up as the season for annual shareholders' meetings approached. The March 15 *Wall Street Journal*'s lead story was headed ''Borrowing Binge: Takeover Trend Helps Push Corporate Debt and Defaults Upward.'' In 1987 corporate defaults totaled nearly $9 billion. Respected financial journalists Lindley Clark and Alfred Malabre speculated, ''Companies may be rushing to buy while the Reagan administration still keeps the antitrust watchdogs on a short leash.''[13] While that story mentioned several companies in financial distress because it might be that they could not pay interest on their debt and would go bankrupt, stories about new takeover attempts were scattered throughout even that single issue of the *Wall Street Journal*. On page 2 it reported that Salant Corporation had extended the expiration date of its $95 million tender for Manhattan Industries[14] and that Ply-Gem Industries Inc. would complete its acquisition of Wolverine Technologies Inc.[15] On page 3, R.H. Macy and Co. ''boosted its friendly tender offer'' to $6.3 billion for Federated Department Stores Inc.[16]; and on page 4, T. Boone Pickens, Jr., and his Mesa Limited Partnership dropped its takeover proposal for Homestake Mining Co.[17] On the same page is an article on the Farmers Group Inc. 's rejection of a $4.5 billion tender offer from Batus.[18] J.P. Stevens had accepted a nearly one-billion-dollar bid by Odyssey Partners and spurned West Point–Pepperell Inc.[19] In the rest of the paper many other takeover stories were reported, including a long story on Cooper Cos.,[20] original parent of Oral-B, and a proxy solicitation by Desert Partners L.P., for USG Corporation.[21] This was heady reading. The stage for the spring season's annual shareholders' meetings was being set, and in general they promised to be contentious.

During March 1988 both parties to the Coniston/Gillette proxy fight sent several letters to Gillette shareholders, each trying to convince recipients to vote for it. Coniston Partners sent letters to Gillette shareholders on March 10, 17, 24, and 31 and an added Mailgram on April 8 with reference to its March 10 letter. Gillette sent letters to their shareholders on February 25, March 7, March 16, April 4, and April 15. Paid advertisements by both parties appeared in newspapers such as the *Wall Street Journal* and the *New York Times*. Coniston's appeared on March 24, April 5 and April 14, the latter being addressed to ''institutional fund members and bank trust departments,'' and Gillette's on March 17, April 6 and April 19.[22] Gillette's March 18 notice of its annual meeting to the stockholders, which included its proxy statement, was sent to all shareholders. By April 19 the media believed that the institutional holders had most of the votes. The *Tangled Web* chart (Figure 7.1), Gillette's last advertisement, was directed primarily to the institutional holders or fund managers. At the head of the chart, in apparent answer to the question "The Coniston Group: Who are they?" was the name "Tito Tettamanti."

Coniston Partners' various letters and advertisements supported their view that the current market price of Gillette shares valued the Company below its sale or merger value. Additionally, Coniston stated that the repurchase of stock by Gillette in November 1986 had constituted payment of *greenmail* and descried the Board's refusal to consider Revlon's August 1987 request to purchase Gillette stock at $47 per share. Coniston's March 10 letter raised other points to support its views, including Gillette's revision of its various benefit plans to increase the protection of existing high-level employees' benefits. Additionally, Coniston charged Gillette with lobbying the Massachusetts legislature to pass antitakeover legislation on July 21, 1987. Other companies in Massachusetts and other states have lobbied their states and even their federal legislators for similar antitakeover laws. Gillette did what companies in like circumstances often do.

The 1988 annual shareholders meeting was scheduled for April 21, only a few weeks after the settlement of the 1986 events. Four directors would be elected for the next three years. Although the settlement of the past takeover attempts seemed very good, the old problems in a new guise were still out there. California Public Employees' Retirement System (CalPERS), owner of over 1.6 million shares of Gillette, had placed on the April ballot an antigreenmail stockholder proposal that would prohibit the company from acquiring "any of its voting equity securities at a price above the average market price of such securities from any person who is the beneficial owner of more than three percent of the company's voting equity securities and has been such for less than two years, unless such acquisition is pursuant to the same offer and terms" made to all other holders. The statement supporting the CalPERS proposal defined greenmail as follows: " 'Greenmail' refers to the situation in which a potential hostile takeover bidder demands and is paid, as a condition of not pursuing its takeover, a premium price for the targeted repurchase of its shares."

Gillette disclosed its record sales of $3.17 billion in 1987 with profits of $515.3 million, a 16 percent margin. A fourth fight over the control of Gillette was about to occur.

In Massachusetts it is generally agreed that the antitakeover bill was introduced early in the 1987 legislative session and that it was Ronald Perelman's second takeover attempt, despite the ten-year standstill agreement not to buy Gillette, that spurred action on the measure.[23] Gillette, although incorporated in Delaware, was subject to the laws of both states. The Massachusetts legislation of July 21, 1987, was patterned after the Indiana antitakeover law that was upheld by the Supreme Court two days before the enactment of the Massachusetts legislation. The bill was signed at the front door of Gillette's South Boston plant. By the time Coniston got involved with Gillette, the Delaware law of

Figure 7.1
Tangled Web Chart

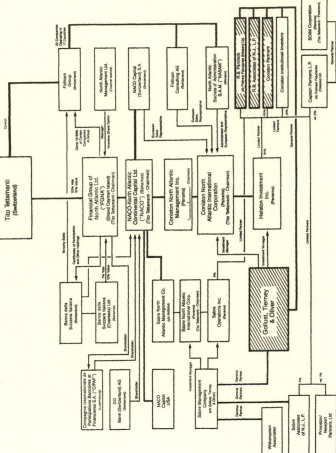

How can you vote for the Coniston Group when you don't know who they are?

- Gillette believes that this chart shows only part of a tangled web of Coniston-related foreign and domestic corporations and partnerships which Gillette has asked about from the beginning.

- Until Monday, April 11, only three entities, in addition to their investment advisor, were identified by Coniston as involved with its attack on Gillette (see chart). Only on that date, more than two months after Coniston announced its investment in Gillette, did Coniston in its fourth amended SEC filing begin to disclose some additional facts.

- In order to protect the rights of Gillette stockholders, in light of Coniston's most recent SEC filing, Gillette believed it was necessary to file a lawsuit alleging violations of the disclosure provisions of the Federal securities laws by Coniston. Gillette alleges in the lawsuit that additional information should have been disclosed to stockholders.

- Gillette believes that stockholders voting in this election contest, especially fund managers with fiduciary responsibility, should know who is behind those for whom they are being asked to vote.

Gillette's Board believes that a vote for its nominees is a vote for present and sustainable growth significantly above industry averages, which should lead to continued investment performance significantly above stock market averages. The Board believes that a vote for its nominees is also a vote for the continued commitment to take all steps necessary in the current environment to maximize value for all stockholders.

(signature)

Colman M. Mockler, Jr.
Chairman of the Board and
Chief Executive Officer   April 19, 1988

IMPORTANT

YOU CAN VOTE BY A TOLL-FREE TELEPHONE CALL

To ensure that your Gillette proxy is received prior to the April 21 Annual Meeting, we have established a toll-free telephone procedure by which **ALL** Gillette stockholders are encouraged to vote their shares.

Your Datagram voting instructions will be received by us, or by your bank or broker if your shares are in Street name, within minutes, and will ensure the representation of your shares at this important meeting.

All Gillette stockholders were mailed instructions on using the TOLL-FREE Datagram voting procedure. Should you have any questions, or need any assistance in making sure your vote FOR the Gillette Board's nominees counts at this critical meeting, please call the Company's proxy solicitor, Georgeson & Company Inc. at 212-440-9800 (call collect) or TOLL-FREE at 1-800-223-2064.

Wall Street Journal, April 19, 1988, p. 47.

February 2, 1988, was also effective. It requires, for an acquirer to vote, that it either have board approval or own 85 percent of the voting stock not owned by employee-directors or have shareholder approval by a two-thirds vote of the shares. This statute had been made effective retroactive to December 23, 1987, in order to protect Texaco from a takeover bid. In essence, it was predicted to bar for three years hostile takeovers of companies incorporated in Delaware. Although some acquirers might be able to meet the requirements, others like Coniston chose the proxy route.

Gillette filed a complaint, and Coniston filed a counterclaim in April, each alleging that the other had violated the federal securities law in seeking proxies. Hearings began June 16, 1988.

GILLETTE'S CORPORATE CULTURE

Gillette, an international manufacturer, had in 1988 about 30,000 employees, and Coniston Partners had about ten employees. Gillette was an old company; Coniston, a newly formed entity with hardly any staff, had no sales or even planned future production or sales. It was an investment company specializing in takeovers, formed solely to take over other companies, and thus appealed to different kinds of people than Gillette did.

It is not surprising that the corporate culture of Gillette seems to be diametrically opposite to that of the Coniston Partners. Gillette's top management certainly didn't fit the description of "Ivy League buccaneers." Rather, the words that readily come to mind to describe Gillette management are *stolid, bureaucratic* and *traditional*. Management dressed conservatively in dark business suits, except for Derwyn Phillips, who at times wore boldly striped shirts with large polka-dot ties and colorful suspenders. In most organizations there is usually at least one maverick. All of Gillette's top management was male, and all wore their hair short. One of the Coniston Partners had shoulder-length hair. One could not imagine at that time a single top executive of Gillette having long hair. However, the lack of beards among Gillette's managers is probably related to the fact that its primary product is razors and blades. This is not to say that the top level of Gillette, based on all characteristics, was a homogeneous group of people, although all were white men who seemed to love baseball, a major advertising venue for Gillette. Only Al Zeien and the corporate secretary, Kathryn de Moss, enjoyed in a literal, as well as possibly a figurative sense, sailing his or her own boat. Although most European ethnic strains were represented in top management, I do not recall ever seeing a black, a Japanese, a Chinese, a Vietnamese, or a Filipino working at the top level of Gillette. However, an East Indian wearing a turban and one woman of Gillette's staff each made one presentation to the Board. Compared to many Californian companies, Gillette seemed to lack diversity.

Even though many of Gillette's management were born in countries other than United States and cities other than Boston, many of them did go to Harvard

University as undergraduates or earned an MBA at that school. Colman Mockler was born in St. Louis, but his degrees were earned at Harvard, as were those of many other Gillette executives and board members. This may help explain why I, with a Harvard Ph.D., fitted in well with this group of businessmen.

The Gillette Company, headquartered in Boston and in existence for almost ninety years, has evolved its own common set of values, which include an emphasis on international production and marketing. Like IBM, Gillette transfers individuals in top management to several different countries in order to give them wide experience of different cultures. But Coniston was of a culture apart, one with which Gillette had no prior experience.

Gillette has a male atmosphere pervasive throughout the company, probably stemming in part from the emphasis on the successful use of male sports to advertise its major male-specific products, razors and blades. I had to learn more than the infinitesimally small amount of knowledge I already had about big-league baseball, especially before the board meetings, in October when the World Series occurred, if I were to take part even occasionally in the informal conversational exchange. Although Gillette's world-famous slogan, *"Gillette: The Best a Man Can Get,"* is of recent origin, it evolved naturally from the Company's male-dominated atmosphere. My fellow directors did not "get" any tinge of sexism in that slogan. This was a male culture.

Less than 1.5 percent of the over 100 top executives of Gillette listed in the Company's 1977 Annual Report, just printed when I went on the board, were women. In 1990, when I left, that percentage had improved but was still under 4 percent. In 1995 it was about 5 percent.

The willingness of Coniston Partners to help Harvard Business School professors prepare a case about the proxy battle for classroom discussion while The Gillette Company did not initially so participate indicates another difference between the two companies. Gillette always avoided publicity, except when it involved advertisements for its products. Coniston, on the other hand, used publicity very well to support its positions to acquire other companies. This was not their first time around in the use of publicity as a tool for takeover. Probably I was more aware than most of the other directors of the use of publicity as a means to an end because the Hoover Institution, where I worked, was at the time perceived as a target by at least some people for a takeover by Stanford University,[24] and the media were used in part to fight this perceived intention.

TITO TETTAMANTI

The full name of Tito Tettamanti is Tito Pier Domenico Tettamanti. He was the mystery man of Coniston Partners and remained a mystery man in financial circles well after the proxy battle with Gillette. Information about Tettamanti made available to the Board was always presented with a veil of mystery. That he might be a perfectly respectable financier was never even hinted. But in their characterization Gillette's lawyers were not unique. The few articles in the fi-

nancial press about him were similar in tone. For example, a quotation from a
Business Week article asks, ''Where does Tettamanti get his money? Given the
persistent efforts of the Mafia and Italian tax evaders to use Lugano [where he
works] banks and investment houses for money laundering and as conduits for
capital flight, Tettamanti is exposed to suspicion that some of his funds may be
dirty.''[25] This charge was not proven. The article characterizes some of his
holdings involved with Coniston as follows: ''His Panama-based Coniston North
Atlantic International Corp. funded as much as a third of Coniston Group's 5.9%
stake in Gillette. But Paul E. Tierney Jr. . . . insists that Tettamanti 'has no influence or control over what we do.' ''[26] It may be that these remarks are overdrawn, as was a Swiss television claim at the time that Tettamanti was aiming
to become ''the Warren Buffett of Europe.''

Yet, despite this type of media publicity over six years ago, there had not
surfaced by July 1996, even with use of computer searches, any really new,
harmful information that taints Tettamanti's reputation. The main source of my
information about Tettamanti is a long article in *Barron's* that describes Tettamanti as being ''respected in financial circles and is not associated with any
known unethical or illegal practices.''[27] Reference was made to somewhat questionable practices dating back to 1977 in a Canadian Lockheed sale of a nuclear
reactor to Argentina but concluded that the matter ''ended with no charges being
brought, though the Royal Canadian Mounted Police has never closed the
case.''[28] At 57 years of age in 1988, Tettamanti, who gave his deposition in the
Gillette case in Monaco, was reported by *Barron's* to have amassed

a $2 billion portfolio, with holdings stretching from Kenya to Marseilles to Argentina,
though most of it was in Canada.

There, Tettamanti rewarded thousands of anonymous, tax-sensitive, European investors
with a 9%–15% return on their money by setting up shell companies in Panama or
Liechtenstein, and then funneling the money into real-estate developments. Thus, the
411-room Holiday Inn in Winnipeg was built by Winnihotel Investments Corp. of Panama, and a bunch of properties in Saskatoon and Regina were built by Prairie Towns
Investment Corp.

Because of Swiss banking laws, it was never clear where Tettamanti's money came
from. . . .

By 1977 Tettamanti was running 20 separate corporate units in a dozen countries, with
real-estate assets totaling $2 billion.[29]

Both the *Business Week* and *Barron's* articles ran in 1988 after the proxy
battle, and even then neither was definitive. The August 15 article in *Barron's*
concludes, in part, that ''Tettamanti controls entities that had a 34% stake in
Coniston's Gillette position.''[30]

The author of this article, Joe Queenan, a well-known business journalist,
apparently had access to the trial and some of the depositions. He points out
that neither Gollust, Tettamanti nor Colman Mockler could easily identify where
Tettamanti fitted in; ''at one point in the trial, Gollust himself couldn't remember

who owned the common stock of North Atlantic Continental Capital. (Financial Group North Atlantic Ltd., as a matter of fact.)"[31] Coniston's attorney also had problems remembering who was connected with whom. "Even Tettamanti had trouble keeping things straight. . . . And when asked if he had ever become a limited partner in Coniston Partners, he replied: 'It could be. I don't remember if the name was Coniston Partners, but it was something similar to Coniston Partners, let's put it this way.' " As Queenan states, "Cynics will not easily be persuaded that an international wheeler-dealer on the order of a Tito Tettamanti would be content with a supine role vis-à-vis his money managers or exert no influence on such critical decisions as calling off the epic legal battle with Gillette".[32] In support of these kinds of conclusions, it seems sufficient to point out that Tettamanti met with Coniston "nine or ten times a year in New York," and that Gollust testified, "He meets with us basically so that he can be an effective salesperson in meeting with potential investors in Europe."[33] Tettamanti remained a mystery man even into July 13, 1988, when Judge Wolf commented, "But you know, if you've got a narrow amount on this great mystery of Dr. Tettamanti and his role, maybe he would like to come and answer the questions."[34]

To own one-third of the Coniston position in Gillette or of their specially formed "RB" Partners (that is Razor Blade Partners, formed to take over Gillette) was in itself such a substantial ownership share that it really did not matter to most observers, but did apparently matter legally, that Gillette could not prove that Tettamanti belonged at the top of the *Tangled Web* chart.

In the July 13, 1988, "scheduling hearing" held in the federal district court in Boston, Tettamanti's lawyer, Mr. Henn, claimed that when Mr. Tettamanti first met Keith Gollust he "didn't know a strategic block from [a] sun block."[35] This is hard to believe. For example, Tettamanti had in early April 1988 in another matter sold 20 percent of his stake (worth about $147 million) of the machinery maker Gebrueder Sulzer AG[36] and apparently then used that money to buy 55 percent of another Swiss machinery company, Adolph Saurer AG. Whereupon, it is reported that Sulzer maintained, "Tettamanti intended to take over the company and strip its assets."[37] Tettamanti knew about and had exercised pressure stemming from ownership of strategic blocks of shares in other instances. He was at that time an international wheeler-dealer involved in an astounding number of business strategies.

Judge Wolf in his June 30, 1988, "Findings . . ." had clearly stated:

Tito Tettamanti had an interest in RB Partners and the overall investment in Gillette. He personally had a 2.4 percent interest in the combined RB Partnerships through Helston, Sabre Operations and Captain, Captain being a newly formed entity to provide a vehicle for $5 million which Dr. Tettamanti agreed to raise and raised for the investment in Gillette.

In addition, the companies in which Dr. Tettamanti had ownership interest, companies reflected on the chart which emerged in the ad which is Exhibit 1 to this opinion, that is FGNA, NACO, and FIMSA had a 9 percent interest in the partnerships. In addition, the companies in which Dr. Tettamanti directly or indirectly had a leading role, and these include Helston Investors, Captain, and Sabre Operations, had a 34 percent in the combined RB Partnerships.[38]

The private investigator hired by Gillette "reported to the lawyers that Dr. Tettamanti 'although . . . a well-known raider . . . Swiss public records contain no derogatory information relative to Dr. Tettamanti or his business ventures.' "[39] This information favorable to Tettamanti was not passed on to the Gillette Board nor to me individually during the proxy fight.

The remarks of Judge Mark L. Wolf both in his June 30 "Findings of Fact and Conclusions of Law" and his later July 13 "Scheduling Hearings" shed little additional light on Tettamanti, although they do illustrate why the court found the chart to be misleading, although it was also found to be accurate. The accuracy of the chart was not denied. "Accuracy, however, does not, as a matter of law end the inquiry. Something may be literally true but misleading. Common sense suggests this, the law plainly recognizes it."[40] However, many laymen believe that accuracy alone should be sufficient to prove compliance with legal regulations, and I belong to that school. However, it was held that, even though the facts were accurate, accuracy was insufficient because the "presentation can make accurate information misleading,"[41] and examples were given:

As described in the Findings of Fact, the ad is deliberately designed to mislead. In addition, accurate information is presented in an unnecessarily confusing and misleading manner. This is true with regard to the relative roles of Mr. Tettamanti, GTO, Coniston Partners and Coniston Institutional. It's also true with regard to the placement of Mr. Tettamanti at the top, and the size and placement of the boxes, and the lines with and without arrows.[42]

Despite the fact that "the SEC gave accelerated approval to the publication of the ad,"[43] the SEC did not realize, Judge Wolf clarified, that the letter and ad would be read together. Further, the SEC did not consider that the placement of the boxes, with Mr. Tettamanti at the top, and the sizes of the boxes would together convey a message. The SEC thus did not consider the question before the court. Almost a year and half later *Forbes* carried a story stating that Tito Tettamanti "is controversial. He and his companies reportedly have been involved in kickbacks, insider trading and political corruption."[44]

In the June 30 "Findings" Judge Wolf stated that he felt pressured because "the legitimacy of the 1988 Gillette annual meeting and the present composition of its board have been called into question"[45] and therefore he gave an oral opinion asking that each party file by July 11th, reporting what were the matters still not settled. Then he pressured the parties further in saying that he was vacationing and would have little time to settle the case until at least October 1988.

NOTES

1. Michael C. Jensen, "The Takeover Controversy: Analysis and Evidence," in *Knights, Raiders, and Targets: The Impact of the Hostile Takeover*, ed. John C. Coffee, Jr., Louis Lowenstein and Susan Rose-Ackerman (New York: Oxford University Press, 1988), p. 321.

2. Carolyn Kay Brancato and Patrick A. Gaughan, "Institutional Investors and Capital Markets: 1991 Update," Columbia University Center for Law and Economic Studies, Table 21, September 1991, unpaged.

3. Stratford P. Sherman, Charles C. Krusekopf and Alan Farnham, "Dealmakers: The Trio That Humbled Allegis," *Fortune*, July 20, 1987, p. 54.

4. Ibid., pp. 52–53.

5. Ibid., p. 52.

6. Stephen Taub, "Knowing a Company's Worth," in "Shark Alert," *Financial World*, April 1, 1986, p. 28.

7. *Annual Report 1987* (Boston: The Gillette Company, 1988), p. 16.

8. Alison Leigh Cowan, "Markets and Investments: Three Raiders Who Are Cleaning Up—Without Junk Bonds," *Business Week*, December 1, 1986, p. 124.

9. Scheduling Hearing for Phase II of Trial, Before Honorable Mark A. Wolf, Civil Action No. 88-0862-WF, United States District Court, District of Massachusetts, *The Gillette Company, Plaintiff v RB Partners et al., Defendant*. Boston, July 13, 1988 mimeo, p. 55. (Hearafter Scheduling Hearing.)

10. James B. Stewart and Daniel Hertzberg, "Insider Focus: Small Securities Firm Links Drexel's Milken, Goldman's Freeman," *Wall Street Journal*, April 6, 1988, p. 1.

11. Gillette full-page advertisement: "An Open Letter to Fund Managers from Gillette: The Coniston Group—Who Are They?" *Wall Street Journal*, April 19, 1988, p. 47.

12. Stuart Flack, "Marion Gilliam's Two Faces," *Forbes*, April 2, 1990, p. 42.

13. Lindley H. Clark, Jr., and Alfred L. Malabre, Jr., "Borrowing Binge: Takeover Trend Helps Push Corporate Debt and Defaults Upward," *Wall Street Journal*, March 15, 1988, p. 1.

14. "Salant Corp. Extends Offer for Manhattan Industries to Friday," *Wall Street Journal*, March 15, 1988, p. 2.

15. "Ply-Gem to Acquire Balance of Wolverine Technologies Shares," *Wall Street Journal*, March 15, 1988, p. 2.

16. Bryan Burrough, "Macy Sweetens Federated Offer to $6.3 Billion," *Wall Street Journal*, March 15, 1988, p. 3.

17. Elliott D. Lee, "Mesa Scuttles Its Takeover Bid for Homestake; Pickens's Dropped Proposal Is the Latest in Series of Setbacks for Raider," *Wall Street Journal*, March 15, 1988, p. 4.

18. "B.A.T. Unit Seeks Any Data Farmers Group Gave Others," *Wall Street Journal*, March 15, 1988, p. 4.

19. Frank E. James, "J. P. Stevens Accepts $939.4 Million Bid, Spurning West Point–Pepperell Proposal," *Wall Street Journal*, March 15, 1988, p. 4.

20. James P. Miller, "Ex-Fans Give Cooper's Montgomery the Cold Shoulder; Unpredictable Deal Maker May Be Alone in Understanding His Vision," *Wall Street Journal*, March 15, 1988, pp. 4, 6.

21. Richard Gibson, "Desert Partners Sets Proxy Fight for USG Seats," *Wall Street Journal*, March 15, 1988, p. 20.

22. It has been helpful in compiling the dates of advertisements to use the Harvard Business School's revised "Communications in a Proxy Fight: Coniston vs. Gillette," July 27, 1989. On page 1 of this study, it is noted, "Norman Klein and Professor Stephen A. Geyser with the cooperation of Coniston Partners prepared this case as a basis for class discussion. Apparently, Gillette did not cooperate until a later version, February 6, 1990, where Gillette letters, as in press releases, are given.

23. State Law Amendments: Massachusetts, "How the Massachusetts Statute Was Adopted," June 1, 1994, Corporate Governance Service: State Takeover Laws, Fourth Quarter 1992, p. Massachusetts-3 (Washington, D.C.: Investor Responsibility Research Center Inc., 1994).

24. The Hoover Institution on War, Revolution and Peace is "an independent institution within the framework of Stanford University," which means in practice that no faculty committee governs or oversees it. "The director reports directly to the president of Stanford University and through him to the Board of Trustees." *The Hoover Institution on War, Revolution and Peace Report 1984*, Stanford University, September 1984, p. 27.

25. John Templeman, "The Spotlight Falls on a Swiss Mystery Man: Tito Tettamanti Wants to Be 'the Warren Buffett of Europe,' " *Business Week*, June 20, 1988, p. 76.

26. Ibid.

27. Joe Queenan, "Silent Partner: Will the Real Tito Tettamanti Please Stand Up?" *Barron's*, August 15, 1988, p. 6.

28. Ibid., p. 28.

29. Ibid., p. 29.

30. Ibid., p. 31.

31. Ibid.

32. Ibid.

33. Ibid.

34. Scheduling Hearing, p. 29.

35. Ibid., p. 53.

36. "Corporate Report: Swiss Financier Tettamanti Sells a 20% Stake in Sulzer," *Wall Street Journal*, April 6, 1988, p. 20.

37. Ibid.

38. Judge Mark L. Wolf, "Findings of Fact and Conclusions of Law," mimeo, June 30, 1988, pp. 17, 18. This chapter quotes from the uncorrected drafts of Judge Wolf's "Findings" and "Scheduled Hearing" that I received as a director; both, I understand from Judge Wolf, are in the public domain. The published version of the "Findings" is available in "693 Federal Supplement, *The Gillette Company, Plaintiff, v. RB Partners et al., Defendants*, Civ. A. No. 88-0862-WF, United States District Court, D. Massachusetts, June 30, 1988." I prefer to use the uncorrected draft versions because these are the ones that each director received during the period of decison-making by the Board.

39. Ibid., p. 20.

40. Ibid., p. 59.

41. Ibid., p. 59.

42. Ibid., p. 61.

43. Ibid., p. 62.

44. Stuart Flack, "The Cayman Connection," *Forbes*, December 11, 1989, p. 42.

45. "Agreed Order" appended June 30, 1988, U.S. District Court, Massachusetts, C.A. No. 88-862-WF, June 20, 1988, typescript, p. 3.

8

Proxy Contest
and Legal Outcome

SETTING FOR THE PROXY CONTEST

The Securities and Exchange Commission (SEC) first issued rules governing proxy contests in 1935 that were designed to promote corporate democracy. These regulations have been almost continuously amended since. They were substantially changed in 1956, when extensive disclosure requirements were mandated for anyone who wished to communicate about issues up for vote and required that all such statements be cleared by the SEC in advance. Federal regulation imposed high costs on communication and, in the minds of some such as myself, has limited free speech about the issues involved far more than is done in political elections.

The voting public apparently remained in favor of such regulation until after the extensive proxy takeover period in the late 1980s. The public distrusted both corporate management and potential takeover raiders and at the same time wanted some protection for individual shareholders. Therefore, they accepted requiring disclosures and even requiring that all communication about proxy issues be cleared by the SEC in advance. This latter seemed to interfere with the principle of free speech protected during political campaigns for federal and state office. The regulations were weakened in October 1992.

It is claimed that the targeted company in a proxy battle has an advantage because it has a list of shareholders to whom it can send letters pressuring for the company's position. The dissidents, here the Coniston Partners, do not have such a list. The SEC requires a target company on request to mail to the dissidents a list of shareholders or mail to their shareholders the dissident's material as long as the latter pay the costs. However, getting an up-to-date list of a company's shareholders with addresses is not just that simple, because many holders register their stock under their investor's street names, not theirs, and also because of the high frequency of buying and selling of shares of a company in play. A target company has the potential to delay the dissidents' getting out information about themselves by doing the mailings for the dissidents.

There is, relative to other articles on corporate governance, little written about proxy contests and the everyday problem of compiling an up-to-date list with correct addresses of the owners of the company's shares. Registration in a so-called street name occurs because most individuals do not want to store their own stock certificates but prefer to leave them with the broker in whose name they are registered. In 1987 roughly 70 percent of all corporate stock was held in street name, and of these 30 percent were in broker name and 70 percent in a bank nominee account. The latter figure is so high because the Employment Retirement Income Security Act of 1977 (ERISA), which governs some pension funds, requires that these funds keep their assets in trust. Moreover, the shareholder of the set record date, ten to sixty days before the annual meeting, retains the right to vote, even though the shares in a volatile proxy fight may be sold and change hands several times before the vote count. Who has the right to vote does not change from the owner after the record date. Many heavily traded votes are not even cast. Only about 50 percent of shareholders vote in most annual elections of directors of a company.

The target company in a proxy fight does not always have as great an advantage in having a list of shareholders as it seems to have on the surface. The list may be out of date. The large institutional holders, because of the size of their trades, are usually known by both sides. Old, large companies, such as Gillette, also have older shareholder lists that can be used to solicit votes even though they are inaccurate.

Would-be acquirers sometimes sue their target for a list, as was done by Coniston unsuccessfully against Gillette. However, after the proxy fight, Gillette amended its bylaws, April 20, 1988, to add among other items that "the secretary shall prepare and make, at least ten days before every meeting of stockholders, a complete list of the stockholders entitled to vote at said meeting, arranged in alphabetical order and showing the address of each stockholder and the number of shares registered in the name of each stockholder."[1]

It has been claimed that the "biggest barrier to entry" into the top ranks of proxy solicitors is not knowing "the data base that each of the top leading players has accumulated since it entered the hostile takeover business—cracking the code that disguises the true ownership of so much publicly held stock."[2] Initially, telephone calls or in-person visits are made by the proxy solicitors, and then the proxy solicitor and its client company—target or dissidents—determine together whom specific individuals might call, sometimes in person. Considerable pressure is exerted by both sides as they telephone top management of the institutions that hold large blocks to lobby in favor of one party or the other. "As one proxy solicitor put it, 'Sure the calls are made. They're made in an effort to inform and persuade. There's nothing wrong with that. There's nothing coercive about it.' Indeed, in the case of a proxy contest, a number of individuals interviewed agreed that it is often useful to exchange views with the parties involved.''[3]

When involved in a proxy contest, companies hire an additional set of advisers and consultants who are specialists in obtaining votes for the employing company's side. These are proxy solicitors—in Gillette's case, Georgeson and Company; in Coniston's, the Carter Organization. They usually can profile the investors in a company and especially the large stockholders. The regular investment bankers sit on the sidelines while the proxy pros concentrate on the larger investors and encourage management to make personal calls. Each tried to gain an advantage from monitoring changes in Gillette's shareholder base. Individuals usually own a very small percentage of company stock, and thus their monitoring costs would be quite high in relationship to the little benefit that they might gain from improving the company's operation. Institutions, on the other hand, own a relatively high percentage of stock and thus have a greater incentive to monitor a company more closely. Individual holders often invest for the long run and are not as quick to shift ownership of their shares to benefit from an immediate price rise in stock. Their assessment of long-run value is important. Many individual investors maintain that although the price of stocks goes up and down, it is the long-run trend in which they are most interested, not churning the stock, paying taxes on capital gains or accumulating unnecessary broker's fees. In fighting the proxy contest, Gillette had to overcome the relative indifference of most individual shareholders as compared to institutional holders. Gillette needed their votes, which were more likely to side with Gillette.

Managers of pension funds and other institutional groups are interested primarily in the short-run gain—the stock price today, not a year from now. Only a few pension funds today still hold to the principle ''Vote with management or sell the stock.'' Very large holders of any company's stock will depress the price if they sell their holdings in one block. The Coniston Partners look at shares in a company from the same point of view as any institutional money manager: how to make an immediate gain on the shares that they own. They want to see a sizeable short-run increase in the price of the stock in order to sell the high number of shares that they hold at a sizable profit. Most institutional holders voted with Coniston. In a short snapshot of Coniston Partners, an article in *Fortune* magazine gave them ''high marks for investment savvy, doing their homework, clever proxy tactics, and brilliant timing.''[4]

An individual holder of stock almost always weighs their individual options: How much in taxes will I have to pay, and is it worth paying them and the brokerage fees and the effort in search to find a new investment if I sell immediately when I do not need cash, rather than hold in the hope, or even belief, that the price will rise? A one-dollar rise on 100,000 shares is $100,000, but on 100 shares it is only $100. The difference in magnitude affects the decision-making process. The fight heated up.

GILLETTE'S PROXY STATEMENT

The Company mailed out to their known holders of shares a 24-page proxy statement on March 7, a little over six weeks ahead of the annual meeting scheduled for April 21. It carried slightly fuller biographies of the members of the Board of Directors than in past years and a more detailed financial report on the Company, as well as four shareholder proposals and the Company's recommendation of Peat Marwick Main and Co. as auditors. The four directors up for election, each nominated for three-year terms that would expire at the 1991 annual meeting, were Lawrence Fouraker, a past dean of the Harvard Business School; Herbert Jacobi, a banker; the CEO and chairman of Gillette's Board, Colman M. Mockler, Jr.; and Joseph Turley, who would be retiring on April 30 from being Gillette's president and chief operating officer, at 62 years of age. It is interesting that Director Herb Jacobi owned only 400 shares, as did two other directors at that time; Lawrence Fouraker owned 2,000 shares and Colman Mockler, who had spent 31 years with the Company, owned 219,000; Joseph Turley, who had been there 28 years, owned 90,000. All directors and officers of Gillette, as a class, owned only 1.3 percent of the outstanding shares—a very small percentage among the major corporations. As others have pointed out, this low percentage is a trademark of companies targeted for a hostile takeover. Some economists have found a causal linkage between a company's having a low percentage of shares owned by directors and its being a target for a takeover. It is argued that directors who own very little stock do not think as do shareholders or owners but rather are more interested in doing whatever will ensure retention of their director's job and pay. This generalization is debatable.

Among the four shareholder proposals were two that would have the corporation make no new investments in South Africa and in effect fully pull out of that country. The Board of Directors recommended a vote against these proposals. Gillette employed in South Africa approximately 350 persons, of whom 216 were nonwhite, and those operations accounted for approximately 1 percent of the Company's sales and earnings. The Board strongly believed and the proxy so stated that pulling out from South Africa would be detrimental to many employees who would lose their jobs and would also remove the Company's ability to improve the lives of South Africans through existing community programs, "such as scholarships for needy black university students, funds and equipment for technical and secondary schools, adult education programs, and, most recently, funds and equipment for medical care." Additionally, Gillette sponsored a legal-aid clinic.

Another stockholder proposal was the perennial against the practice of testing on living animals some of Gillette's cosmetics and toiletry products including antiperspirants and antidandruff shampoos classified by the Food and Drug Administration (FDA) as *over-the-counter* (OTC) drugs because they affect bodily functions. Because of their classification as drugs, the FDA requires that these products be tested on living animals. The FDA has similar requirements to test any substance considered to be a drug, such as *color additives* used in the manufacture of cosmetics. The FDA stated in its October 11, 1988, test policy, "Because it is unreasonable that people be exposed to substances whose safety has not been established, initial safety studies, by necessity, are conducted on animals."[5] By 1994 Gillette managed to eliminate all tests that used research animals for cosmetic products but still used them as required by law for those products classified as OTC drugs. The dilemma for the Board was, if the tests were eliminated, how to know that the products would not harm human beings. Moreover, a company cannot sell products that are classified as drugs without the FDA's blessing. The most vociferously agitated protestors at the annual meetings of Gillette were the animal-rights groups. The Board believed that the welfare of human beings should have a higher priority than the welfare of animals, but a very vocal minority do not view the issue in this fashion.

ANTIGREENMAIL SHAREHOLDER PROPOSAL

The remaining shareholder proposal was, in essence, an antigreenmail proposal. Again, on the recommendation of the in-house lawyers, the Board of Directors, after some discussion, recommended a vote against this proposal. In hindsight this was probably a mistake. Board members were sensitive to criticism of their November 1986 action, but the Board had already informally discussed and, it seemed to me, agreed that they would not in the future make any payments that were or could even be perceived as greenmail. Why not reaffirm this position and clear the muddy waters?

Why do I say it was probably a mistake to recommend a turndown of this proposal? In part because the shareholders had voted narrowly to approve it on April 21 and the Board should have been more perceptive of the investment climate. Another major reason is that boards should not turn down every shareholder proposal, especially one with considerable merit. If shareholders are to monitor a company and to believe that they can influence a company's actions, shareholder proposals should be an acceptable route. No shareholder proposal in the twelve years that I was on the Board was ever endorsed by the Board. The shareholders are the owners. The in-house lawyers seemed to me to have an arrogance in quickly recommending dismissal of every shareholder proposal while I was on the Board. Most of the proposals were extreme, but this one was not.

The main reasons given for the antigreenmail provision by its proponent, CalPERS, were that (1) greenmail wastes corporate assets, leaving the Company with additional debt, (2) it attracts would-be raiders and (3) it treats shareholders unequally.

The Gillette's proxy statement defends its specific action of November 24, 1986, when Gillette purchased stock from Perelman/Revlon for $29.75 ($59.50 before split). The company does not call this greenmail but rather in defense points out that the repurchase price was "below or slightly above the weighted average closing price for the preceding periods of ten ($30.57), twenty ($29.23) or thirty trading days ($28.74); was equal to the highest price at which the stock had traded on the immediately preceding trading day ($29.75); and was slightly above the closing price on the preceding day ($28.31)." The Board statement in the proxy concluded that, even if the price were considered greenmail, "the Board believes the transaction was justified." The Board statement did not endorse the practice of greenmail in general.

Coniston Partners charged that Gillette in November 1986 had paid Perelman/ Revlon greenmail, and they supported the CalPERS resolution to amend the Company bylaws to ban future greenmail payments. Coniston's advertisement of March 24, 1988, stated that, "On November 24, 1986, the Gillette Board authorized the payment of Greenmail to the Revlon Group. . . . In our opinion, the Gillette Board is now asking you in effect to allow them to pay Greenmail again by urging you to vote against proposal number six—a resolution banning Greenmail proposed by one of the Company's largest institutional stockholders."

A later Coniston-paid advertisement, April 14, asked institutional fund managers and bank trust departments in bold letters: "How Can You Endorse a Board That Endorses Greenmail?"

Would Board approval of the antigreenmail proposal have weakened the pressure Coniston Partners put on the Gillette Board and top management for recognition after the vote, even though they had been narrowly defeated in the proxy election? This is interesting speculation. The proposal to ban greenmail passed, while Coniston's nominees were narrowly defeated. Some of the votes for Coniston may have rested almost entirely on the greenmail issue.

It is well to recall here that directors' actions in a takeover are protected by the business judgment rule, if the following conditions are met: they act in good faith, are adequately informed and have a rational business purpose. Gillette's directors met all these requirements in November 1986. The rational business purpose was to follow the Company's business plan. Management and the Board's perception of the prospects of the Company were exceedingly bright, if the already-begun restructuring and development of the Sensor razor and blade could be finished and the new product be marketed worldwide. The matter of greenmail and whether Gillette paid it is discussed more in depth a little further on in this chapter.

CONISTON GROUP'S PROXY STATEMENT

The Coniston Group mailed to their list of Gillette shareowners a twelve-page printed "Proxy Statement in Opposition to the Board of Directors of The Gillette Company." No potential buyers of the Company were named, but Coniston promised that election of Coniston's nominees "will ensure that the sale of the Company is both actively pursued and fairly considered." In Coniston's view, "the current market price is well below its sale or merger value." Coniston charged further that the Company's management has been "greenmailing" Revlon and the Company's refusal to consider Revlon's $47 per share bid was injurious to stockholder interests. "Recent market volatility, exemplified by the crash on October 19, 1987, suggests, in the Coniston Group's opinion, that reliance on the stock market to safely and consistently reflect the underlying value of the Company is questionable at best."[6]

The Coniston Group stated that they had "approximately 6% of the outstanding shares, with an aggregate cost, including commissions, of $213,260,228 and an aggregate market value, based on the closing price of the stock on The New York Stock Exchange on March 9, 1988, of over $268,000,000."[7] Their tactics were already paying off with an unrealized gain of $50 million in the value of Gillette's stock. Although Gollust, Oliver and Tierney are each listed as owning 5.9 percent of shares, a footnote in their proxy makes clear that their holdings cannot be totaled to 17.7 percent of shares. Their fourth nominee, David H. Strassler, chairman of Weston Associates, a small investment firm, is listed as owning no shares, although a footnote states that his wife owns 150 shares, "to which Mr. Strassler disclaims beneficial ownership."[8] The Coniston proxy wanted each of their nominees to be elected to three-year terms, and Coniston also supported the antigreenmail amendment. Additionally, it supported election of Gillette's current auditing firm, Peat Marwick Main and Co., but it had no recommendations on the other stockholder proposals about South Africa and the use of animals in testing Company products for safety. The Coniston Group also stated that they "will seek reimbursement from the Company for"[9] their estimate of the $3 million that their solicitation of stockholders would cost them!

Columbia Law School Professor Bernard S. Black argues that when dissidents such as Coniston try to gain control of a *minority* number of board seats, their action does not imply that they are seeking control.[10] I question this assertion. Although in staggered board elections often only a minority of seats are up for election, winning some seats can be a first step in what could be only a two-year process. Although only four director seats were up for election at Gillette each year, Coniston would need only two elections to gain formal control of a twelve-person board. Several members acting as a cohesive unit can exert considerable pressure during board meetings for change, especially when as in the Gillette case winning the votes for the Coniston slate would have meant a concomitant ouster of the chairman of the board and the soon-to-be-retired president of the company.

GREENMAIL

The issue of whether greenmail was or was not paid in November 1986 became very important in the 1988 proxy battle and the legal suits following. Before analyzing the greenmail charge, I disavow any knowledge of Gillette's legal defense in this issue and of the depositions of my fellow directors, except for a very brief look, June 5, 1991, at a few in the Boston Courthouse reading room. In the subsequent legal settlement all the documents were sealed. My recollection of events may differ from that of other directors; I have not consulted with them.

Greenmail is generally viewed as a pejorative term that describes the act of a target company in repurchasing its own shares from a large stockholder, who typically in return signs a standstill agreement not to buy any more shares. The repurchase is made at a premium price above market price, often not precisely defined, but usually stated as a price above what others can sell their stock for. There are many parts to that definition, and Gillette's repurchase of shares from Ron Perelman can be viewed as fitting all parts of the definition. However, how the level of the repurchase price or the *premium* paid is precisely determined is ignored by the definition. The tax act passed at the end of 1986 states that "Greenmail is considered to have been paid if the recipients held their stock for less than two years and threatened a public tender offer in the two years before the payments were made."[11] Under this definition Gillette paid greenmail. Again, the definition ignores the problem of how to define the market price and a premium over that price. Whether or not the Gillette repurchase was greenmail depends, I believe, on whether one views the price paid as a premium price, and it is debatable that it was not.

Would Perelman have signed the ten-year standstill agreement at a lower price? I do not know. He made a profit of $34 million, but got $5.50 less per share than he would have paid out in the tender. In November 1986 Perelman/Revlon sold to the Company their 9,226,300 shares of Gillette. Would he have signed for $20 million and the $9 million of expense reimbursement? I do not know. Would $28 a share ($56 on a pre-split basis) have been greenmail? My answer to this is unequivocally that it would not, even if Perelman went away. At $28 Perelman would have gotten about $14 million less. The averages of the market price 10, 20 and 30 days prior and on the close of the day before were all higher than $28.

The practical details of how the price, at which shares are repurchased, is established is often overlooked. For example, a 1993 business handbook, states that "greenmail . . . is essentially an effort to 'buy off' the raider, the target of the takeover enters into a transaction whereby it pays the raider a premium (greenmail) well over the shares' market price."[12] This definition does not even attempt to discuss the level of the premium, what is meant by "well over," nor over what time period the market price is obtained. A quick glance at textbooks on corporate finance finds that older textbooks did not even use the term *greenmail*; while later reference handbooks, such as *Barron's Finance and Investment Handbook*, may define greenmail payment, they also do not attempt to define the base above which a premium is set.[13] The *Wall Street Dictionary* defines *greenmail* only from the point of view of a hostile acquirer who is bought off, rather than that of the target company that pays.[14]

The eighth edition of James C. Van Horne's *Fundamentals of Financial Man-*

agement barely mentions the term *greenmail* and then primarily as a trade for a standstill agreement. Van Horne argues against both greenmail and standstill agreements as follows: "However, standstill agreements appear to have a negative effect on shareholder wealth, as do stock repurchases by a company from a large block owner. The later are often associated with 'greenmail,' where the large block owner threatens the company with a hostile takeover, and the company buys the owner out at a favorable price to eliminate the threat. Unfortunately there is a wealth transfer away from nonparticipating shareholders."[15] Van Horne emphasizes that in greenmail "the idea is to get the threatening party off management's back by making it attractive for the party to leave. Of course the premium paid to one party may work to the disadvantage of stockholders left 'holding the bag.' Greenmail is a controversial topic that has led to cries for reform, the simplest version of which is simply to require that the same offer be made to all stockholders."[16]

Again, there is no discussion of how to determine the statistical limits of the premium paid. The textbook approach reflects that the authors have probably never been in a situation of negotiating a price that would make a raider go away and sign a standstill agreement to stay away. Each such situation has unique qualities. There probably have been very few, if any, other instances where a large holder of shares, other than the bidder, has dumped them after a tender and before a repurchase, as did Ivan Boesky, because of the threat of a federal suit over his alleged insider trading in other stocks. How much did this action squeeze from a prior price rise in Gillette stock due to buyers and sellers anticipating a takeover?

A definition of greenmail, I believe, should be more precise in respect to the price paid than merely specifying a premium over the prevailing market price for the stock at the time of the repurchase. Among others, Professor Ronald J. Gilson of Stanford University Law School maintains that a "market price at the time of the repurchase already incorporates a premium for the greenmailer"[17] and thus should act as a ceiling price on the amount of greenmail that can be paid. Gilson believes that when a potential acquirer announces that he has already bought a significant portion of a company's shares, then already "there is a significant increase in the stock's price,"[18] because "the market anticipates that a takeover may take place."[19] In the Gillette case, a rise in the stock price did occur at the time of the tender and ahead of the repurchase announcement, but then a substantial fall in price occurred because Boesky dumped stock. This was a unique event.

Gilson objects specifically to an approach that defines "market price as the average price of the company's stock over the thirty days prior to the repurchase,"[20] on the grounds that this method picks up some of the rise after the actual announcement of a tender and a subsequent repurchase. Gilson's assumption of 30 days elapsing between these two events weakens his argument substantially for the Gillette case. In the Gillette case, within five days after the tender and before the repurchasing announcement, Gillette's stock price had dropped 11 points because of the Ivan Boesky sell-off and scandal. The Gillette share price peaked on Friday, November 14, at 67¾; remained high on Monday at 67¼; but dropped sharply on Tuesday, November 18, to only 60; and on Friday, before the repurchase announcement, the price had fallen already to 56⅝. With a tender outstanding for 20 business days at $65, this was a very unusual turn of events. In the Gillette case, the period of time between the tender and the announcement of a repurchase was only six business days, Friday, November 14, and the week of November 17 through 21. The deal was done before the market opened on Monday, November 24.

Only after these events did I become aware of Gilson's proposal to set the price of a repurchase by averaging the market prices over the "three days— after public announcement of the intended repurchase transaction."[21] Gilson, in supporting the use of a postdisclosure price (that is, after announcing a repurchase would take place), gives credit to Joseph Grundfest, former SEC commissioner and a Stanford University Law School professor. Gilson states that the California legislature passed a postdisclosure valuation in 1987, but that it was vetoed by Governor Deukmejian on September 19, 1987.[22]

It is difficult for me to imagine a board of directors defining a market price for a repurchase payment as the average of three days after the board announced that the company would buy back stock from a hostile acquirer at then an unknown price. It is also difficult for me to imagine a would-be acquirer agreeing to this. Neither the target board or the acquirer would know to what they were committing. To argue that the price in three days would level at the *intrinsic*, or long-run value of the company is illogical, to my mind, unless the company released detailed information about its thinking and future plans. This would not be done, because it would hurt the company's competitive position. In most cases the process would open up the potential of a huge gamble with lottery-like returns. Although a company's share price "typically drops immediately on announcement of a repurchase from a potential acquirer," reflecting that the announced takeover will not occur, the degree of drop is not known and each company's case is unique; and Gillette's, it could be argued, was more unique than others.

On December 15, 1986, *Barron's* published a perceptive article by Benjamin Stein, a lawyer and economist, entitled "Who Owns This Company Anyway?— Greenmail Leaves Shareholders Out in the Cold." This is how many shareholders feel when greenmail is paid because they cannot get at that point in time the same high price for the stock that they own. The article paints a snapshot view of Gillette and attributes common characteristics to all companies buying back shares, including Goodyear, Phillips and Disney Companies in a typical scenario: "An entrenched management. . . . A 'raider' . . . usually simultaneously criticizing management and suggesting a new way of running the company . . . the 'raider' sells his stock at a large profit. . . . Entrenched management embarks upon a massive reorganization of the company, often along the lines suggested by the 'raider.' "[23] But in the case of Gillette and Perelman and later of Coniston Partners, the would-be acquirers did not criticize management, nor did they detail any future plans to run the Company, but rather Coniston announced that it would sell the Company. The article is correct, however, in stating that for a short period of time a greenmail payment is "a secret deal" and "When the deal—the inside knowledge—became public, the shares' prices plummeted."[24] The antigreenmail amendment to the bylaws submitted by the California Public Employees Retirement System (CalPERS), which passed in April 1988, used in its definition of greenmail "a price above the average market price," but CalPERS did not state over what period of time that "average" was to be computed. Rather, the supporting statement said that "Greenmail" refers to the "situation in which a potential hostile takeover bidder demands and is paid as a condition of not pursuing its takeover, a premium price for the targeted repurchase of its shares."[25]

The CalPERS resolution was approved in 1988 by 55.7 percent of the Gillette shares voted. The Gillette directors stated in their 1988 proxy that

On November 24, 1986, when the Company purchased its stock from the Revlon Group for $29.75 per share, [before split $59.50] that price was well within the range of prices at which the stock had traded in the period immediately preceding the purchase. . . . Furthermore, by early February 1987, the price of the stock had reached and even exceeded the price per share paid to the Revlon Group. In terms of those stock prices and in terms of the long-term value of the Company, the directors do not believe a "premium price" was paid to purchase the stock from the Revlon Group.[26]

The Gillette proxy statement continued that the Company had negotiated a "settlement agreement" with parties in sixteen consolidated lawsuits and in these "the market price" was "defined as the preceding 10 days' weighted average closing price."[27]

There is difficulty during a period of a takeover in determining the market price of a very volatile stock, but some price has to be selected. An average over a period of time seems more defensible than a price for one day.

A company, because of its need for cash to buy back the stock, will usually be forced into borrowing large amounts to repurchase its equity capital. Then some justification by the target company to buy back the would-be acquirer's position may be made because the action leads to changing the company's ratio between its equity and debt capital. There are those who argue that more borrowing and less equity capital is per se a good thing. Interest payments on borrowings, unlike dividends, are deductible from operating income before the company computes its taxes on profits. In 1985, a boom year, Gillette was faulted by some analysts for having relatively little long-term debt, less than half-a-billion dollars, and thus paying higher taxes than if it were financed more from borrowing. Interest on loans is deductible as an expense in determining the base of taxable corporate income, while dividends paid to obtain the use of equity capital are not deductible. This difference in tax treatment is in some people's opinion sufficient reason to finance more from loans rather than selling ownership shares or stock. However, if there is a recession, equity capital is favored over debt capital because interest, unlike dividends, must be paid and its rate cannot be changed. Thus there is an outside restraint on the amount of debt a company incurs, because if debt is too high, the company can be forced into bankruptcy in nonprofitable years in order to meet its interest payments.

Members of the Gillette Board were well aware of the company's relatively low debt on its balance sheet. Some board members argued for diversification of products through new acquisitions almost solely because it would force more debt and make the Company appear less attractive to so-called takeover artists. Well before November 1986, the Board had adopted several antitakeover measures, such as a staggered board and a poison pill. The purchase of another company, which would force more debt capital, was viewed by some board members to be desirable primarily because it would deter a potential takeover. This opinion seemed to be held by some irrespective of the other merits of such a purchase. This line of argument did not appear sensible to me and others. Most directors argued on the merits of how good a fit with Gillette the purchase would be. These discussions occurred during board meetings prior to November 1986.

By buying back shares from Perelman, the Board signaled "its private information (e.g., that it has not found a white knight),"[28] and the repurchase resulted in a subsequent fall in the share price. This, I believe, reflected in large part "the market's response to learning this information, rather than a negative evaluation of the action itself."[29] Gillette's share price fell after the payment to Perelman largely because short-term speculators and arbitrageurs pulled out when the $65 price was no longer immediately available to all shareholders. The Board's action, coupled with the subsequent substantial rise in the market price of Gillette shares and its subsequent fall in the October 1987 stock market crash, I believe, induced Coniston Partners "to explore taking over the firm."[30] It is logical that a company that attracts a hostile bid and then eliminates the bidder must have takeover gains that another acquirer or the target company itself could attain.

Whether or not the Gillette Board's repurchase in November 1986 should be termed *greenmail* was not as important, I believe, as whether the Board's action was justified. In Gillette's case, as this book as a whole points out, the Board acted wisely, by most financial measures, and shareholders who held the stock gained. The company's revenues, net asset value, profitability and other measurable areas of growth increased. Among the drivers for growth are usually believed to be leadership, technology and use of information. On these Gillette scored high.

INSIDER TRADING

Gillette was well aware of the SEC rules against insider trading and timed its negotiations as many firms in similar situations do to weekends, thus minimizing the possibility of leakage. The announcement of the repurchase was timed to the opening of Gillette trades on Monday morning. The final decision for Gillette to repurchase Perelman's shares at $59.50 was not made until shortly after 1:00 A.M. on that Monday, November 24, 1986. There was disclosure of the terms well before the market opened. The stock market had not been open since its close on Friday afternoon, November 21.

The importance of timing in all actions connected with takeovers is important, yet textbook definitions ignore this. If a company is involved in negotiations where the outcome will affect the price of the stock and the final outcome is not known, it is illegal to trade during that negotiating period. Once agreement is made, then immediate disclosure of the information is required. It is no accident that corporate boards that are targets of takeovers often meet on weekends. The markets are closed, and a charge of delay in disclosure for insider benefit is minimized. It is important that no insider be charged with trading on insider information.

Henry Manne's 1966 book, *Insider Trading and the Stock Market*, still considered to be the classic in this area, has a brief section on "Delay in Disclosures." It does not discuss company actions on weekends.[31] Nor do I know of more recent discussions about how access to the Internet will affect future charges of insider trading.

ANNUAL MEETING, APRIL 21, 1988

Colman Mockler must have viewed with considerable anxiety the upcoming annual shareholders meeting of April 21, although he showed no signs of apprehension. A few directors recalled the advice of Ed Littlefield, who had been chairman of the board and CEO of Utah, International, Inc., and who gave a talk on July 17, 1983, that advised those in a similar position, facing the chairing of an annual shareholders meeting in a proxy battle, "Not to worry. . . . Nothing . . . will be decided at [that] meeting that has not already been decided. [Almost all the] proxies have been . . . [voted leaving] no discretion . . . [to] the proxy holder."[32]

This good common-sense advice, delivered with a saving grace of humor, may have helped Colman Mockler retain his remarkably calm composure throughout a somewhat difficult meeting. At no time did anyone inside the meeting tent even shout. On both sides speakers exhibited controlled, polite demeanor. This was my only experience with such a tension-filled meeting of shareholders. Academics whom I have associated with are somewhat less temperate in manner and speech in similar circumstances.

The Gillette Board had a special meeting at 3:00 P.M. on Wednesday, April 20, the day before the annual meeting. Minutes of the Board's March 1988 meeting were approved and the financial results of the first quarter reported. Of course, the proxy fight was discussed, and several large institutional holders were identified.

The regular quarterly dividend of 21½ cents per share was declared to holders of record, May 2, 1988. Additionally, the definition of *change in control* of the Company in the various benefit plans was clarified to mean change defined as only by shareholder election of a majority of the Board's members, which then totaled eleven. This was done on advice of in-house counsel to avoid any potential dispute if Coniston's four nominees were elected and some could claim that a change of control had taken place by including the as yet not voted-on directors Juan Steta and Derwyn Phillips to make a majority. These two directors had been approved initially and earlier by only the Board, as was customary, and shareholder approval would be sought at the next year's election. Some newspaper articles interpreted this action as a method of greatly diminishing any power the Coniston nominees would have, even if they were elected.

Several of the directors, including Colman Mockler, had dinner together at the Harvard Club on Commonwealth Avenue the night before the vote. A newspaper story was discussed in which two Harvard Business school professors conjectured whether they would probably write up this whole affair as a business school case study. At least one director said that would be great. Then I remarked that after I left the board I might write it up myself. Immediately, a director asked, "Do you have such detailed notes?" I retorted, "No, but there are written minutes and I have a good memory." A coolness in the air developed. I was thinking of a scholarly academic book, but were some of my fellow directors thinking of a *Barbarians at the Gate*–style book, although that book had not yet been published?

During the Wednesday meeting in the afternoon we had been briefed about the large institutional holders. CalPERS held 1,664,100 of Gillette shares and apparently was the Company's third-largest holder, with Investors Research Corp. of Kansas City, holding about 2.7 million and Mutual Shares of New York about 2.4 million. The fourth-largest holder of Gillette shares was Wells Fargo Bank of San Francisco with 1.56 million shares. Although I had volunteered much earlier to telephone and/or write people whom I knew in California about the proxy fight, I was told not to do so until the meeting of April 20; by then, when it was suggested that I go ahead, the late afternoon of the day before the proxy meeting, I believed that it was too late. The institutional holders had presumably already voted. However, I later read that CalPERS' final vote was made at the annual meeting.[33]

Colman Mockler personally had called on several persons in California during the first week in April to solicit proxy votes. Unfortunately, his mother died during that period, forcing his return to the East before he could really make Gillette's case. Paul Tierney of Coniston was also reported to have lobbied large institutional shareholders in California.

I had read on the plane flight to Boston an article on Greta Marshall, "investment manager of the more than $40 billion California Public Employees' Retirement System [CalPERS] Pension Fund"[34] since 1985. She had announced plans to leave that post in June 1988 when her contract expired. I believed that several large California holders including CalPERS might have been persuaded to support Gillette. I knew several directors on the boards of these organizations, and additionally the article I read quotes Greta Marshall as saying ''I don't think pension funds are the appropriate vehicle to correct apartheid even though I disagree with apartheid as policy.''[35] This was a paraphrase of Gillette's position. CalPERS was about to be forced under California law to sell its Gillette stock because of Gillette's South African plant. There appeared to me to be some common intellectual ground here. Among Gillette's 27,000 shareholders, eleven of the twelve large institutional holders that held an estimated 60 percent of shares voted with Coniston. The third and fourth largest were headquartered in Sacramento and San Francisco, respectively. Individual holders in general voted for Gillette.

Whether Gillette management's reluctance to ask directors to use their connections is common in proxy fights, I do not know, and I even don't know whether Gillette's hesitation was specific to me, but it surprised me. To invite directors to make telephone calls the day before a vote was too late. Almost all institutional holders had already voted and could not reasonably be dissuaded to change that late in the game.

Gillette's share price on the Wednesday before the Thursday vote was down by 1¾ and closed at $40¼, and some viewed that as an indication that Gillette would win. The Gillette share price had closed at $46.75, as recently as March 25, 1988. Continual comment in the press by interested parties kept speculation at fever pitch. For example, Ronald Perelman was reported as saying in a speech to a thousand or more people at Drexel Burnham Lambert's conference in Beverly Hills, California, on April 14, 1988, ''that Revlon would bid if invited by Gillette's board and he is more likely to have the board's support if Coniston wins its proxy fight.''[36]

The shareholders' meeting was held in Andover, Massachusetts, the traditional spot for Gillette's annual meetings. Andover is about 25 miles north of Boston. Suggestions over the years to move the shareholder meeting to a more convenient—that is, convenient for shareholders—place in Boston had always been overruled by management. In a year with a proxy contest, no one at Gillette argued to make it more convenient for dissenting shareholders. However, the expressed historical reasoning for selecting Andover was that it is an early site of a Gillette plant, and the original South Boston Gillette factory was unable to handle large numbers of people. The Andover plant, largely a warehouse, is in an attractive, almost rural setting with room to erect a very large tent for the meeting. (The site of the April 1992 annual meeting was the John F. Kennedy Library and Museum, Columbia Point, Boston, where it has been held at least through April 1997.)

The number of people in attendance was the largest of any other annual Gillette shareholders meeting that I can recall. Newspaper articles and analysts' reports held that the vote for directors was too close to call. The four Gillette nominees to the Board were Lawrence E. Fouraker, Herb H. Jacobi, Colman M. Mockler, Jr., and Joseph F. Turley. These gentlemen, already briefly described, were reelected. That both the chairman of the board, Mockler, and the soon-to-be-retired president of the Company, Turley, were up for reelection was significant. The three Coniston Partners, Keith R. Gollust, Paul E. Tierney, Jr., and Augustus K. Oliver, and a David H. Strassler were the four nominees of Coniston. The last, a general partner in a small investment company, had joined Coniston in their dissident slate for Allegis in 1987 and Storer in 1985. The reelection of the four directors proposed by Gillette, including the chairman of the board, was the main item of business and approved by 52 percent of voted shares. The antigreenmail provision passed, by a slightly higher percentage, 55.7 percent of the vote.

Among the larger holders of Gillette stock were Bear Stearns and Co., Merrill Lynch, Morgan Guaranty, Chase Manhattan Bank, and Bankers Trust. Ownership of large amounts of stock had moved from individuals to banks and brokers as well as to major investment funds such as CalPERS. The Teachers Insurance Annuity Association (TIAA) reported holding over one million shares. Most of the large holders had already voted their shares. Gillette had meanwhile repurchased only about three million of the fourteen million shares that had been authorized for Company repurchase in November 1986.[37]

The flow of letters and newspaper advertisements continued almost to the meeting date. Gillette made available a toll-free number and sent a one-page Datagram proxy to ''fellow stockholders,'' dated April 14, and also a four-page letter and blue proxy card of the same date. Coniston's last advertisement was, I believe, in the *New York Times* of April 14, while Gillette published the *Tangled Web* advertisement that highlighted Tito Tettamanti April 19. Gillette announced that it would speed up its buy-back of stock. Possibly significant in the outcome was Colman Mockler's April 15, 1988, letter mailed to 175 CEOs of the top U.S. corporations on Coniston's strategic-block investment technique. The two-page letter, enclosed with the April 14 letter to all stockholders of record, pointed out that every large public company with discrete units that could be sold off were at risk from strategic-block investing tactics.

The final results of the voting were not available at the end of the meeting, although a margin of 4 percent for Gillette's slate of directors held early on. Mockler chaired the annual meeting and made a long presentation that reviewed the financial results of Gillette for 1987. Its thrust was that 1987 net earnings were 41 percent higher than 1986 earnings and that these substantial financial gains reflected the Company's world leadership position in blades and razors, pens, electric shavers and other Braun small household appliances and Oral-B toothbrushes. The success of other leading Gillette brands was also described, and Liquid Paper and Right Guard were named. Restructuring, as in the sale of S.T. Dupont Luxuries Products and Misco Computer Supplies, was also reported. The heavy spending on R & D, $76 million in 1987, represented a 35 percent increase over the $56 million annual expenditure five years ago. Also, the very heavy spending on advertising and sales promotion of $520 million, a 44 percent rise over the average of the past five years, was reported. The main interest of the shareholders present was in which four persons would be elected as directors for the ensuing year and therefore would run the company.

The question period that followed the chairman's report centered on this issue. Very wisely Mockler without comment called on Paul E. Tierney, Jr., of Coniston Partners, to answer any questions about Coniston and RB Partners. Shareholder Chester Novoychek asked Coniston directly what their long-term program was. Mr. Tierney responded, "upon election to the Board of Directors, the Company will solicit offers to be purchased. If it takes longer than a year and it's in the best interests of the shareholders, we will continue it after a year." Further, he commented, "We have not made a major objection to the way in which the Company is operated. We are talking about a financial sale or merger of the business."[38]

Charles Gammel, another shareholder, followed up with, "It seems to me that, if they had anything to bring to the Company for the benefit, the long-term benefit, of all shareholders, they would come up to us and say, 'Hey, we have a plan to maximize shareholder value,' without selling it off and letting someone else do it. They are admitting that there are people out there who can do a better job than them."[39] There was no response to this remark from the Coniston people who were present.

Another shareholder, James L. Dallas, self-described as a long-time shareholder of Gillette, pointed out the tax disadvantages of being forced to sell his investment, which he claimed had had "an 88 per cent capital gain; and Uncle Sam wants about a third of that the minute I realize that capital gain, and I end up with about two-thirds of my capital."[40] To the tax question, there was no response; rather, Mr. Gollust spoke to Mr. Dallas's differentiation between persons who speculate and "a real investor" as follows: "This is corporate democracy. There's a principle of one share/one vote and, when you own your shares, for whatever reason, for whatever your motivations, you're entitled to vote."[41] Nor did Mr. Gollust respond to Mr. Dallas's request, "I wonder if they will advise me, right now, what I will do with two thirds of my present day value to invest it in something that will give me just as good an investment as I now have for the long term."[42]

Some individuals present then voted, but of course most of the voting had already been completed before the meeting was held. The media had predicted a close election, and indeed so close was the vote that the next day, April 22, a *Wall Street Journal* article reported that "Coniston Partners said it believes it won its proxy fight to unseat four Gillette Company directors."[43] Very early Gillette attained a 4 percent margin over Coniston that held throughout the count. Generally speaking, institutional holders were expected to vote for Coniston and individual holders for Gillette. Among the claims made after the election was that all institutional shareholders had not voted, whereas virtually all individual holders had voted, mostly for Gillette. Gillette also claimed victory immediately, but the final outcome was not filed until May 3, when Gillette announced it had won, by 52 percent to 48 percent. After the voting was over, the Corporation Trust Company, a Delaware bank, counted the ballots; with time for either side to make challenges, the final count could not be completely certain until early May.

After the shareholders meeting, the directors resumed meeting informally. To me it seemed that a consensus existed on the Board to retain Mockler as CEO regardless of the shareholder vote. Even if all four seats were lost, the remaining eight directors were sufficient to make that election. At least one of the eight said that he wanted no part of staying on the board if Coniston prevailed. There were some who believed that a foreign buyer could be found. Others wanted to be "fair" to Coniston, which apparently had won eleven of the twelve large institutional holders. One director even suggested, during the ride to the airport, that if we won we could magnanimously drop two of the nominated directors and then offer the two seats to Coniston.

AFTER THE PROXY FIGHT

My first reaction to the 52 percent versus 48 percent of votes in the proxy election going for Gillette was, "We have won!" All of my previous experience with contested elections has been in political elections and not in corporate board elections.

In a political election everyone who wishes can convey what they think about the individuals and the issues. Not so in a corporate proxy fight. Not only must the statement of why the people are running be approved by the SEC, but any other future letters or newspaper advertisements by either side must also have their text approved by the SEC before they are allowed to be issued. At least this was so in 1988. (The SEC issued in 1991 proposed proxy rule changes; in July 1992 a somewhat weaker, revised proposal on SEC control over communications between contestants in a proxy fight was announced and final new regulations were issued late in 1992.) Communications by the Company and the dissidents to shareholders, whether in letters or newspaper advertisements, were reviewed by the SEC. In this regard Gillette's *Tangled Web* advertisement, although initially cleared by the SEC, eventually became a risk (see Figure 7.1). The required SEC pre-clearances added to the costs of a proxy contest that were estimated to total about $3 million for Coniston and nearly $8 million for Gillette.

In political elections in the United States it would be considered extreme to attempt to censor communications to the degree that the SEC did in corporate elections. Moreover, prior to the new 1992 SEC regulation, individuals who were not even parties to either side were also apparently restricted in expressing their opinions and restricted from circulating "analyses about issues pertaining to voting decisions."[44] But this type of restriction did not noticeably limit the number of newspaper and other articles on the April 1988 Gillette-Coniston proxy fight. Headlines varied but they told the story: "Gillette's Future on the Line" (*Boston Globe*, April 20, 1988, p. A1), "Analyst Picks Coniston over

Gillette'' (*Boston Globe*, April 19, 1988, p. 41), "Gillette in Proxy Fight, Speeds up Stock Buy-Back" (*Wall Street Journal*, April 20, 1988, p. 45), and "D-Day for Gillette" (*Boston Herald*, April 21, 1988, p. 1). The election was too close to call and it went "down to the wire."

In the weeks that followed it became clear to me that a close win in a corporate election was not really a win in the political sense. The party with a slim loss acted as if it were only a delay in calling for a change in tactics to gain their goals. The contrast between the political and the corporate world's handling of outcomes of elections amazed me. A win in the corporate world is not necessarily a defeat for the other side over a long period. Only one year would pass before a new election, and pressure can build on the winning company. The closer the vote, the greater the pressure. Coniston sought a recount, but Gillette's win was upheld on appeal. This only slightly decreased the pressure Coniston placed on Gillette.

Gillette announced the Sensor's successful development in March 1988, during the proxy fight. It was the promise of this revolutionary new product that permitted Gillette to project that the Company's net income during the next four years would grow at an annual average compound rate well above 12 percent. Milton Glass, Gillette's vice president of finance, was quoted as saying, "Test customers are saying 'Wow' " in a speculative article about what the new features of the new shaving system would be; considering Glass's usual careful, conservative demeanor, "Wow" was a strong word.[45]

Coniston Partners filed suit charging Gillette with making false and misleading statements during the proxy contest, most notably in heading the April 19 "The Coniston Group—Who Are They?" chart with the name of Tito Tettamanti. Coniston stated that the advertisement had induced some major institutional holders to switch promised votes to Gillette. Others held that Coniston lost because they could not surface a buyer. One observer commented that "Mockler's main mistake was to allow his major shareholders to believe he cared more about keeping his job than about the price of their stock."[46]

Gillette had already filed a suit claiming that Coniston Partners' nondisclosure of all its partners also misled shareholders. The hearing on both suits was set for June 13. On June 14 the *Boston Globe* reported that Judge Rya Zobel removed herself from the Gillette case "because both she and Gillette's chairman serve on Harvard University boards [and] . . . she became aware for the first time last Friday that the credibility and performance of Gillette's chairman and chief executive officer Colman M. Mockler"[47] would be questioned. Both were on Harvard's Board of Overseers. In her place Judge Mark L. Wolf was appointed. He has a Yale University undergraduate degree, cum laude, and a Harvard law degree, also cum laude, and a very good reputation.[48] By narrowing the issues in question primarily to the Tettamanti chart, the standstill agreements and events of November 1986, he was able to make initial findings as early as June 30.

Depositions were given by Colman Mockler, Joe Mullaney, Milton Glass,

William McMorrow, Al Zeien and Paul Fruitt—Gillette's top brass—and also by directors Fouraker and Sisco and by others such as Eric J. Gleacher of Morgan Stanley and Gus Oliver and Tito Tettamanti and others from Coniston. In fact, Coniston claimed that Gillette was tying up all their people in making depositions and that they wanted a court order to stop it.

All the various depositions that I saw at the Boston Courthouse for a few hours on one day in early June 1991 had many redacted or blacked-out sections. (There are few precise footnotes because I had intended to return to take notes, but did not return. Then, I believe, the records were sealed.) In that all-too-brief look, I read that the *Tangled Web* chart was initially conceived to be a form of road map to understand the relationships among Coniston's many parts. It was drafted as a talking point, to illustrate in short form what Gillette knew, and it was apparently done by legal counsel. The chart became important because Judge Wolf held in his June 30, 1988, ruling that The Coniston Group had proved that the chart "The Coniston Group—Who Are They?" violated Rule 14a-9 and that Gillette therefore had "unclean hands."[49] Further, Judge Wolf also states in the "Findings" that in response to SEC's early comments in giving approval of the chart, Gillette "modified some language and deleted some language" in the *Tangled Web* chart. The chart appeared in full-page, newspaper advertisements throughout the country on April 19. The questions of "The Coniston Group—Who Are They?" and "what the role of Dr. Tettamanti was," Judge Wolf held to be "fair." But then, despite the earlier SEC approval, the court held that to use the chart as a graphic response to the questions was deliberately and materially "false and misleading"[50] because "It did not reflect all of the relevant information of which Gillette was aware."[51] However, it was all the information of which the Gillette Board that approved its use was aware, and according to Judge Wolf this was as outside Director Lawrence Fouraker testified.[52] Objections by Judge Wolf were that the size of the boxes did not reflect the size of the ownership shares and that "Presentation can make accurate information misleading. Mr. Ziegler on behalf of The Coniston Group graphically conveyed that message by holding up a commonly alleged *New Yorker* cover regarding a Bostonian's view of the world." That cover picture shows Boston buildings—The Custom House, Fanueil Hall, and so on—on two-thirds of the page and beyond a Charles River dividing line, the remaining one-third of the space representing the rest of the country all the way to the Pacific Ocean and the world beyond, to Hawaii and Australia.[53] This comparison seems to me to exaggerate the chart's errors of omission. What was presented was accurate.

But accuracy alone was held to be insufficient for compliance with legal regulations. Judge Wolf also criticized the chart as containing irrelevant information about foreign entities that he believed were unrelated to the proxy contest. "They were included to create, and did create, a distorted impression. Similarly, the chart omitted information regarding comparable U.S. companies."[54]

Judge Wolf states in support of his opinion of Gillette's errors that "Gillette knew . . . about many of the U.S. limited partners of certain investors in The Coniston Group, including the Common Fund, which managed money for Harvard and Yale, among others,''[55] but they are not included in the chart. In respect to Tito Tettamanti, Judge Wolf held that "The chart might be a fair response to the question who is Tito Tettamanti,''[56] but that "Dr. Tettamanti did not dominate The Coniston Group for the purposes of the proxy contest. The companies he was involved with had a 34 percent investment.''[57] The latter was to the Gillette Board a major finding. One-third is a dominant share where there are multiple partners.

A July 7, 1988, newspaper article reported that the *Tangled Web* chart "was compiled by a team of more than a dozen lawyers from the Cleveland law firm of Jones, Day, Reavis & Pogue. . . . As the web grew, we just kept adding to it. The diagram was a direct result of all that work.''[58]

Other matters of interest surfaced in the June 30 hearings. Judge Wolf quoted from Gillette's April 14 letter to stockholders that "The Gillette Board has not said that a sale of the company could never be the best way to maximize value.''[59] Rather, the Board could not find a buyer for the whole company. Both Coniston and Gillette believed that to maximize value Gillette would have to be sold as a whole.

Further, Judge Wolf reported on the ten confidentiality agreements with potential purchasers made late November 1986 and a few proposals to acquire parts of the Company. Gillette did not pursue these because they would not maximize shareholder values. They also could make Gillette harder to take over because they would have entrenched management. Further, reference was made by Judge Wolf to a February 1988 offer from KKR to buy a part of the Company, 40 percent of equity, and he speculated that KKR would have opposed the Coniston group.

Eric J. Gleacher, then Morgan Stanley's head of mergers and acquisitions and investment banker for Gillette, testified in his deposition of April 27, 1988, about other companies' interests in Gillette. Gleacher maintained under questioning that no one wanted to buy the whole company. KKR was interested in a convertible security so that KKR could get income but was willing to buy only up to 40 percent of Gillette. Gleacher saw no sense in this offer and did not tell Gillette about it until much later. Others, such as Metro Media, never made an offer. Among those companies that signed letters of confidentiality were Anheuser-Busch, PepsiCo, and Forstmann Little. The latter really was interested in the same type of financing as KKR. Unilever and Ralston-Purina wanted "a cross minority ownership" interest. RJR Nabisco said they were not interested as the price was too high, and they believed that Eric Gleacher was shopping the company for what amounted to an inclusion in the price of $4.5 billion to $5 billion worth of goodwill, thus inflating the price. Some concluded that that was why there was no interest.[60] Gleacher said that he had not received one phone call during the proxy fight from any company that expressed interest in buying the whole company. During this period Gleacher did talk over the telephone with Al Zeien, who was voted chairman of the board in January 1991. Gleacher also stated that he had nothing to do with the *Tangled Web* chart.

Judge Mark L. Wolf upheld Gillette's claim that Gollust, Tierney and Oliver deliberately failed "to register or publish" the required information regarding the RB Partnership, which was 45 percent Coniston Partners, 12 percent Coniston Institutional Investors, 31 percent Helston Investment, Inc., 5 percent Sabre Operations, 2 percent Captain Partners L.P., 4 percent Sabre Associates of New Jersey, and 1 percent the Princeton/Newport fund.[61]

Only after a Gillette delegation, including its lawyers, visited the SEC on April 7 did GTO file a fourth amended 13D on April 11, 1988, in which for the first time GTO disclosed all the limited partners of the RB Partnership. The New Jersey law does not require public disclosure of the identities of limited partners.

The entities disclosed on the 13D of April 11, in addition to those already listed, included Coniston North Atlantic International Corporation, Sabre Associates of New Jersey, Sabre Management Company, Witherspoon Associates, a company known as SNAIC, and SOIM Corporation. Some of these companies were revealed in the April 19 ad by Gillette. "Many other companies on that ad, however—for example, the Fidinam Group of about five companies on the right side—were not mentioned in the 13D."[62] The Boston newspapers, the *New York Times* and the *Wall Street Journal* all reported on Gillette's search for a white knight in November 1986 and gave details of Gleacher's testimony. They also reported on two companies seeking to buy into Gillette in February during the looming proxy battle period.

For example, a *Wall Street Journal* article reported that Forstmann Little and Company and Kohlberg Kravis Roberts and Co. (KKR) in February 1988 had

separately offered to buy 20% to 40% of Gillette stock, a Gillette spokesman confirmed. KKR's offer was made in a letter received by Gillette in February, Gillette said. Forstmann approached Gillette shortly before that, it added.

The maker of personal-care products rebuffed both overtures after discussing the offers with Morgan Stanley & Co., its investment adviser. "The proposals were very informal and it was not in the best interest of Gillette stockholders," the Gillette spokesman said.[63]

It was upsetting to read the June 1988 newspaper accounts of February offers for partial equity of Gillette because the Board, as far as I knew, had not been told about these when they occurred. I telephoned Colman Mockler to ask why the directors hadn't been informed. As I recall, he stated correctly that we had been informed about similar partial equity approaches in November 1986, which the Board had turned down, and thus he did not believe it necessary again to seek Board approval. The earlier offers were, however, in connection with Perelman's attempts and made over a year earlier. The *ancient history* allusion did not seem sufficiently forthright to me. I even drafted a letter to convey more strongly my opinion about informing the Board, but did not send it and marked it *not sent*. To this day I do not know with certainty whether other directors might have been informed about these overtures at the time that they occurred, but I was not.

Coniston charged that Gillette had violated securities law because "Gillette misled stockholders into believing that no one was interested in buying Gillette even though two concerns approached Gillette earlier this year with offers."[64] Gillette's attorney stressed that these firms were interested in buying only a portion or stake of the company, and not the whole company. Meanwhile, the mystery of Tito Tettamanti had invaded the court. Judge Wolf states in the "Scheduling Hearing" of July 13 that although he saw "excerpts from Dr. Tettamanti's deposition . . . I've never seen the whole thing myself."[65] Further, a Mr. Henn, Dr. Tettamanti's lawyer, remarks, "that Judge Zobel was actually quite candid at our last pretrial conference with her when she said that I would be sort of curious to see him. . . . THE COURT: If we are really curious, we'll all go to Switzerland."[66]

A July 12 article in the *Wall Street Journal*,[67] reported that Judge Wolf was considering alternative options: one was to move up the annual shareholders meeting to some time in the fall and possibly to require that all eight Gillette directors be up for election—that is, the four from 1988 and the four who normally would be up in 1989. This might permit a takeover of Gillette, with eight of the twelve directors being elected at one time. The second option would have been to require a shareholder referendum on whether Gillette should be sold. Trading on Gillette's stock was halted on the news of Judge Wolf's comments.[68] No wonder Gillette agreed to negotiate a settlement.

It was the balancing of Coniston's errors in not disclosing all its partners and Gillette's alleged misuse of the chart that drove the Gillette Board's actions in July and August 1988. Judge Wolf observed in the July 13 "Scheduling Hearing," "My present view is not my final view. But my general inclination is to believe that if Gillette committed one significant violation of a proxy which I have found, then Coniston committed at least one."[69] Coniston and Gillette settled out of court in August, as detailed in Chapter 9.

Judge Wolf correctly observed that "The shareholders' rights are at the core of this dispute,"[70] and then stated that "I will consider accelerating next year's Gillette annual meeting, and having the contest involve the election of eight directors rather than four. . . . [I] may suggest the wisdom of the parties seeking some mutually tolerable resolution of this matter."[71] I repeat, no wonder Coniston and Gillette settled out of court.

NOTES

1. The Gillette Company, "Bylaws, As Amended April 20, 1988," mimeo, Article VII, "Proxies and Voting," pp. 5–6.

2. Alison Leigh Cowan, "The Trench Warriors," *New York Times*, May 29, 1988, Business Section, p. 5.

3. James E. Heard and Howard D. Sherman, "Conflicts of Interest in the Proxy Voting System" (Washington, D.C.: Investor Responsibility Research Center, Inc., 1987), p. 50.

4. Thomas Moore and Wilton Woods, "Money & Markets: How the 12 Top Raiders Rate," *Fortune*, September 28, 1987, p. 45.

5. "LD$_{50}$ Test Policy," Food and Drug Administration Notice, Docket No. 86P-0224, *Federal Register* vol. 53, no. 196 (October 11, 1988), p. 39650.

6. The Coniston Group, Proxy Statement in Opposition to the Board of Directors of The Gillette Company, Annual Meeting of Stockholders, April 21, 1988, p. 3.

7. Ibid., pp. 4–5.

8. Ibid., p. 6.

9. Ibid., p. 10.

10. Bernard S. Black, "Next Steps in Proxy Reform," Working Paper #90, Center for Law and Economic Studies, Columbia University School of Law, 1993, p. 14.

11. "Washington Update: Shattering the Mirror," *Mergers & Acquisitions* vol. 22, no. 5 (March/April 1988), p. 18.

12. Joel G. Siegel, Jae K. Shim and David Minars, *The Financial Troubleshooter: Spotting and Solving Financial Problems in Your Company* (New York: McGraw-Hill, 1993), p. 201.

13. John Downes and Jordan Elliot Goodman, *Barron's Finance and Investment Handbook*, 3d ed. (New York: Barron's, 1990), p. 302.

14. R. J. Shook and Robert L. Shook, *The Wall Street Dictionary* (New York: New York Institute of Finance, 1990), p. 173.

15. James C. Van Horne and John M. Wachowicz, Jr., *Fundamentals of Financial Management*, 8th ed. (Englewood Cliffs, N.J.: Prentice-Hall, 1992), p. 712.

16. James C. Van Horne, *Financial Management and Policy*, 8th ed. (Englewood Cliffs, N.J.: Prentice-Hall, 1989), p. 666.

17. Ronald J. Gilson, "How to Draft a Prohibition on Greenmail," Working Paper No. 38, John M. Olin Program in Law and Economics, Stanford Law School, Stanford, Calif., October 1987, p. 16.

18. Ibid., p. 16.

19. Ibid., p. 17.

20. Ibid., p. 18.

21. Ibid., p. 28.

22. Ibid., footnote 35, p. 28.

23. Benjamin J. Stein, "Who Owns This Company Anyway? Greenmail Leaves Shareholders Out in the Cold," *Barron's*, December 15, 1986, p. 9.

24. Ibid.

25. The Gillette Company, Proxy Statement, March 7, 1988, p. 21.

26. Ibid., p. 22.

27. Ibid., pp. 22, 23.

28. Andrei Shleifer and Robert W. Vishny, "Greenmail, White Knights and Shareholders' Interest," *Rand Journal of Economics* vol. 17, no. 3 (Autumn 1986), p. 295.

29. Ibid.

30. Ibid.

31. Henry Manne, *Insider Trading and the Stock Market* (New York: Free Press, 1966), pp. 151–153.

32. E. W. Littlefield, "Enjoying the Corporate Clime," lakeside talk, Bohemian Grove, July 17, 1983, mimeo, pp. 9–10.

33. John Paul Newport, Jr., "The Stalking of Gillette," *Fortune*, May 23, 1988, p. 101.

34. Julianne Malveaux, "Risky Business," *Ms.* (March 1988), p. 57.

35. Ibid., p. 58.

36. Alison Leigh Cowan, "Company News: Perelman Says Quest for Gillette Isn't Over," *New York Times*, April 15, 1988, p. D4.

37. David Stipp, "Gillette, in Proxy Fight, Speeds Up Stock Buy-Back," *Wall Street Journal*, April 20, 1988, p. 45.

38. Transcript of Annual Meeting, April 21, 1988, Burt Reporting Associates, p. 14.

39. Ibid., p. 16.

40. Ibid., p. 19.

41. Ibid., p. 20.

42. Ibid., pp. 19–20.

43. Lawrence Ingrassia and Joseph Pereira, "Coniston Claims Proxy Victory over Gillette," *Wall Street Journal*, April 22, 1988, p. 3.

44. John Pound, "Proxy Contests," *American Enterprise* (September/October 1991), p. 61.

45. Joseph Pereira, "Gillette's Next-Generation Blade to Seek New Edge in Flat Market," *Wall Street Journal*, April 7, 1988, p. 30.

46. "Newport, Stalking of Gillette," p. 101.

47. Mary Sit, "Judge Zobel Steps Out of Gillette Case," *Boston Globe*, June 14, 1988, p. 43.

48. See *Almanac of the Federal Judiciary* vol. 1, Lawletters, Inc., 1988, 10—1st circuit.

49. Judge Mark L. Wolf, "Findings of Fact and Conclusions of Law, Civil Action No. 88-0862-WF, United States District Court, District of Massachusetts, *The Gillette Company v RB Partners et al.*, June 30, 1988," mimeo, p. 5. I use the uncorrected draft versions because these are the ones that each director received during the period of decision-making by the Board. See also Chapter 7, n. 38.

50. Ibid., p. 33.

51. Ibid., p. 34.

52. Ibid., p. 39.

53. Ibid., p. 59, Exhibit Four.

54. Ibid., p. 61.

55. Ibid., p. 42.

56. Ibid., p. 39.

57. Ibid., p. 42.

58. Joseph Pereira and Bryan Burrough, "Judge Rules Gillette Ran Misleading Ad on Coniston during Their Proxy Fight," *Wall Street Journal*, July 7, 1988, p. 17.

59. "Findings," p. 53.

60. Joseph Pereira, "Gillette Trial Told of a Long Search for White Knight," *Wall Street Journal*, June 28, 1988, p. 44.

61. "Findings." p. 15.

62. Ibid., p. 26.

63. "Gillette Discloses Bids from 'Squires' against Coniston," *Wall Street Journal*, June 22, 1988, p. 50.

64. Ibid.

65. Scheduling Hearing for Phase II of Trial, Before Honorable Mark A. Wolf, Civil Action No. 88-0862-WF, United States District Court, District of Massachusetts, *The Gillette Company, Plaintiff, v RB Partners et al., Defendant*, Boston, July 13, 1988, mimeo, p. 50.

66. Ibid., p. 51.

67. Joseph Pereira, "Judge May Overturn Gillette Proxy Win over Coniston and Order New Election," *Wall Street Journal*, July 14, 1988, p. 2.

68. Alison Leigh Cowan, "Judge Says He May Order New Election at Gillette," *New York Times*, July 14, 1988, p. C-1.

69. "Scheduling Hearing," p. 43.

70. "Findings," p. 68.

71. Ibid.

9

Proxy Fight Overhang

PRESSURES TO NEGOTIATE

The events of July 1988 were stressful. Pressure was placed on both the Company and its directors from various sources to mollify Coniston, which had lost by only four percentage points. For example, Moody's Investors Service Inc. reduced its already lowered debt ratings for Gillette from Baa-1 to Baa-2.[1] These ratings had been placed under review in April because Gillette had announced it would accelerate its buy-back of stock. The Company could not argue with the lower rating, although it could make the next two months more difficult. If Gillette acted in a costly way to mollify Coniston, it could greatly increase Gillette's need for cash, and as a result the rating would fall again. Alternatively, Gillette could act to use a costless method in money terms of appeasing Coniston, such as two board seats, or could take no specific action at all.

Pressure also came from Judge Wolf's mentioning the possibility of his nullifying the election of directors in April and calling for a new election. Additionally, a legal cloud hung over the Company because Judge Wolf had stated that Gillette had "unclean hands" in respect to the April 19 advertisement, which he found "deliberately misleading." If his comments became a legal decision, rather than "a finding," and were so reported by the media, Gillette feared that other legal suits based on the Court's ruling would be filed against the Company. The second part of the trial was scheduled for August 22, and at the end of that trial the interim ruling would become legal doctrine. It was tempting to risk an appeal, but the Gillette Board was risk adverse.

On May 4, 1988, "more than 5.1 million Gillette shares changed hands on the New York Stock Exchange," and it was rumored that Carl Icahn was buying.[2] This was the day after Gillette formally announced that it had won the proxy. So much speculation occurred in the newspapers that trading in Gillette's stock was temporarily stopped for one day, but on reopening, the stock closed up $2.25 on that day, at $40.50. Although the proxy fight seemed to have been won, the matter was not fully resolved. Negotiations began.

Coniston was continually pressing for some recognition in the governance of Gillette. After all, their slate of officers had gained 48 percent of shares voted. Although in politics that would be a defeat, those in the corporate world seemed to believe that some redress should be granted Coniston; and it was this point that the lawyers, even those working for Gillette, emphasized. A July 14 letter from Paul E. Tierney, Jr., of Coniston was sent to all outside directors. It requested a meeting with outside directors to explore a way to "benefit stockholders, employees and other concerned parties" and referred to Gillette's "tainted solicitation" of votes. Meanwhile, Coniston was also approaching Gillette's lawyers.

Although interests of the minority political parties exist in U.S. federal elections through the possibility of state election of senators and representatives from minority parties to Congress, there is no such avenue for corporations. In the federal government power is divided among the presidency, the legislature and the judiciary, creating a balance. This type of solution was not possible in a corporate proxy outcome. Whereas in most political elections in the United States the winners have two or more years before a new challenge is mounted, corporate elections are annual and dissidents can almost immediately regroup and focus anew to take a target company.

In corporate control contests, even when the original firm wins the majority of the vote, the existing company may in actuality lose control. For example, only one-fifth of a sample of targeted firms that were in a proxy contest during 1978–1985 remained at the end of three years still publicly held and under the same management as prior to the proxy contest. About two-thirds of the firms had defeated the dissidents, but even among these, resignations of CEOs and also sales of companies occurred in 50 percent and 25 percent of the cases, respectively.[3] Coniston Partners believed that a 48 percent vote for them should have some tangible recognition, and they were pressing for it. Coniston was under pressure also because it had bought over two hundred million dollars worth of Gillette's shares, and there was no immediate promise that the stock price would rise soon enough and high enough to enable Coniston to realize gains sufficient to justify that kind of investment.

As events show, although Gillette had won the battle, it had not necessarily won the war. Takeover speculation persisted, and Coniston, as the Company's largest shareholder, continued to push for a higher gain than the current market share price would yield them. They had paid an average price of $32 for 7.4 million shares, an expenditure of $236.8 million, plus an estimated $7 million for expenses. Of course, they could sell the stock for a price that was fluctuating between $36 a share when Gillette's legal prospects looked bright and $40 a share when Coniston's legal prospects looked bright. Coniston would gain, but if they sold over seven million shares in a short period of time, it would place downward pressure on the stock price. Minimally a net gain of $20 million was about what they could expect via the market route—and, if they were lucky, double that amount.

Judge Wolf's seemingly casual offhand comments in the court were assiduously picked up, interpreted and reinterpreted by each side and the newspapers. Would the judge order or wouldn't he order a new election? Would he or wouldn't he require that it be for eight directors, or was that really not legally viable? Uncertainty was the name of the game. This, in part, was a public relations war—and at this Coniston was better, it seemed, than Gillette. When Coniston did agree to a settlement, writers of most media stories were puzzled by Coniston's withdrawal, and some informed observers commented that they were surprised because they believed that Coniston Partners were winning and their decision to settle and withdraw was "inexplicable."

Legal suits had been filed by each side. Charges and countercharges were absorbing time and money and with little hope of soon ending. These and the uncertainty were driving both Coniston and Gillette toward a settlement out of court.

Indicative of the pressures was a request that I arrange a dinner on the night before the scheduled July 21 Board meeting at the Hotel Westin (Copley Place) for not only director Herb Jacobi and myself but also for Joe Sisco and Colman Mockler, Gillette's CEO. Juan Steta also joined us. This was very unusual because, although Herb and I sometimes had dinner the night before a board meeting, the other outside directors did not usually come in the night before, or if so, they already had had dinner and were tired. Joe Sisco often took a very early morning plane from Washington, D.C., as did Dick Pivirotto from New York City; and Colman Mockler, except for the night before the December meeting, never before to my knowledge joined during this period any group of directors at dinner the night before a board meeting. I believe that many corporate boards that have directors who live at a distance have regularly scheduled dinners the night before a meeting, for example, Raytheon Company in the Boston area. Meetings of even small groups of directors give an opportunity for informal discussion of the more pressing events that lie ahead. My recollection of the July 20, 1988, dinner is that we sat in the back of the main dining room of the hotel where I stayed and that almost all of us had lobster for dinner while Colman, as usual, had roast beef. Colman was a very reserved man, with traditional food tastes, and also a heavy smoker. We informally discussed, among other things, Judge Wolf's rulings and the possibility that he might legally be able to push up the 1989 election of directors to this fall or even appoint a new outside referee. We discussed that the longer it took before a final settlement that would free us from Coniston's pressure, the more probable it became that a larger number of shares would change hands. For the judge to order a new election on the grounds that this would treat the shareholders more equitably would become less defensible as time passed. The names of shareholders of record changed each month.

The proxy fight and its immediate aftermath were very costly to Gillette: about $11 million in expenses and a very considerable loss in management time that was distracted from running the business. A second proxy battle was not wanted by either side. There also were lawsuits filed against the directors (and two of top management) in Delaware's Chancery Court claiming breaches by the directors of their fiduciary duties in connection with the Coniston proxy contest. Directors were reminded that they had signed an agreement to reimburse Gillette if later the courts determined that they were not entitled to their directors' insurance benefits or indemnification. This added to the pressure on directors.

According to the newspapers, there were lawyers who believed that Coniston Partners "were on the verge of winning the litigation"[4] even as late as August 1, when the settlement was announced. However, there were two sides to this issue. It was true that Gillette was found with "unclean hands" with respect to the *Tangled Web* chart, but that finding was debatable, as I hope my discussion in chapter 8 points out. Even if the preliminary ruling were wrong, there was no assurance that the court would see it that way. Gillette's board and management discussed whether an appeal would be successful. Gillette had been absolved of any wrongdoing in not letting the public know about the ten standstill agreements, all but one signed in November 1986. Coniston's activities and the Gillette charges that Coniston had not revealed their partners were issues yet to be decided during Phase II of the hearings presided over by Judge Wolf.

Merely quoting some of the July 13 remarks of Judge Wolf indicates the degree of pressure Judge Wolf was placing on both Coniston and Gillette. For example, the court states, "The Coniston Group now seems to suggest that we skip the unclean-hands issue because a remedy, that is most likely a new election . . . is likely in any event without regard to the merits of the unclean-hands argument."[5]

Further, "It's possible that somebody might have discerned in my opinion last week that I was disturbed by The Coniston Group's decision on one hand to try to get the benefits of Bahamian law, and on the other hand not—deliberately not comply with it."[6]

Judge Wolf also questioned whether Coniston should have disclosed Mr. Tettamanti as a participant in the proxy contest as early as October 19, because he had by then raised five million dollars for strategic block investment in Gillette. This type of questioning by the court implies that the Coniston Partners were not necessarily going to be happy with the final ruling of Judge Wolf in Phase II.

Judge Wolf elaborated on his suggested potential remedies: "If there's a new election, for example, Coniston shares might be neutered, that is other shareholders can vote, but under the circumstances, Coniston ought not to be permitted to vote its shares."[7]

In a jocular and mildly threatening vein, Judge Wolf went on for sixty-two pages; it is possible, although I have not tried to count, that his comments were equally detrimental to Coniston and to Gillette, but certainly the pressure of the jovial tongue-in-cheek remarks throughout the July 13 hearing did not reassure either side as to the certainty of a favorable outcome from continuing litigation.

In conclusion the court set dates that gave Gillette until July 18 to supply Coniston with a statement of issues for the next phase of the trial, gave Coniston until July 19 for its response, and gave until July 20 for both sides to state for the court the issues and identify their expected evidence, testimony and discovery. These requirements indicate the extent of the pressure placed on both sides. A lot of work, time and therefore money is involved prior to a trial, not just during the actual days of the trial. Taking discovery or unearthing facts and writing briefs are very labor-intensive activities, and sometimes nonlawyers are not aware of the degree of pressure that can thus be placed on participants in a litigation.

Paul Tierney's attempt through a letter to each outside director to open a back channel of communication did not work. Rather, each director invited management to comment on the letter that he or she had received, and a draft reply common to all directors was fashioned. As with Ronald Perelman, no direct discussion between any of the Coniston Partners and Gillette's directors ever took place (to the best of my knowledge).

In retrospect, it is amazing to me that the outside directors' discussions did not operate as a separate body. There were only a few instances when management was excluded during board meetings from the discussions of the outside directors. No overtures were made by the outside directors during November 1986 or in the spring of 1988 to find separate investment and/or legal advisors. Those who advised the management and the Board's outside directors were the same individuals. In many similar situations, outside directors do seek to hire their own lawyers and investment advisors. As I recall, the little dissatisfaction expressed, and then by only a few outside directors of Gillette, was in the area of public relations, not on the more substantive issues. However, perception is sometimes more important than reality.

The trial on Coniston's alleged misdeeds was set for a yet-to-be-selected precise time between August 22 and August 26. Meanwhile, Judge Wolf would soon go on vacation and not return until August 15. Negotiations between Gillette and Coniston began, and they were lawyer-driven. It was Coniston, not Gillette, that made the first proposal for a complex $720 million buy-back of Gillette stock by issuance of transferable put rights. This procedure would permit Coniston to convert what would have been, if they sold their Gillette stock, "highly-taxed capital gains into dividend income. (Unlike individuals, corporations need pay no taxes on 70% of these dividends.)"[8] The favorable terms to Coniston and all other shareholders of the pro-rata buyback, one for every seven Gillette shares held that is 16 million of 112 million shares outstanding, was at $45, which was at least $5 above the volatile price of Gillette stock in this period. Coniston accepted that Gillette directors and management could not pay anything that was or could be perceived as greenmail, and in fact the Board was legally bound not to pay greenmail because of the antigreenmail shareholder proposal that had passed April 21, 1988.

TRANSFERABLE PUT RIGHTS

A *put* is an option to sell a given number of shares at a set price within a predetermined brief period of time. Transferable put rights as a vehicle for re-purchase of stock in 1988 was a generally unknown, complicated version of a put. This financial transaction had been used only once before in the United States, by Millicom in April of 1987. *Transferable put rights* (TPR) were not written about in the economic or business literature until a comprehensive article was published in late 1989 in the *Journal of Financial Economics*. Some of the information in this section is taken from that article. ''The first company to use TPRs was Millicom, a small cellular telephone and electronic paging company, which in April 1987 issued transferable puts to its shareholders as a method of share repurchase. Millicom justified its action by saying that it did not want arbitrageurs, who drive up the prices in a fixed-price tender offer, to get into the act.''[9]
As I recall, none of the directors had ever heard of transferable put rights and the company Millicom.

The prime argument placed by management before the Board to issue trans-ferable put rights was to get rid of Coniston and not pay greenmail. Their is-suance would offer equal benefits to all shareholders. Because the ''puts'' were tradable in the market, individual holders of Gillette stock who did not wish to sell their Gillette shares either for tax reasons alone or also because they viewed them as a form of annuity paying good and reliable dividends would still benefit because they could sell separately their repurchase right to others. Gillette an-nounced that the Company would repurchase one in seven of outstanding shares, or 16 million shares, that were put back to the firm. Individual shareholders, 95 percent of whom had voted in the proxy, would gain. There was no risk of more shares being offered than Gillette was willing to repurchase, as can occur in a straight buy-back. Moreover, all shareholders, even those not dealing in the puts, would benefit because there would be fewer shares outstanding and each share held would represent a higher portion of the Company. Thus, greenmail was not paid and yet Coniston gained.

A market was created for the puts which could be bought by speculators, such as Coniston Partners, who had over 7 million shares and were ''able to buy over two million puts, in addition to its allotment of approximately one million''[10] under the initial one-in-seven award. The puts were heavily traded, and virtually all ended up in the hands of persons who wanted to sell back their shares. Coniston sold back 3 million shares for $135 million, over half their dollar investment.

This was an intricate financial maneuver, not a simple buy-back. It required that Gillette issue the put options in the form of share buy-back rights to holders of record as of August 9. The puts then would trade on the open market prior to the final exercise date of September 19. Shareholders who did not want to sell back any shares at $45 could sell their repurchase right, which had a "market value of $10.81¼ when issued, or $1.54½ per Gillette share."[11] The market price of the transferable put fluctuated from a high of $11.125 to a low of $9.50 during the 24-day trading period, August 16 through September 19. Over eight-and-one-half million puts traded.[12] The maneuver had the advantage of not being greenmail. The details were fashioned so that it was just within the financial capabilities of The Gillette Company to do.

The price of Gillette's stock fell from $40.125 on July 31 with the August 1 announcement to $37.50 and to $33.75 on August 16, the first day of trading the puts. On August 1, Gillette and Coniston issued a joint statement, including "Questions and Answers" on their settlement of the Company's control issue involving transferable put rights, or TPRs, approved by a July 31 Gillette Board meeting the day before.

I stress here, as with the handling of the tender and repurchase payment to Ronald Perelman, that the directors were never directly present during the negotiations with Coniston, rather the lawyers negotiated within the guidelines set by the Board. Lawyers on both sides had met several times prior to the July 21 board meeting, where the directors as a group first heard of the transfer puts proposal. I was naive in thinking that we might discuss any substitute, such as two board seats for Coniston as an alternative to the cleverly designed cold-cash offer. The major points of negotiation during the July 21 and July 31 board meetings were how many shares Gillette could afford to buy back and at what price. The latter was fairly quickly settled, but the number of shares was not. The market share price rose to $40 on July 29. Some directors argued that one in eight shares was sufficient to repurchase as this would not put the Company into negative equity. Coniston was arguing, of course, for repurchase of a higher number of shares, one in seven. At $45 a share, it would cost $720 million to buy back 16 million shares, a purchase that would force Gillette to borrow close to this amount. If only one in eight of the 112 million shares outstanding were repurchased, the cost at $45 a share would be $630 million, still sufficient nearly to wipe out the company's shareowners equity (estimated at that point of time at only $600 million),[13] but not enough, as the share price was fluctuating, to force the Company definitely into negative equity in an accounting sense.

A low-cost proposal made during the bargaining was to issue one put for every ten shares. Discussion over the terms froze out any discussion of alternatives such as seating Coniston representatives. The management and the directors wanted a clean break from Coniston, not the continual harassment this option would entail, as I saw it. As I recall, from the very beginning the lawyers on both sides came in with the one-for-seven proposal; during the discussion I and at least one other director argued for the one-for-eight. The cost differentials were considerable, at $720 million for one-for-seven, $630 million for one-for-eight, and $450 million for one-for-ten. Apparently, it was a *deal breaker* for Coniston for Gillette to offer one-for-eight, and on the Gillette directors' side it was a deal breaker if we had to reimburse Coniston's expenses directly. At the July 31 meeting, Coniston opened up with requesting consideration of a one-in-six buy-back and used, apparently as a lever, a proposal for one in five. The Board never took these proposals seriously. The $45 and one in seven were firm.

The directors were not physically included in the actual negotiation. Face-to-face negotiation between principals would do away with some of the functions of business lawyers, but the use of lawyers as go-betweens means that those ultimately responsible for the decision are denied the opportunity to read body language and actively be engaged and dilutes the function of directors. It is understood that if the principals negotiate directly that then what might be considered to be premature disclosure is legally required.

At best a delicate waltz takes place, whether or not the principals on both sides are involved in direct negotiations. Some inkling of what I perceive might occur if the principals were in direct negotiations in tender offers and in situations such as the settlement after the proxy vote can best be illustrated with a quotation from a book by Dorman L. Commons, who was CEO of Natomas Company, a San Francisco firm targeted in a hostile takeover attempt by Diamond Shamrock of Dallas, Texas, in 1983. Commons's description of their initial negotiations follows:

It is certainly difficult to read a man during a first meeting, but we were all experienced in such encounters. We had never met the Diamond management team, and "reading" them correctly was vitally important to our negotiating position. Jackson said little and showed little emotion. But Rush was voluble, responding smilingly or knowingly to my comments and echoing or embellishing on Bricker's statements. He oozed sincerity and concern. I put it down to posturing. Bricker was more difficult to read, but he seemed anxious to keep the meeting friendly. Ken and I exchanged glances. I think we simultaneously had the same gut reaction: Bricker had come to make a deal.

Now the maneuvering began. . . . Our attorneys now proposed one of those legal niceties of the corporate world that would free us from having to prematurely disclose counteroffers made in direct negotiation: "conversations" would be carried on between the investment bankers representing their respective clients.[14]

Thus it was described how it comes about that directors are not involved in face-to-face negotiations and what they may lose in forgoing face-to-face exchanges. A third party can make a recommendation to another nonprincipal, and because the principals are not directly talking the immediate disclosure of the interim jousting is not required.

I had read this book shortly after November 1986 and before 1988; and at times I felt, along with Commons, that if we could get rid of the bankers and lawyers, maybe the Board and Coniston could have agreed more easily and possibly more favorably to Gillette. At any rate, I felt very strongly that one in eight shares were quite sufficient to buy back.

Coniston's lawyers were also their principals: Mr. Oliver and Mr. Tierney and, in the July 18 meeting, their investment advisor Mr. Gollust were all involved. Mr. Flom of Skadden, Arps and in-house counsel Joe Mullaney represented Gillette, while Mr. Gleacher and Mr. Liu from Morgan Stanley acted as Gillette's investment advisers. Thus, Coniston's principals were involved in the negotiation, but not Gillette's. Do principals on one side of a bargaining table and not on the other spell an advantage to the party with their principals in the negotiation? I believe so.

Requiring the use of outside experts as lawyers and investment advisers to act as go-betweens during negotiations means that those ultimately responsible for the decision are denied access to the verbal interplay and body language of the opposite party. Such outside professionals' main incentive is to make money, while the expressed main motive of directors is to maximize the company's profit and, in a long-term sense, its reputation.

Opinions about the role of outside advisors differ. Gillette had announced in March 1988 a $3 million bonus to Morgan Stanley if the company were not taken over in three years. This was recognition that investment bankers, like lawyers, are driven by the size of the deal, because they usually get a percentage of the amount that is involved. This creates pressure for larger deals and could work to increase the price for Gillette if it were up for sale as Coniston wanted. A few shareholders saw the $3 million as a waste of corporate funds and assets and wrote to the directors in an angry vein. The directors realized that $3 million represents 1 percent of only $300 million, an amount far below the range of a deal for any company with over $3.6 billion revenues. To change the incentives for the investment banker away from a bigger deal even by a small degree seemed to be a reasonable action. Any negotiation involving the sale of Gillette would surely be in the billions, and 1 percent of that amount would be many multiples of $3 million. Offering Morgan Stanley a return if no deal took place should have lessened their zeal to spend lots of time to fashion a big deal.

The outside advisors of the Company had brought the put proposal in from Coniston at the same terms as were finally approved by the Board: a price of $45 and one of seven shares repurchased. Both investment and legal outside counsel and Gillette's in-house lawyers and top management supported this action. The directors were given the information about this method of letting Coniston get some return on their investment without Gillette paying greenmail, and it was presented to the Board as such. It was Coniston's plan. The argument for it was that the Company's largest shareholder, Coniston, had received 48 percent of the votes and thus could not be completely shunted aside. From the directors' point of view, it was believed better to accept this proposal than to award Coniston Partners seats on the board from which Coniston could continually harass with the object of selling the Company at what they would hope to be well above the current market price. Management would find it difficult to focus on business with Keith Gollust continuing to be quoted as saying, "We're a lot more interested in finding a buyer for the company than sitting on the board."[15]

The directors continued to believe that the best outcome for shareholders was that the Company remain independent and finally market its new product, the Sensor, and that the Company continue to pursue its business plans for widespread geographic expansion. A telephone conference call among the board members thrashed out details. With all the information spread before the Board and with full opportunity to ask questions and discuss the issue, it was clear that issuance of TPRs would also serve to entrench the Company's top management. But this outcome would also ensure quick and widespread marketing of the Sensor. The directors had confidence in the CEO and top management and in the Company's strategic business plans and approved the issuance of the transferable put rights on July 31.

This negotiated settlement would have become null and void if Gillette had not received assurances from investment banks and lawyers before the issue date, August 12, that the financing was available and that the action was legal under Delaware law, despite the fact that Gillette would have to go into $85 million of negative equity. This would be for a short period and only in an accounting sense. The Company's valuable asset, goodwill, is not valued on the balance sheet. If goodwill is viewed as an asset in a nonaccounting sense, then the Company should not be held insolvent because its more broadly defined assets exceed liabilities. The directors believed that the valuation outcome would be favorable. In essence, a negative equity position, even for a brief period of time, meant that top management had to get letters of confidence about the availability of loans and an evaluation opinion from investment bankers and lawyers stating that the negative equity position would not materially affect Gillette's financial ability to conduct its business and pursue its strategic business plan. Even though the proposed TPRs would push the net debt to about $1.8 billion, Gillette's cash flow was large enough that its negative equity position could be reversed during the following year, 1989. Fortunately, Gillette had excellent overseas financial contacts and a very astute financial officer, Milton Glass, who believed that he could borrow about $300 million abroad at 7 percent. Within the United States, the rate would be about 10 percent, and about two-thirds of that cost would be tax deductible. The deal was viable.

On July 29, 1988, the Company received from J. P. Morgan and also from Morgan Stanley assurances that obtaining the needed financing "would not materially affect Gillette's financial ability to conduct its business" and not materially affect its ability to pursue its business plans, including payment of current dividends. But to meet the requirements of Delaware's law, Gillette had to go further and get a positive opinion from a firm that specialized in assessing, in depth, the valuation of companies. To go into $85 million of negative equity, even for a short period and if only in an accounting sense, was not something to be ignored. Delaware's law on corporations requires a formal valuation, including "solvency and capital impairment" tests, to be positive before the action of issuing TPRs at $45 and one-for-seven could be finalized. Although the Board had been briefed on this issue at the regular July 21 board meeting, it was not until the July 31 board meeting that Valuation Research Corporation (VRC) made a presentation to the Board of its preliminary findings; on the next day, August 1, the settlement was announced. The TPRs would not be issued until August 12.

Valuation Research had to do balance-sheet tests and cash-flow tests, assess the effect on capital and conduct other solvency assessment tests. From already reviewing Gillette's strategic business plans and financial statements, VRC saw no reason to doubt that they would give a positive opinion by August 11, their deadline. They needed time to do the computations and perform what was a form of a financial audit. Cash flow had to be sufficient to provide working capital, dividends and the repayment of debt.

Once again, the Board became informed in depth about a new aspect of business finance that was yet in concept a familiar topic, how the *value* of a company is determined. The directors were accustomed to assessing the value of a going enterprise from estimating the present worth of projected future revenues. Gillette's revenues were growing and seemed to the directors to carry hardly any risk of falling. The goodwill value of Gillette's many trade names was high, and the directors were determined to keep them high in part by not cutting advertising expenses. VRC would put hard data behind the directors' softer, more intuitive estimate of Gillette's worth.

Obviously, borrowing most of the $720 million needed for the TPRs would increase the interest load or expense and decrease earnings per share. Yet, despite this, our investment advisers stated that the share repurchase would not have a long-term negative effect. I recall, for example, Eric Gleacher of Morgan Stanley arguing that the one-in-seven TPR action would not have a long-term negative effect on the price of Gillette shares. Whether this could ever be proved, I doubted. All the variables were changing over time, and one cannot even guess what would have occurred if the TPRs were not issued or if the one-in-eight option had been taken. No one argued against the belief that the immediate effect would be to depress the price of the stock. And, indeed, after the announcement on August 1, the stock price fell to $36⅝ on August 3 from $38⅞ the previous Wednesday. Although financing was assured, at apparently close to 7 percent interest for overseas loans and 10 percent for U.S. loans, it was probable that Gillette's credit rating would be decreased. Financing for the $720 million was arranged and debt projected to be less than $1 billion by 1992 because of high cash flow and use of foreign loans at lower interest rates than in the United States. The Company's long-term debt for 1992 was reported at $554 million.

Joe Flom of Skadden, Arps argued strongly that because TPRs would eliminate the harassment by Coniston, they would in the long run benefit stockholders because the Company could pursue its business plans in a new period of stability and relative certainty. Maintaining the payment of existing dividends and projections for long-run increases in the dividend rate were included in the plan. Lawyers assured the directors that they would be entitled to the protection of the business judgment rule. The TPRs issue and accompanying necessary financial arrangements were approved during the Sunday, July 31, special meeting that started at 6:00 P.M. Boston time. I attended by telephone because my nonstop 9:00 A.M. flight from San Francisco was canceled shortly after noon San Francisco time and then it was far too late to make a 6:00 P.M. meeting in Boston, where Eastern standard time was three hours later. The Board needed a favorable opinion of Gillette's solvency after the deal: sufficient cash flow to make interest payments, to pay off debt eventually and to meet working-capital needs. Gillette—like all companies—has several areas of potential liability, from known and unknown environmental deficiencies, product liability and pensions; and the Company, the Board believed, should continue to pay dividends. Could the Company cover all this? A firm positive opinion was received on August 11, but the decision to go ahead was made earlier, albeit contingent on receiving a positive opinion by August 11. The Board's actions here and later were made because the directors relied in good faith on in-house counsel's advice that under Delaware law they could rely on Gillette's management and its advisers about the financial position of the Company and specifically about the amount of surplus from which dividends could be paid.

The near-term imbalance effect, an $85 million negative equity, was held not to be a potential hindrance to receiving a fully unqualified legal opinion promised by August 11. On that date a special meeting was scheduled, however, just in case an unqualified positive opinion had not come in and the issuance of the TPRs already announced would have to be canceled. This was a risk the Board was willing to take.

During the negotiations Coniston had also asked for their proxy expenses to be reimbursed. All the directors were adamantly opposed. There is something galling about people trying to take over a company, whether by tender or proxy, to ask when they fail that the target pay the cost of trying to take it over. I believe that, for most people, to acquiesce would be outside the realm of rationality. To me, this request might have been a bargaining ploy, to be dropped when Coniston could be assured of getting what they really wanted. The directors even discussed a $47 put and letting Coniston get $2 million more in that fashion, rather than to pay up front their legal expenses. However, the $45 buyback price remained. Gillette announced simultaneously with the settlement that no change was planned in the current dividend and also agreed not to enforce the confidentiality agreements with other companies for the remaining short period of the designated two years, from late November 1986 and one agreement from September 1987. Ten companies had looked at Gillette's books and had agreed not to make offers of purchase of Gillette stock for a two-year period. The ten-year standstill agreement with Perelman/Revlon continued. Coniston in this negotiation agreed not to purchase additional significant numbers of shares of Gillette stock and not to conduct any proxy contests or seek control of Gillette for three years.

This was a lawyer-run transaction. The special 3:00 P.M., August 11 board meeting during the usually already-scheduled summer vacation period had no outside directors present in person; however, all but one were on a telephone hookup. The meeting was a rather routine affirmation of the actions already taken on July 31. A draft of a legal opinion had been distributed, stating that the issuance of TPRs is a valid repurchase of stock under the Delaware law. Further, it stated that a company's surplus may be defined as the present fair market value of a corporation's net assets less the total value of its common stock. Although qualifiers such as ''suggest'' and assumptions such as that the directors would as usual act ''with informed judgment and in good faith'' were used in the draft opinion, my reading was that it is okay to declare dividends out of surplus, partly unearned funds, but that still the directors might be sued in connection with this action. This was primarily a telephone conference call and directors could not read each other's body language. There was ''no controlling precedent'' for the proposed actions of the Gillette Board. But the Board had risked before. The individual directors were firmly convinced that the Company needed time free of continuous harassment to pursue its strategic business plan, which promised earnings growth at above 12 percent annually, compounded through 1992. The probable sales value of Company assets exceeded liabilities including identified contingent liabilities, and with sufficient capital left over for business operations and payment of dividends the directors were satisfied and voted to not stop the action. The Board had been assured that they could call off the TPR issue if Gillette did not get an appraisal valuation that cleanly stated that under Delaware law the whole transaction was legal; the Board also could reconsider if private parties filed to enjoin the issue. Although VRC's preliminary letter of approval was dated August 11, it was not until September 19, the last day of the share repurchase rights program, that VRC completely signed off on these actions.

Various informal commentators and market analysts commented that Coniston's agreement and withdrawal in August 1988 could not be explained, despite the face-saving and profitable rescue that was finally negotiated. Some observers believed that Coniston's agreement to settle proved that no one was out there intending to buy the whole Company, and in fact this was the case. Others believed that there was a third party quietly bidding but that the decks had to be cleared before they would finally commit. This was not true, as events proved.

The scheduled date of the second phase of the trial, August 22, had come and gone. I found it strange that although nothing specifically in the *Tangled Web* chart was found to be false, that the Judge's interpretation of it as ''misleading'' had such power. But then I had at that time no knowledge of other respected investors in Coniston. Remaining unknown was that if a new election had been ordered, would Gillette have won?

BUSINESS REQUIRES ATTENTION

Gillette's business did not stand still in this hectic period. The directors committed over $120 million for production of the Sensor (not yet named as I recall) to be launched in January 1990. New machinery had to be built in order to manufacture the new Sensor to be sold initially in Canada, major European markets and Japan in 1990 and later in the United States. Much smaller amounts were approved to expand production of and, in some instances, improve the manufacture of the disposable razors, Waterman Pen and Oral-B ultra/plus toothbrush and to carry out geographic expansion into Egypt and Turkey. All of these items were also acted on during the July 21, 1988, meeting.

Analysts' sheets were stating, ''Gillette is posting one super quarter after another,'' but until the final outcome from the proxy fight was decided, the price of Gillette stock depended on expectations of how the Coniston challenge and continuing fight would be resolved. Three million eight hundred thousand shares had been repurchased during May and June, leaving 7 million shares still authorized for repurchase. The restructuring program increased profitability in blades and razors. Profits grew 26 percent on a 15 percent sales growth during the first quarter of 1988, and by 16 percent on 12 percent sales growth in the second quarter. The Oral-B toothbrush was also doing well, and the purchase of the Waterman pen had pushed profits in the stationery area up by 84 percent on a 43 percent rise in sales during the first quarter of 1988 and by 25 percent on a 21 percent increase in sales the second quarter. Toiletries and Braun products were somewhat less than spectacular in either sales or profits performance but overall for the first half of 1988 operating profits rose 20 percent and sales 16 percent. Streamlining the labor force was creating profits.

In its restructuring Gillette sold its 40 percent interest in Eye Optics and finalized sale of its 81 percent ownership of Elizabeth Grady Face First beauty salons during August. Earlier in 1988, Gillette bought Antica Erboristeria, an Italian-based herbal toiletries line, as part of a European sales push. But here, as with other products deliberately designed for women, this did not produce large profits. The only such product that has consistently done well at Gillette has been White Rain shampoo, and recently the women's version of the Sensor has been selling exceptionally well. Jafra, which uses a direct marketing technique based on ''party plan'' marketing, also has been consistently quite profitable.

Despite the turmoil created by the proxy fight and subsequent sizable repurchase of stock, Gillette during 1988 returned to its shareholders a rate of return of 25.7 percent in appreciation and dividends, well above the 16 percent average rate for the stocks in the Dow Jones Industrial Average.

Gillette continued, as it had ever since 1906, with one deferral in 1931, to pay dividends in 1988. The Company was profitable and enjoyed a high cash flow. It was deemed better to borrow all that was needed to pay for the TPRs and not create a cash squeeze within the Company.

Although Coniston's pullout in August 1988 seemed inexplicable to some observers, such as Joe Queenan, Gillette believed that there were two reasons: one, holding a potential lawsuit over Coniston's head for its breaking the disclosure law on partners, and two, the face-saving and profitable rescue offered in early August of Coniston's investment in Gillette stock. Queenan, in his *Barron's* article (August 15, 1988), said that the amount of debt that Gillette assumed in doing the TPR, even into negative equity in an accounting sense, was so staggering that all potential acquirers would go away.[16] After all, *negative equity* means that the Company owed more than it owned. Although most individuals would look at this with dismay, Warren Buffett, as future events show, was not dissuaded from investing heavily in Gillette.

After the TPR share repurchase was completed in October 1988 and Coniston was reported to have reduced its ownership to 4.5 percent of outstanding shares, Gillette continued to be viewed by many market analysts as a potential takeover target. The stock remained in the stockbrokers' category of a *buy*. The price gradually rose as earnings per share increased and as the Company's new strategy in preparation for the marketing of the Sensor was developed. Most of Gillette's advertising and marketing monies were put behind the more profitable permanent razors and blades and diverted from supporting the less profitable disposables. In 1987, 70 percent of the advertising budget was for disposables and 30 percent for the razors and blades. This allocation was reversed two years later.[17] The announced new advertising campaign using one slogan worldwide, "Gillette—The Best a Man Can Get," would help launch the Sensor. The Company was going all out in gearing up for the manufacture and sale of the new razor and blade.

An October 21, 1988, *Value Line* release concluded that "though increased financial leverage has magnified the risk here and perhaps diminished Gillette's appeal to some as a takeover candidate, we still think another offer is possible. . . . Indeed, based on our projections of bottom-line improvement to 1991–93, these shares appear to be a worthwhile 3- to 5-year holding."[18] The price of the stock at times rose into the upper $30s, for example, $37⅛ reported October 25, 1988; and Morgan Stanley after a lengthy analysis continued to conclude the stock was still a buy because it will continue to generate free cash flow. Shearson Lehman published as late as November 29, 1988, that it "believed Gillette would lose its court case against Coniston and the judge would order another proxy contest. . . . Of course, we never anticipated that Coniston would walk away from the prize it said it desired. Accordingly, our takeover scenario was dependent upon an outside force that now appears absent."[19] Coniston had executed such a convincing public relations maneuver that some observers could not believe the facts.

On November 23, Gillette announced it was phasing out its two Canadian plants, one in Montreal and the other in Toronto, beginning in April 1989. It would take somewhat over a year to complete the phase-out. Montreal's was primarily a razor blade plant; with the production of the Sensor, it made sense to consolidate that operation into the South Boston and Andover plants. The directors received quite a bit of direct mail from workers who would lose jobs in these plants and even, as newspapers reported, criticism by the Canadian government. The Toronto Paper Mate plant was sold in the spring of 1989, and in late 1989 and early 1990 Gillette bought, from Storer AB, the Wilkinson's blade and razor business that was outside of the United States and the European Community.

Additionally noteworthy during the fall of 1988 was agreement with CalPERS that the definition of *average market price* would, under the antigreenmail amendment to the bylaws, be the same as that which was ratified and adopted by the directors for the Perelman-related stockholder suits. It was virtually identical to the way Gillette determined its repurchase price of shares in November 1986. The bylaws amendment, October 20, 1988, defines the average market price as the average of the closing sale price for each of the ten full trading sessions prior to the first public announcement of an intended purchase, weighted by the number of shares trading in each session.

A somewhat backward step—at least, so I interpreted it—for Gillette was its introduction of Epic Waves home permanents early 1989. These were kits that Gillette hoped would repeat the success of the Toni home permanents. But again in the area of women's toiletries, Gillette did not seem to be able to grasp the basic essentials. Times had changed; and despite the $21 million spent on advertising and promotions, Gillette could not switch women's desires for nearly straight hair to a preference for curly hair such as existed during the period of the great gains from the "Toni Twins" promotion. The natural look was in. Moreover, with more women working, probably fewer women were interested in trying to replace beauty-shop visits with an at-home, time-consuming chore. Epic Waves home permanents flopped. "Domestic sales of toiletries and cosmetics were virtually unchanged [in 1989], and profits decreased somewhat."[20]

Confirming that 1988, despite the share repurchases, was overall financially a successful year, the Board voted a 10-cent increase in the dividend rate payable in June 1989. The payout ratio of dividend to profits after taxes was about one-third; but if the value of the one-for-every-seven shares repurchase right were included as a dividend, the dividend payout ratio for 1988 was 98 percent. The peak payout ratio in recent years was 50 percent in 1985, before all the takeover furor began. The Board and management were confident that Gillette's future continued to be bright despite the Company's huge debt. Plant and manufacturing consolidation continued, and Gillette became leaner and with higher profits as the lower-margin disposables became less important.

Coniston was finally reported as having sold all its Gillette shares by the end of March 1989; about the same time, it was reported that overall institutional ownership of Gillette had dropped to 34 percent. Despite strong operating profits, it seemed that Gillette was, at least for the time being, not in play, and the Company could concentrate on making money.

The 1989 annual meeting was called for April 20 to elect three directors for terms to expire in 1992: Dick Pivirotto, president of his own management-consulting firm; Juan Steta, a lawyer from Mexico City; and Al Zeien, vice chairman of the Board. Charles Meyer did not stand for reelection because he was 70 years old. No dissidents were running for the Board. Compared to that of 1988, this meeting was cut and dried. The 1971 stock option plan was amended to extend the awarding of options to a broader group of key employees. Among the five stockholder proposals, two were for the Company to plan withdrawal from South Africa, two would stop the use of animals in testing and one would require use of a confidential ballot. The directors did not endorse any of these and none passed; however, in respect to the confidentiality-in-voting issue, the directors answered in part that there was a new "confidential voting procedure being employed for the Company's 1989 Annual Meeting" and in essence the Board would rather wait to see how that new procedure, although somewhat different from the proposal, worked out.

The heavier debt and the brief period of negative equity in 1988 stemming from the company's repurchase of one of seven shares of stock outstanding at $45 reinforced any sensitivity that the Board and management had to criticism charging poor management. Although in February 1931, almost fifty years earlier, Gillette had deferred dividends during its financial upheaval at that time, it did not do so in the period immediately subsequent to November 1986 or in 1988. In 1986–1988 Gillette not only maintained payment of its dividends but actually raised their annual rate. Recollection by management of the earlier Gillette history may have been why the question of whether to defer or to pay a lower dividend rate was not even raised in 1988. However, I do not recall any actual discussion of the events of 1931 during the 1988 board meetings after the proxy fight and the repurchase decision. Gillette prior to the events of 1986 through 1988 had deliberately avoided incurring large long-term debt. Acquisitions were not made or even discussed if sizeable debt would result from the purchases. It was recognized that interest payments on debt have to be met, while dividends for equity capital can be unilaterally delayed, lowered or just not paid. In retrospect it is interesting that in an image crunch Gillette acted as if the payment of dividends were also legally mandated in order to retain financial respectability.

The shaving wars had resurged. In June of 1989, Wilkinson Sword Inc., a much smaller company than Gillette, filed counterclaims to Gillette's suit charging Wilkinson with falsely advertising the superiority of their blades with a lubricating strip as compared to the Gillette Atra with its lubricating strip. Wilkinson countercharged Gillette with false advertising and monopolistic practices. This was like a warm-up practice before the big game, the introduction of the Sensor. On July 7, 1989, a U.S. District Court in southern New York found that the Wilkinson ads were false in claiming that its product was "six times smoother" than Gillette's, and the Wilkinson's television commercial so claiming was enjoined, effective July 21. With Wilkinson then having about 4 percent of the wet-shave market against Gillette's over 60 percent, this continued the no contest market status.

Late in 1988, legal suits over Gillette's November 1986 action were filed in the Delaware and Massachusetts courts charging Gillette directors with breach of fiduciary duty. All but two of the suits were consolidated and settled before the printing of the proxy statement for the April 1992 annual stockholders meeting. One, with Albert E. Evans as plaintiff, was filed as late as January 9, 1990. This was finally settled out of court March 31, 1994, and finalized by May 1; all the records, including depositions, involving Gillette and Coniston were sealed.

WARREN BUFFETT ENTERS

Gillette had in the summer of 1989 a higher long-run value than its low market price. Looking at Gillette's consistent earning power, good cash flow, its management in place and its everyday products, such as razors and blades and pens, it would have been hard for Warren Buffett to miss that Gillette was a real opportunity for his investment arm, Berkshire Hathaway. Buffett's Berkshire Hathaway portfolio has no computer stocks, no semiconductor companies and no companies in the complex fields of biomedical products and wireless communication. Gillette fits. Razors and blades, along with Coca-Cola, both nondurable consumer products, not only fit, they have become the backbone of the Berkshire Hathaway investments. Manufacture of nondurable consumer goods and marketing them geographically worldwide make Buffett's picks big winners.

That Joe Sisco of the Gillette board on GEICO's (Government Employees Insurance Company) board along with Buffett was a major instrumental factor in Buffett's decision to invest in a big way in The Gillette Company. Sisco was a very well informed and articulate spokesman for Gillette. Sisco became the conduit for Warren Buffett to approach Gillette for a "negotiated purchase of large, but not controlling, blocks of stock," as it is referred to under the Berkshire Hathaway's acquisition criteria described in their annual reports. This move became even more attractive to Gillette's directors when they also read the disclaimer, "We will not engage in unfriendly takeovers."[21] The Gillette Board was easily swayed to accepting a Buffett investment, but the terms had to be negotiated.

Warren Buffett might be termed a *microinvestor* in the same sense in which the term *microeconomist* is used. He bases his investment decisions on an individual business, more than on the probable future trends of interest rates, money supply and the general economy. His interest centers on the long-run, intrinsic value of a company in relation to the price he has to pay. For him, the time to buy is when a company has a problem and its price is down. The Gillette Company could be so characterized in this period, the summer of 1989. Buffett not only fully understood Gillette's products, he also appreciated the growing high value of using Gillette's brand names worldwide concomitant with world-wide TV advertising. The brand name *Gillette* could be used similarly to *Coca-Cola*, in which Berkshire already had a heavy investment. Gillette's subdivisions—Braun, Oral-B toothbrushes, writing instruments—all were doing well, with the exception of toiletries and cosmetics. Gillette had plans to leverage its name and its new slogan "Gillette: The Best A Man Can Get" over a selected upscale group of its male grooming products, thus spreading the appeal of its brand name worldwide.

Colman Mockler had with Joe Sisco's urging and the Board's support met Warren Buffett in June 1989 for the first time in Omaha, Nebraska. As I recall, Colman reported to the Gillette Board that Warren Buffett had taken him to lunch and that they immediately formed a liking for each other, only in a very small part based on the fact that they liked the same foods: meat, potatoes and ice cream. The two men genuinely admired each other. As Warren Buffett wrote in his 1989 letter to shareholders of Berkshire Hathaway, "We only want to link up with people whom we like, admire and trust. John Gutfreund at Salomon, Colman Mockler, Jr., at Gillette . . . meet this test in spades."[22]

Obviously, each man appreciated the other; and from the point of view of Gillette as a company, its directors welcomed a person whose record showed that he does not engage in hostile takeovers. This move could not have come at a better time for Gillette. Buffett's entrance into the affairs of Gillette as an investor and a director gave the company time to develop its strategic business plans to launch the Sensor and continue its geographic expansion worldwide to sell its products.

Who is Warren Buffett that by one major investment he could remove Gillette as a target of the takeover wars? According to *Forbes* magazine, Warren Buffett, with $9.2 billion net worth, was in 1994 the second wealthiest man in the United States. As head of Berkshire Hathaway Inc., a holding company primarily in the property and casualty insurance business, Buffett has been in the limelight of the financial press for several years. Attention in the fall of 1991 became enormous as he rode to what was hoped to be the rescue of the investment house Salomon Brothers and also, incidentally, to protect Berkshire Hathaway's $700 million investment made in 1987 in that firm. He was considered to be an ideal person for that position, being known as "Mr. Clean" and having a mathematical mind and superb memory cloaked by a folksy Omaha, Nebraska, demeanor.

Warren Buffett bought Berkshire Hathaway, a declining textile mill, in 1965 as an investment vehicle. Its early acquisitions include the *Washington Post* in 1973 and GEICO in 1977, both of which were enormously successful investments, in 1995 worth more than thirty times their original price.

Berkshire Hathaway also owns or has owned blocks of bonds, as of the government, RJR Nabisco and the Washington Public Power Supply System—and, of special interest to readers of the Gillette story, redeemable, convertible preferred stocks of Champion International, Salomon, and USAir. Some of these have been converted into common stock. Although primarily an insurance company, Berkshire Hathaway also owns Furniture Mart (a retailer of carpet, furniture and appliances, and the like), See's Candy Shops Inc., Kirby Vacuum Cleaners, and others.

Berkshire Hathaway also owns or has owned stock of Wells Fargo and Company, Coca-Cola and Capital Cities/ABC Inc. When the Disney Company in 1995 bought Capital Cities/ABC, Buffett's Berkshire Hathaway stock value soared. Holding good stock pays. The $57 million Berkshire had spent for 20 million shares in 1985 of Capital Cities/ABC rose to $2.3 billion.

But not all of Berkshire's investments were or are winners. Berkshire wrote off millions against its USAir and Salomon Brothers holdings. Sales of its *World Book Encyclopedia* were early slowed by the impact of computers on accessing information, but its new CD-ROM products may have regained sufficient market to recover fully. In Berkshire's 1994 report, Warren Buffett refers to "Our $358 million purchase of USAir preferred stock, on which the dividend was suspended in September" as "a case of sloppy analysis, a lapse that may have been caused by the fact that we were buying a senior security or by hubris. Whatever the reason, the mistake was large."[23] Despite all the current hype on Buffett, it is nice to know that he is human and, like us, also makes mistakes.

All of Berkshire's investments are detailed in the Berkshire Hathaway annual reports, which are a delight to read. Straightforwardly, with a sense of humor, Warren Buffett portrays his philosophy, compliments his readers and cajoles Berkshire Hathaway shareholders. For example, "Charlie [Munger] and I always enjoy the meeting, and we hope you can make it. The quality of our shareholders is reflected in the quality of the questions we get: We have never attended an annual meeting anywhere that features such a consistently high level of intelligent, owner-related questions."[24]

Warren Buffett runs about a $21 billion (December 1994) insurance and investment fund from his office in Omaha, Nebraska, where some imagine that he feeds into nearly one hundred computers the financial data of thousands of companies from their SEC filed 10-K forms and annual reports in order to direct his astute investments. This is apparently not true. Peter Lynch, another well-known stock investor (who for many years ran Fidelity's Magellan Fund) states in his foreword to Robert G. Hagstrom's 1994 book, *The Warren Buffett Way*, that "To be able to play more bridge, early in 1994 Warren learned how to use a computer so he could join a network where you can play with other individuals from their locations all over the country."[25] This comment runs true to me. When I first met Warren Buffett at the first Gillette board meeting, which he as a new director attended in November 1989 (Warren Buffett had agreed in July to join the Gillette Board but was not formally elected by the Board until October 1989), we discussed, among other things, hobbies and playing bridge, which he takes very seriously, being newly involved at the international level in duplicate bridge tournaments. In duplicate bridge the same hands or deals are played by all taking part, thus placing the stress on strategy and tactics. In

Omaha, Nebraska, there are probably few bridge partners close by with whom he can play at his level. Of course, his private plane, bought in 1986, can take him expeditiously all over the country, and he probably combines, at times, playing bridge with business meetings.

Berkshire Hathaway acts as an investment vehicle for Warren Buffett, and I envision from talking with him that the excellence of his investment choices is possible because he reads carefully the newspapers and the financial press, has an excellent memory, reads carefully company annual reports and 10-Ks and also analyzes all the information he has gathered to decide whether or not to invest in a company. Additionally, he has eleven employees and the astute Charles T. Munger, the vice chairman of his board of directors, with whom he consults. Munger is a knowledgeable lawyer based in Los Angeles. Warren Buffett has stated that he uses the precepts of Benjamin Graham in selecting those companies in which Berkshire Hathaway invests. Graham, the dean of financial analysts, advocated buying those stocks whose market price was two-thirds or less than the long-run or intrinsic value of the Company and had a low market price to future earnings ratio.

Buffett, over the years, has advertised for acquisitions in the Berkshire annual report and did so in the 1994 annual report, from which the following acquisitions criteria are taken:

Acquisition Criteria

We are eager to hear about businesses that meet all of the following criteria:

(1) Large purchases (at least $10 million of after-tax earnings),

(2) Demonstrated consistent earning power (future projections are of no interest to us, nor are "turnaround" situations),

(3) Businesses earning good returns on equity while employing little or no debt,

(4) Management in place (we can't supply it),

(5) Simple businesses (if there's lots of technology, we won't understand it),

(6) An offering price (we don't want to waste our time or that of the seller by talking, even preliminarily, about a transaction when price is unknown).

The larger the company, the greater will be our interest: We would like to make an acquisition in the $2–3 billion range.[26]

With a few exceptions, such as the criterion for little or no debt, which Gillette was rapidly paying down, and the need for an offering price, Gillette fitted the criteria of a desirable Berkshire acquisition.

Warren Buffett initially proposed that he (Berkshire Hathaway) buy $600 million of a newly issued, convertible, preferred stock of The Gillette Company. The proposal was that the stock carry a dividend of 9 percent and a conversion price of $45, or alternatively a dividend of 9.5 percent and conversion price of $50 after eight years. The final terms were negotiated. Colman Mockler was very critical of the initial proposal. The final, specific provisions evolved in bargaining during July 1989 between Charlie Munger on Buffett's behalf and Joe Flom on Gillette's behalf and eventually between Warren Buffett and Colman Mockler. The resulting final terms, 8¾ percent and a $50 conversion price within two years if certain conditions were met, were better for Gillette than the original proposal and better than the earlier Buffett/Salomon deal of a 9 percent preferred convertible at $38 per share. The price in the latter was about $5 over its common stock trading price at the time or about 13 percent higher than market as compared to Gillette's conversion price, which was 20 percent higher than market.

Buffett's Berkshire Hathaway Inc. on July 20, 1989, bought 600,000 newly issued Gillette preferred stock, with a high quarterly dividend of 8 3/4 percent, for $1,000, with each share convertible to 20 shares of common stock. In essence Buffett paid $50 a share, well above the then market price of about $40. Further, the agreement provided that if the market price of Gillette's common stock for twenty consecutive trading days closed at at least 125 percent of the issue price during the following two-year period, then Gillette could call Berkshire's shares for redemption into common. If after two years the preferred had not been called, then the required premium need be only 110 percent of the issue price, and after ten years the shares must be redeemed. Obviously, Warren Buffett hedged his bets.

Gillette viewed Buffett's stock purchase primarily as giving the company time to continue to develop its business plans. Gillette planned to use the $600 million of Buffett's equity investment to pay back its high-interest loans, thus substituting equity for debt and reducing its current interest expenditures. It would greatly strengthen the balance sheet and allow for a continued capital spending program.

Gillette was criticized in the press for giving Buffett too good a deal. There were, as I recall, no alternative deals sought by Gillette or offered to it. A lump-sum investment of $600 million dollars is not easily found, and the Board knew of no recent public offerings of this size by other companies for comparison. Gillette's advisors said that the investor's return would probably be about 25 percent. From Buffett's point of view, there is a risk in any investment, including convertible preferreds, as his USAir and Salomon holdings illustrate. However, Berkshire's $600 million worth of Gillette stock at the end of 1991 was worth $1,347 million, a gain, without counting the dividend payments, of over 100 percent.[27] The immediate gain on conversion had been nearly 46 percent, and then also Berkshire owned 11 percent of Gillette. Buffett made about $279 million when he converted Berkshire's Gillette preferred to 11 percent of Gillette outstanding stock on February 21, 1991, when the common closed at $73.25, far above Buffett's $50 per share payment.[28] Salomon, like Gillette, had also been a takeover target of Ronald Perelman and Buffett was also that company's white knight. Although the outline of the Gillette deal was close to the one Buffett had made with Salomon Brothers in September 1987 and in which he has invested $700 million in preferred (and years later additional millions in common) stock, the outcomes have been very different. On Gillette, Buffett has won big; not so on Salomon.

From Gillette's point of view, this was a dream white-knight deal. Buffett, admired worldwide for his investment acumen, became a director of Gillette and informally agreed not to try to take over the Company. Gillette directors recognized Buffett as an investor, not a raider. He would give Gillette time to pursue their business plans and meanwhile by being on its board add luster to the Company's name and make available his valuable advice. From Buffett's point of view, the market value of Gillette's stock in July 1989 was far less than the discounted value of its potential earnings power from the new Sensor, its newly pared down workforce and its ever-increasing geographic expansion.

Gillette's July 20, 1989, press release reads in part as a mutual-admiration exercise.

"We are pleased in the confidence shown by Berkshire Hathaway and Warren Buffett in the Company's prospects and look forward to his counsel as a director. His record as an astute long-term investor is widely recognized and his investment in Gillette is a highly favorable development for the Company, its stockholders and employees," Mr. Mockler said.

"Gillette is synonymous with highly-successful, international, consumer marketing and is exactly the sort of business in which we like to invest for the long term. We are delighted to be associated with the Gillette management team," Mr. Buffett said.[29]

However, Gillette's action to accept Warren Buffett's investment in Gillette was not approved by all. One newspaper columnist stated, "Mr. Buffett is getting 'whitemail' to stick around and hold management's hand,"[30] and some criticized the action in almost the same words as a *Wall Street Journal* headline, "Buffett's Savior Role Lands Him Deals Other Holders Can't Get." One answer to such criticism of the deal lies in Buffett's experience with USAir, which in August 1989 also sold to Buffett convertible preferred stock, this time with a 9.25 percent dividend. But here the risk turned out to be sizeable. No one has perfect knowledge of the future, and although determining the "correct" price of such deals might be done in hindsight, such deals always involve a degree of risk.

Preferred securities with high dividends are safer investments for the buyer than common stock with much lower dividends. But from Gillette's point of view, two years free of time-wasting harassment was crucial in 1989. The call provisions set a limit on Buffett's gains, and Gillette's Sensor was waiting to be launched.

Some newspaper articles have stated that Gillette approached Buffett, but that is not accurate. The approach was from Buffett to Gillette. The deal was definitely a negotiated one in which the terms were improved during the short period between late June and July 20 and became more favorable to Gillette. As would be expected, one of the intense public critics of Gillette's action was Paul Tierney of Coniston Partners, because this action would remove Gillette from being in play and end any possibility of Coniston taking over the company for a period of years. Buffett promised Gillette that at least for ten years Berkshire Hathaway wouldn't join with any other group holding 5 percent or more of the stock. Warren Buffett as a friendly investor owning 11 percent of the stock would, under the new *"freeze-out"* Delaware law on hostile takeovers and the Delaware Chancery Court decision of July 14, 1989 (upheld by Delaware's Supreme Court ruling of July 24, 1989, in *Paramount Communications v Time, Inc.*), would work effectively to rule out future takeover attempts. The law in Delaware, where Gillette is incorporated, restricts a targeted company for three years from entering into a business combination with any hostile 15 percent shareholder. It prevents the use or sale of a corporation's own assets, as when an acquirer issues junk bonds and then sells off parts of the targeted company to complete a hostile takeover. Coniston did not appear to have access to cash sufficient to purchase 15 percent of Gillette in mid-1989, when the Company's value was well over four billion dollars. Coniston's power to pressure Gillette with Buffett owning 11 percent of the stock and sitting on the board would be sharply curtailed. The Delaware law was intended to protect incumbent managers. It pushed would-be acquirers into the proxy mode. Further, as Joe Grundfest wrote in 1993, the emergence of legal and political "barriers in mid to late 1989 coincided with a sea change in financial market conditions that tightened the supply of available credit and made capital for hostile takeover activity exceedingly difficult to obtain."[31] I do not recall long discussions during the June and July board meetings that Gillette would gain because of Buffett's investment. Probably it was so obvious to all concerned that it did not warrant discussion. Gillette needed a quiet period to conduct its business. Gillette had continued to be a target of takeover speculation up to the Buffett investment. For example, in early July, one could still read an investment company's assessment: "As a takeover candidate, we value Gillette in a range from the low-$50's to the low-$60's per share," this when the stock price was $40¼.[32] Being a target had become a way of life for Gillette.

To me it was amazing how many of the board members knew of the reputation of Warren Buffett, and yet apparently I was the only investor in Berkshire Hathaway on the Gillette board, although for such a minimum amount that there could be no question of conflict of interest.

Warren Buffett is an independent, tough-minded businessman. In November 1985, just one year before the first takeover attempt of Gillette, several board members discussed informally prior to the scheduled board meeting an academic conference held at Columbia Law School's Center for Law and Economic Studies on "Takeovers and Contests for Corporate Control." The papers, which are printed in an Oxford University Press volume, include one by Michael Jensen and also remarks by Warren Buffett, who comments,

You notice I don't include the board of directors, because my experience overwhelmingly has been that the boards of directors (there are exceptions) tend to go along with what management wants. So I put them in the management classification. And managements are usually going to resist sale, no matter how attractive the price offered. They will advance all sorts of high-sounding reasons, backed up by legal and investment banking opinions, for rejection. But if you could administer sodium pentathol, you would find that they, like you or me, simply don't want to be dispossessed—no matter how attractive the offer might be for the owner of the property. Their personal equation is simply far different from that of the owners. If they can keep the keys to the store, they usually will.[33]

This realistic appraisal of corporate boards is right on target.

To me, Warren Buffett is a sophisticated, well-read man who loves playing duplicate bridge and reading classical economists such as David Ricardo and enjoys most portraying himself as the investor's equivalent of a small-town lawyer, fond of saying, "With me, what you see is what you get." But along with the author of a long *Wall Street Journal* article that quotes this phrase in 1991, I ask, "Or is it?"[34]

NOTES

1. "Credit Ratings: Securities of Amax, Unit Are Upgraded in Moody's Ratings," *Wall Street Journal*, July 11, 1988, p. 25.

2. *San Francisco Chronicle*, May 5, 1988, p. C1.

3. Harry DeAngelo and Linda DeAngelo, "Proxy Contests and the Governance of Publicly Held Corporations," *Journal of Financial Economics* vol. 23, no. 1 (June 1989), pp. 29–59, and especially pp. 51–52.

4. Alison Leigh Cowan, "Gillette and Coniston Drop Suits," *New York Times*, August 2, 1988, p. C5.

5. Scheduling Hearing for Phase II of Trial, Before Honorable Mark A. Wolf, Civil Action No. 88-0862-WF, United States District Court, District of Massachusetts, *The Gillette Company, Plaintiff v RB Partners et al., Defendant*, Boston, July 13, 1988, mimeo, p. 6.

6. Ibid., p. 7.

7. Ibid., p. 20.

8. Robert Willens, "Put and Take: New Ways to Buy Back Shares, Cut Payouts," *Barron's*, August 22, 1988, p. 20.

9. Jayant R. Kale, Thomas H. Noe and Gerald D. Gay, "Share Repurchase through Transferable Put Rights: Theory and Case Study," *Journal of Financial Economics* vol. 25 November 1989, p. 152.

10. Ibid., p. 156.

11. *Annual Report 1988* (Boston: The Gillette Company, 1989), p. 2.

12. Kale, Noe and Gay, "Share Repurchase," p. 158.

13. Cowan, "Gillette and Coniston Drop Suits," p. C1.

14. Dorman L. Commons, *Tender Offer: The Sneak Attack in Corporate Takeovers* (Berkeley: University of California Press, 1985), pp. 97–98.

15. Alison L. Cowan, "Judge Says He May Order New Election at Gillette," *New York Times*, July 14, 1988, p. C-3.

16. Joe Queenan, "Silent Partner: Will the Real Tito Tettamanti Please Stand Up?" *Barron's*, August 15, 1988, pp. 6, 28, 29, 31.

17. Andrea Rothman, "Gillette, in a Shift, to Emphasize Cartridge Blades over Disposables," *Wall Street Journal*, November 18, 1988, p. B6.

18. Marilyn M. Royce, "Gillette NYSE-GS," Value Line, p. 811, October 21, 1988.

19. Andrew Shore, "Consumer: Gillette Company," Shearson Lehman Hutton, November 29, 1988, p. 1.

20. *Annual Report 1988* (Boston: The Gillette Company, 1989), p. 6.

21. *Berkshire Hathway Annual Report, 1994*, p. 21.

22. Letters to Shareholders 1987–1990, Berkshire Hathway Inc., Omaha, Neb., p. 59.

23. *Berkshire Hathaway Annual Report, 1994*, p. 17.

24. *Berkshire Hathaway Annual Report, 1990*, p. 21.

25. Peter S. Lynch, Foreword to Robert G. Hagstrom, Jr., *The Warren Buffett Way: Investment Strategies of the World's Greatest Investor* (New York: John Wiley and Sons, 1994), p. v.

26. *Berkshire Hathaway Annual Report, 1994*, p. 21.

27. *Berkshire Hathaway Annual Report, 1991*, pp. 15, 27.

28. Diane Tracy, "Gillette's Net Jumps; Payout Is Set to Rise," *Wall Street Journal*, February 22, 1991, p. A3.

29. "Gillette Reports Second Quarter Results and Sale of Convertible Preferred to Berkshire Hathaway," *The Gillette Company News*, July 20, 1989, p. 3.

30. Linda Sandler, "Heard on the Street: Buffett's Savior Role Lands Him Deals Other Holders Can't Get," *Wall Street Journal*, August 14, 1989, p. C1.

31. Joseph A. Grundfest, "Just Vote No: A Minimalist Strategy for Dealing with Barbarians inside the Gates," *Stanford Law Review* vol. 45, no. 4 (April 1993), p. 861.

32. "The Gillette Company," Equity Research Bulletin, Dean Witter Consumer Group, July 7, 1989.

33. John C. Coffee, Jr., Louis Lowenstein and Susan Rose-Ackerman (eds.), *Knights, Raiders, and Targets: The Impact of the Hostile Takeover* (New York: Oxford University Press, 1988), p. 16.

34. Ron Suskind, "Legend Revisited: Warren Buffett's Aura as Folksy Sage Masks Tough, Polished Man," *Wall Street Journal*, November 8, 1991, p. A1.

10

In Retrospect

In 1990, New York's Greenwich Village promoted the cause of shareholders in an aptly titled, widely praised play, *Other People's Money*. This drama, written by Jerry Sterner, details the painful anticipation by the management of an old-line New England company in the wire and cable business, which was financed primarily by equity capital, of a hostile takeover that would be financed primarily by debt capital. The CEO did not feel comfortable with the prospect of a heavy load of high-interest-bearing loans forcing high annual payouts for years to come. Although the corporate raider, "Larry the Liquidator," and the company's board chairman are overdrawn caricatures, many lines rang true for the Gillette situation. For example, the chairman of the board states in the play at the annual shareholder meeting where the proxy vote occurs:

At least the robber barons of old left something tangible in their wake. A coal mine. A railroad. Banks. This man leaves nothing. He creates nothing. He builds nothing. He runs nothing. In his wake lies nothing but a blizzard of paper to cover the pain.

If he said, "I could run this business better." Well, that's something worth talking about. He's not saying that. . . .

A business is more than the price of its stock. It is the place where we make our living, meet our friends and dream our dreams. It is, in every sense, the very fabric that binds our society together.[1]

Although Colman Mockler, to the best of my knowledge, never uttered such words, they were in character. This play, which appeared in forty U.S. cities and several foreign countries, illustrates the wide appeal of the takeover theme. And indeed the wire and cable company is taken over, but not The Gillette Company.

ASSESSMENT

Some believe that a board of directors should "adopt a posture of strict neutrality in connection with hostile tender offers made to shareholders." The primary arguments for this position are that the premiums normally offered by bidders to shareholders are large and that the board and management have a potential conflict of interest when a tender is announced because a takeover threatens their incumbency. In contrast, a major financial audit firm states that

> the courts have uniformly rejected the notion that tender offers concern only the shareholders and have reaffirmed the authority of the board as protectors of the corporation. . . .
> The board should consider the long-term interests of the corporation and its shareholders. The company is not for sale unless and until the board decides that it is. The board is not obliged to accept an offer simply because it exceeds the current market price of the company's shares. In fact, it should not accept an offer unless it determines that there is no other reasonable likelihood that it can produce a larger gain for its shareholders by some other means, including maintaining the independence of the company.[2]

This quotation summarizes what the Gillette Board members assumed and acted upon during 1986 through 1988. A board is responsible, and it is the board that makes the decisions. The Gillette Board firmly believed that the Company would produce a larger gain for its shareholders continuing the Company business plans rather than by selling it for a somewhat higher price than market, and the Board was correct. "The company's most optimistic pre-launch projections [for the Sensor] were for the sale of 18m razors and 200m blades in 1990. The actual totals were 27m and 350m. Sensor grabbed 7% of both the (at the time) $850m American blade market and the $1.1 billion European one, and an astonishing 42% of the $150m combined American and European market for non-disposable razors. Sensor was a phenomenal success,"[3] and profits from Sensor blades with *The Economist*'s estimate of "a gross margin of nearly 90%"[4] meant huge profits. Gillette's Board and management risked big and gained big.

However, the defenses that already had been adopted were insufficient to protect fully Gillette's control. Even a poison pill and a staggered board seemed to be of little help in maintaining Gillette's independence in the face of Ronald Perelman's cash tender. Whatever response the Board might have adopted, legal suits would begin. Indeed, suits were initiated concomitant with the Revlon/Perelman cash tender. The suits claimed that the Board's failure to waive its poison pill was a violation of the Board's fiduciary duties.

Whatever action they took, the directors knew that they were individually liable. Disgruntled shareholders of other companies have filed legal actions against board members because their board accepted an offer that was not high enough. In the Van Gorkom, Trans Union case, the courts ruled that the board in selling Trans Union at a 30 percent premium over market should have negotiated a higher price because the company's intrinsic value was higher; this claim was upheld, and individual board members were held personally liable. However, in July 1995 in the Ronald Perelman 1983 acquisition of Technicolor Inc. case, the Supreme Court of Delaware upheld the dismissal of a shareholder suit charging director negligence. John Coffee, a corporate law professor, is quoted as saying that this ruling puts ''one more set of ramparts and moats around the citadel'' before you hold directors liable.[5] The suit had charged that Technicolor's board had not considered all offers for that company. During late 1986 and well into the future, most directors of major companies believed that they would always be held liable unless they acted to maximize short-run shareholder value. This 1995 ruling coupled with protective legislation by the states may have weakened this belief.

Others have filed suit against a board because it authorized a buyback of shares from an unsought bidder at a more favorable price than was offered by the market to other shareholders, most notably, those bringing suit. This was the charge made against Gillette's action in November 1986, designated by many as greenmail. But the later dramatic rise in Gillette's stock price essentially made the charge moot, and the cases were settled out of court.

In the mid-1980s and again in the 1990s, mergers, takeovers and leveraged buyouts, followed by restructuring, have occurred. There is little agreement, however, on what drives these or earlier periodic spurts in the number of mergers followed by lulls in activity. The merger periods of the 1980s and that of the 1990s are different.

In the mid-1980s, the availability of easy cash as via junk bonds played an important role in hostile takeovers. In 1995 the wide impact of sophisticated computers and software and increasing wireless telecommunications have been driving huge, apparently friendly takeovers, such as Walt Disney Company's purchase of Capital City/ABC for $19 billion and the merger of Chase Manhattan and Chemical Bank to form the largest U.S. bank, with over thirty billion dollars in assets and much larger custodial accounts and a stock market valuation of close to $25 billion illustrate. These large transactions represent the two major industries where technological innovation in the mid-1990s has had the greatest impact: the media and banking. Recent media mergers to form multimedia companies stem from innovation and desire for efficiency and bigness as corporations with creative ideas link up with the corporations that have the technology to disseminate more efficiently their substantive ideas, for example, through producing creative movies and widely appealing music via cable systems. Bank mergers reflect vertical integration. Technological change is also encouraging formation of very large banks in the United States that are more efficient than smaller banks. It is estimated that the merger of the Chase Manhattan and Chemical Bank corporations, now ''Chase Manhattan Bank,'' will result in the elimination of 12,000 jobs out of a total of pre-merger approximately 75,000 employees. These numbers reflect horizontal integration. Some years ago, Walter Wriston, then head of Citicorp, predicted that computers would help tear down banking as we know it, and only the U.S. antitrust laws and prohibitions on branch banking have stopped this from occurring earlier. Many of the 1980s mergers resulted from hostile takeover attempts, while in the mid-1990s, mergers were noticeably more friendly and were primarily technology driven.

Gillette offers an example of a company targeted by the two most common methods of acquisition: a tender offer and a proxy contest. In neither case did the would-be acquirers claim that Gillette was badly managed, and in neither case did they present a plan to restructure the Company, nor was new technology an important stimulus for the acquirers. Perelman and Coniston were raiders, not managers. Although Ronald Perelman said that such an acquisition would in 1986 be synergistic, he never spelled this out, and the Coniston Partners actually openly approved of Gillette's management. This does not mean that Gillette during the early part of the 1980s was not somewhat bloated, did not have excess middle management and or did not need to streamline or downsize. The Perelman attempt was opined by some to be a needed impetus to force Gillette to become more efficient. Subsequently, the Company did release 8 percent of its workforce and did become more efficient. In fact, one might say that Perelman's attempt pushed Gillette ahead of the game in international competition, coming as it did in late 1986. The Company thus began its restructuring early, completing it well before 1990.

Hostile acquirers seem more intent than friendly acquirers on diverting cash into their own pockets than on improving efficiency for longer-run gains and expanding a company's presence in the international markets. This seemed to be true in the case of The Gillette Company. Both Perelman and Coniston wanted to sell the Company primarily for immediate gain and were not really concerned about the long-run future of Gillette. The friendly mergers of the mid-1990s are touted as primarily attempts to improve the efficiency of the companies involved. But to a cynical observer, not a player, it may seem that the current players just have good public relations departments.

Gillette had and still has the prime characteristic that lures others to try to acquire it—a stable, large, predictable cash flow from the sale of razors and blades. Unless some harmless chemical were found to stop beard growth, the close to universal human desire to eliminate facial hair ensures a worldwide, very profitable market for the most effective and comfortable shaving device possible, and Gillette claims to be the company that produces that. Since ridding itself of unwanted suitors, Gillette has done extraordinarily well. By the end of 1994, using pre-merger with Duracell (the "historical financial summary" data in Gillette's 1996 annual report gives different 1994 data because it reflects merger-related activity with Duracell), it was a company with $6 billion in annual sales, compared to just under $3 billion sales in 1986 when this story began. Profits from operations had risen to over $1.2 billion, and long-term debt had dropped to $715 million, down from its peak in 1988 of $1.675 billion. Whereas in that year, as a result of the stock repurchase, there was a negative shareholder equity, minus $85 million, in 1994 shareholder equity grew to over $2 billion. The change in six years was remarkable.

Gillette's 1967 purchase of Braun AG in West Germany for $50 million resulted in eventual domination of the electric shaver market. The launch of the Sensor in 1989, followed by SensorExcel, permits Gillette to dominate all shaving markets, except possibly the disposable razor-blade market, worldwide. Gillette's cash flow seems assured for the immediate future, and its razor and blade sales, which are directly related to the size of the male population exposed to its advertisements, are predictable for several years ahead. The Company's efforts to reduce costs prior to 1986 were intensified by the takeover attempts. Divisions that were losers were sold off, which increased profits.

In the restructuring of 1987–1988, Gillette sold many small divisions, but it still owns its primary core: Braun, Paper Mate, Waterman and more recently Parker pen, Liquid Paper, Oral-B toothbrush, Jafra Cosmetics with over $1 billion sales and several well-known toiletry brand names such as White Rain shampoo and Right Guard deodorant which have stood the test of competition over many years. Once Gillette, attracted by the promise of even greater profits in fields its management did not know enough about, stopped using its excess cash flow to diversify in its effort to halt the loss of razor and blade sales to disposables, its restructuring held promise of great economic returns.

At year's end 1995, the Company had 33,500 employees, somewhat above the 29,600 in 1988, reflecting in part the recent acquisition of Parker Pen. And with the acquisition of the battery manufacturer, Duracell, in September 1996, its labor force continues to grow. Restructuring after 1986 reduced the work force by 8 percent, but new acquisitions, new products and geographic expansion increased the number of Gillette workers. The ratio of dollar sales to employees greatly improved from the 1986 measure of only $88,000 generated per worker to over twice that amount, or $189,000 per worker in 1994 and over $200,000 per worker by the end of 1995, far more than price inflation during that period would account for. Today Gillette is a far more efficient company than in 1986 and is realizing that bright future optimistically promised in late 1986.

Very early during the attempted takeovers, a debatable point was whether the Gillette Board should have hired outside advisors, investment bankers who reported only to the Board and not also to the management. This was suggested by one board member, but after long discussion and despite the mistrust by some directors of Morgan Stanley that held up renewal of its contract to gain greater economic reward, the consensus was that top management and the Board would act as one, with one set of investment and legal advisers.

Some board members continued to be skeptical of investment advisers who had used the felicitous timing of the expiration of their contract to force up their advisory fees substantially. As a result, the payments were restructured after the November 1986 takeover attempt so that the returns to outside advisers were no longer directly linked to the size of any completed deal, a practice that acted to encourage negotiating ever-larger deals. Rather, a set amount, $3 million, was negotiated in 1988, whether a future deal would be concluded or not. In other words, Morgan Stanley was forced to take a lump sum rather than a percentage of the deal.

In respect to the outside legal advisers, very early a second firm (Jones, Day, Reavis and Pogue) was hired in addition to the legendary takeover lawyer Joe Flom and his colleagues at Skadden, Arps, Slate, Meagher and Flom. As a director, I was grateful for this when during the Board discussion of the second Perelman/Revlon attempt, June 1987, Joe Flom argued that the Board would have to get a second outside valuation of the firm's intrinsic value. I and a few other board members argued that a well-informed board that included an investment banker and an economist could update an existing valuation, which had been made in late 1986, only seven months previously. The representative of Jones, Day strongly supported that point of view. The Company thus did not pay out an extra several hundred thousand dollars that a second valuation probably would have cost. The Board's judgment in refusing as too low, after considerable discussion, the $40.50 per share offer in June 1987 was reinforced by Perelman/Revlon's third and still higher offer in August 1987 of $45 in cash and $2 in securities. The Board also considered this amount to be below the long-run value of the stock. These dollar amounts are after the stock was split in the spring of 1987. In judging these actions one needs to note that the new offers were per share $81 and $94, respectively, on a basis comparable to the original $65 tender. By the end of 1995, two more two-for-one splits had occurred.

A few scholarly articles support my earlier observation that what is important in computing the gains or losses from actions resolving hostile takeovers is the interval of time over which one computes the gains or losses of targets and acquirers. After analysis of several thousand hostile acquisitions 1976–1981, authors Magenheim and Mueller conclude that the shorter the period of time considered, the more the data support that the shareholders of the *acquiring* firm benefit. But alternatively, "if three years . . . prior . . . and . . . three years . . . after"[6] are considered, then the market has a long-run view of the consequences, and completed hostile takeovers have less favorable results. Although their data analysis is of acquirers and Gillette was a target, a long-run view from either point of view, I believe, gives a truer picture.

The implications for a company of being the target of a hostile takeover bid has been ably described by an analogy to ice hockey.

But the peculiar genius of a takeover bid is that the management is taken off the ice, put in the penalty box, so to speak, long enough for the bidder to make a "score." We need to think more, therefore, about whether such a playing field is ever level or appropriate. The decision to put a company into play, almost irrevocably we might add, is made neither by the shareholders, who are not active participants, nor by management, which the tender offer process is designed to circumvent, but by persons outside the company who may or may not intend to operate the business or to do anything more than exact tribute. Should the decision to liquidate the venture be lodged there?[7]

There are those who believe management alone makes the strategic decisions of response, and not the board of directors. Management can, by controlling the information flow to the board, influence the board's decisions. There is no federal legislation nor should there be any that requires management to make full disclosure to the board of all the details of running a business. Any such legislation could interfere with the day-to-day running of a business. Successful corporate governance depends on full disclosure to the board by management of the past and planned large expenditures and future policy direction. Audit committees and other post facto reviews may at times be inadequate in obtaining that disclosure, which includes plans for the future. Customarily, audit committees review the financials of the firm, and the directors sign the Form 10-K, the annual detailed financial report that a corporation files with the SEC. On this information about past actions the directors depend in part in order to make decisions about the future; but in such rare and sometimes unique situations as are involved in hostile takeover bids and/or proxy contests, there may be at times other information that the board may not fully know and yet may not necessarily know that it is not fully informed. For example, in the matter of Gillette's proxy contest the Board had not been informed fully about Tito Tettamanti. All that the in-house lawyers knew was not fully passed on to the Board; although this may seem like a minor matter, in essence it became the legal linchpin on which Judge Wolf held Gillette at fault. Boards have to be more diligent in their oversight functions, Closer questioning of what may seem to be a forthcoming management during extraordinary periods is in order. This recommendation can be difficult to implement because it is not always clear what questions need to be asked.

The complications in judging the long-term price of a company's shares should be self-evident. Although Gillette's market share price fell sharply on Black Monday of October 1987 along with the rest of the market, it recovered quickly and by the beginning of 1988 was at a new high level. The stock has been split, two-for-one, four times: in 1986, 1987, 1991 and 1995. Whereas at year-end the stock price in 1986 was 6⅛; in 1987, 7⅛; and in 1988, 8¼, the stock price at year end 1990 was 15⅝ or over double the 1986 year-end price[8] and in November 1996 had reached over $74 a share, roughly nine times the initial tender offer. The enormous gain is due in large part to the superb performance of Al Zeien, chairman from 1991 forward.

January 25, 1991, marked the end of an era, with the unexpected and untimely death of the chairman of the board, Colman M. Mockler, Jr. On February 25, a month later, Gillette share price closed 15 percent higher, reflecting shareholder confidence in the Board's selection of its new chairman and CEO, Alfred M. Zeien. The continuing rise in price to $52⅛ at year's end 1995 and to over $74 in November 1996 reaffirms the wisdom of the Board's actions to repel takeovers and develop its own long-run plans to launch the Sensor, to concentrate on Braun, Oral-B and its writing instruments division and to continue expansion geographically.

Al Zeien and Michael Hawley in their letter to stockholders, March 1, 1996, stated that "Over the last 10 years, the compounded rate of return on Gillette stock has been 31%, about twice that of the market averages. The value of a $1,000 investment in Gillette stock at the end of 1985 grew to $14,924 by the end of 1995—more than three times the value of a comparable investment in either of the market averages."[9]

The following table was added for emphasis.[10]

	Investment 12/31/85	Value 12/31/95	Compounded Rate of Return
Gillette	$1,000	$14,924	31%
DIJA	$1,000	$4,590	16%
S&P 500	$1,000	$3,983	15%

Gillette still has tremendous growth potential because it is just beginning to benefit from earlier expansion into countries new to Gillette. There are very long-run lead times involved. For example, Gillette opened an office in India in the city of Calcutta in 1919, and only 64 years later, in 1983, did Gillette receive permission from the Indian government to establish a joint-venture manufacturing company, the Indian Shaving Products, Limited. With India projected by year 2000 to have one billion people in its population, it is a prime market for razors and blades and also for writing instruments. India places great emphasis on learning, and not only is the income per capita rising, but also their literacy rate. Forty percent of the Indian venture was attained in 1992. Gradually Gillette has been trying to increase its share in this joint venture to obtain 51 percent or more. In 1995 Gillette bought Wiltech, India, increasing its thriving blade business in India. Similarly, in 1982 Gillette started a joint venture to manufacture blades and razors in Shenyang, a northern city of the People's Republic of China (PRC). With 1.2 billion persons already in the PRC, the demographics were quite clear, not only for razors and blades but also for writing instruments, where Gillette is also the world's leading manufacturer. Gillette has expanded in the PRC since that time, building a joint manufacturing plant in Shanghai. The PRC company's name, Shenmei Daily Use Products Limited, is an example of the clever use of words by Gillette's advertising department. The name alone suggests that the Chinese male makes use of his razor and blade daily and not, as many Chinese normally do, especially in the countryside, once or twice a week. The name was an attempt to impress on the Chinese that shaving every day was the western way and the desirable way to live. Shaving in a sense becomes a lifestyle.

Colman Mockler, from the time I became a member of the Board, always expressed interest in demographics and was fascinated by what a country's given population data meant for the potential markets of Gillette. Indeed, this made detailed board presentations on different economies very interesting. Every time the Company was considering expansion into new geographical areas, an in-depth, academic type of presentation was made. Management covered the broad socioeconomic characteristics of the area's population and projected estimates of markets for the Company's products. Razors and blades, I believe, were always the initial product manufactured in a country new to Gillette, usually in a joint venture, with the Company sometimes building a new plant, but many times renting an existing one. In the long run the opening of plants in new geographical areas will pay off big for Gillette.

The Gillette Board can be criticized—and during the takeover period was— for its wide product diversification and at times concomitant waste of money in seeking new products to replace what it saw as a potential large decline in sales and profits because of the rise in worldwide sales of disposable razors and blades. However, some of this investment paid off. It would be nice to answer, if one could before a purchase or stock swap, exactly what will be a good fit. Hindsight is always better. The person primarily responsible for Gillette's extensive, often unrelated, diversification during the 1980s was (according to Thomas Skelly, Senior Vice President for Finance) Derwyn Phillips, who then headed up a very informal group within the Company named the Venturists. It was Derwyn who was responsible for such new, at least to Gillette, types of services as Elizabeth Grady Beauty Salons and the retail eyewear ventures. The latter always seemed to me to be a good business bet, but the former I never could understand as a Gillette business line. Sandra Lawrence, the only woman from Gillette management who during the twelve years I was a member of the Board ever presented to the Board, was for a brief period during the 1980s head of new business development. She replaced Robert Ray, who resigned for personal reasons to pursue a line of less demanding work. Sandra Lawrence was one of the few women who was listed in this period as an officer of the Company in Gillette's annual reports. The others were the two corporate secretaries in that period—Jan Day, founder and head of Jafra Cosmetics, and Judith Herald, vice president for human resources and also of Jafra—and additionally Francine Gomez, who sold her Waterman S.A. Company to Gillette in 1987. More women than earlier are cited in Gillette's 1995 annual report, totaling about 5 percent of 160 names. Still the Board has only one female director, who replaced me when I retired, but as the pool of qualified women continues to grow, Gillette can be expected to join many other large companies by having at least two female directors. At the April 1996 annual shareholder meeting of Gillette, the chairman, Al Zeien, stated in reply to a comment from the floor that Gillette should have more women than one on its Board, that "the Company hopes to recruit a woman as part of its objective to further diversify and internationalize the Board."[11] The Board in 1996 has three directors who live outside the United States.

FEDERAL GOVERNMENT POLICY

There is little conceptual framework of public policy that can be used to assess hostile corporate control events such as the tenders and proxy contest in which Gillette was involved.

This may be in part because regulation of the stock markets and corporations exists at both the state and the federal level, and there was legal dispute over which of the two took precedence in takeovers at the time. Although a 1982 Supreme Court ruling held that the federal 1968 Williams Act that specifically regulates takeovers did preclude state takeover laws, that did not in practice occur. Legal debate ensued. In 1985, only three years later, the Supreme Court greatly narrowed its earlier decision and in 1987 overturned it in *Dynamics Corporation v CTS Corporation, Indiana*, in which case Dynamics had tried to take over through a hostile tender the CTS Corporation. The Supreme Court also in 1987 upheld Indiana's strong 1986 antitakeover law, which acted as a green light for all the other states to legislate. In 1987 Massachusetts passed an antitakeover law, and in 1988 Delaware, where over 50 percent of U.S. corporations are incorporated, also passed antitakeover legislation. "By 1990, more than forty states had adopted antitakeover legislation, creating a 'de facto' national antitakeover regime."[12] It is no wonder that congressional Bill S-1323, originally introduced in the Senate in September 1987, was pulled by its main sponsor William Proxmire (D-Wisconsin) from the Senate floor in June of 1988. That bill would have required greater disclosure of takeover intentions to the SEC, as for example, requiring disclosure within five rather than ten days after the purchase of 5 percent of a company's stock. The bill had provisions against payment of greenmail and golden parachutes and enactment of poison pills. To my knowledge it has never been revived in part or in whole.

Legal indecision during the 1980s probably contributed greatly to the number of hostile takeovers at that time. For three years the states were apparently unable to enforce their antitakeover laws, and the federal government did not act. State antitakeover laws could not apparently be enforced after the 1982 ruling, which could have played a real part in stimulating the number of takeover attempts, including hostile ones.

The then single largest golden parachute, $35–36 million, was paid to the Revlon CEO, Michel Bergerac. In 1985 Gillette in line with the income tax code had a 2.99 times annual salary limit. Gillette's executives were not in the same league in size of their reported total annual compensation as compared to Keith Gollust and Paul Tierney at $11 million each or even Gus Oliver at $7 million.[13]

There was considerable debate between those who would and those who would not like to regulate further takeover attempts of corporations during the 1980s. The SEC commissioners were split. Many Chicago school economists took the stand to say that takeover attempts generally had produced a more efficient U.S. economy by replacing poor management with better management. However, others, as did the chairman of the Council of Economic Advisers in reporting on a national committee's conclusions, opposed "legislation to curb hostile takeovers [as it] could hurt shareholders, lead to a loss of jobs, preempt state regulations, and deter benefits [*sic*] takeovers."[14] Far better in promoting economic welfare than more government regulation of corporations and their governance is the favorable impact from the effective workings of the marketplace. International competition in product markets can eliminate poor managements. It is not necessary for a company to attract a hostile takeover bid that it be poorly managed or have potentially greater value if broken up and its parts sold. Takeover attempts are also attracted by large cash flow that creates the potential for an acquirer to make large gains. The states-rights issue with over forty states having laws that govern some takeover actions and a general feeling that the federal government interferes too much helped to defeat any intent for more government control and regulation. Corporate restructuring was left to the private parties involved, primarily the shareholders, management and corporate boards.

The decline in hostile takeover attempts that subsequently occurred in the late 1980s was in part a result of the legal force of the states' new antitakeover laws, the drying up of available loans at viable interest rates to finance them and, to a lesser degree, changes in the tax law on greenmail payments. The new state laws induced would-be acquirers to seek a proxy vote rather than the outright purchase of stock to take over a company.

Some individuals believe that the Economic Recovery Tax Act of 1981 also spurred the growth in the number of mergers that peaked in 1986 and that the Tax Reform Act of that year caused the number of takeover attempts subsequently to fall.[15] Although most of the 1986 Tax Act was not effective until January 1987, the tax rule on making greenmail payments subject to tax applied to payments made from March 1, 1986, forward. This explanation correctly places a high responsibility on the tax system for corporate actions.

During 1986–1988, there was also legal controversy over whether costs and legal fees involved in mergers were deductible in all cases from the corporate income tax base. This indecision surfaced in friendly mergers where case-by-case rulings were made. Because benefits were assumed to occur from friendly mergers, the costs involved were often denied deductibility. However, "the IRS, in ruling on specific cases, generally has allowed costs involved in defending against hostile takeovers to be deducted, albeit with some shifting positions along the way."[16] The Supreme Court stated in its February 1992 decision on National Starch that "There still are no clear, concise criteria to differentiate hostile takeovers from friendly deals for tax purposes."[17] That decision, however, made clear that expenses in a friendly takeover are not deductible because such costs would benefit the company over many years. As recently as mid-October 1995 the Tax Court denied deductions to the A. E. Staley Manufacturing Company on these or similar grounds for bankers fees incurred in fighting a hostile takeover offer: The target company would eventually get a long-term benefit.[18] This area of tax law was still unsettled in 1996.

During and after the two years in which Gillette was in play, legal changes in the laws and the regulations that govern takeovers occurred, involving both tenders and proxy fights. The extent of government regulations over corporations, communications and the expense of meeting SEC filing requirements during a proxy contest was a surprise to me and apparently to many other people.

Anyone who wished to comment about a proxy contest had to file and get clearance from the SEC. One excellent analysis of proxy voting prior to 1992 legislation observes that "after the 1956 revisions, no major campaign used full-page newspaper ads, presumably because strategists had not developed techniques necessary to clear them in a timely fashion as now required by the SEC. Ads resurfaced shortly thereafter, but were significantly fewer in number and have remained so up to 1991."[19] That Gillette did issue a full-page ad in 1988 that became a target of the regulators and the courts was significant. It is also noted in the same article that the number of total communications to the shareholders during "modern campaigns" has been substantially lessened. Prior to the federal legislation, dissidents campaigned more vigorously for votes. Extensive advertising as in Robert Young's attempt to take over the New York Central was common. There were 272 written statements and advertisements in that proxy contest, with each adversary taking out 40 ads in the *New York Times* alone. In this regard, Gillette and Coniston followed the practice of the 1980s with far fewer advertisements.

The Gillette/Coniston proxy fight and other events did result in some eventual weakening of the SEC regulations. In October 1992, three-and-a-half years later, SEC finally issued its revised shareholder communication regulations, effective October 22, exempting from all proxy requirements persons without any special interest in the issues being voted and also not having a special relationship with the company. This reduced expenses created by SEC preclearance requirements for business, dissidents and others wishing to comment on such issues. In the past, SEC "proxy rules have prohibited even telephoning more than ten other institutions to discuss such matters"[20] as proposals on antitakeover amendments or executive compensation. As access to the Internet increases, federal regulation that depends for enforcement almost entirely on restrictions on disclosures and communication will be greatly weakened. The contents of communication on the Internet and all types of electronic mail are very difficult, if not impossible, to monitor and regulate, which alone will weaken the effectiveness of government regulation.

Into the 1990s there has been a resurgence of friendly mergers where proxy contests do not occur. In the mid-1990s friendly mergers and spin-offs greatly increased in number as corporations in order to compete have been forced to restructure and take advantage of gains from acquiring higher levels of computers, getting into cyberspace and using wireless telecommunications equipment. In all types of restructurings, some people are likely to lose jobs primarily because of technological change concomitant with the information age. Changes in ownership are secondary to the prime driver of technological change. It is technological change and competition that force many companies to reduce the size of their labor force. Downsizing, in the lingo of the 1990s, occurs. But new jobs open elsewhere as in manufacture of the new equipment, and the overall societal effect is usually favorable, as the overall growth in the real gross national product indicates.

REFLECTIONS

Colman Mockler, who had some very trying moments during the lengthy hostile takeover period starting in 1986, experienced intense personal stress resulting from the picketing of his Wayland, Massachusetts, home in 1990 by the animal-rights activists who charged that Gillette's product testing subjected some laboratory animals to unnecessary pain. The calm control of emotions in events such as these was a trademark of Mockler, who died before he could enjoy his announced retirement at the end of 1991. It is ironic that Gillette's medical care program, which has a comprehensive cardiac program and clinic offices within the Prudential Boston headquarters building close to Mockler's office, could not prevent Mockler's premature death. (A 1979 booklet describes the plan as follows: "Each Gillette Medical Department is equipped with a crash cart carrying necessary cardiac emergency equipment, including drugs, oxygen and a cardiac defibrillator. In recent years, Gillette staff physicians have resuscitated four of six individuals who experienced cardiac arrest while at work." Gillette's cardiac program was an early pioneer in cardiac rehabilitation, permitting cardiac patients to return to work on a four-hour-a-day basis, and, in essence, easing them back to being full-time, productive employees.) It is improbable that more than an hour could have elapsed after Colman Mockler's heart attack without someone becoming aware. The company physician, who was a good friend of Colman Mockler, William C. Greer, refused to comment to me on this matter, but it was well known that Mockler's health habits (heavy smoker, lack of exercise and preference for a high-cholesterol diet) and the stress from takeover attempts probably would make him prone to an early heart problem.

William Holmes, president of Simmons College, who knew him well, commented that "He was a quiet, compassionate man who had an overwhelming belief in education, and great respect to those who caused it to happen."[21] Colman Mockler was chairman of the Simmons College Corporation from 1974 until 1991, and he also served on Harvard University's Corporation and Board of Overseers and was an overseer of the New England Medical Center, the Boston Museum of Fine Arts and the Boston Symphony Orchestra and a trustee of the New England Conservatory of Music. His interests are indicated by the names of the organizations listed. These many commitments meant a very busy schedule.

My one-on-one conversations with Mockler usually concerned his children and grandchildren, the latest mystery he had read (he especially liked books by P. D. James), Harvard University, art and general national and international affairs.

Warren Buffett in his 1990 annual report to the Berkshire Hathaway shareholders (p. 19) stated, "No description better fitted Colman than 'gentleman'—a word signifying integrity, courage and modesty. Couple these qualities with the humor and exceptional business ability that Colman possessed and you can understand why I thought it an undiluted pleasure to work with him and why

I, and all others who knew him, will miss Colman so much.'' With all this, I concur.

During the mid-1980s, I was a member of an international business roundtable that included several Japanese top business leaders. Through that and SRI International, on whose advisory board I served, I had one-on-one conversations with Akio Morita, then chairman of Sony, and Ryuzaburo Kaku, then board chairman of Canon. The Japanese emphasis on long-run profits really was very similar to Gillette's. Kakusan explained that the Japanese manufacturing strength is derived from incremental technological change, which a large Japanese company encourages by fostering lifetime employment. Professor Haruo Shimada, a Japanese labor economist whom I knew and met with from time to time, concluded that ''the American system . . . places a ceiling on the performance gains that can be achieved by improving human resource effectiveness—a ceiling *not* in place in the Japanese system. Japanese companies emphasize human resource effectiveness because it is a technological imperative to achieve *continued gains in performance* (emphasis added).''[22] Japanese firms try to maximize market share, and profits will follow. This also is Gillette's philosophy.

In any even partially autobiographical writing, I must acknowledge the influence of my Harvard economics professor, Joseph A. Schumpeter, from whom I took a course in money and banking and who also was an intellectual friend. In the mid-1940s, when I was a research assistant to Professor Sumner Slichter, Professor Schumpeter frequently would come to my office in the Littauer Center at Harvard to chat in the late afternoon about various topics. Born in 1883, Schumpeter was sixty years of age in 1943, and it was commonly observed that he still had an eye for any young lady he believed to be attractive. We enjoyed talking about art, architecture, music and other cultural affairs. Professor Schumpeter may have found it refreshing to relax thus, although at times he would expound on economic subjects such as the importance of profits and the true entrepreneur—one who is willing to take risks in a capitalist economy. I can see him at this point in time, a dapper man, usually in a gray suit, with black, highly polished shoes, legs crossed, smoking a cigarette in a silver holder, after having taken it from his silver cigarette case from his vest pocket. He would tap the cigarette on the case before lighting it and visibly enjoyed it immensely. At that time I had not read all of his new book, *Capitalism, Socialism and Democracy*, published in 1942, but appreciated his general thesis presented in class that capitalism in a social democracy would eventually destroy itself via an inflation that would be created from a redistribution of income from rich to poor, middle-income to low-income in order to finance various social schemes. He was, in my opinion and at that time, a true prophet of what could occur. In lectures, Professor Schumpeter, from day one, emphasized the dynamism of a changing economy. He would put an enlarged dot on the right side of the blackboard and from the left side would start to draw a straight line towards it and then stop, because he would explain, as you approach a goal, the goal itself will change. This is a dynamic economy. He would then move the dot and break the line, starting a new line toward the new dot and he would say, "but the goal has changed," and make another new dot and again would change the direction of the line. His concepts have stayed with me all these years. Persons in a social democratic economy will vote to redistribute income for overall expensive goals, and the resulting tax load can be too high for the economy to bear. Business firms can set goals that they wish to achieve, but the world keeps changing, and the firm must change with it.

A less dominant precept which was also part of his teaching was that debt financing is dangerous to the health of a firm and an economy. Profits were rewards for taking risks with money. Entrepreneurs take risks and are innovators and thus they get high profits. If an entrepreneur fails to make money, that is the essence of risk. Capitalism entails the freedom to fail and start again.

In the years since I knew Professor Schumpeter, to whose home I at times went to dinner, I have realized the great influence he had on my thinking. This was true whether I was studying the social security system and the huge debt that it has accumulated or the national health policy reforms proposed in 1994. While on the Board of The Gillette Company, his teaching helped me understand the dynamism that a profitable company must have for success. Gillette, and I know I am repeating, has always started a new product on the drawing boards as soon as they market an old one, which of course was especially true of razors: Trac II, Atra, Sensor and, currently, SensorExcel.

It was fortunate that in 1986 through 1988 I was neither writing a book nor in charge of erecting sizable buildings at the Hoover Institution, as I did in 1978. Takeovers absorb enormous amounts of time from any conscientious outside director. It amazed me then and now that CEOs of other companies, who are, of course, an ideal type of outside director because they know firsthand the problems that a chief executive of a company faces, would have the time to be involved not in one but several boards other than the companies they run. Recently the National Association of Corporate Directors were reported to recommend that "senior executives should sit on no more than three boards, including their own. Retired executives or professional directors should serve on no more than six."[23] Although the article from which this is taken does not discuss the geographic location of board meetings, of course, generally the greater the distance from the director's home, the greater the demands on his or her time. However, long plane flights do give one time to read. Gillette was fortunate in that during 1986–1988 only two active chairmen of even a nearly sizable company were directors: Ray Foster, chairman until January 1988 of Stone and Webster Inc., and Herb Jacobi, chairman of the managing partners of Trinkaus and Burkhardt.

It astounds me that there are persons who are reported to be on ten or more boards at one time; whether or not they are retired, to me that is too much for one individual to handle. It is true that what one learns at one board meeting sometimes can be carried to another board meeting, as in reference to the Financial Accounting Standard Board's (FASB) changes or legislative changes, but this does not offset the need to learn a company's specifics and also the details of the industry in which it operates.

In ending my twelve-year relationship with Gillette I ask myself why it became such a highlight of my life. As an academic, already four years on the board of a defense electronics manufacturer that had then about $300 million in annual sales, I had some contact with businessmen. Additionally, as a senior fellow, an economist, and wife of the director of the Hoover Institution, I had intermingled with the businessmen on the Board of Overseers of that institution. Many of these men were CEOs of their companies. As the only woman member of President Reagan's Economic Policy Advisory Board, I had gained some stature among businessmen, but immediate acceptance as an equal by top business people came first and most strongly from being a director of Gillette, and this acceptance is very different from derived acceptance as a wife or even that derived from being an academic economist at a prestigious university.

Although it may seem contradictory, being a director of Gillette also created more time for myself. During the long cross-country airline flights, no one could bother me, and in traveling to Boston I also gained more personal space to enjoy dinners and museums, take a Boston harbor ferry ride and even to wander among interesting shops, renew friendships with old Bostonian friends and on a regular basis take to dinner my mother, who lived alone in Boston. As the scheduled business demands on my time increased, I learned to factor into my busier schedule more time for myself. As the mother of three children, the youngest aged 14 when I went on Gillette's board, dealing with a shortage of time had become a way of life for many years. As personal demands decreased—in 1985 my youngest was 21 years old—it was not difficult to accommodate the increasing demands of work, and to do so was enjoyable.

To be back in the city of my birth and youth was pleasing. Changes in Boston's architecture over the past fascinated me. The Copley Place area was built during the first part of my years on the board, and prior to that the whole wharf area had been renovated. With the new Boston Harbor Hotel at Rowe's Wharf, the retail shops and restaurant development at Fanueil Hall market and the computer museum and its older art museums and symphony, Boston was a top city to visit, even though it has been held back by racial problems and in recent years by a lack of money and transportation difficulties, the latter hopefully to be solved in part by the new Ted Williams tunnel under the harbor.

But with all these gains in becoming a board member, did the Gillette shareholders get a bad deal? I believe not. I was able to give a Californian and a Washingtonian (D.C.) and, yes, a woman's perspective to the debates over Gillette's policy.

I believed that leaving a board on which one has served for twelve years might be emotionally trying. Therefore, I arranged to stay an extra day in Boston during my last meeting as a member of the Gillette Board in April 1990 to view the exhibit of the series of Monet paintings at the Boston Fine Arts Museum. Although I arrived just after opening, the museum was already crowded; hours later, when I left, it was more crowded. The opportunity to view master paintings of the same scene, whether poplar trees or the Rouen Cathedral, in different lights—morning, noon with strong sunlight, mid-afternoon and dusk—was mildly exhilarating. In winter, snow was highlighted, while in summer bright sunlight yielded an extraordinary variation of colors. Dull beige in the morning light moved towards bright orange and yellow in the hot afternoon sun, to evening's soft purples, pinks, gray, blue and golds. The variety was amazing. The genius of Claude Monet elated me. This brief interlude was primarily intended to lessen any sense of loss, and I found it a fitting way to end this special part of my life.

NOTES

1. Jerry Sterner, *Other People's Money: The Ultimate Seduction* (New York: Applause Theatre Book Publishers, 1990), pp. 82–83.

2. KPMG, *A Practical Guide for the Corporate Director*, prepared by Michael P. Dooley and the Center for Corporate Governance Education and Research, January 1990, p. 24.

3. "Management Brief: The Best a Plan Can Get," *The Economist*, August 15, 1992, p. 59.

4. Ibid., p. 60.

5. Edward Felsenthal, "Liability of Directors," *Wall Street Journal*, July 19, 1995, p. B10.

6. Ellen B. Magenheim and Dennis C. Mueller, "Are Acquiring-Firm Shareholders Better Off after an Acquisition?" in John C. Coffee, Jr., Louis Lowenstein and Susan Rose-Ackerman (eds.), *Knights, Raiders and Targets: The Impact of the Hostile Takeover* (New York: Oxford University Press, 1988), p. 190.

7. Edward S. Herman and Louis Lowenstein, "The Efficiency Effects of Hostile Takeovers," in Coffee, Lowenstein and Rose-Ackerman, *Knights, Raiders and Targets*, p. 232.

8. All stock price data taken from The Gillette Company's *1995 Annual Report* (Boston: The Gillette Company, 1996), p. 43.

9. "Letter to Stockholders," *1995 Annual Report* (Boston: The Gillette Company, 1996), pp. 3–4.

10. Ibid., p. 4.

11. *1996 Annual Meeting and First Quarter Report* (Boston: The Gillette Company, 1997), p. 13.

12. Joseph A. Grundfest, "Just Vote No: A Minimalist Strategy for Dealing with Barbarians inside the Gates," *Stanford Law Review* vol. 4, no. 4 (April 1993), p. 861.

13. Congressional Record—Senate, Tender Offer Disclosure and Fairness Act, June 21, 1988, pp. S-8269, S-8271 and S-8272.

14. Congressional Record—Senate, Tender Offer Disclosure and Fairness Act, June 20, 1988, p. S-8211, as quoted from E. Sussman, *Wall Street Journal*, June 24, 1987.

15. C. Clinton Stretch and Frank C. Devlin, Jr., "The 1986 Tax Reform Act: The New Rules for Business," *Practical Accountant* vol. 19, no. 11 (November 1986), p. 58.

16. Ray A. Knight and Lee G. Knight, "The Point of No Return for Tax Deductions of Acquisition Costs," *Mergers and Acquisitions* (September/October 1992), p. 41.

17. Ibid., p. 41.

18. Deborah Lohse, ''Hostile Takeover Expenses Will Be Harder to Deduct,'' *Wall Street Journal*, October 18, 1995, p. A-1.

19. John Pound, ''Proxy Voting and the SEC: Investor Protection Versus Market Efficiency,'' *Journal of Financial Economics* (October 1991), p. 277.

20. Pound, ''Proxy Voting and the SEC,'' p. 279.

21. *Simmons Now*, March 1990 [*sic*, actual 1991], p. 3.

22. Alan Blinder, ''International Perspective: Trading with Japan: Why the U.S. Loses—Even on a Level Playing Field,'' *Business Economics* (January 1992), p. 28.

23. John A. Byrne, ''Listen Up: The National Association of Corporate Directors' New Guidelines Won't Tolerate Inattentive, Passive, Uninformed Board Members,'' *Business Week*, November 25, 1996, p. 104.

Bibliography

BOOKS

Adams, Russell B., Jr. *King C. Gillette: The Man and His Wonderful Shaving Device.* Boston: Little, Brown and Company, 1978.

Anderson, Charles A. and Robert N. Anthony. *The New Corporate Directors: Insights for Board Members & Executives.* New York: John Wiley & Sons, 1986.

Auerbach, Alan J. (ed.). *Corporate Takeovers: Causes and Consequences.* Chicago: University of Chicago Press, 1988.

Bhagat, Sanjai, Andrei Shleifer and Robert W. Vishny. "Hostile Takeovers in the 1980s: The Return to Corporate Specialization." In Martin Neil Baily and Clifford Winston (eds.), *Brookings Papers on Economic Activity: Microeconomics*, pp. 1–84. Washington, D.C.: Brookings Institution, 1990.

Bottom, Norman R., Jr. and Robert R. J. Gallati. *Industrial Espionage: Intelligence Techniques and Countermeasures.* Boston: Butterworth Publishers, 1984.

Browne, Lynn E. and Eric S. Rosengren (eds.). *The Merger Boom: Proceedings of a Conference Held at Melvin Village*, New Hampshire, October 1987, sponsored by the Federal Reserve Bank of Boston. Boston: Federal Reserve Bank of Boston, 1988.

Burrough, Bryan and John Helyar. *Barbarians at the Gate: The Fall of RJR Nabisco.* New York: Harper and Row, 1990.

Cody, Thomas G. *Strategy of a Megamerger: An Insider's Account of the Baxter Travenol–American Hospital Supply Combination.* Westport, Conn.: Quorum Books, 1990.

Coffee, John C., Jr., Louis Lowenstein and Susan Rose-Ackerman (eds.). *Knights, Raiders, and Targets: The Impact of the Hostile Takeover* (Columbia Law School Symposium, November 1985). New York: Oxford University Press, 1988.

Coleman, James S. "Social Organization of the Corporation." In John R. Meyer and James M. Gustafson (eds.), *The U.S. Business Corporation: An Institution in Transition.* Cambridge, Mass.: American Academy of Arts and Sciences, 1988.

Commons, Dorman L. *Tender Offer: The Sneak Attack in Corporate Takeovers*. Berkeley: University of California Press, 1985.

Davidson, Kenneth M. *Mega-Mergers: Corporate America's Billion-Dollar Takeovers*. Cambridge, Mass.: Ballinger Publishing Company, 1985.

Downes, John and Jordan Elliot Goodman. *Barron's Finance and Investment Handbook*, 3d ed. New York: Barron's, 1990.

Fleischer, Arthur, Jr., Geoffrey C. Hazard, Jr. and Miriam Z. Klipper. *Board Games: The Changing Shape of Corporate Power*. Boston: Little, Brown and Company, 1988.

Friedman, Benjamin M. *Corporate Capital Structures in the United States*. Chicago: University of Chicago Press, 1985.

Gillette, King C. *The Human Drift* [1894]. Delmar, N.Y.: Scholars' Facsimiles & Reprints, 1976.

Hagstrom, Robert G., Jr. *The Warren Buffett Way: Investment Strategies of the World's Greatest Investor*. New York: John Wiley and Sons, 1994.

"Insider Trading." *The New Palgrave Dictionary of Money and Finance*, vol. 2. London: Macmillan, 1992.

Juran, J. M. and J. Keith Louden. *The Corporate Director*. New York: American Management Association, Inc., 1966.

Kelly, Edmund J. *The Takeover Dialogues: A Discussion of Hostile Takeovers*. Arlington, Va.: Washington Network Press, 1987.

Lampe, David (ed.). *The Massachusetts Miracle: High Technology and Economic Revitalization*. Cambridge, Mass.: MIT Press, 1988.

Leonard, Albert S. *The Gillette Company 1901–1976*, ed. Patricia Holland. Boston: The Gillette Company, 1977. (A special issue of *Gillette News* commemorating the 75th anniversary of the Company's founding.)

Lewis, Michael. *Liar's Poker: Rising through the Wreckage on Wall Street*. New York: Penguin Books, 1989.

Lichtenberg, Frank R. with Donald Siegel. *Corporate Takeovers and Productivity*. Cambridge, Mass.: MIT Press, 1992.

Lorsch, Jay W. with Elizabeth MacIver. *Pawns or Potentates: The Reality of America's Corporate Boards*. Boston: Harvard Business School Press, 1989.

Lynch, Peter S. Foreword to Robert G. Hagstrom, Jr., *The Warren Buffett Way: Investment Strategies of the World's Greatest Investor*. New York: John Wiley and Sons, 1994.

Manne, Henry G. *Insider Trading and the Stock Market*. New York: Free Press, 1966.

McAllister, Margaret (ed.). *The Merger Yearbook '87: Yearbook on Corporate Acquisitions, Leveraged Buyouts, Joint Ventures and Corporate Policy*, 9th ed. Boston: Cambridge Corporation, 1987.

McKee, David L. (ed.). *Hostile Takeovers: Issues in Public and Corporate Policy*. New York: Praeger, 1989.

Poole, William T. (ed.). *Patterns of Corporate Philanthropy: Funding False Compassion*. Summary essay by Marvin Olasky. Preface by Rady A. Johnson. Washington, D.C.: Capital Research Center, 1991.

Ravenscraft, David J. and F. M. Scherer. *Mergers, Sell-Offs, and Economic Efficiency*. Washington, D.C.: Brookings Institution, 1987.

Scholes, Myron S. and Mark A. Wolfson. *Taxes and Business Strategy: A Planning Approach*. Englewood Cliffs, N.J.: Prentice-Hall, 1992.

Shook, R. J. and Robert L. Shook. *The Wall Street Dictionary*. New York: New York Institute of Finance, 1990.

Siegel, Joel G., Jae K. Shim and David Minars. *The Financial Troubleshooter: Spotting and Solving Financial Problems in Your Company*. New York: McGraw-Hill, 1993.

Smith, Roy C. *The Money Wars: The Rise and Fall of the Great Buyout Boom of the 1980s*. New York: Truman Talley Books/Dutton, 1990.

Stern, Paul G. and Tom Shachtman. *Straight to the Top*. New York: Warner Books, 1990.

Sterner, Jerry. *Other People's Money: The Ultimate Seduction*. New York: Applause Theatre Book Publishers, 1990.

Van Horne, James C. *Financial Management and Policy*, 8th ed. Englewood Cliffs, N.J.: Prentice-Hall, 1989.

Van Horne, James C. and John M. Wachowicz, Jr. *Fundamentals of Financial Management*, 8th ed. Englewood Cliffs, N.J.: Prentice-Hall, 1992.

Weidenbaum, Murray L. and Kenneth W. Chilton (eds.). *Public Policy toward Corporate Takeovers*. New Brunswick, N.J., and Oxford: Transaction Books, 1988.

Weston, J. Fred, Kwang S. Chung and Susan E. Hoag. *Mergers, Restructuring, and Corporate Control*. Englewood Cliffs, N.J.: Prentice-Hall, 1990.

Wriston, Walter B. *Risk and Other Four-Letter Words*. New York: Harper and Row, 1986.

ARTICLES

Anders, George. "Boesky Fund Sold Big Blocks of Securities." *Wall Street Journal*, November 20, 1986, p. 3.

Anders, George. "KKR in Peril: The Fight to Save RJR." *Wall Street Journal*, April 6, 1992, p. B8.

Anderson, Leonard. "Seagram to Go Slowly on Any Purchase Using $2.3 Billion from Properties Sale." *Wall Street Journal*, September 16, 1980, p. 2.

Bagwell, Laurie S. and John B. Shoven. "Cash Distribution to Shareholders." *Journal of Economic Perspectives* vol. 3, no. 3 (Summer 1989).

Bagwell, Laurie Simon. "Dutch Auction Repurchases: An Analysis of Shareholder Heterogeneity." *Journal of Finance* vol. 47, no. 1 (March 1992).

"B.A.T. Unit Seeks Any Data Farmers Group Gave Others." *Wall Street Journal*, March 15, 1988, p. 4.

Beam, Alex. "T.G.I.W.: Gillette: Who Are They?" *Boston Globe*, July 13, 1988, p. 67.

Bhagat, Sanjai and Richard H. Jefferis, Jr. "The Causes and Consequences of Takeover Defense: Evidence from Greenmail." *Journal of Corporate Finance* (1994).

Black, Bernard S. "Bidder Overpayment in Takeovers." *Stanford Law Review* vol. 41 (February 1989).

Black, Bernard S. "Institutional Investors and Corporate Governance: The Case for Institutional Voice." *Continental Bank: Journal of Applied Corporate Finance* (Fall 1992).

Black, Bernard S. *Next Steps in Proxy Reform*. Working Paper #90, The Center for Law and Economic Studies, Columbia University School of Law, 1993.

Bleakley, Fred R. and Peter Pae. "Clark Is Barred from American Express Meeting." *Wall Street Journal*, January 25, 1993, pp. A3–A4.

Blinder, Alan S. "International Perspective: Trading with Japan: Why the U.S. Loses—Even on a Level Playing Field." *Business Economics, The Journal of the National Association of Business Economists* (January 1992).

Brancato, Carolyn Kay and Patrick A. Gaughan. "Institutional Investors and Capital Markets: 1991 Update." Columbia Institutional Investor Project, Center for Law and Economic Studies, Columbia University School of Law, Table 21.

Brauchli, Marcus. "Dickson, Hong Kong Luxury Goods Company, Sees Gold in Opening 'Status' Shops in China." *Wall Street Journal*, March 1, 1993, p. A10.

Burrough, Bryan. "Gillette Is Placed on Restricted List of Oppenheimer." *Wall Street Journal*, September 11, 1987, p. 41.

Burrough, Bryan. "Macy Sweetens Federated Offer to $6.3 Billion; Firm Also Secures Option to Buy Two Big Units; Market Is Disappointed." *Wall Street Journal*, March 15, 1988, p. 3.

Burrough, Bryan and David Wessel. "Gillette Shares Advance Amid Signs That Big Buyer Is Accumulating Stock." *Wall Street Journal*, July 15, 1987, p. 4.

Chakravarty, Subrata N. "We Had to Change the Playing Field." *Forbes*, February 4, 1991, p. 83. (Cover story: "Triumph for Gillette's Colman Mockler: Technology as a Marketing Tool.")

Chatterjee, Sayan. "Sources of Value in Takeovers: Synergy or Restructuring—Implications for Target and Bidder Firms." *Strategic Management Journal* vol. 13 (May 1992).

Chipello, Christopher J. and Laurie P. Cohen. "Gillette's Rejection of Revlon's Proposal Isn't Likely to Deter Chairman Perelman." *Wall Street Journal*, June 22, 1987, p. 7.

Chipello, Christopher J. and Ann Hagedorn. "Revlon Proposes to Buy Gillette and Is Rebuffed." *Wall Street Journal*, June 19, 1987, p. 3.

Chutkow, Paul. "Her Nibs." *New York Times Magazine*, December 4, 1988, p. 28.

Clark, Lindley H., Jr. and Alfred L. Malabre, Jr. "Borrowing Binge: Takeover Trend Helps Push Corporate Debt and Defaults Upward; Analysts Worry That Load Will Worsen Downturn in the Next U.S. Recession; Reaping the Reagan Harvest?" *Wall Street Journal*, March 15, 1988, p. 1.

Cohen, Laurie P. "Revlon Offers to Buy Interest in Salomon Inc." *Wall Street Journal*, September 29, 1987, p. 3.

Cole, Robert J. "Jacobs Calls Holdings in Gillette 'Substantial.' " *New York Times*, June 20, 1987, p. 37.

Cole, Robert J. "Rumors Swirling around Gillette." *New York Times*, June 4, 1987, p. D2.

Committee on Corporate Laws. "Guidelines for Directors: Planning for and Responding to Unsolicited Tender Offers." Report approved for submission for future publication in *The Business Lawyer*. November 1985.

Coniston Group. "An Open Letter to the Stockholders of The Gillette Company." *Wall Street Journal*, March 24, 1988, p. 33.

Cooper, Wendy. "The Case of the Exploding Cigarette Lighters." *Institutional Investor*, December 1987, p. 210.

Congressional Quarterly, No. 193 S1323, "Corporate Takeovers/Golden Parachutes," Washington, D.C., June 25, 1988, p. 1777.

"Corporate Report: Swiss Financier Tettamanti Sells a 20% Stake in Sulzer." *Wall Street Journal*, April 6, 1988, p. 20.

Cowan, Alison Leigh. "Company News: Perelman Says Quest for Gillette Isn't Over." *New York Times*, April 15, 1988, p. D4.

Cowan, Alison Leigh. "Gillette and Coniston Drop Suits." *New York Times*, August 2, 1988, pp. C1, C5.

Cowan, Alison Leigh. "Judge Says He May Order New Election at Gillette." *New York Times*, July 14, 1988, pp. C-1, C-3.

Cowan, Alison Leigh. "Markets & Investments: Three Raiders Who Are Cleaning Up—Without Junk Bonds." *Business Week*, December 1, 1986, p. 124.

Cowan, Alison Leigh. "The Trench Warriors." *New York Times*, May 29, 1988, Business Section, p. 5.

"Credit Ratings: Securities of Amax, Unit Are Upgraded in Moody's Ratings." *Wall Street Journal*, July 11, 1988, p. 25.

Crock, Stan. "Insider Trading: There Oughta Be a Law." *Business Week*, December 12, 1994, p. 82.

Crudele, John. "Buyout Rumors Spur Gillette's Stock." *New York Times*, December 4, 1986, p. 35.

DeAngelo, Harry and Linda DeAngelo. "Proxy Contests and the Governance of Publicly Held Corporations." *Journal of Financial Economics* vol. 23 (1989).

Dunkin, Amy, Laurie Baum and Lois Therrien. "People/Dealmakers: This Takeover Artist Wants to Be a Makeover Artist, Too." *Business Week*, December 1, 1986, p. 110.

English, Mary B. *The Gillette Company*. Analyst's Sheet, Furman Selz Mager Dietz & Birney Incorporated, May 26, 1989.

Feinberg, Andrew. "Antic Observations: Fanciful Theories on Perelman's Obsession with Gillette." *New York Times*, August 23, 1987, p. F8.

Felsenthal, Edward. "Liability of Directors." *Wall Street Journal*, July 19, 1995, p. B10.

Flack, Stuart. "The Cayman Connection." *Forbes*, December 11, 1989, p. 42.

Flack, Stuart. "Marion Gilliam's Two Faces." *Forbes*, April 2, 1990, p. 42.

Flax, Steven. "How to Snoop on Your Competitors." *Fortune*, May 14, 1984, pp. 29, 31.

Gibson, Richard. "Desert Partners Sets Proxy Fight for USG Seats." *Wall Street Journal*, March 15, 1988, p. 20.

Gibson, Richard and John Andrew. "Jacobs Considers Move in Takeover Fight for Gillette, Confirms McGraw-Hill Stake." *Wall Street Journal*, August 26, 1987, p. 2.

Giese, William. "Gillette Pays, Revlon Scrams; Greenmail Is In." *USA Today*, November 25, 1986, p. 1B.

Gillette Company. "An Open Letter to Fund Managers from Gillette: The Coniston Group—Who Are They?" Full-page advertisement, *Wall Street Journal*, April 19, 1988, p. 55.

"Gillette Discloses Bids from 'Squires' against Coniston." *Wall Street Journal*, June 22, 1988, p. 50.

"Gillette Review: Hat in Hand." *Fortune* vol. 4, no. 4 (October 1931), p. 48.

"Gillette Stake of Substantial Size Is Held by Investor Irwin Jacobs, Sources Say." *Wall Street Journal*, February 6, 1987, p 6

"Gillette's Sharp Identity." Editorial, *Boston Globe*, August 21, 1987.

Gilson, Ronald J. "How to Draft a Prohibition on Greenmail." Working Paper No. 38, John M. Olin Program in Law and Economics, Stanford Law School, Stanford, Calif., October 1987.

Gilson, Ronald J. and Reinier Kraakman. "What Triggers *Revlon?*" Working Paper no.

54, John M. Olin Program in Law and Economics, Stanford Law School, Stanford, Calif., August 1989.

Grundfest, Joseph A. "Just Vote No: Minimalist Strategies for Dealing with Barbarians *inside* the Gates." *Stanford Law Review*, vol. 45, no. 4 (April 1993).

Guenther, Robert. "Gillette Is Severing Ties with Citibank over Bank's Role in Hostile Revlon Plan." *Wall Street Journal*, August 14, 1987, p. 4.

Hagedorn, Ann. "Gittis Opts for a Low Profile at Revlon." *Wall Street Journal*, June 25, 1987, p. 30.

Hammonds, Keith. "Turnarounds: How Ron Perelman Scared Gillette into Shape." *Business Week*, October 12, 1987, p. 40.

Harris, Robert S., Julian Franks and Colin Mayer. "Means of Payment in Takeovers: Result for the U.K. and U.S." Working Paper No. 2456. Cambridge, Mass.: National Bureau of Economic Research, December 1987.

Heard, James E. and Howard D. Sherman. "Conflicts of Interest in the Proxy Voting System." Investor Responsibility Research Center, Inc., Washington, D.C., March 1987.

Hill, G. Christian. "Buffett Is Said to Hold 9.8% of Wells Fargo." *Wall Street Journal*, October 25, 1990, p. A2.

Ingrassia, Lawrence. "The Cutting Edge." *Wall Street Journal*, April 6, 1992, p. R6.

Ingrassia, Lawrence. "Face-Off: A Recovering Gillette Hopes for Vindication in a High-Tech Razor." *Wall Street Journal*, September 29, 1989, p. A6.

Ingrassia, Lawrence. "Keeping Sharp: Gillette Holds Its Edge by Endlessly Searching for a Better Shave." *Wall Street Journal*, December 10, 1992, p. A6.

Jacobs, Margaret A. "Settlement Closes Trial Pitting Perelman against Fired Executive." *Wall Street Journal*, July 19, 1995, p. B10.

James, Frank E. "J. P. Stevens Accepts $959.4 Million Bid, Spurning West Point–Pepperell Proposal." *Wall Street Journal*, March 15, 1988, p. 4.

Jensen, Michael. "Agency Costs of Free Cash Flow, Corporate Finance, and Takeovers." *American Economic Review* vol. 76, no. 2 (1986).

Kale, Jayant R., Thomas H. Noe and Gerald D. Gay. "Share Repurchase through Transferable Put Rights: Theory and Case Study." *Journal of Financial Economics* vol. 25 (November 1989).

Kaplan, Steven N. and Michael S. Weisbach. "The Success of Acquisitions: Evidence from Divestitures." *Journal of Finance* (March 1992).

Knight, Ray A. and Lee G. Knight. "The point of No Return for Tax Deductions of Acquisition Costs." *Mergers and Acquisitions* (September/October 1992), p. 41.

Kurz, Mordecai. "On the Structure and Diversity of Rational Beliefs." Technical Report No. 39. Stanford Institute for Theoretical Economics, Stanford, Calif., November 1991.

Laabs, Jennifer J. "Gillette: Building a Global Management Team." *Personnel Journal* vol. 72, no. 8 (August 1993).

Lee, Elliott D. "Heard on the Street: 'Poison Pills' Benefit Shareholders by Forcing Raiders to Pay More for Targets, Study Says." *Wall Street Journal*, March 31, 1988, p. 53.

Lee, Elliott D. "Mesa Scuttles Its Takeover Bid for Homestake: Pickens's Dropped Proposal Is the Latest in Series of Setbacks for Raider." *Wall Street Journal*, March 15, 1988, p. 4.

Lenzner, Robert. "Gillette Can Hear the Footsteps," *Boston Globe*, September 27, 1987, pp. A1, A5.

Lichtenberg, Frank R. and Donald Siegel. "The Effect of Ownership Changes on the Employment and Wages of Central Office and Other Personnel." *Journal of Law and Economics* vol. 33 (1990).

Lipton, Martin, Theodore N. Mirvis and Andrew W. Brownstein. "Takeover Defenses and Directors' Liabilities." Unpublished manuscript, 1986.

Littlefield, E. W. "Enjoying the Corporate Clime." Talk delivered to Bohemian Club meeting along the Russian River in California, July 17, 1983. Typescript.

Lohse, Deborah. "Hostile Takeover Expenses will Be Harder to Deduct." *Wall Street Journal*, October 18, 1995, p. A-1.

Malabre, Alfred L., Jr. "Stocks May Face More Than a Correction: Past Linkage with Bond Market Suggests So." *Wall Street Journal*, October 15, 1987, p. 6.

Malatesta, Paul H. and Ralph A. Walkling. "Poison Pill Securities: Stockholder Wealth, Profitability, and Ownership Structure." *Journal of Financial Economics* vol. 20 (January/March 1988).

Malveaux, Julianne. "Risky Business." *Ms.* (March 1988), pp. 57, 58.

"Management Brief: The Best a Plan Can Get." *The Economist*, August 15, 1992, p. 59.

Marr, Wayne. "The Persistent Borrowing Advantage in Eurodollar Bonds: A Plausible Explanation." *Journal of Applied Corporate Finance* vol. 1, no. 2 (Summer 1988).

McGoldrick, Beth, Gregory Miller, Beth Selby, Fiammetta Rocco, Ellen James, Fayette Hickox. "America's Best CFOs (cover story)." *Institutional Investor* vol. 20, no. 9 (September 1986), pp. 87, 101.

McIntyre, Kathryn J. "Fighting Crime: Name Recognition Makes Gillette Target for Fraud, Theft." *Business Insurance*, April 18, 1988, p. 53.

Mergerstat Review, ed. Andre F. Rhoads, 1986; ed. Janet L. Neiman, 1987. Chicago: W. T. Grimm and Co.

Metz, Tim. "Heard on the Street: Promoter of the Poison Pill Prescribes Stronger Remedy." *Wall Street Journal*, December 1, 1988, p. C1.

Milken, Michael, as told to James W. Michaels, and Phyllis Berman. "My Story— Michael Milken." *Forbes*, March 16, 1992, p. 83.

Miller, James P. "Ex-Fans Give Cooper's Montgomery the Cold Shoulder; Unpredictable Deal Maker May Be Alone in Understanding His Vision." *Wall Street Journal*, March 15, 1988, p. 5.

Miller, Michael W. and William M. Bulkeley. "Revlon Begins $4.12 Billion Bid for Gillette Co." *Wall Street Journal*, November 14, 1986, p. 3.

Miller, William H. "Gillette's Secret to Sharpness." *Industry Week*, January 3, 1994, p. 28.

Montgomery, Cynthia A. "Corporate Diversification." *Journal of Economic Perspectives* vol. 8, no. 3 (Summer 1994).

Moore, Thomas and Wilton Woods. "Money and Markets: How the Twelve Top Raiders Rate," *Fortune*, September 28, 1987.

Morgenthaler, Eric. "At Council on Ideas, It Is Helpful to Be a Daydream Believer." *Wall Street Journal*, July 29, 1994, p. A5.

Mullaney, Joseph. "Gillette after the Tender Offer." In House Committee on Banking, Finance and Urban Affairs, *Oversight Hearing on Mergers and Acquisitions*, May 12, 1987, Serial No. 100-20. Washington, D.C.: U.S. Government Printing Office, 1987, p. 181.

Nash, Nathaniel C. "How Bic Lost the Edge to Gillette." *New York Times*, April 11, 1982, p. F7.

Newport, John Paul, Jr. "The Stalking of Gillette." *Fortune*, May 23, 1988, p. 101.

Pare, Terence P. "Yes, You Can Beat the market." *Fortune*, April 3, 1995, p. 74.

Peers, Alexandra. "Are Big Insider Purchases 'Buy Signals'?" *Wall Street Journal*, October 21, 1992, p. C1.

Pereira, Joseph. "Gillette Trial Told of a Long Search for White Knight." *Wall Street Journal*, June 28, 1988, p. 44.

Pereira, Joseph. "Gillette's Next-Generation Blade to Seek New Edge in Flat Market." *Wall Street Journal*, April 7, 1988, p. 30.

Peers, Alexandra. "Inside Track: Insiders Are Not Always Best Judges of Future Course of a Company's Stock." *Wall Street Journal*, April 3, 1991, p. C19.

Pereira, Joseph. "Judge May Overturn Gillette Proxy Win over Coniston and Order New Election." *Wall Street Journal*, July 14, 1988, p. 2.

Pereira, Joseph. "Trial Discloses Identity of Ten Firms Gillette Co. Contacted as White Knights." *Wall Street Journal*, June 27, 1988, p. 8.

Pereira, Joseph, and Bryan Burrough. "Judge Rules Gillette Ran Misleading Ad on Coniston during Their Proxy Fight." *Wall Street Journal*, July 7, 1988, p. 17.

Peterson, Jonathan. "Junk Bonds: A Financial Revolution That Failed." *Los Angeles Times*, November 22, 1990, p. A34.

Phillips, Derwyn. "Product Development: Where Planning and Marketing Meet." *Journal of Business Strategy* (September/October 1990).

"Ply-Gem to Acquire Balance of Wolverine Technologies Shares." *Wall Street Journal*, March 15, 1988, p. 2.

Porter, Michael E. "From Competitive Advantage to Corporate Strategy." *Harvard Business Review* vol. 65, no. 3 (May–June 1987).

Pound, John. "Proxy Contests." *American Enterprise* (September/October 1991).

Pound, John. "Proxy Voting and the SEC: Investor Protection Versus Market Efficiency." *Journal of Financial Economics* vol. 29, no. 2 (1991).

"Proxy Contests and the Efficiency of Shareholder Oversight." *Journal of Financial Economics* vol. 20, no. 1 (January/March 1988).

Queenan, Joe. "Silent Partner: Will the Real Tito Tettamanti Please Stand Up?" *Barron's*, August 15, 1988, pp. 6, 28, 29, 31.

Ramirez, Anthony. "A Radical New Style for Stodgy Old Gillette." *New York Times*, February 25, 1990, p. F5.

Ramirez, Anthony. "The Year's 50 Most Fascinating Business People: Revlon's Striving Makeover Man." *Fortune*, January 5, 1987, p. 54.

Rauters. "Gillette Trading Heavy On Reports About Icahn." *San Francisco Chronicle*, May 5, 1988, p. C1.

Reese, Jennifer. "News/Trends: Buffett Buys Junk." *Fortune*, April 22, 1991, p. 14.

Rothman, Andrea. "Gillette, in a Shift, to Emphasize Cartridge Blades over Disposables." *Wall Street Journal*, November 18, 1988, p. B6.

Royce, Marilyn M. "Gillette NYSE-GS" VALUE LINE, No. 811, October 21, 1986.

Royce, Marilyn M. "Gillette NYSE-GS" VALUE LINE, No. 818, October 21, 1988.

Rusitzky, Louis M. "View from New England." *Barron's*, April 2, 1979, p. 4.

Ryngaert, Michael. "The Effect of Poison Pill Securities on Shareholder Wealth." *Journal of Financial Economics* vol. 20 (1988).

Ryngaert, Michael. "The Effects of Poison Pills on the Wealth of Shareholders." Securities and Exchange Commission Staff Paper, September 5, 1985.

"Salant Corp. Extends Offer for Manhattan Industries to Friday." *Wall Street Journal*, March 15, 1988, p. 2.

Sandler, Linda. "Heard on the Street: Buffett's Savior Role Lands Him Deals Other Holders Can't Get." *Wall Street Journal*, August 14, 1989, p. C1.

Sandler, Linda. "Heard on the Street: 'Pale Green Greenmail' Is Spreading as Firms Buy Out Raiders as Part of Broader Purchases." *Wall Street Journal*, November 25, 1986, p. 59.

Sherman, Stratford P., Charles C. Krusekopf and Alan Farnham." The Trio That Humbled Allegis." *Fortune*, July 20, 1987, pp. 52–53, 54.

Shleifer, Andrei and Robert W. Vishny. "Greenmail, White Knights and Shareholders' Interest." *Rand Journal of Economics* vol. 17, no. 3 (Autumn 1986).

Shleifer, Andrei and Robert W. Vishny. "The Takeover Wave of the 1980s." *Science* vol. 249 (August 17, 1990).

Shore, Andrew. "Consumer: Gillette Company." Shearson Lehman Hutton, November 29, 1988, p. 1.

Shore, Andrew. "The Gillette Company." Shearson Lehman Brothers, May 4, 1987, p. 1.

Sidak, J. Gregory and Susan E. Woodward. "Takeover Premiums, Appraisal Rights and the Price Elasticity of a Firm's Publicly Traded Stock." *Georgia Law Review* vol. 25 (1991).

Sit, Mary. "Judge Zobel Steps Out of Gillette Case." *Boston Globe*, June 14, 1988, p. 43.

Sloan, Allan. "Pyramid Power." *Forbes*, January 27, 1986, pp. 30–31.

Sloan, Pat. "Perelman Eager to Snare Gillette: Bitter Takeover Fight Expected." *Advertising Age*, November 17, 1986, p. 108.

Smith, Lee. "The Boardroom Is Becoming a Different Scene." *Fortune*, May 8, 1978, pp. 150–170.

Smith, Randall and Ann Monroe. "New Insecurity: Insider-Trading Jitters Deal Another Setback to Junk-Bond Market." *Wall Street Journal*, November 20, 1986, p. 1.

Stein, Benjamin J. "Who Owns This Company Anyway? Greenmail Leaves Shareholders Out in the Cold." *Barron's*, December 15, 1986, p. 9.

Stewart, James B. and Daniel Hertzberg. "Insider Focus: Small Securities Firm Links Drexel's Milken, Goldman's Freeman; Oakley Sutton, Also an Ally of the Coniston Partners, Is Target of Investigation, Subpoenas and Flak Jackets." *Wall Street Journal*, April 6, 1988, pp. 1, 10.

Stipp, David. "Gillette, in Proxy Fight, Speeds Up Stock Buy-Back." *Wall Street Journal*, April 20, 1988, p. 45.

Stone, Dominic. "Rational Thinking." *Design* (March 1992), pp. 35–37.

Stout, Lynn A. "Are Takeover Premiums Really Premiums? Market Price, Fair Value, and Corporate Law." *Yale Law Journal* vol. 99 (1990).

Stretch, C. Clinton and Frank C. Devlin, Jr. "The 1986 Tax Reform Act: The New Rules for Business." *Practical Accountant* vol. 19, no. 11 (November 1986).

Suskind, Ron. "Legend Revisited: Warren Buffett's Aura As Folksy Sage Masks Tough, Polished Man." *Wall Street Journal*, November 8, 1991, p. A6.

Swartz, Steve. "Home to Roost: Raid on Salomon Inc. Has Turned the Tables on Wall Street Firms." *Wall Street Journal*, October 2, 1987, p. 16.

Taub, Stephen. "Knowing a Company's Worth." In "Shark Alert." *Financial World*, April 1, 1986, p. 28.

Templeman, John. "The Spotlight Falls on a Swiss Mystery Man: Tito Tettamanti Wants to Be 'the Warren Buffett of Europe.' " *Business Week*, June 20, 1988, p. 76.

Tracy, Diane. "Gillette's Net Jumps: Payout Is Set to Rise." *Wall Street Journal*, February 22, 1991, p. A3.

Ulman, Neil. "Gillette Chairman Takes a Long View in Program to Brighten Profit Picture." *Wall Street Journal*, June 28, 1977, pp. 12, 14.

"Washington Update: Shattering the Mirror." *Mergers and Acquisitions* vol. 22, no. 5 (March/April 1988), p. 18.

Waters, Richard. "Merger to Create Largest U.S. Bank." *Financial Times*, August 29, 1995, p. 1.

Weiss, Gary. "Razor Sharp: Gillette to Snap Back from a Dull Stretch." *Barron's*, August 25, 1986, pp. 15, 37.

Wessel, David. "Gillette Reaffirms Refusal of Revlon Bid, Argues for Stronger Anti-Takeover Law." *Wall Street Journal*, June 29, 1987, p. 8.

Wessel, David and Ann Hagedorn. "Gillette Refuses Revlon's Bid of $47 a Share." *Wall Street Journal*, August 25, 1987, p. 4.

Willens, Robert. "Put and Take: New Ways to Buy Back Shares, Cut Payouts." *Barron's*, August 22, 1988, p. 20.

Wines, Richard A. *Poison Pill Impact Study II*. Georgeson and Company Inc., October 31, 1988, unpaged.

Wise, Deborah. "Waterman Rift: A Tearful Farewell." *New York Times*, December 16, 1988, p. D1.

Yerger, Ann and Elizabeth Lightfoot. "Voting by Institutional Investors on Corporate Governance Issues." Investor Responsibility Research Center, Corporate Governance Service (IRRC), Washington, D.C., December 1991.

MISCELLANEOUS: ANNUAL REPORTS, ANALYSTS SHEETS, ETC.

"Agreed Order." Appended June 30, 1988, U.S. District Court, Massachusetts, C.A. No. 88-862-WF, June 20, 1988, p. 3 (mimeo).

Almanac of the Federal Judiciary vol. 1. Lawletters, Inc., 1988, 10–1st circuit.

Berkshire Hathaway Annual Report 1987, "Letter to Shareholders," Omaha, Nebraska.

Berkshire Hathaway Annual Report 1990, "Letter to Shareholders," Omaha, Nebraska.

Berkshire Hathaway Annual Report, 1990, Omaha, Nebraska.

Berkshire Hathaway Annual Report, 1991, Omaha, Nebraska.

Berkshire Hathaway Annual Report, 1994, Omaha, Nebraska.

"Bulletin: Cosmetics." Smith Barney Research, July 27, 1987.

Class Action Complaint for Breach of Fiduciary Duty; Intentional Interference with Prospective Economic Advantage; Conspiracy. No. 620975. *Sandra Miller v Gillette Corporation*, Superior Court of the State of California. Filed January 29, 1987.

"Chronological History of Gillette, as Delineated by the Company." Shearson Lehman Hutton report on Gillette, October 19, 1989.

Congressional Record—Senate. Tender Offer Disclosure and Fairness Act, June 20, 1988, p. S. 8211.

Congressional Record—Senate. Tender Offer Disclosure and Fairness Act, June 21, 1988, pp. S. 8269, S. 8272 and S. 8271.

The Coniston Group, Proxy Statement in Opposition to the Board of Directors of The Gillette Company, Annual Meeting of Stockholders, April 21, 1988.

Council of Economic Advisers to the President. *Annual Report*. Washington, D.C.: U.S. Government Printing Office, 1985.

Dean Witter Research, Gillette North American Venture Council, October 31, 1984, table 5.

Delaware Supreme Court, *Ivanhoe Partners v Newmont Mining Corporation*, No. 341, November 18, 1987.

Esty, Benjamin. In collaboration with Professor Pankaj Ghemawat. "The Gillette Company." Equity Research Bulletin. Dean Witter Consumer Group, July 7, 1989.

"Gillette's Launch of Sensor." Harvard Business School case study 9-792-028. September 15, 1992.

The Hoover Institution on War, Revolution and Peace. *Report 1984*. Stanford, Calif.: Stanford University, September 1984.

"In Memoriam." *Simmons Now*, March 1990 [*sic*, actual, March 1991]. Boston: Simmons College, p. 3.

KPMG Peat Marwick (National Association of Corporate Directors). *A Practical Guide for the Corporate Director*, prepared by Michael P. Dooley and the Center for Corporate Governance Education and Research, January 1990.

Mockler, Colman M., Jr., "Strategic Block Investing." Letter to 175 presidents of other companies, April 15, 1988.

Report of the Committee on Banking, Housing, and Urban Affairs, United States Senate, to accompany S. 1323. Tender Offer Disclosure and Fairness Act of 1987. Washington, D.C.: U.S. Government Printing Office, 1987.

U.S. Congress. House. Subcommittee on Telecommunications, Consumer Protection, and Finance of the Committee on Energy and Commerce. *Corporate Takeovers: Public Policy Implications for the Economy and Corporate Governance*. 99th Congress, 2d session, 1987. Committee Print 99-QQ.

U.S. Congress. Senate. Hearings before the Committee on Banking, Housing, and Urban Affairs, June 23, 24, and 25, 1987. *Regulating Hostile Corporate Takeovers*. 100th Congress, 1st session, Senate Hearing 100-183.

U.S. Congress. Senate. *Tender Offer Disclosure and Fairness Act of 1987*. Committee on Banking, Housing, and Urban Affairs, December 17, 1987. 100th Congress, 1st session, Senate Report 100-265.

Gillette Company Publications

The Gillette Company, *Annual Meeting of Stockholders, April 16, 1992 and First Quarter Report 1992*, "Stockholder Participation," by Al Zeien.

The Gillette Company, *Annual Meeting of Stockholders, April 20, 1978 and First Quarter Report 1978*, Boston, 1979.

The Gillette Company, *Annual Report 1987*, Boston, 1988.

The Gillette Company, *Annual Report 1988*, Letter to Stockholders, Boston, 1989.

The Gillette Company, *Annual Report 1989*, Letter to Stockholders, Boston, 1990.

The Gillette Company, *Annual Report 1990*, Boston, 1991.

The Gillette Company, *Annual Report 1995*, Letter to Stockholders, Boston, 1996.

The Gillette Company, Bylaws, amended April 20, 1988, mimeo, Article VII, "Proxies and Voting."

The Gillette Company, Bylaws, amended October 20, 1988, Article XI, "Acquisitions of Stock."

The Gillette Company, *Chronology*, issued by Corporate Public Relations, The Gillette Company [1989].

The Gillette Company, General Bulletin No. 138-86, November 5, 1986, memo signed by Joseph F. Turley.

The Gillette Company, *1996 Annual Meeting and First Quarter Report*, Boston.

The Gillette Company, Notice of Annual Meeting and Proxy Statement (1977), March 22, 1977.

The Gillette Company, Notice of Annual Meeting of the Stockholders, March 17, 1994.

The Gillette Company, Proxy Statement, March 11, 1986.

The Gillette Company, Proxy Statement, March 7, 1988.

The Gillette Company, Transcript of Annual Meeting, April 21, 1988, Burt Reporting Associates.

The Gillette Company News vol. 11, no. 21 (July 1984).

The Gillette Company News vol. 12, no. 2 (October 1985).

The Gillette Company News, press release, "Gillette Files Suit against Perelman-Revlon Group." November 17, 1986.

Zeien, Alfred M. and Michael C. Hawley. "Letter to Stockholders," March 3, 1997. *1996 Annual Report*. Boston: The Gillette Company, 1997.

Index

About the Author

RITA RICARDO-CAMPBELL is Senior Fellow Emerita at the Hoover Institution, Stanford University. She was the first woman director of the Gillette Company, held positions at Tufts University and Harvard University, and has written numerous books and articles.

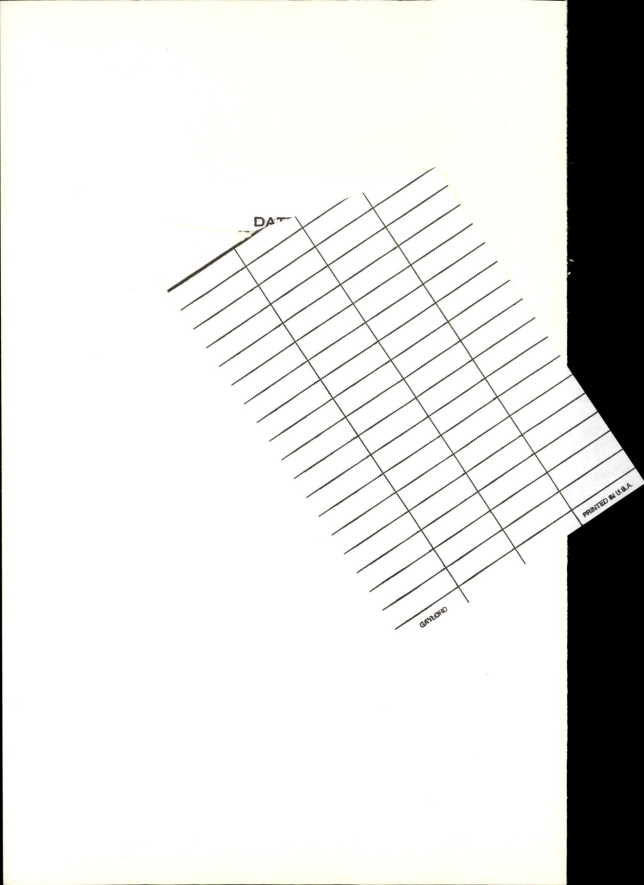

DATE

GAYLORD

PRINTED IN U.S.A.